New Men

New Men

Manliness in Early America

EDITED BY Thomas A. Foster

FOREWORD BY Mary Beth Norton
AFTERWORD BY Toby L. Ditz

NEW YORK UNIVERSITY PRESS
New York and London

NEW YORK UNIVERSITY PRESS
New York and London
www.nyupress.org

© 2011 by New York University
All rights reserved

References to Internet websites (URLs) were accurate at the time of writing.
Neither the author nor New York University Press is responsible for URLs
that may have expired or changed since the manuscript was prepared.

Library of Congress Cataloging-in-Publication Data

New men : manliness in early America / edited by Thomas A. Foster ;
foreword by Mary Beth Norton ; afterword by Toby L. Ditz.
p. cm.
Includes bibliographical references and index.
ISBN 978–0–8147–2780–5 (cl : alk. paper) — ISBN 978–0–8147–2781–2
(pb : alk. paper) — ISBN 978–0–8147–2822–2 (e-book)
1. Masculinity—United States—History. 2. Men—United States—History.
I. Foster, Thomas A.
HQ1090.3.N492   2010
305.310973'09032—dc22   2010033743

New York University Press books are printed on acid-free paper,
and their binding materials are chosen for strength and durability.
We strive to use environmentally responsible suppliers and materials
to the greatest extent possible in publishing our books.

Manufactured in the United States of America
c 10 9 8 7 6 5 4 3 2 1
p 10 9 8 7 6 5 4 3 2 1

For Marlon

Contents

Preface   ix
    Mary Beth Norton

Acknowledgments   xi

Introduction: New Men: 1
Feminist Histories of Manliness in Early British America
    Thomas A. Foster

PART I. Settlement

1. Gentlemen and Soldiers: 9
Competing Visions of Manhood in Early Jamestown
    John Gilbert McCurdy

2. Indian and English Dreams: Colonial Hierarchy and   31
Manly Restraint in Seventeenth-Century New England
    Ann Marie Plane

PART II. Warfare

3. "We are MEN": Native American and Euroamerican   51
Projections of Masculinity During the Seven Years' War
    Tyler Boulware

4. Real Men: Masculinity, Spirituality, and Community in   71
Late Eighteenth-Century Cherokee Warfare
    Susan Abram

PART III. Atlantic

5. "Blood and Lust": Masculinity and Sexuality in   95
Illustrated Print Portrayals of Early Pirates of the Caribbean
    Carolyn Eastman

6 "Banes of Society" and "Gentlemen of Strong Natural Parts": 116
Attacking and Defending West Indian Creole Masculinity
Natalie A. Zacek

7 "Impatient of Subordination" and "Liable to Sudden 134
Transports of Anger": White Masculinity and Homosocial
Relations with Black Men in Eighteenth-Century Jamaica
Trevor Burnard

PART IV. Enactment

8 "Effective Men" and Early Voluntary Associations in 155
Philadelphia, 1725–1775
Jessica Choppin Roney

9 "Strength of the Lion . . . Arms Like Polished Iron": 172
Embodying Black Masculinity in an Age of Slavery and
Propertied Manhood
Kathleen M. Brown

PART V. Revolution

10 Of Eloquence "Manly" and "Monstrous": The Henpecked 195
Husband in Revolutionary Political Debate, 1774–1775
Benjamin H. Irvin

11 John Adams and the Choice of Hercules: Manliness and 217
Sexual Virtue in Eighteenth-Century British America
Thomas A. Foster

12 "Play the Man . . . for Your Bleeding Country": 236
Military Chaplains as Gender Brokers During the American
Revolutionary War
Janet Moore Lindman

Afterword: Contending Masculinities in Early America 256
Toby L. Ditz

About the Contributors 269

Index 271

Preface

MARY BETH NORTON

According to the *Oxford English Dictionary*, the term *masculinity* was coined in 1748. As the insightful essays in this volume show, however, long before that men in North America were thinking about and living out the traits represented by the word: "the assemblage of qualities regarded as characteristic of men; maleness, manliness." From Captain John Smith in early Jamestown to John Adams in late eighteenth-century Massachusetts, from soldiers and Native warriors who fought early America's many wars to men who recorded their dreams (and those of others) quietly in their diaries, from Jamaica to New England, colonial men worried about defining and meeting standards of masculinity—regardless of whether they had a word for that characteristic.

Exhibiting manly qualities in early America was a complicated task, as all the men discussed in this book knew. Should one show self-restraint or aggression? Independence or cooperation? Deference or superiority? The answers to those questions depended on circumstances: what behavior worked for a man in one instance would be inappropriate in another. And a man had to recognize which was which. Failure to do so could result in charges by one's peers that he was somehow less than a man—or worse. Under certain conditions, a perceived lack of manliness could even lead to death.

In a sense, the range of behavioral choices confronting early American men was nothing new: Englishmen and enslaved Africans who sailed to the colonies did not suddenly acquire the attributes and anxieties of manhood somewhere in the middle of the Atlantic Ocean.[1] Native Americans did not learn how to be manly from their contacts with the invaders; their societies had long since developed cultural definitions of what traits men should display and which ones they should eschew if they wished to have the esteem of their peers. Rather, what was "new" about the "new men" of North America were the complex patterns in which such groups interacted with one another. Native standards of manhood conflicted with English standards:

what, a white colonist might think, could possibly be manly about torturing a captive to death? What could be manly about fighting battles by "skulking" behind trees in ambushes? Conversely, a Native man could think, how could a "real man" do the agricultural work commonly assigned to women? Or how could a master both differentiate himself sharply from his bondsmen and simultaneously recognize their prerogatives as husbands to give them preference over women for skilled and managerial plantation jobs? How could an enslaved man prove his masculine worth when he had neither property nor independence in a larger colonial society that placed great emphasis on both?

One striking aspect of these essays, in short, is the complexity of the cultural relationships they disclose and the intricacy of the interweaving of different sets of masculine values in the North American context. American feminist scholars have for years addressed the connections of gender, race, and status. This book shows that utilizing the same parameters to study men best illuminates American masculinity. And it perhaps suggests that there is something after all to the old idea of American exceptionalism. What made the "new world" novel was not the fact of its "discovery" by Europeans, but rather the interplay of cultural forces that brought new pressures and new opportunities to its many male and female residents. After decades of enlightening feminist scholarship on women, it is time to have similarly enlightening feminist scholarship focusing on men.

NOTE

1. On early modern English masculinity, see the following useful review essays: Alexandra Shepard, "From Anxious Patriarchs to Refined Gentlemen? Manhood in Britain, Circa 1500–1700," *Journal of British Studies* 44 (2005): 281–95; and Karen Harvey, "The History of Masculinity, Circa 1650–1800," ibid., 296–311.

Acknowledgments

This book could never have come together without the help of all those who suggested potential authors, submitted their work for consideration, or offered advice and support. I especially thank my editor, Deborah Gershenowitz, and the staff at New York University Press. I also acknowledge the financial support of the University Research Council at DePaul University. I am grateful to my students, colleagues in the departments of history and women's and gender studies, and the staff at DePaul for giving me a place to continue to develop as a lifelong student of gender in early America. Finally, I would like to thank each of the authors for sharing their work.

THOMAS A. FOSTER

Introduction

*New Men: Feminist Histories of
Manliness in Early British America*

THOMAS A. FOSTER

> What, then, is the American, this new man?
> —J. Hector St. John de Crevecoeur, 1782[1]

In 1782, when J. Hector St. John de Crevecoeur published his description of American society and wrestled with what it meant to be an American, he articulated a question that many were asking: "What, then, is the American, this new man?" For every generation that followed, the question has resonated. *New Men* takes up Crevecoeur's question and applies it to early America using the insights of gender history. It approaches the history of masculinity as a feminist project in that it signals the gendered subjectivity of men and highlights the social and cultural construction of that subject position, especially with regard to power relations.[2] While scholarship on women in early America has demonstrated the centrality of gender to understandings of womanhood, men, long at the center of historical studies, have only relatively recently been examined as gendered subjects.

New Men examines masculinity in British America from European settlement through the Revolutionary era. It argues that understandings of manliness significantly shaped the founding and development of early America. Historians have shown that in early America successful manhood rested on the establishment of a household, the securing of a calling or career, and the self-control over one's masculine comportment.[3] Within this broad framework, the essays in this volume examine how the conditions of early America affected those norms and ideals of masculinity and linked them to ever-changing regional and nascent American identities. The essays here collectively address the variety of standards and ideals of manliness in early America and highlight the breadth of differences among them.

• • •

It has become increasingly popular for mainstream media to report on the latest scientific finding about "male" and "female" brains. Evolutionary biologists and other scientists garner widespread attention for postulating genetic and biological explanations for generalized social differences observed in male and female behavior. Gender, or the social expression of and meanings given to biological difference between men and women, is recognized as an important aspect of society and history, but not all disciplines agree on the origins of gender difference.

Virtually all historians of gender approach differences between male and female historical subjects as the product not of evolutionary brain chemistry, but rather with the theoretical position that gender is socially constructed.[4] Following the French theorist Michel Foucault, most scholars approach gender as a social and cultural construction. Joan Scott, drawing from Foucault, explained that gender is "knowledge about sexual difference"—understandings that get "produced in complex ways" and that are not limited "only to ideas but to institutions and structures, everyday practices as well as specialized rituals."[5] The earliest major histories of American masculinity employed this theoretical framework, as do the most recent. Anthony Rotundo, in his study of nineteenth-century Northern manhood, argued that "manliness is a human invention . . . learned, used, reinforced, and reshaped by individuals in the course of life."[6] Similarly, Michael Kimmel, in his study of modern American manliness, approached gender as "the sets of cultural meanings and prescriptions that each culture attaches to one's biological sex."[7] All the essays in *New Men* follow this theoretical underpinning and focus on how society and culture develop understandings of masculinity that are in turn frequently naturalized—or culturally defined or masqueraded as if from nature, not culture.[8]

Although books on masculinity in colonial America are relatively few and quite recent, a larger selection of articles and book chapters has expanded our understanding of masculinity in the colonial context with a cross-Atlantic perspective. But the essays on manliness in early America are largely scattered and serve the purposes and intellectual pursuits of a range of fields, including histories of slavery, sexuality, Native America, and cross-cultural and cross-border histories of early America, among others. As Toby Ditz cautions, a growing body of literature on masculinity runs the "risk of occluding women and downplaying men's power over women," and creates the "danger of restoring men—however particularised, differentiated and socially constructed—to the centre of our historical narrative."[9]

One of the reasons that the work has been able to recenter men is that much of it has been easily integrated in a variety of fields whose primary concern is not with gender studies. This is in part because of the traditional focus on men and men's experiences. Men, long at the center of historical studies, are still written about as un-gendered subjects, despite decades of scholarship that has established gender as central to societies and has critiqued the age-old use of the "universal" historical subject—as that subject was virtually always male, white, and middle class.

By focusing explicitly on the construction of manliness in early America, this book heeds the call of women's and gender scholars to deepen our understanding of the historical formation and deployment of gendered power in America. Within the broad understanding of masculinity in early America, the essays in this volume examine how gender operated specifically in terms of oppositional identities, social interactions, and the cultural development of norms and ideals.

Several essays highlight how understandings of manliness affected social and cultural developments. The first two chapters (part I) examine manliness in the seventeenth-century era of settlement in Virginia and New England. John Gilbert McCurdy's examination of early Jamestown rereads the failure of the Virginia Company with an eye toward gendered norms of masculine comportment. Thus he concludes that Anglo-American masculinity was being defined on the ground at the same time that definitions of masculinity were threatening the cohesion of the fledgling colony. Ann Marie Plane's work on dreams and dream recording in colonial New England traces a fascinating medium for self-reflection and highlights the ways dream interpretation informed and reflected manliness for Anglo-Americans and Algonquians. She also finds that white men formulated their masculine identities in opposition to Native Americans and other perceived threats to white patriarchal order.

Colonial warfare and conflict figures in the second pairing of essays. Susan Abram's ethnographic study of Cherokee manhood and warfare finds a spiritual aspect of manliness. Tyler Boulware's chapter builds on the gendered order of Native American societies and examines how discourses of masculinity among British, Americans, and Native Americans during the Seven Years' War informed that conflict.

As illustrated by the chapters by Boulware, Brown, and Plane, masculine identities were often developed in oppositional relationships across racial, gender, and class divides. Several essays in this book, including those in part

III, focus on Atlantic world constructions of manliness. Natalie Zacek's study of white masculinity in the Leeward Islands makes the compelling point that even within a racialized society, relations among white men mattered significantly. Trevor Burnard's chapter finds that in Jamaica white masculinity was defined in opposition to black masculinity as much as in opposition to white womanhood. Carolyn Eastman finds that in the Atlantic world of print representations of pirates, the tropes of deviant gender and sexuality reflected some realities and popularized others.

The pairing of essays in part IV illustrates the various ways that manliness could be performed or enacted depending on social and cultural circumstances. In contrast to the social development that was stymied by gendered notions of manhood in McCurdy's Jamestown, Jessica Roney finds that understandings of white masculinity in eighteenth-century Philadelphia fueled charitable and philanthropic (white) men's societies in a host of venues. Kathleen M. Brown's essay on black masculinity traces a broad narrative from the earliest days of colonial settlement to the early republic, arguing that the body served to perform and illustrate masculinity for black men—who, in contrast to Roney's subjects, generally had neither property nor independence.

The final chapters underscore the varieties of ways that manly identities were forged in the context of the American Revolution. Janet Lindman's study of masculinity and ministry during the American Revolution examines how models of manliness emphasized self-control, and often did so in a Christian framework. Cultural messages both reinforced and developed new notions of manliness at the same time that they also gave voice to radical and deviant models of manliness. Benjamin H. Irvin similarly locates constructions of manliness at work in the political (and personal) rhetoric of the Revolutionary era. Irvin examines the figure of the henpecked husband as a measure of manly standards wielded by both loyalists and patriots as they attacked the authority of Congress to enter in a war of colonial independence. As this trope of manhood motivated factions in the American Revolution, Irvin suggests the figure of the henpecked husband might well be thought of as a "forgotten foot soldier" in the war.

Political figures and structures also play a role in this study of early American manhood. In my own essay, John Adams's emphasis on the classical story of the Choice of Hercules as a lesson in the importance of masculine virtue and sexual self-restraint highlights but one aspect of masculinity in the broader political world of the Revolutionary era.

Through these essays, *New Men*, with its focus on colonial and Revolutionary America, shows that long before industrial and capitalist models of masculinity became central to U.S. culture, manliness was defined in a variety of important ways—and conversely, that notions of manhood affected the development of what would become the United States.

NOTES

1. J. Hector St. John de Crevecoeur, *Letters from an American Farmer and Sketches of Eighteenth-Century America*, edited and with an introduction by Albert E. Stone (New York: Penguin, 1981), 69.

2. On the relationship between feminism and masculinity studies, see, for example, Judith Kegan Gardiner, ed., *Masculinity Studies and Feminist Theory: New Directions* (New York: Columbia University Press, 2002). See also Toby L. Ditz, "The New Men's History and the Peculiar Absence of Gendered Power: Some Remedies from Early American Gender History," *Gender and History* 16 (April 2004): 1–35.

3. On early American masculinity, see, for example, Toby L. Ditz, "Shipwrecked; or Masculinity Imperiled: Mercantile Representations of Failure and the Gendered Self in Eighteenth-Century Philadelphia," *Journal of American History* 81 (1994): 51–80; Thomas A. Foster, *Sex and the Eighteenth-Century Man: Massachusetts and the History of Sexuality in America* (Boston: Beacon Press, 2006); Jane Kamensky, "Talk Like a Man: Speech, Power, and Masculinity in Early New England," *Gender and History* 8 (1996): 22–47; Mark E. Kann, *A Republic of Men: The American Founders, Gendered Language, and Patriarchal Politics* (New York: New York University Press, 1998); Ann M. Little, *Abraham in Arms: War and Gender in Colonial New England* (Philadelphia: University of Pennsylvania, 2007); Anne S. Lombard, *Making Manhood: Growing Up Male in Colonial New England* (Cambridge: Harvard University Press, 2003); John G. McCurdy, *Citizen Bachelors: Manhood and the Creation of the United States* (Ithaca: Cornell University Press, 2009); and Lisa Wilson, *Ye Heart of a Man: The Domestic Life of Men in Colonial New England* (New Haven: Yale University, 1999).

4. Histories of masculinity draw on these theories and approaches of gender history, yet as a subfield of women's and gender history, they have also developed their own approaches for best understanding how manhood was historically informed. As Robert Connell reminds us, we must study *masculinities*—there is no singular model for all men. R. W. Connell, *Masculinities*, 2nd ed. (Berkeley: University of California Press, 2005); and Michael Kimmel, *Manhood in America: A Cultural History* (New York: Free Press, 1996). Scholars have also argued that masculinity should be studied as it formulates itself in opposition to womanhood. Historians have called for the need to maintain one eye on "relations of power" while examining "the complex distribution of authority both between and within the sexes and the ways in which this was mediated by gender." See Alexandra Shepard, *Meanings of Manhood in Early Modern England* (Oxford: Oxford University Press, 2003), 3–4.

5. Joan Wallach Scott, *Gender and the Politics of History* (New York: Columbia University Press, 1988), 2.

6. E. Anthony Rotundo, *American Manhood: Transformations in Masculinity from the Revolution to the Modern Era* (New York: Basic Books, 1993), 7.

7. Michael Kimmel, *Manhood in America: A Cultural History* (New York: Free Press, 1996), 2–3.

8. It has become commonplace to view *gender* as distinct from *sex*—a conceptual separation that helped enormously to drive home the point that the cultural and social meanings we attach to the biological difference of male and female should be critically engaged, both historically and in contemporary society. But studies today are increasingly informed by the notion that even our understanding of biology is culturally constructed and that therefore the distinction so carefully drawn between sex and gender in the 1980s and 1990s is flawed. As Judith Butler has argued, it makes "no sense . . . to define gender as the cultural interpretation of sex, if sex itself is a gendered category." Gender, she argues, "must also designate the very apparatus of production whereby the sexes themselves are established." This insight has largely tempered the once strictly guarded division of the terms *sex* and *gender*. See Judith Butler, *Gender Trouble: Feminism and the Subversion of Identity* (New York: Routledge, 1990), 7.
Judith Butler's insights into gender construction have also informed a recent wave of literature on the history of gender and gender identity. Butler argued that gender was "performative." Gender, she argued, is "a doing," and "there is no gender identity behind the expressions of gender; that identity is performatively constituted by the very 'expressions' that are said to be its results." Building on Butler's insight, Gail Bederman in her study of ideal nineteenth-century manhood argues that masculinity is a "continual, dynamic process" in which "individuals are positioned or position themselves," and through which "men claim certain kinds of authority." Butler, *Gender Trouble*, 25; and Gail Bederman, *Manliness and Civilization: A Cultural History of Gender and Race in the United States, 1880–1917* (Chicago: University of Chicago, 1995), 7.

9. Toby L. Ditz, "The New Men's History and the Peculiar Absence of Gendered Power: Some Remedies from Early American Gender History," *Gender and History* 16 (April 2004), 3, 7.

I

Settlement

1

Gentlemen and Soldiers

*Competing Visions of Manhood
in Early Jamestown*

JOHN GILBERT MCCURDY

On May 14, 1607, 104 men and boys landed on a small peninsula in the Chesapeake and established Jamestown. The colonists sailed not for themselves but for the Virginia Company, whose shareholders were financing this foray into the New World. Consistent with the company's instructions, the colonists organized a government, built a settlement, and made contact with the indigenous people. Almost immediately, however, Jamestown was on the brink of collapse. Starvation and disease struck first, followed by internal dissention and war with the Powhatan Indians. In the decade that followed, the Virginia Company continued to resupply Jamestown and send hundreds of new colonists, but large numbers continued to die and no one could find gold or any other resource that might profit the investors. Hoping to salvage the colony as well as his own investment, Sir Edwin Sandys took control of the Virginia Company in 1619 and implemented a series of changes. For Sandys, the colony's problem was that it contained too many men. Too many men led to too much fighting and ultimately diverted the colonists from their original mission of enriching the Virginia Company. "For the remedying of that mischiefe," Sandys demanded that the company send young women for the men to marry, as "wifes, children and familie might make them lesse moueable and settle them."[1]

Four centuries have passed since the settlement of Jamestown. While Sir Edwin was ultimately unsuccessful at rescuing the company's fortunes, the colony survived to become the first permanent English settlement in the New World. The recent quadricentennial celebrations of Jamestown's founding testify to the continued relevance of the settlement and its place at the beginning of American history. Nor is Jamestown just a fixation of the popular imagination. In recent years, professional historians have continued to unearth—literally and figuratively—new meaning from the Virginia colony, such as the origins of American racism and the creation of an Atlantic world.[2] Studies of Jamestown have also proved instrumental to understanding gender at the beginning of American history. As historians like Mary Beth Norton and Kathleen Brown have demonstrated, gender was critical to the conquest and subjugation of the native Virginians. It also informed concepts of power, dividing the English settlers along the lines of social rank, and was even used in the justification of African American slavery. As these historians have been careful to note, divisions of gender did not only separate men from women; they were also used by men to suppress other men and to deny them power in the early Chesapeake.[3]

It is possible to build on this work to gain a better understanding of the struggles that beset early Jamestown. Although historians have sought to understand the experience of the first female colonists, we actually learn much more from a gendered analysis of the colony's male population.[4] After all, early Jamestown was decidedly a man's world. The first English women did not arrive until September 1608—more than sixteen months after settlement—and they remained a distinct minority for the next decade, totaling only three percent of the population in 1613.[5] Yet the problem may not have been as simple as too many men. While Sir Edwin Sandys treated all male colonists the same, it is now widely accepted that manhood is anything but monolithic. Instead, distinct variations exist, sometimes peacefully coexisting and other times leading to conflict. Nor is manhood static. It has changed markedly over time, shifting in response to political and economic trends.[6] In early Jamestown, the varieties of manhood were particularly contentious *because* the very concept of manhood was undergoing significant revision and change.

The key to understanding manhood in early Jamestown is to recognize first that the colony was established as a military outpost. Concerned with the extraction of resources and fearful of a hostile native population, the Virginia Company purposely outfitted the early colony like an army unit. It organized the colonists as soldiers, settling them in a fort and denying them the comforts of civilian life such as private property and political rights. Individual interests were subordinated to the mission of the company. Nine of the eleven men who led the colony between 1607 and 1619 had considerable experience leading troops into battle.[7] Indeed, the military mission partly explains the limited number of women in the early colony.[8]

Studies of gender in the contemporary military have concluded that part of the process of making one a soldier is to inculcate him with the values of hegemonic masculinity. New recruits are taught that they must be strong, aggressive, unemotional, and refuse to complain. Any sign of weakness is dismissed as effeminate or homosexual.[9] Building on these observations, Marcia Kovitz has suggested that notions of military masculinity have not always been constant, but rather they changed dramatically with the rise of the state and the centralization of authority.[10] At the moment when Jamestown was settled, the English military was undergoing a profound transition. Labeled the "military revolution" by scholars, the change reordered the weapons, organization, and ideas of war.[11] The constructions of manhood in early Jamestown reflected these changing ideas. The earliest settlers brought with them medieval notions of military masculinity that stressed the importance of social status to military rank and preserved the right of men to resist their mistreatment, while later leaders rejected these ideas and attempted to enshrine a modern military masculinity that prized obedience and promotion through the ranks. These contrasting interpretations led to conflict, thus destabilizing the colony.

This chapter explores gender in early Jamestown; specifically, how conflicting ideas of manhood arising from changes in the military led to conflict among the settlers. Although race often affected gender in the early Chesapeake, here only English manhood is considered, partly for brevity and partly because the colonists insisted that men of color were not really men. In sum, understanding the different interpretations of manhood at the beginning of American history helps us to understand the struggles of the first English colonists and to appreciate the ways in which different interpretations of manhood can divide society.

Social Rank and Military Manhood

For much of medieval English history, manhood was tied to mastery. A man was defined by economic independence as well as his ability to assert control over dependents. In the typical life course, a boy left home in his early teens to begin an apprenticeship or work as a servant in husbandry, and thus became a dependent of a master who housed, fed, and disciplined him. It was only when he completed his apprenticeship, received his inheritance, or saved up enough money to purchase land that a boy became a man. Only then could he begin the process of taking on dependents of his own: a wife, children, servants, and apprentices. Notions of domestic mastery also permeated the society as a whole. Kari Boyd McBride has written that the late medieval country estate remained the symbol of English society writ large, with its "static, hierarchical, socioeconomic structure."[12] Authority flowed from the monarch to the aristocracy and from the aristocracy to the people. A small landholder was expected to defer to his social betters and recognize that his manhood was naturally inferior to that of an aristocrat.

Two early Jamestown leaders exemplified this medieval notion of manhood based on rank and title: Edward Maria Wingfield and George Percy. The eldest son of a distinguished family, Wingfield had a position in society secured by birth. His father was a member of Parliament, although his early death meant that Wingfield was largely raised by his Uncle Jacques. Jacques Wingfield held several high positions in Ireland, including membership in the Irish Privy Council, and he no doubt helped secure young Wingfield's entrance into law school at Lincoln's Inn. While still a young man, Wingfield briefly held a seat in Parliament and governed the Kimbolton School. George Percy also hailed from a distinguished background. The son of the Earl of Northumberland, Percy attended Oxford before completing a degree in law at the Middle Temple. To be sure, neither Wingfield nor Percy inherited great riches, but their social position was sufficient to allow them to obtain officers' commissions in the English army.[13]

The military long had been a noble profession for the well-born of English society. Under feudalism, the aristocracy was required to assemble troops from among the people and lead them into battle when the kingdom was threatened. In the High Middle Ages, the image of the knight atop a horse was the very embodiment of masculinity.[14] Leadership positions in the military remained the exclusive preserve of the nobility and an expression of manhood well into the sixteenth century, although by the time Wingfield and Percy entered the army, the officers' corps was increasingly populated by sons of the gentry or younger sons of the nobility whose families purchased them an officers' commissions in place of a landed estate.[15] The fact that Wingfield's father was dead and Percy was not an eldest son probably influenced their decision to join the military. Once in the army, mastery—and thus manhood—was secure. Entering the service as captains, both men immediately acquired a company of infantry to command. They expected the same respect from these men that a lord received from his villeins.

Moreover, Wingfield and Percy entered the army at a moment of great opportunity. Beginning in the reign of Henry VIII, England entered a series of wars in Europe and Ireland that increased in intensity over the course of the sixteenth century. By the 1590s, Queen Elizabeth had committed tens of thousands of troops to fighting two large-scale conflicts: the Anglo-Spanish War (1585–1604) in the Low Countries and the Nine Years' War (1594–1603) in Ireland. These conflicts provided ample opportunities for young captains to make a name for themselves.[16] Wingfield and Percy held leadership positions in both Ireland and the Netherlands in the decades before they ventured to America. Henry J. Webb has observed that captains in the Elizabethan army, "often having no knowledge of military discipline, conducted their army affairs as they might have conducted their civilian lives." Lacking any professional training for the military, many captains went to war to line their pockets, and often abandoned their companies so that they could spend more time "in great towns feasting, banqueting, and carousing with their dames."[17] While it is unclear whether Wingfield or Percy engaged in such shenanigans, both men did use military service as a means to an end. In Ireland and the Low Countries, they ingratiated themselves with men like Sir Fernando Gorges and Ralph Lane who promoted English colonization, and began scheming for ways to parlay their military experience into colonial profit.

While the well-born saw the military as a vehicle for maintaining their social position, and along with it their manhood, the lesser-born viewed the army as an opportunity for adventure and a vehicle to demonstrate their manhood. Over the course of the sixteenth century, manhood in England was in the midst of a prolonged and profound crisis. The cause of the troubles was an economic transformation by which manorialism was slowly replaced by agrarian capitalism. The accompanying enclosure of open fields and engrossing of farms forced tens of thousands of people off their lands. A simultaneous population explosion drove wages down and food prices up, leading to mass unemployment and dislocation. By 1600, some thirty percent of England was destitute. Although this prolonged financial calamity affected all segments of the population, young men took the brunt of it. They were forced to seek work far from the towns of their birth, effectively ending the feudal loyalties that underscored much of medieval domestic arrangements. Instead of being dutiful tillers of the soil, they became "masterless men" who roamed the countryside seeking work or charity. In short, the medieval feudal order that guaranteed Wingfield and Percy a place atop the society was verging on collapse just as they came of age.[18]

The economic crisis inhibited the path to manhood for many young Britons. Bereft of steady income or property, more and more young men were unable to establish independent households and thus delayed marriage and family formation. Age at first marriage crept steadily upward as the hard times continued, topping twenty-nine for men in the second half of the sixteenth century, with one in five having not married by the age of forty.[19] As men remained single longer, they found themselves increasingly exploited by a government that mandated they obtain yearlong labor contracts. A generation of men in their late twenties and early thirties thus found themselves in a demeaning and subordinate position at the age at which they expected to attain mastery. Accordingly, men at the middle and bottom of English society were increasingly desperate for a new means to demonstrate manhood.

Many of these men looked to the military. In cultures the world over and dating back millennia, warfare has been an effective path to manhood. More than any other activity, combat effectively separates the men from the boys as well as the men from the women. A ritualized cycle of leaving home, training to use weapons, bonding with comrades, and surrendering one's will to a commander earns a man a place in society based on his ability to defend it. In this, warfare is a male rite of passage as a young man cannot marry and father children until he has proved himself in battle.[20] Early modern England was no different. An English soldier gained a sense of purpose as well as a source of income. He attained power through the possession of firearms and was able to exercise sexual license unimaginable in his hometown. In a world where hard times undermined the path to gender privilege, the military offered an alternative.

In many ways, John Smith embodied the martial manliness of early modern England. Born in 1580, Smith grew up the son of a yeoman in rural Lincolnshire. His family was comfortable and Smith could have easily married a local girl and settled down to a life of farming and fatherhood. Yet this version of manhood held little appeal for Smith. By age thirteen he had grown weary of the English countryside. His parents attempted to prepare him for the new economy by sending him to village schools and apprenticing him to a merchant, but this had little effect. When his father died in 1596, Smith sold his inheritance and joined the military. He saw combat in the Low Countries at the age of sixteen and this only whetted his appetite for more. He left the English service to fight in eastern Europe and probably received the title "Captain" from a foreign prince. By the time he sailed for Virginia in 1607, Smith had already traversed Europe and visited Hungary, Turkey, Russia, and North Africa. He became the antithesis of his father, never marrying or settling down, yet he successfully laid claim to manhood. Instead of a wife, he took lovers. While other men achieved immortality through fatherhood, Smith praised his own adventures in his many histories, recasting himself as a swashbuckler and a conquistador for all the yeoman farmers of Lincolnshire to envy.[21]

Some ninety thousand young Englishmen followed Captain Smith into the military between 1588 and 1627, and we might speculate as to the role of manhood in motivating their participation. Unlike Smith, most did not have the luxury of choosing military service over farming. Elizabethan commentators described soldiers as "the dregs of society" or "scoundrels, thieves and murderers," and historians have found little in these assessments that needs revision. They were the quintessential victims of the economic transformation: men from poor regions and vulnerable occupational groups who had no other means of support, or desperate men who turned to crime only to be punished with conscription. For such men, military service did not bring accolades or communal respect. If anything, it lowered their position in society. They were overworked and underpaid, shipped far from home to fight in foreign wars where they faced disease and near-certain death.[22]

Nevertheless, foreign service allowed even the dregs to attain manhood. Contemporary reports of English soldiers' behavior depict not a class of broken degenerates but proud men who exercised masculine privilege. "The common sort of our countrymen that go to war, of purpose more to spoil than to serve," complained officer Geoffrey Gates, "they put themselves to the liberty and use of swearing, drunkenness, shameless fornication, dicing, and thievery, in slow wars and under loose government in the tumultuous state of a foreign nation."[23] Emasculated at home, soldiers found plenty of ways in Ireland and on the Continent to demonstrate their manhood. Denied wives, the men sought lovers and prostitutes in Dutch garrison towns. Denied property, they plundered and claimed booty. As civilians, the men were forced into labor contracts and a dependent status, but as soldiers, they refused to cower before authority. Idleness was rampant and desertion drained some twenty percent of the army annually. Men frequently abandoned the service in Ireland, while in the Low Countries, the Earl of Leicester lost some 300 of his 1,100 recruits. Those who did not desert stood their ground and mutinied when times got tough and supplies ran low. Loyalty to one's country ebbed particularly low among men who had no home to return to. Perhaps the height of indignity came in January 1587 when several English garrisons in the Netherlands, tired of their mistreatment, defected to the Spanish and handed over several key defenses in the process.[24]

The caveat to disaffected young men claiming their manhood in foreign wars was that it became difficult for them to transition back to civilian life. Having learned a masculine ethos that relied on conquest, pillaging, and mutiny, the more staid manliness of agricultural labor and domesticity seemed disappointing. Former convicts returned to a life of crime, while those who had been unemployed became vagabonds. Between 1560 and 1640, soldiers and sailors were the fastest growing occupational groups among vagrants.[25] We might thus observe that while military service in other places and times typically was a prerequisite to marriage and a household, in early modern England it was an alternative to it. Once again, the example of John Smith is instructive. Upon returning from his adventures, he chose not to settle down in Lincolnshire, but rather sank his earnings and hopes into the Virginia Company.

John Smith and the Self-Made Soldier

In December 1606, Edward Maria Wingfield, George Percy, and John Smith boarded ships destined for America. All three men had purchased shares in the Virginia Company and all three sought the adventure and profits that a colonial enterprise was sure to bring. Arriving at the Chesapeake in April the following year, the men unsealed the official instructions sent by the company and discovered that Wingfield, Smith, and five others were to constitute the colony's governing council. Although Percy was inexplicably excluded, the seven named members quickly assembled and immediately elected the highest-born member to be president of the colony. Landing at Jamestown a few weeks later, President Wingfield called on his experience leading men into battle to plant the colony. Security was paramount and so he set the men to work building a fort and making contact with the Powhatan Indians. Only then did the colonists begin building houses and planting crops.

The conflicting approaches to manhood that divided sixteenth-century England accompanied the colonists to Jamestown. From the start the colony was divided between the well-born who came to profit from the labor of others, and the economically desperate who saw America as an overseas adventure not unlike Ireland or the Netherlands. According to John Smith, councilors and gentlemen just outnumbered the carpenters, artisans, laborers, and boys on the first voyage.[26] Division became apparent in late summer 1607 when the colonists' health rapidly deteriorated. In early August, the first colonist died from the bloody flux, a disease contracted from contaminated water, and within a month nearly half the colonists were dead. As death stalked the camp, differences of social rank emerged in bold relief. The well-born reminded the colonists to respect the social order while the lowly born recalled the prerogative of soldiers to mutiny when conditions became unbearable.

The divisions of social rank made their first emphatic appearance in September 1607 when a cabal of councilors challenged Wingfield's leadership. Later reflecting on the experience, Wingfield blamed the colony's troubles on men who had no respect for the traditional order. Wingfield saw the problems foreshadowed in June when Captain Christopher Newport warned the colonists "to be myndefull of their dutyes to his Majestie and the Collonye." But as the summer wore on, Wingfield and three councilors—including John Smith—fell out over the proper distribution of the colony's supplies. Wingfield claimed that although the councilors demanded "some better allowance for themselves," he attempted to retain the social order by insisting "every man should have his portion according to their places." Further attempts to reason with the three proved futile as the president began to suspect a conspiracy against him. "Thus had they forsaken his Majesties government sett us downe in the instruccions," opined Wingfield, who chided the men for subverting the will of their superiors. Unable to answer the charges against him, Wingfield was removed from power by Smith and two other councilors. Not being men of proper station, the three had no idea how to care for their subordinates. The councilors "beate men at their pleasures," remembered Wingfield, who added, "Wear this whipping, lawing, beating, and hanging in Virginia knowne in England I feare it would drive many well affected myndes from this honorable action of Virginia."[27]

Not surprisingly, John Smith remembered Wingfield's removal quite differently. Personal ambition had not motivated him; rather, he and his compatriots were merely embodying the will of the people. "Captaine Wingefield having ordred the affaires in such sort that he was generally hated of all," Smith wrote, "in which respect with one consent he was deposed from his presidencie."[28] George Percy, who was no admirer of Smith, lent credence to the captain's interpretation in his own account of the first summer. He described a desperate colony of men who slept "lying on the bare cold ground what weather soever came" and starved by a diet of "Barlie sod" and water "full of slime and filth." His military experience taught him that such living conditions threatened the security of the encampment, as "this miserable distresse" meant "not having five able men to man our Bulwarkes upon any occasion." It was chilling to hear Percy, who had served in both the Low Countries and Ireland, lament, "There were never Englishmen left in a forreigne Countrey in such miserie as wee were in this new discovered Virginia." Having seen what happened when soldiers suffered such a situation, it was of little surprise to Percy that Wingfield was deposed.[29]

With the removal of Wingfield, the council elected John Ratcliffe (alias Sicklemore) from among the councilors to serve as president of the colony. For his part, Smith ventured into the wilderness to seek assistance from the Powhatans. When he returned in July 1608, it was clear that Wingfield's prognostications had been correct. Smith chastised "the needlesse crueltie of the silly President," who had "riotously consumed the store" and forced the colonists to build him a palace in the woods.³⁰ He forced Ratcliffe from power and assumed the office himself in September. Neither Ratcliffe nor Smith could claim membership in England's elite, but considerations of birth were less important to Smith than they had been to Wingfield. He formulated an ideal of leadership that downplayed social rank and relied instead on the successful demonstration of manhood. In many ways, John Smith's vision for Jamestown was in keeping with his military experience. A man of modest means who rose through the ranks because of his bravery and skill, Smith believed that anyone could be a successful leader as long as he subscribed to a manly set of values that included strength, dedication, and selflessness.

For Smith, physical strength was the first test of manhood. Although nearly everyone—himself included—suffered from the debilitating effects of "seasoning" once they reached the Chesapeake, Smith viewed with deep skepticism the man whose health never recovered. Soon after Wingfield's removal, Smith lost faith in his coconspirators once their "never mending sicknes" forced him to take the lead in building houses and trading with the Indians. He saw a weak constitution as evidence of a lack of commitment to the colony, and thus was not surprised when "the still sickly President" Ratcliffe sold the colony's stores for profit and tried to steal a pinnace to sail back to England. In contrast, Smith praised the masculine vigor of those who marched into battle against the Powhatan Indians. Never shy about praising himself, Smith told of the time he discovered that Opechancanough was plotting to kill him. Instead of backing down in fear, Smith challenged the warrior to a duel. "Take therefore your Armes, you see mine," he told Opechancanough. "My body shall bee as naked as yours: the Isle in your river is a fit place, if you be contented: and the conquerour (of us two) shall be Lord and Master over all our men." In his various histories of the colony, Smith praised the physical prowess of the men and disparaged those who shrunk in fear before the Indians. He admired the courage of George Forrest, who "had seaventeene Arrowes sticking in him, and one shot through him, yet lived six or seaven dayes, as if he had small hurt," but rebuked "the patient Councell that nothing would move to warre with the Salvages." A man was strong and fought vigorously in his own defense.³¹

Smith also believed that a man should be able to subordinate his personal desires for the good of the unit. Having led men into battle, Smith knew the dangers of greed and constantly rebuked those men in Virginia who placed their love of money before the colony. "There was no talke, no hope, no worke, but dig gold, wash gold, refine gold, loade gold," he complained, and much to his dismay, it was his fellow councilors who were the worst offenders. "Captaine Martin being always very sickly and unserviceable" demanded that space in a supply ship returning to England be reserved for a shiny substance he mistook to be gold. Similarly, Smith's respect for Captain Newport declined when he discovered that Newport was "a refiner" who "guilded mens hopes with great promises." Such men cared little for the success of the colony and abandoned it as quickly as possible. More admirable to Smith was Captain Francis Nelson, who visited the colony in early 1608 and generously provisioned the colonists: "He had not any thing but he freely imparted it, which honest dealing (being a Mariner) caused us admire him: we would not have wished more then he did for us."[32]

Throughout his writings, John Smith repeatedly depicted common men more favorably than the well-born. Among the leaders who left accounts of the early years, he alone listed the names of immigrants regardless of social rank.[33] He also singled out the elite for scorn. Among the settlers who arrived with the Second Supply in October 1608 were "two gallants" named Gabriel Beadle and John Russell, whom Smith disparaged for being "both proper Gentlemen." At first, the two worked without complaint, but after a week "the Axes so oft blistered their tender fingers" that they began to utter curse words with every third swing. Refusing to allow profanity regardless of one's station, Smith devised a plan to pour a can of water down the gentlemen's sleeves each time they took the Lord's name in vain. To be sure, Smith was no Leveler and he faithfully recorded the occupation and title of each colonist. Yet he insisted that every man in the colony be held to a single standard. In early 1609, after having served as president for a few months, Smith began to grow weary with the idle colonists who could do nothing but complain. Accordingly, he appealed to the men's sense of fairness. "Countrymen," he addressed the men, "the long experience of our late miseries, I hope is sufficient to perswade every one to a present correction of himselfe," adding for good measure, "he that will not worke shall not eate."[34]

John Smith's formulation of order predicted a modern version of military masculinity. He asserted that a man's identity and claim to gendered power derived entirely from his ability to demonstrate hegemonic masculinity. High social rank neither exempted one from hard work nor guaranteed him a leadership position, while even the most lowly born could be praised for his service to the colony. Smith no doubt derived some of these ideas from his experience in the Netherlands, but they were also born of circumstances. With the colony still teetering on the brink of collapse, Smith needed to find a way to make the well-born work and keep the low-born from mutinying.

He also needed a means to legitimatize his own leadership, which his common birth undermined. Smith thus connected manliness to military duty in a way that was extraordinary in the seventeenth century but would become common in the twentieth.

Unfortunately for Smith, his ideas fell on deaf ears in Jamestown. The men complained openly about his high-handed style of leadership and resisted him at every turn. One group went so far as to make contact with the Indians and promise the fort's tools in exchange for food. This made Smith livid. "Those distracted Gluttonous Loyterers" were prepared "to sell not only our kettles, hows, tooles, and Iron," but also the colony's "swords, pieces, and the very Ordnance and howses" in order to remain idle. Smith no doubt realized what was happening. Like so many angry and disposed soldiers, the colonists felt wronged by the conditions of life in America and were prepared to hand over Jamestown to the enemy. To counter this, Smith depicted himself as one of the men. He addressed the colonists as "fellow souldiers" and swore, "I will doe my best for my most maligner." Unlike Wingfield, he promised all men an equal portion, stating proudly, "I never had more from the store then the worst of you." This too went unheeded by some colonists, including William Volday, who plotted with the Powhatans to overthrow Smith. Although two colonists betrayed Volday, others plotted Smith's murder. In the fall of 1609 a colonist set fire to a powder bag in the president's lap, "which tore the flesh from his body and thighs, nine or ten inches square in a most pittiful manner."[35] In excruciating pain, Smith finally admitted defeat and returned to England. His attempt to hold all men to the same standards of manhood had failed.

Thomas Dale and the Obedient Soldier

After John Smith abandoned the colony, Jamestown rapidly descended into chaos and anarchy. By September 1609 all seven of the original councilors had died, returned to England, or been discredited, and so the presidency finally devolved to George Percy. Highly skeptical of Smith's egalitarian principles, Percy attempted to govern the colony much as Wingfield had two years earlier. By this point, however, Percy had taken ill, and as Smith could have predicted, this weakened the colonists' respect for him. With winter approaching and supplies dwindling, Percy sent John Ratcliffe to trade with the Powhatans for food. After unwisely angering the Indians, Ratcliffe was captured, tied to a pole, and "his fleshe was skraped from his bones with Mussell shelles." When Percy then sent Francis West to seek maize, "Capteyne

Weste by the perswasion or rather by the inforcement of his company hoysed upp Sayles and shaped their Course directtly for England and lefte us in thatt extreme misery and wantte." After these failed attempts to supply the colony, Percy noted that "all of us at James Town" began "to feele the sharpe pricke of hunger." The population of the colony halved. Many were lost to starvation, while others "did Runn away unto the Salvages whome we never heard of after."[36] The medieval military model had returned, with the well-born leading and the soldiers mutinying.

Even before "the starving time" of the winter of 1609–10, the directors of the Virginia Company had become convinced of the need to change course. With death a common occurrence and instability rampant, the colony had yet to turn a profit. Accordingly, the directors sought and received a new charter from the king, which allowed for a reorganization of the government in Virginia. Although the council was retained, a powerful governor (to be appointed by the company and answerable to it alone) replaced the president. Specifically, the second charter empowered the governor "to use and exercise martial law, in cases of rebellion or mutiny."[37] In observing the failed presidencies of Wingfield and his successors, the company directors deduced that the military model for Jamestown still made sense but that the leader on the ground had to be given near absolute power to make it work.

These changes reflected larger shifts in ideas about the military. The wars in the Low Countries marked a turning point, when the medieval military model collapsed and a new, modern model was formulated. Change had begun in the 1580s under the leadership of Dutch Prince Maurice of Nassau, although similar ideas were evident among the Spanish forces as well. The reassessment of the military stemmed from the introduction of small arms fueled by gunpowder, which increased the importance of the gun-armed infantry at the expense of pikemen and the cavalry. This, in turn, led to an enlargement of scale and the creation of military science as a field of academic study. Modern warfare demanded more men, more money, and more planning than had been typical in the medieval era. Although the full extent of this "military revolution" would not be felt until the Thirty Years' War (1618–48), a movement for change was apparent in England at the turn of the seventeenth century. Having fought in the Low Countries, English officers embraced these new ideas when American colonization was in its infancy.

One of the changes that English planners seized almost immediately was a new attention to discipline in the ranks. Commentators like Matthew Sutcliffe and Thomas Digges used their experience serving as officers in the Low Countries to call for a reformation of the common soldier. Digges advised that the widespread practice of conscripting the dregs of society be ended, while Sutcliffe recommended that recruits be scrutinized based on "first, the strength of the body; secondly, the vigor and virtues of the mind; and thirdly, the manner and trade of the parties' living."[38] After attempts to end the practice of drafting rogues failed, military planners began to promote teaching new values to recruits. William Garrard insisted that soldiers be imbued with "obedience, silence, secretiveness, sobriety, valor, truthfulness, and loyalty." To enforce these standards, officers were to keep soldiers constantly at work. The spade acquired new significance as soldiers dug trenches, ramparts, and redoubts. These defensive structures were needed as weapons and tactics evolved, but they also kept the men busy. The new emphasis on values and work ultimately required new leaders. Another piece of the feudal past slipped away as writers disparaged officers appointed for social rank alone.[39]

To enforce the new philosophy, the English army adopted harsh new military laws. In 1585, the Earl of Leicester issued a legal code that regulated three aspects of a soldier's life: divine, moral, and martial. The code strictly prohibited blasphemy and mandated religious service attendance; it prohibited idle diversions such as playing cards and forbade soldiers from bringing women into the camp; and it specified the soldier's actions in battle, banned stealing another man's rations, and established a clear chain of command. Most important, desertions were to be curtailed and mutinies prevented. It is possible that Leicester derived his laws from the Dutch code, which sought to protect civilians by controlling soldiers. In both the Dutch and the English versions, rape was a capital crime, and pillaging and looting were to be harshly punished as well. Such actions on the part of English troops had aroused the animus of the Dutch populace and Leicester no less than his Dutch counterparts sought to suppress them. Above all, Leicester's code placed a great deal of power in the hands of officers to keep order.[40]

Appropriately, the Virginia Company turned to three officers who had extensive experience leading men in the Low Countries to fill the new position of colonial governor: Baron De La Warr, Sir Thomas Gates, and Sir Thomas Dale. The three had earned considerable acclaim for their military service and each had been knighted for leadership in battle. That the company hoped these men would replicate their successes in Virginia is evident by the fact that it sought them out and negotiated with the Dutch army for their temporary release. De La Warr and Gates sailed in the fall of 1609, while Dale followed two years later.

The military revolution ultimately affected manhood. For some, the new formulation meant promotion for distinguished service. Although De La

Warr was born to an aristocratic family, Gates and Dale hailed from unmemorable backgrounds. Accordingly, while De La Warr inherited an Oxford education and membership in Parliament, Gates and Dale had no other path to success except the military. In many ways, the three fulfilled John Smith's formulation of military masculinity once they reached Virginia. De La Warr soon sickened after he arrived in Jamestown, and thus his governorship was ineffectual and brief. By contrast, Gates survived a shipwreck in Bermuda on his way to Virginia and had to suppress a mutiny and build new ships to reach the mainland. Between them, Gates and Dale governed for six years and oversaw the erection of new settlements and the successful conclusion of the First Anglo-Powhatan War (1609–14). The two then returned to England, where they were praised for their service. Unlike the case with common soldiers of the sixteenth century, the military was not an alternative to civilian manhood for Gates and Dale but a path to it. Both used their success on the battlefield and in America to gain powerful friends, distinguished wives, and landed estates.[41] While Gates and Dale realized the social mobility that modern military masculinity afforded them, neither man extended the same opportunity to the Virginia colonists. Like Smith, the two rejected the medieval regime and with it the right of the well-born to be captains and the soldiers to mutiny. Yet whereas Smith held all his men to the same code of manliness, Gates and Dale reduced them to mindless drones. To them, the military revolution meant that they no longer had to worry about social rank—only military rank mattered. Subordinates were not to be reasoned with or given the opportunity to prove their manhood. Instead, they were to obey their commanders and be punished ruthlessly if they failed to follow instructions.

Upon taking over the governorship of Virginia, Gates and then Dale began to implement the lessons they had learned in the Dutch service. First, they published a military code to govern the colony. When he arrived in May 1610 and discovered (in the words of colonial secretary William Strachey) "all things so contrary to our expectations, so fully of misery and misgovernment," Gates immediately posted on the meetinghouse door "certaine Orders and Instructions, which hee enjoyned them strictly to observe."[42] Published in England in 1612 as the *Lawes Divine, Morall and Martiall*, these edicts imposed martial law on the colony. Darrett Rutman has argued persuasively that these laws owe a debt to Leicester's military code and thus transferred the military order established in the Netherlands to Virginia.[43] The *Lawes* announced to the colonists in Virginia that they were soldiers in a new military regime and that they would have to modify their behavior to fit the model. All were required to work, obey their superiors without question, and live an orderly life. Tellingly, the first law informed men of their obligation to worship Christ, "the King of kings, the commaunder of commaunders." The *Lawes* also prescribed the death penalty for "any Souldier" who attempted "to depart from, and abandon the Colony" as well as for "hee that shall begin a mutiny." Mirroring the laws on the Continent, the Virginia version also sought to prevent friction with the natives by spelling out severe punishments for men who stole from or raped Indians.[44]

Dale also created a model community to demonstrate what Virginia could be like if it was placed under the proper authority. In September 1611, he led about two hundred men up the James River to found a settlement at Henrico. Sufficiently removed from the continued insolence of Jamestown, Dale implemented his vision. Two years later he claimed success in a letter to England. His first act was to divide the men into groups based on skill and industry. "Some of them be officers and commanders," he wrote, "others of my men be either soldiers or workmen." A third group, which he deemed "fit neither to fight nor for the mechanic trades," he termed "farmers." In this system, each man was set to the station best fitting his ambition, and as Dale promised the company, "if they work they shall be kept here, and then they shall subsist of themselves without England." But Dale was coy about how he managed to compel such discipline. "Oh sir, my heart bleeds when I think what men we have here," he reported. "Did I not carry a severe hand over them they would starve one the other by breaking open houses and chest[s] to steal a pottle of corn from their poor brother, and when they have stolen that the poor man must starve."[45] In short, Dale used military organization to compel his men to obedience.

The interpretation of the military revolution by Gates and Dale actively curtailed the manhood of the common soldier. Under the new regime, all the elements that made military life undeniably masculine were slated for elimination: women, booty, and a sense of personal autonomy. Not surprisingly, the colonists resisted the reign of Gates and Dale. In 1624, eight years after Dale returned to England, the Virginia Company teetered toward collapse.

Following a devastating Indian attack that killed 347 colonists, King James I began an investigation of the company that ultimately led to its dissolution. Hoping to shed light on the abuses of leadership in Jamestown, a group of colonists known as "the Ancient Planters of Virginia" issued a pamphlet that traced their troubles back to Gates and Dale. Unflinching in their defiance, the colonists condemned Dale for adding "to that extremity of misery under which the colony from her infancy groaned" when he "made and published most cruel and tyrannous laws, exceeding the strictest rules of martial discipline." They also condemned Henrico as "no better than the slaughter of His Majesty's free subjects." Apparently, the Henrico colonists treated Dale much as the Jamestown colonists had once treated John Smith; they confronted his discipline by running off to live with the Indians, stealing food, and attempting to return to England. Yet Dale made no appeal to the men's sense of duty and fairness. Instead, the defiant ones "were shot to death, hanged, and broken upon the wheel." Doling out such punishments had not earned the governors the respect of the colonists but rather their enmity.[46]

For Gates and Dale, the new military order was not entirely without a role for manhood, yet it was counterintuitive for the early colonists. Obedience was the first mark of a man, and thus a soldier had to demonstrate his ability to serve without complaint before anything else. This was the lesson they had learned in the Low Countries and now they applied it in America. There was no longer any place for a soldier to mutiny; rather, he was expected to obey his commander regardless of condition. He who obeyed might be rewarded with a promotion, but this was entirely contingent on the whims of his commander.

Civilian Manhood and Jamestown

Ultimately, the martial cast for Jamestown failed. Regardless of whether the Virginia Company appointed leaders based on their social status or their individual accomplishments, organizing the colony like a military expedition had not led to profits for investors or internal stability. Accordingly, it was left to Sir Edwin Sandys to institute civilian government in Jamestown. In 1618, the company began to patent land for individual colonists, thus instituting private property, and a year later the colonists received a voice in their own governance when the House of Burgesses first convened. When the company started sponsoring the immigration of women, the military regime finally came to a close.

That a military regime led to instability seemed ironic to the Virginia Company and remains so to us today. In the sixteenth century the Spanish had been highly successful in colonizing the Americas under the leadership of the quasi-military conquistadores, and the British would build a second empire along the same principles in the nineteenth century. But the military was in transition during the era of American colonization and this compromised its effectiveness as a model. Indeed, in those North American settlements that followed immediately after Jamestown—Plymouth, Massachusetts, and Maryland—civilian organization would prove more effective than the military model. The rules of membership in the military were in flux, and this disrupted the connection between service and manhood. Within a generation the puzzle would be put back together with Smith's and Dale's formulation melded effectively, but in the meantime the transition led to divisions among leaders and between governors and colonists.

In the end, the lasting vision of manhood in early Jamestown was probably the one modeled by John Rolfe. Like Smith and Dale, Rolfe hailed from an undistinguished lineage, yet he was a man of economic rather than military ambition. In 1609, he sailed for Virginia with his pregnant wife. Although his family died en route, once Rolfe made it to the mainland he bypassed much of the bitter divide engendered by the military regime. He experimented with growing tobacco, eventually introducing to Virginia the variety that would salvage the financial relevance of the colony. He even moved to Henrico while Sir Thomas Dale was governor; but while Dale and the colonists struggled for supremacy, Rolfe planted his tobacco and took the newly Christianized Pocahontas as his wife. For Rolfe, manhood came through earning profits and establishing himself as a patriarch over a new generation of Virginians. As more men aspired to following his path, observers like Sandys rarely commented that there were too many men like John Rolfe in Virginia.[47]

NOTES

This chapter would not have been possible without the careful comments of my Eastern Michigan University colleagues Steven J. Ramold and Matt Schumann, and the participants of 2008 American Men's Studies Association conference. I am also indebted to the students of "Jamestown, 1607–2007: An Interdisciplinary Exploration" (EMU, 2007), whose inspiration made this essay possible.

1. Susan Myra Kingsbury, *The Records of the Virginia Company of London*, 4 vols. (Washington, D.C.: Government Printing Office, 1906–35), 1:269.

2. James Horn, *A Land as God Made It: Jamestown and the Birth of America* (New York: Basic Books, 2005); Karen Ordahl Kupperman, *The Jamestown Project* (Cambridge, Mass.: Harvard University Press, 2007); William M. Kelso, *Jamestown: The Buried Truth* (Charlottesville: University of Virginia Press, 2006); Camilla Townsend, *Pocahontas and the Powhatan Dilemma* (New York: Hill and Wang, 2004); Robert Appelbaum and John Wood Sweet, eds., *Envisioning an English Empire: Jamestown and the Making of the North Atlantic World* (Philadelphia: University of Pennsylvania Press, 2005); Edmund S. Morgan, *American Slavery, American Freedom: The Ordeal of Colonial Virginia* (New York: Norton, 1975).

3. Mary Beth Norton, *Founding Mothers and Fathers: Gendered Power and the Forming of American Society* (New York: Knopf, 1996); Kathleen Brown, *Good Wives, Nasty Wenches, and Anxious Patriarchs: Gender, Race, and Power in Colonial Virginia* (Chapel Hill: University of North Carolina Press, 1996). See also Karen Vieira Powers, *Women in the Crucible of Conquest: The Gendered Genesis of Spanish American Society, 1500–1600* (Albuquerque: University of New Mexico Press, 2005); Joan Pong Linton, *The Romance of the New World: Gender and the Literary Formations of English Colonialism* (Cambridge: Cambridge University Press, 1998).

4. Virginia Bernhard, "'Men, Women and Children' at Jamestown: Population and Gender in Early Virginia, 1607–1610," *Journal of Southern History* 58 (1992): 599–618; David R. Ransome, "Wives for Virginia, 1621," *William and Mary Quarterly*, 3rd ser., 48 (1991): 3–18; "Heroines of Virginia," *William and Mary College Quarterly Historical Magazine* 15 (1906): 39–41; H. R. McIlwaine, "The Maids Who Came to Virginia in 1620 and 1621 for Husbands," *Reviewer* 1 (1921): 105–13.

5. John Rolfe, "A True Relation of the State of Virginia," in James Horn, ed., *Captain John Smith: Writings, and Other Narratives of Roanoke, Jamestown, and the First English Settlement of America* (New York: Library of America, 2007), 1182; John Clark, "Confession of the English Pilot of Virginia, 18 February 1613," in Edward Wright Haile, ed., *Jamestown Narratives: Eyewitness Accounts of the Virginia Colony, the First Decade, 1607–17* (Champlain, Va.: Roundhouse, 1998), 693; Irene W. D. Hecht, "The Virginia Muster of 1624–5 as a Source for Demographic History," *William and Mary Quarterly*, 3d ser., 30 (1973): 65–92; Evarts B. Greene and Virginia D. Harrington, *American Population Before the Federal Census of 1790* (New York: Columbia University Press, 1932), 127–31, 143–51.

6. On types of manhood, see R. W. Connell, *Masculinities*, 2nd ed. (Berkeley: University of California Press, 2005); Ruth Mazo Karras, *From Boys to Men: Formations of Masculinity in Late Medieval Europe* (Philadelphia: University of Pennsylvania Press, 2003); Jennifer Low, *Manhood and the Duel: Masculinity in Early Modern Drama and Culture* (New York: Palgrave Macmillan, 2003); John Gilbert McCurdy, "'Your Affectionate Brother': Complementary Manhoods in the Letters of John and Timothy Pickering," *Early American Studies* 4 (2006): 512–45. On change over time, see E. Anthony Rotundo, *American Manhood: Transformations in Masculinity from the Revolution to the Modern Era* (New York: Basic Books, 1993); Michael Kimmel, *Manhood in America: A Cultural History* (New York: Free Press, 1996).

7. The exceptions were Matthew Scrivener and Francis West, whose presidencies totaled three months of the first twelve years. John W. Raimo, *Biographical Directory of American Colonial and Revolutionary Governors, 1607–1789* (Westport, Conn.: Meckler Books, 1980), 453–67.

8. Darrett B. Rutman, "The Virginia Company and Its Military Regime," in Darrett B. Rutman, ed., *The Old Dominion: Essays For Thomas Perkins Abernethy* (Charlottesville: University Press of Virginia, 1964), 1–20; Edmund S. Morgan, "The Labor Problem at Jamestown, 1607–18," *American Historical Review* 76 (1971): 595–611; Stephen Saunders Webb, "Army and Empire: English Garrison Government in Britain and America, 1569 to 1763," *William and Mary Quarterly*, 3rd ser., 34 (1977): 1–31; Karen Ordahl Kupperman, "Apathy and Death in Early Jamestown," *Journal of American History* 66 (1979): 24–40.

9. Joshua S. Goldstein, *War and Gender: How Gender Shapes the War System and Vice Versa* (Cambridge: Cambridge University Press, 2001); Frank J. Barrett, "The Organizational Construction of Hegemonic Masculinity: The Case of the U.S. Navy," in Stephen M Whitehead and Frank J. Barrett, eds., *The Masculinities Reader* (Cambridge: Polity, 2001), 77–99; David H. J. Morgan, "Theater of War: Combat, the Military, and Masculinities," in Harry Brod and Michael Kaufman, eds., *Theorizing Masculinities* (Thousand Oaks, Calif.: Sage, 1994), 165–82; Paul Higate and John Hopton, "War, Militarism, and Masculinities," in Michael S. Kimmel, Jeff Hearn, and R. W. Connell, eds., *Handbook of Studies on Men and Masculinities* (Thousand Oaks, Calif.: Sage Publications, 2005), 432–47; Carol Burke, *Camp All-American, Hanoi Jane, and the High-and-Tight: Gender, Folklore, and Changing Military Culture* (Boston: Beacon, 2004); Mark Moss, *Manliness and Militarism: Educating Young Boys in Ontario for War* (Don Mills, Ont.: Oxford University Press, 2001). Studies of military masculinity before the twentieth century are still relatively few. Two notable exceptions are Ann M. Little, *Abraham in Arms: War and Gender in Colonial New England* (Philadelphia: University of Pennsylvania Press, 2007); and Steven J. Ramold, *Baring the Iron Hand: Discipline in the Union Army* (DeKalb: Northern Illinois University Press, 2009).

10. Marcia Kovitz, "The Roots of Military Masculinity," in Paul R. Higate, ed., *Military Masculinities: Identity and the State* (Westport, Conn.: Praeger, 2003), 1–14.

11. The "military revolution" was first proposed by Michael Roberts in 1955 and has been subjected to considerable dispute ever since. Historians agree that a change took place, but where, when, and how is a matter of considerable dispute. Michael Roberts, *The Military Revolution, 1560–1660* (Belfast: Boyd, 1956); Geoffrey Parker, *The Military Revolution: Military Innovation and the Rise of the West, 1500–1800* (Cambridge: Cambridge University Press, 1988), 1–5; Jeremy Black, *A Military Revolution? Military Change and European Society, 1550–1800* (London: Macmillan, 1991); David Eltis, *The Military Revolution in Sixteenth-Century Europe* (New York: Barnes and Noble, 1995); Andrew Ayton and J. L. Price, "Introduction: The Military Revolution from a Medieval Perspective," in Andrew Ayton and J. L. Price, eds., *The Medieval Military Revolution: State, Society, and Military Change in Medieval and Early Modern Europe* (New York: St. Martin's, 1995), 1–22.

12. Kari Boyd McBride, "Introduction: The Politics of Domestic Arrangements," in Kari Boyd McBride, ed., *Domestic Arrangements in Early Modern England* (Pittsburgh: Duquesne University Press, 2002), 5. See also Brown, *Good Wives*, 15–24; Susan Dwyer Amussen, *An Ordered Society: Gender and Class in Early Modern England* (Oxford: Basil Blackwell, 1988).

13. John A. Garraty and Mark C. Carnes, eds., *American National Biography*, 24 vols. (New York: Oxford University Press, 1999), s.vv. "Wingfield, Edward Maria," "Percy, George"; Jocelyn R. Wingfield, *Virginia's True Founder: Edward-Maria Wingfield and His Times, 1550–c. 1614* (Athens, Ga.: Wingfield Family Society, 1993).

14. M. Bennett, "Military Masculinity in England and Northern France, c. 1050–c. 1225," in D. M. Hadley, ed., *Masculinity in Medieval Europe* (London: Longman, 1999), 71–88.

15. Lawrence Stone, *The Family, Sex, and Marriage in England, 1500–1800* (New York: Harper and Row, 1977), 377–78.

16. C. G. Cruickshank, *Army Royal: Henry VIII's Invasion of France, 1513* (Oxford: Clarendon Press, 1969); Jonathan Israel, *The Dutch Republic: Its Rise, Greatness, and Fall, 1477–1806* (Oxford: Clarendon Press, 1995); Paul E. J. Hammer, *Elizabeth's Wars: War, Government, and Society in Tudor England, 1544–1604* (Hampshire: Palgrave Macmillan, 2003); Pieter Geyl, *The Revolt of the Netherlands, 1555–1609* (London: Williams and Norgate, 1932).

17. Henry J. Webb, *Elizabethan Military Science: The Books and the Practice* (Madison: University of Wisconsin Press, 1965), 70, 68.

18. A. L. Beier, *Masterless Men: The Vagrancy Problem in England, 1560–1640* (London: Methuen, 1985), 16–22; McBride, "Introduction," 5–6; Brown, *Good Wives*, 22–23. See also James Horn, *Adapting to a New World: English Society in the Seventeenth-Century Chesapeake* (Chapel Hill: University of North Carolina Press, 1994), 48–52; John Pound, *Poverty and Vagrancy in Tudor England*, 2nd ed. (London: Longman, 1986).

19. E. A. Wrigley and R. S. Schofield, *The Population History of England, 1541–1871: A Reconstruction* (Cambridge, Mass.: Harvard University Press, 1981), 424. See also Alan Macfarlane, *Marriage and Love in England: Modes of Reproduction, 1300–1840* (Oxford: Basil Blackwell, 1986), 20–27; John Gilbert McCurdy, *Citizen Bachelors: Manhood and the Creation of the United States* (Ithaca, N.Y.: Cornell University Press, 2009), 15–29.

20. Goldstein, *War and Gender*, 264–72; David D. Gilmore, *Manhood in the Making: Cultural Concepts of Masculinity* (New Haven, Conn.: Yale University Press, 1990), 120–21, 142, 148–51.

21. Philip L. Barbour, *The Three Worlds of Captain John Smith* (Boston: Houghton Mifflin, 1964), 3–73; Alden T. Vaughan, *American Genesis: Captain John Smith and the Founding of Virginia* (Boston: Little, Brown, 1975), 1–13.

22. C. G. Cruickshank, *Elizabeth's Army*, 2nd ed. (London: Oxford University Press, 1966), 27; H. L. Zwitzer, "The Eighty Years War," in Marco van der Hoeven, ed., *Exercise of Arms: Warfare in the Netherlands, 1568–1648*(Leiden: Brill, 1997), 48. See also Lindsay Boynton, *The Elizabethan Militia, 1558–1638* (London: Routledge and Kegan Paul, 1967). On the number of soldiers in foreign wars, see Parker, *Military Revolution*, 52.

23. Quoted in Webb, *Elizabethan Military Science*, 72.

24. Cruickshank, *Elizabeth's Army*, 165, 168–71; Israel, *Dutch Republic*, 220–30, 265; Parker, *Military Revolution*, 55, 58; Morgan, "Labor Problem at Jamestown," 607–8. For comparisons, see Cruickshank, *Army Royal*, 94–104; Gilbert John Millar, *Tudor Mercenaries and Auxiliaries, 1485–1547* (Charlottesville: University Press of Virginia, 1980); Geoffrey Parker, *The Army of Flanders and the Spanish Road, 1567–1659: The Logistics of Spanish Victory and Defeat in the Low Countries' War* (Cambridge: Cambridge University Press, 1972), 179–200.

25. Webb, *Elizabethan Military Science*, 75; Beier, *Masterless Men*, 93–95; Cruickshank, *Elizabeth's Army*, 26; Parker, *Army of Flanders*, 180. For present-day comparison, see Samantha Regan de Bere, "Masculinity in Work and Family Lives: Implications for Military Service and Resettlement," in Higate, *Military Masculinities*, 91–109; Bruce Allen Watson, *When Soldiers Quit: Studies in Military Disintegration* (Westport, Conn.: Praeger, 1997).

26. John Smith, *The Generall Historie of Virginia, New-England, and the Summer Isles*, in Horn, *Captain John Smith*, 332–34.

27. Edward Maria Wingfield, *A Discourse of Virginia*, in Horn, *Captain John Smith*, 951, 953–54, 959.

28. John Smith, *A True Relation*, in Horn, *Captain John Smith*, 8. See also Smith, *Generall Historie*, 312–13.

29. George Percy, *Discourse*, in Horn, *Captain John Smith*, 933.

30. Smith, *Generall Historie*, 341. See also Leslie Stephen and Sidney Lee, eds., *Dictionary of National Biography*, 66 vols. (New York: Macmillan, 1885–1901), s.v. "Sicklemore or Ratcliffe, John."

31. Smith, *Generall Historie*, 315, 329, 331, 377, 399.
32. Ibid., 328–31, 355.
33. Ibid., 310–12, 332–34, 365.
34. Ibid., 359–60, 385.
35. Ibid., 391–92, 402. See also Horn, *Land as God Made It*, 169–70.
36. George Percy, *A Trewe Relacyon*, in Horn, *Captain John Smith*, 1099–1100.
37. William Waller Hening, ed., *The Statutes at Large; Being a Collection of All the Laws of Virginia, from the First Session of the Legislature in the Year 1619*, 13 vols. (New York: Bartow, 1819–23), 1:96.
38. Quoted in Webb, *Elizabethan Military Science*, 59–60.
39. Webb, *Elizabethan Military Science*, 51–77; J. A. de Moor, "Experience and Experiment: Some Reflections upon the Military Developments in 16th- and 17th-Century Western Europe," in van der Hoeven, *Exercise of Arms*, 17–32; Israel, *Dutch Republic*, 267–71; Cruickshank, *Elizabeth's Army*, 28–29; Paul A. Jorgensen, "Moral Guidance and Religious Encouragement for the Elizabethan Soldier," *Huntington Library Quarterly* 13 (1950): 241–59.
40. Cruickshank, *Elizabeth's Army*, 159–63; Israel, *Dutch Republic*, 228–29, 268.
41. Garraty and Carnes, eds., *American National Biography*, s.vv. "Dale, Sir Thomas," "De La Warr, Baron," "Gates, Sir Thomas."
42. William Strachey, *A True Reportory*, in Horn, *Captain John Smith*, 1014–15.
43. Rutman, "Virginia Company," 15n51. See also David Thomas Konig, "'Dale's Laws' and the Non–Common Law Origins of Criminal Justice in Virginia," *American Journal of Legal History* 26 (1982): 354–75.
44. D. H. Flaherty, ed., *Laws Divine, Moral, and Martial Compiled by William Strachey* (Charlottesville: University Press of Virginia, 1969), 9–25.
45. Dale, "Letter from Henrico," in Haile, *Jamestown Narratives*, 778–79. On Henrico, see Charles E. Hatch, Jr., *The First Seventeen Years: Virginia, 1607–24* (Charlottesville: University Press of Virginia, 1957), 50–52.
46. The Ancient Planters of Virginia, "A Brief Declaration," in Haile, *Jamestown Narratives*, 899–900.
47. Garraty and Carnes, eds., *American National Biography*, s.v. "Rolfe, John."

2

Indian and English Dreams

Colonial Hierarchy and Manly Restraint in Seventeenth-Century New England

ANN MARIE PLANE

In the last months of his life, Samuel Sewall—a prominent merchant and chief justice of the Massachusetts Superior Court of Judicature—had a dream so remarkable that he recorded it in his diary in great detail:

> Last night I dreamed that a little boy had got away with my watch. I found him on the Common, and by giving him another Watch, persuaded him to give me that round which was engraven *Auris, mens, oculus, manus, os, pes; munere fungi Dum pergunt, praestat discere velle mori.*
>
> When I awaked I was much startled at it. The Lord help me to watch and pray that I may not enter into Temptation.[1]

Sewall had his dream in 1728, when he was already an elderly man, recently retired from his post on the bench; he would die a little over a year later.[2] Sewall the diarist would never fully unravel the pun that Sewall the dreamer had constructed in the night. The little boy had stolen the old man's "watch"—given form in the dream as a timepiece "engraven" with some cautionary lines in Latin. Of course, the little thief also carried away a second type of "watch"—whose meaning, as watchfulness or inner vigilance, is contained in Sewall's comments immediately following his dream report: "The Lord help me to watch and pray that I may not enter into Temptation." The type of punning in this dream is an example of a phenomenon that Freud noted more than a century ago—that dreams often code abstract concepts through concrete imagery, so that a vigilant "watch" becomes, literally, a timepiece.[3] It is possible that, at the least, the dream speaks of the aging Sewall's anxieties about death, as foreshadowed by recent events in his life—his retirement from the Massachusetts Superior Court and his bouts with ill health. Indeed, in the last lines of the previous entry, made about a month before, Sewall noted, "[I] Pray that the Retirement and Leisure I am seeking for may be successfully improved in preparing for a better world [i.e., heaven]."[4] Certainly the Latin lines on the watch in the dream speak about the struggle against death and decay; they read: "While ear, mind, eye, hand, bone, foot continue to perform their functions, it is better to want to learn than to stagnate [fade, die]."[5] The central image itself—a mischievous boy, willfully taunting his elder—represents both Sewall's attempts to control unruly parts of himself, as well as, more directly, his struggle to maintain dominance over inferiors (the mischievous boys) in his own society.

This chapter argues that dreams and dream reporting served a variety of purposes for men in colonial New England. For Anglo-American men, dreams offered a challenge: unruly and ungovernable, dreams presented a nightly feast of unrestrained impulses, temptations, and delusions that had to be mastered, contained, and redirected in waking life. This mastery and containment mirrored the sort of containment of social disorder that was required of male patriarchs in early modern Anglo-American society—especially that of nonconformists or "Puritans." Dreams were mostly dismissed as inconsequential, and therefore it is hard to find records of them. The records we do have come mainly from diaries, which were, of course, kept mainly by men of higher status or those who had official duties that required they keep a personal record. Thus, the recorded dreams of Anglo-American colonists are almost always those of men (there are no existing seventeenth-century New England diaries kept by women); and while the diary genre by its nature privileges private reflection, the recorded dreams we have show a concern with restrained self-scrutiny that cannot be explained by the nature of the records alone. Dream reports offered the diarist an opportunity to display his caution, discipline, and disinterest—all of them important parts of the proper performance of masculine identity among New England patriarchs.

Another set of dream beliefs, however, also pervaded seventeenth-century New England. For the Algonquian-speaking Native peoples of southern New England, the careful attention to dreams was a closely held spiritual value. Dreams were assumed to be significant; both their study and their central role in shamanic rituals required a public and enthusiastic embrace of dreams and dream reporting. In the colonial context, records of Indians' practices of dreaming—including the use of trance states in ritual—are largely drawn from reports about male shamans. Anglo-American observers, frightened by the (erroneous) assumption that Satan was actively sought in Indian ritual, cast Native dream beliefs as strong evidence of the unrestrained and wildly feminized nature of Indian men. And this became a means through which the colonial "gender frontier"—identified by Kathleen Brown as a key feature of the Anglo-Indian encounter—was inscribed yet more deeply.[6] Thus dreaming, visioning, and their associated belief systems became a vehicle for the elevation of one sort of masculine performance at the expense of another—and in that way, dreaming became a part of the process of colonization, whereby the Anglo-American cultural approach was advanced as superior to that of New England's indigenous peoples.

Manly Restraint

At least nine New England men of the seventeenth century recorded dreams in a diary or diary-like work, and these dream reports—like Sewall's—often revolve around questions of hierarchy, power, status, and the maintenance or loss of control over self and others.[7] No New England women recorded dreams in the diary format, although there are sometimes women's dreams reported in records generated by men. Women also were charged to approach their dreams with restraint. Just as they had to serve as exemplars in other realms, however, New England's husbands and fathers bore a special burden in having to contain unruly night thoughts. The dream reports bear this out. As Sewall's dream about the little boy and his "watch" suggests, recorded dreams reveal a strong preoccupation with obedience before authority, along with its opposite: willful defiance.

It should be no surprise that men in this hierarchical society were deeply concerned throughout their lives with the attainment, proper exercise, and loss of dominance, as well as with exerting control over unruly emotional states. This is consistent with the separate findings of Anne S. Lombard and Lisa Wilson in their studies of New England men in the seventeenth and eighteenth centuries.[8] As Lombard put her argument, "The ideal of responsible, rational manhood was formulated as part of a conscious attempt to suppress the rowdy, disorderly, sometimes violent behavior endemic to the popular culture of early modern England."[9] Dreams and dream reporting represented both a challenge to and an opportunity for the exercise of self-control. Dreams often present the dreamer with unbridled and unruly feelings, which are then understood and channeled in culturally specific ways.[10] As Thomas Foster has theorized in the area of sexual reputation, men in later colonial New England who failed to exercise self-control faced grave consequences to their reputations, which sometimes caused financial consequences as well as social embarrassment.[11]

Rather than conceptualizing a dream, as would Freud two centuries later, as an attempt at repression, seventeenth-century men and women understood them as appropriate and necessary resistance to the unbalancing of the body and mind either by outside forces (Satan) or by the overflow of internal humoral forces and sinful desires.

Dreams themselves were thought to be tricky—ways in which God or Satan or merely carnal desires might penetrate the mind and body while vigilance was relaxed during sleep. Citing Luther, one nonconformist author on dreams, Philip Goodwin, wrote, "Now a knowing Christian strives to be above a Dream, to rise unto Realities in Religion, that his hopes of Heavenly felicity, may be more then an imaginary fancy, his apprehensions more then apparitions: that though he Dreames in sleep, and sleepes in Dreames, yet awake he may work and live above Dreames, being in all things, serious, solid, and well settled."[12] As slippery and potentially deluding phenomena, dreams had long been regarded with suspicion. This restraint redoubled with the rise of Protestantism and a Reformation rejection of supposed Catholic "credulity" about dreams. In "these latter days"—close to the Second Coming of Christ and Judgment Day—dreams were to be regarded with caution. A restrained and cautious approach to dreams, visions, and related phenomena became the hallmark of strictly Protestant approaches to these psychic experiences.[13] Male heads of household had a particular duty to exercise restraint. A contrast emerged between the idealized judicious restraint and the "disordered" use of dreams by various "others" in colonial society. This chapter takes up the case of Indian shamans, but the same argument was applied to witches or their victims, and to religious enthusiasts, such as Quakers and Baptists.[14]

Radical Protestants like those who colonized New England in the 1630s were trained to be suspicious of dreams. Prescriptive literature published in sixteenth- and seventeenth-century Europe cautioned dreamers against placing too much store in their "night visions." Yet, as Keith Thomas asserts in his landmark book, *Religion and the Decline of Magic*, most English Protestants, both Reformed and Anglican, continued to believe that dreams could, in rare cases, be a source of divine revelation.[15] There was a stereotype that most Puritans rejected dreams altogether. Indeed, when Gervase Holles, a staunch Royalist during England's Civil War years, reported that he had once had a predictive dream of his wife's death, "hir father and mother . . . being rigid puritanes, made slight of it."[16] But some remained interested in dreams, and nonconformist diarists such as the Parliamentarian Simonds D'Ewes recorded remarkable and predictive dreams.[17] Proscriptions against paying attention to dreams seem to have loosened toward the end of the seventeenth century.[18]

Perhaps because of these cautions, Anglo-American diarists in New England were very selective in which dreams they recorded, usually writing down only those that, as with Sewall, had left them "much startled." Questions of governance thus take center stage, whether that was governance of the self or governance of others. Michael Wigglesworth made brief notations in cryptic shorthand when he had wet dreams or other "filthy" dreams, asking God for better self-control.[19] Thomas Minor wrote of a different struggle for control, and of a curious coincidence in which he and his wife seemed to dream the same dream: "my wife dreamed that I struck her & said that I strucke at a dogg & I dreamed that I was going by a red [bitch] which had a puppie and shee bit at me." When he "struck her [the dog in his dream]," he noted, "[I] struck my wife in the face either with my hand or fist which waked my wife & she waked me & asked me what I did doe."[20] It is perhaps not too farfetched to note that while Minor offered an acceptable act of violence toward the "red bitch" in his dream, this dream experience resulted in an *inadvisable* (if not entirely unacceptable) act of violence and loss of control—striking his wife (perhaps, sometimes, herself another sort of "bitch"?[21])   which she duly protested ("& she waked me & asked me what I did doe.")

Like Minor, diarists tended to record dreams if they fell into the category of "wonders," in part because that suggested they might be the rarest sort of dream: a divinely inspired message.[22] But even these reflected a concern with hierarchy and control. In 1665, John Hull recorded a remarkable dream that was circulating as a wondrous oral story about a man on Long Island who "told his sonns he dreamed he fought with diviles & they took his hatt from him." The poor man "was soone after found dead in the way from his meadow home killed as supposed by lightining & his hatt some few rods from him cutt as iff it was by art."[23] Hull noted that the dreamer's sons had reported this dream. That the Boston merchant wrote this bit of oral culture down is no surprise;[24] this dream-as-text encodes the concerns of Hull and others with symbols that were known to connote authority: the hat cleaved in two—a sign of God's power; the hat knocked off the head—so many contempt of authority cases involved hats not coming off of heads; and, perhaps, an actual beheading—that of King Charles I. This act abrogating the monarchy had greatly troubled Hull, and the restoration of the monarchy with Charles II in 1660 still preoccupied New England in 1665, when Hull recorded this "wonder."[25] One further reading suggests a more troubling possibility: a hat was sometimes used as a symbol to represent Puritan plainness. Could this dream also speak about a chastening fall for Puritan New England—itself the focus, at the time, of an investigating commission representing King Charles II?

Indian and English Dreams | 35

Dreams about heaven and salvation reflect both the greatest concern of devout nonconformists in this society of "saints" and their preoccupations with this highest of achievements. For example, in 1634 John Winthrop, the governor of Massachusetts, recorded a wondrous dream that he had, following a period of religious crisis for his two young sons. Because it had come on the heels of these dramatic stirrings, Winthrop thought it "not impertinent" to record the dream in his diary.[26]

The dream presented Winthrop with a startling scene, "viz., that comminge into his Chamber he fo[u]nde his wife (she was a verye gratious woman) in bedd & 3: or 4: of hir Children lyinge by her with moste sweet & smylinge co[u]ntenances, with Crownes upon their heades & blue ribandes [a symbol of faithful observance] about their necks."[27] This scene provoked a sense of wonder and anticipation, enough to cause Winthrop to shake his wife awake and share the dream with her: "when he awaked he tould his wife his dreame: & made this interpretation of it, that God would take of her Children to make them fellowe heires with Christ in his kingdom."[28] But to feel assured of one's salvation was generally considered a sign of error for strict nonconformists. The radical Reformation teachings were quite clear: one could never be sure that God's mercy would extend to oneself or one's loved ones; indeed, signs of assurance might be satanic tricks, designed to lull the faithful into error. For a Puritan father to know that his wife and children were among the elect, as this dream seemed to suggest, would have been almost too good to be true. Thus Winthrop exercised a manly restraint, tamping down his joy, and offering the common post-Reformation qualification: "(thoughe no Credite nor regard [be] to be had of dremes in these dayes)."[29]

Like Winthrop, Samuel Sewall's earliest reported dream, made during King Philip's War of 1675, centered on making his way to heaven, and was treated with a similar mix of hope and restraint. In it, Sewall climbs a "pair of stairs going to heaven," while carrying a young child in his arms. He reports, "I went up innumerable steps and still saw nothing, so that I was discouraged, doubting with myself whether there was such a place as *sedes beatorum* [seats of the blessed].[30] Yet I strengthened myself as well as I could, considering how apt things only heard of are to be doubted . . . though they be never so true." Eventually he arrived at "a fair chamber with goodly lodgings," but he felt disappointed to not be in heaven: "When I saw that was all, I earnestly prayed that God would help us, or else we should never get to our journey's end. Amazed I was, not being able to conceive how furniture should be brought up those stairs so high." Discovering that the room was a "chamber in the N[ew] Building" at Harvard College, and that "part of an old [house] . . . joined to it, of the same height," he was told by "a scholar" that the furnishings had been "drawn up by a pully, and so took in at a window which was all ranshacled like that in Goff Colledge over the Fellows' chamber, and all things began to seem more vile." He then notes, "Hereabout I waked, being much troubled at the former part, and much wondring at the latter of my dream." By way of explanation of the dream's absurd juxtapositions, he quotes some lines from Horace: "*Desinit in piscem mulier Formosa superne.*"[31]

Sewall's dream report speaks to issues of achievement—literally a "climb"—that would logically be of concern to an ambitious young man on the make. The main imagery of the dream includes multiple references to height and verticality—"herself following me up a pair of stairs going to heaven"; "I went up innumerable steps"; "not being able to conceive how furniture should be brought up those stairs so high"; "those things were drawn up by a pully"; "Goff Colledge over the Fellows' chamber"; "part of an old [house] . . . joined to it, of the same height." At this point in Sewall's life—newly graduating from "the College" (Harvard), before his marriage, and in the context of a fearful "rebellion" of the Indians against the colonial government—questions of gaining and keeping authority, of "rising" in the world, were clearly on this young man's mind. This sequence of hope (climbing) versus doubt (despair) is repeated throughout the dream in the "innumerable steps and still saw nothing"; in arriving at the "fair chamber" that was still not yet heaven; and in the disappointing discovery that things were "brought in at a window." Perhaps heaven (and other good things, such as worldly achievement or success) will, in fact, either be shut to him or, worse still, not exist at all—and then he dreads his sins, his doubt, his worldly ambition.

In a second reported dream, recorded about ten years later, Sewall wrestles with ambition, rebelliousness, and subordination in an even more direct way. On January 2, 1685/6, Sewall reported the following dream:

> Last night had a very unusual Dream; viz., That our Saviour in the days of his Flesh when upon Earth, came to Boston and abode here sometime, and moreover that He Lodged in that time at Father Hull's; upon which in my Dream had two Reflections, One was how much more Boston had to say than Rome boasting of Peter's being there. The other a sense of great Respect that I ought to have shewed Father Hull since Christ chose when in Town, to take up His Quarters at his House. Admired the goodness and Wisdom of Christ in coming hither and spending some part of His short Life here. The Chronological absurdity never came into my mind, as I remember.[32]

Sewall was making his way in the world by this point.³³ He was thirty-three at the time, and he had been married to John Hull's daughter, Hannah, for about ten years. Hull himself had been dead since October 1683. But the peaks and valleys of anxiety over authority seem clear: a son, albeit the exalted Christ, chooses to live at "Father Hull's," the very place where Sewall (a "son," or rather, son-in-law) resided after his marriage to Hannah. Upon hearing this news, Sewall has two thoughts. One reflects a certain grandiosity—"how much more" had Boston to boast of than Rome, which only claimed the residence of Peter. The other was a sense of deflation, shame, and regret, perhaps born of guilt: "a sense of great Respect that I ought to have shewed Father Hull." Such an oscillation between certainty and anxiety, and the attempt to control it, is typical of Sewall, and recurs again and again in his diary.³⁴ As Merle Curti noticed half a century ago, "Sewall's dreams were not always an occasion for distress. In one fantasy of grandeur, he was chosen Lord Mayor of London!"³⁵

But the shift between grandiosity and shame—or, put another way, between superiority and inferiority—while an individual experience, also appears in many facets of New England society and connects to a major preoccupation of Puritan thinking: the sin of pride. In Puritan thought, individual believers oscillated between "hardness" and the "breaking open" of their hearts in relation to conversion (again, a pairing of grandiosity and shame).³⁶ This struggle happened "inside" the self as well as in relation to others in social interaction. In New England society, one might be censured for an "intolerable pride in clothes and hair." Sumptuary laws regulating dress and demeanor were designed to reinstate a proper sense of shame in the overly proud, through restrictions on the wearing of lace cuffs or silk dresses. Or men of standing could be considered prideful, which was tellingly glossed as "high." For example, when the lay delegate Master Wheelock of Medway complained in the 1679 Synod that ministers were not taxed, Solomon Stoddard called him a liar. When Wheelock tried to settle the matter with a private apology, Stoddard refused to soften: "Mr. Stodder was high," noted one witness.³⁷ Proper governance of the self thus was linked directly to proper ordering of society, and the would-be male patriarch walked a daily tightrope between the proper exercise of authority and the dangerous shoals of arrogance. The mantle of authority required that responsible husbands and fathers pay constant attention to duty, self-sacrifice, and control—a task that weighed heavily on the individual. Sometimes that weight manifested itself in the psyche creating judge, jury, and executioner to deal with guilty wishes. Thus, in 1705, Sewall dreamed: "Last night I had a very sad Dream that held me a great while. As I remember, I was condemn'd and to be executed. Before I went out I read Dr. Arrowsmith's Prayer, p. 274 [professor at Cambridge under Cromwell, author of several theological works] which was a comfort to me."[38]

We should never forget that these dream reports are just that—reported dreams. These are the ones that Sewall chose to write down and to ponder, often as a means to stir him to better behavior. This handful of reports does not represent more than an infinitesimal number of the dreams Sewall must have had in his life as a whole. Far from being a liability, however, the select nature of the record is all the more meaningful for being carefully chosen. After all, these were the dreams that reveal Sewall's true concerns.

A Diabolical Exercise

The Puritan emphasis on manly restraint finds its confirmation in colonists' horror at Indians' uses of dreaming. Contrast Winthrop's restrained caution about his hopeful dream or Wigglesworth's self-loathing due to shameful lack of self control with the Indians' intentional use of dreams to access supernatural power. Shamans gained their powers through dreams that brought them spirit helpers or manitous, and they frequently "traveled" in trance visions to commune with these supernatural forces.[39] Daniel Gookin described "extraordinary strange motions of their bodies, insomuch that they will sweat until they foam; and thus continue for some hours together, stroking and hovering over the sick."[40] We know that southern New England Algonquians had an elegant and intricate system of dreaming that was in full flower at the time of first colonization.

To Anglo-American eyes, Indian men were already somewhat suspect in their masculinity. The early travel narratives complain that the land was not properly "improved" (i.e., cultivated by the men in a European style) and that "the country wanteth only industrious men."[41] In one early conflict with the Indians, Myles Standish demanded that a Sachem "come out and fight like a man, showing how base and woman-like he was in tongueing it [parleying] as he did."[42] And, as James Axtell has famously argued, New England Indians experienced a veritable "invasion within" as Anglo-American Protestants attempted to remake their gendered divisions of labor in the process of converting them to Christianity, insisting that men give up the supposedly idle pursuit of hunting and replace their wives in the fields.[43]

Although pawwows could be male or female, almost all the Anglo-American accounts focus on male shamans. And if Indian men were generally woman-like, Indian shamans were unusually credulous and undisciplined in their use of dreams. Like women, witches, and sinners, these Indian men became easy prey for Satan's insinuations into their very thoughts.⁴⁴ Consider the remarkable Indian conversions reported in 1651 by Thomas Mayhew on the island of Martha's Vineyard. Among those who came in and professed themselves Christians were two former pawwows.⁴⁵ One of these made a dramatic confession, saying "that at first he came to be a Pawwaw by Diabolicall Dreams, wherein he saw the Devill in the likenesse of four living Creatures"—"pawwawnomas" or spirit helpers, in this case a man, a crow, a pigeon, and a snake—"and these he said were meere Devils, and such as he had trusted to for safetie, and did labour to raise up for the accomplishment of anything in his diabolicall craft."⁴⁶ The two pawwows acknowledged "that they had served the Devill, the Enemy both of God and Man," and they regretted "that they were so hurtfull in their lives."⁴⁷ But most vividly, they acted out their renunciation of pawwowing, "saying, I throw it from me with hatred of it, being sorry that ever I medled with it. And now [that] I have heard of Jehovah, by his help I put it under my feet, and hope to trample it down in the dust with the Devill and *Pawwawnomas* (or imps) I throw it into the fire, and burn it." Mayhew explains, "Thus they fully made known unto all both by word and gesture, . . . not only their indignation against it, but that they would never make use of it more."⁴⁸ Encounters like this one show us both the drama surrounding Christian conversion and the central position of dreams and dreaming in Native shamanism. The Anglo-American found such a seemingly unrestrained use of dreaming to access supernatural powers terribly threatening—even diabolical.

Such Anglo-American descriptions feminize Indian men, strengthening the "gender frontier."⁴⁹ For example, Anglo-American observers thought that diabolical dreams—such as those experienced by Indian pawwows—would be relatively easy to distinguish by their very form, but they used highly sexualized language to describe dreams sent by Satan. As the nonconformist author Philip Goodwin wrote, dreams inspired by the devil "come in a man *As more Hasty, So more Hidden*. In these Dreamings the Devil[']s drivings are like to the drivings of Jehu, furious and fierce, thoughts throng in and thrust out with violence and force, so that thereby reason is oft darkened, brain distempered and powers disturbed, foot-steps so frequently confused, that little is orderly discerned." As if that sexualized imagery were not enough, Goodwin continued, such "Thoughts be in the minde like Rebekah[']s twins in her womb, struggling together: but they do not like them come forth, one holding the heel of another; but be full of inconsistencies, lubricities, slippery, fevered and unsetled, rushings in and rollings about, Reason so roving from one thing to another, that the minde makes miserable non-sence."⁵⁰ In contrast, and using a language that almost mirrored the rhetoric of "manly restraint" and straightforward action that male colonists strove to embody, Goodwin averred that dreams inspired by God "come in a manner *As more Moderate, So more Manifest[;]* Divine Dreames make a more orderly entrance, and leave a more legible Impress: Thoughts herein as adhering one to another, so declaring one of another."⁵¹

Indian shamanism could not be further from the disciplined, restrained, and cautious use of dreams described by Winthrop, Sewall, and other Anglo-American men in their dream reports. As the primary sources attest, Anglo-Americans identified pawwows and shamanic practices as one of the chief obstacles to Christian conversion. Daniel Gookin complained, "These powwows are reputed, and I conceive justly, to hold familiarity with the devil. . . . Satan doth strongly endeavour to keep up this practice among the Indians: and these powwows are . . . great hinderers of the Indians embracing the gospel."⁵² In 1647, the missionary John Eliot described pawwowing as "that diabolicall exercise."⁵³ William Wood reported that pawwows "betak[e] themselves to their exorcisms and necromantic charms by which they bring to pass strange things."⁵⁴ Wood reported that Passaconnaway, an Indian sachem at Merrimack River (whom Shepard would later call "that old Witch and Powwaw") could "make the water burn, the rocks move, the trees dance, [and] metamorphise himself into a flaming man."⁵⁵ One of the first laws made among the praying Indians at Concord in 1646 outlawed the practice, and specified, "and if any shall hereafter Pawwow, both . . . [the Pawwow] & he that shall procure him to Powwow, shall pay 20 s. apiece."⁵⁶ Yet a full generation later, Gookin noted that many Indians still wondered how they might heal the sick without such practices—a pressing question in the context of continuing waves of epidemic.⁵⁷

That shamans obtained their powers through dreams is confirmed in another conversion narrative, in which two young Christian Indians reported, "if any of the Indians fall into any strange dreame wherein Chepian ["the devil"] appears unto them as a serpent, then the next day they tell the other Indians of it."⁵⁸ The boys' quote continues: "[and for] two dayes after the rest of the Indians dance and rejoyce for what they tell them about this Serpent, and so they become their Pawwaws."⁵⁹

Like many Algonquian peoples, southern New England Indians believed in a dream soul that traveled when the body was asleep. The dream soul also interacted with other dream souls and manitous, as well as Hobbamock (a personification of destructive forces). Indians courted visions in a variety of settings, most formally in puberty rituals, and manitous might appear in dreams, which then required the performance of rituals to properly manage these powerful forces and reintegrate the dreamer.[60]

Pawwowing simply offers a more formalized example of the desire to move between different layers of experience—waking and dreaming. Shamans obtained helpers or "pawwanomas" (guardian spirits obtained by vision questing), who sometimes had "residence" in the shaman's body.[61] Tequanonim, a pawwow on Martha's Vineyard, testified that "he had been possessed from the crown of the head to the soals of the foot with Pawwawnomas, not only in the shape of living Creatures, as Fowls, Fishes and creeping things, but Brasse, Iron, and Stone."[62] These "helpers" were integral to curing. As Edward Winslow notes, sometimes the pawwow would not touch a wound himself, "but *askooke*, that is, the snake, or *wobsacuck*, that is, the eagle, sitteth on his shoulder, and licks the same. This none see but the powah, who tells them he doth it himself."[63] As William Wood noted with some relief, the pawwows had begun to lose power "since the English frequented these parts," and the shaman's former adherents "daily fall from his colours, relinquishing their former fopperies."[64]

A measured control in relation to the dream—a cautious optimism and careful analysis by the awakened dreamer, seemed the only appropriate response for the upstanding Puritan man. Anything else—such as a too-credulous use of dreams—would only expose the weakness and penetrability of the human mind. Such Anglo-American theories bolstered colonial rhetoric about the feminized savage and contrasted appropriate manly restraint with a wildly effeminate abandon. At the same time, the accounts of Indian shamanism give us a heartrending view of the force with which the Anglo-American launched a cultural assault not just on the persons or lifeways of the Indians, but, indeed, on their very cosmology. Male shamans were vilified as communing with the devil, while the Native embrace of the dream vision was attacked as allowing Satan himself to make mischief in New England. In so doing, one form of appropriate masculine behavior was set above all others.

The study of these dream reports allows us to glimpse the ways in which New England men struggled to gain control of the unruly content and disruptive emotions attendant in their dreams. Some struggled with worry about the attainment or loss of power, as well as with moderating their joy as they anticipated a successful reward depicted in the crowns and stairways leading heavenward. Both ambitious youths and successful patriarchs struggled to maintain control—whether over their sexual impulses or their fears of losing status. When taken in context, the study of reported dreams provides a new way for historians interested in gendered experience to build a more nuanced discussion of the masculine "worlds of experience" and the "gender frontiers" that characterized this colonial society. Husbands and fathers exercised manly restraint in governing the strange phenomena revealed in their night visions. Approaching dreams with a sober and cautious reserve was a masculine duty, one that helped to separate civility from savagery.

NOTES

1. Samuel Sewall, *The Diary of Samuel Sewall, 1674–1729*, 2 vols., ed. M. Halsey Thomas (New York: Farrar, Straus and Giroux, 1973), vol. 2, pp. 1062–63, entry for September 10, 1728.

2. He retired July 29, 1728, and died January 1, 1729/30, a year and a half later. See "Chronology of Samuel Sewall," in Sewall, *Diary*: vol. 1, pp. xxvii–xxviii.

3. Sigmund Freud, *The Interpretation of Dreams*, trans. and ed. James Strachey, reprint edition (New York: Avon Books, 1965), pp. 374–79.

4. Sewall, *Diary*: vol. 2, p. 1062, entry for August 16, 1728.

5. I am grateful to Harold and Kathy Drake for the Latin translation. This phrase was one that Sewall had composed by at least December 1709, and he frequently inscribed it into books he would give to friends. See Sewall, *Diary*: vol. 2, p. 682, note 14.

6. Kathleen M. Brown, "The Anglo-Algonquian Gender Frontier," pp. 26–48 in *Negotiators of Change: Historical Perspectives on Native American Women*, ed. Nancy Shoemaker (New York: Routledge, 1995), p. 27.

7. The nine men are John Winthrop, John Hull, Michael Wigglesworth, Peter Easton, John Dane, Thomas Minor, Increase Mather, Cotton Mather, and Samuel Sewall. Of these, three (Hull, Dane, and Increase Mather) recorded others' dreams but not their own. See texts cited throughout the chapter.

8. Anne S. Lombard, *Making Manhood: Growing Up Male in Colonial New England* (Cambridge: Harvard University Press, 2003); Lisa Wilson, *Ye Heart of a Man: The Domestic Life of Men in Colonial New England* (New Haven: Yale University Press, 1999).

9. Lombard, *Making Manhood*, p. 15.

10. Modern psychoanalytic theories allow for dreams to serve more functions than Freud's relatively restricted definition of dreams as the "disguised fulfillments of repressed [and unconscious] wishes." Sigmund Freud, *On Dreams*, trans. and ed. by James Strachey, reprint ed. (New York: Norton, 1952), p. 59. Heinz Kohut allowed that some dreams might simply reflect the "state of affairs" in the dreamer's emotional life at the time, and this "self-state" dream has been generalized to allow for a variety of interpretive approaches. See Douglas Hollan, "Selfscape Dreams," pp. 61–74 in *Dreaming and the Self: New Perspectives on Subjectivity, Identity, and Emotion*, SUNY Series in Dream Studies, ed. Jeannette Marie Mageo (Albany: State University of New York Press, 2003), pp. 64–65. On the importance of understanding the complete cultural context in which dreams are theorized and reported, see Barbara Tedlock, "Dreaming and Dream Research," pp. 1–30 in *Dreaming: Anthropological and Psychological Interpretations*, ed. Barbara Tedlock (Santa Fe: School of American Research Press, 1992), p. 25, and see also pp. 22–25.

11. Thomas A. Foster, *Sex and the Eighteenth-Century Man: Massachusetts and the History of Sexuality in America* (Boston: Beacon Press, 2006), pp. 78-79 and ch. 4.

12. Philip Goodwin, *The Mystery of Dreames, Historically Discoursed* . . . (London: Printed by AM for Francis Tyton, 1658), unpaginated Epistle Declaratory.

13. In noting that moderns should no longer expect divine dreams, the Anglican writer Thomas Cooper wrote, "Seeing now we have the Gospell sufficient to reveale the will of God, therefore we are not in these daies to build upon Dreames." Even if "they were ordinary before and under the Law, yet now if any shall . . . expect resolution heereby, wee are to conclude that it is rather a Satanicall illusion then any warning from the Lord, and therefore at no hand to be heeded of us." Thomas Cooper, *The Mystery of Witchcraft* . . . (London: Printed by Nicholas Okes, 1617), pp. 148-49.

14. This expanded argument will appear in my book, with the working title *"When I Awaked": Colonialism and the Cultural Meaning of Dreams in Seventeenth-Century New England* (Philadelphia: University of Pennsylvania Press, forthcoming).

15. Keith Thomas, *Religion and the Decline of Magic: Studies in Popular Beliefs in Sixteenth- and Seventeenth-Century England* (London: Weidenfeld and Nicolson, 1971), pp. 128-29.

16. Gervase Holles, "Memorials of the Holles Family, 1493-1656," ed. A. C. Wood, *Camden Third Series*, vol. 55 (London: The Camden Society, 1937), p. 231; also cited in Thomas, *Religion*, p. 128.

17. I am grateful to my colleague J. Sears McGee who has shared some of his work in draft on Simonds D'Ewes, including dream reports taken from the *Autobiography and Correspondence of Sir Simonds D'Ewes, Bart.*, 2 vols., ed. J. O. Halliwell (London, 1845), vol. 1, pp. 37-38, 251-54; and from McGee's transcription of Simonds D'Ewes, MS Diary, British Library (London, UK), Harley MS 646 [f. 14r].

18. As shown by the publication of Goodwin's book, and by a more general humanistic interest in dreams as natural rather than supernatural phenomena in the works of Enlightenment thinkers.

19. The entry for February 17, 1652/3, is typical: "The last night [I had] a filthy dream and so pollution escaped me in my sleep for which I desire to hang down my head with shame and beseech the Lord not to make me possess the sin of my youth and give me into the hands of my abomination." After listing his many sins, he noted, "I loath my self, and could even take vengeance of my self for these abominations. Yet I feel, a stone in my heart that knows not how to melt." Examples from Edmund S. Morgan, ed., *The Diary of Michael Wigglesworth, 1653-1657: The Conscience of a Puritan* (New York: Harper & Row, 1965) include: February 17, 1652/3 (p. 5—quoted example); February 25/26, 1652/3 (p. 6); October 18, 1653 (p. 50); a general mention of multiple instances, February 15, 1653/4 (p. 78); nocturnal emission "without any dream that I knew of" February 22, 1653/4 (p. 80); and "some night pollution escaped me notwithstanding my earnest prayer to the contrary," September 16, 1655 (p. 93).

20. Sidney H. Miner and George D. Stanton, Jr., eds., *The Diary of Thomas Minor, Stonington, Connecticut, 1653-1684* (New London: Day Publishing Co., 1899), p. 192. The instance is recorded twice in the body of the diary, in chronological order: Wednesday August 20, 1662: "I & my wife both dreamed . . . " (p. 51); and again in random notes at the end, where the fuller report of content begins, "Agust [sic.] 1662. I & my (wife) dreamed at one time . . . " (p. 192).

21. The *Oxford English Dictionary* indicates that the word had the same double meaning in Minor's period as it does in our own.

22. David D. Hall, *World of Wonders, Days of Judgment: Popular Religious Belief in Early New England* (Cambridge: Harvard University Press, 1989), p. 86, and ch. 2.

23. [John Hull], "The Diaries of John Hull, Mint-master and Treasurer of the Colony of Massachusetts Bay, from the original manuscript in the collection of the American Antiquarian Society," *Transactions and Collections of the American Antiquarian Society*, vol. 3 (1857), p. 220, entry for November 22, 1665.

24. Cf. Hall, *Worlds of Wonder*, pp. 83–85.

25. [John Hull], "The Diaries," pp. 216–217, entries spanning April 12–29, 1665.

26. Richard S. Dunn, James Savage, and Laetitia Yeandle, eds., *The Journal of John Winthrop, 1630–1649*, 3 vols. (Cambridge: Belknap Press of Harvard University Press, 1996), p. 112.

27. Ibid. One reference to blue ribbons is found in Numbers 15:37–40: "And the Lord spake unto Moses, saying [v. 38] Speake unto the children of Israel, and byd them that thei make them fringes upon the borders of their garments, throughout their generations, and put upon the fringes of the borders a rybande of blewe silke. [v. 39] And he shal have the fringes, that when ye loke upon them, ye may remember all the commandements of the Lord, & do them. & that ye seke not after your owne heart, nor after your owne eies, after the which ye go a whoring. [v. 40] That ye may remember and do all my commandements, and be holy unto your God." Lloyd Berry, ed., *The Geneva Bible: A Facsimile of the 1560 Edition* (Madison: University of Wisconsin Press, 1969), p. 69. I am grateful to Warren Hofstra of Shenandoah University for noting the reference.

28. [Winthrop], *Journal*, p. 112.

29. Ibid.

30. I am grateful to Harold Drake for this translation, which he also renders as "home of the saints," since "beatus" ("blessed") came to mean saints generally.

31. Sewall, *Diary*: vol. 1, p. 12. The quotation reads, "A woman, beautiful above, has a fish's tail." And then he offers a prayer in Latin: "*Deus det, deus misericors et benignus, me, et comites meos, non tantum et de somnis, sed vere tandem divinis gradibus ad coelum usque ascendere.*" (O God, compassionate and kind, grant me and my comrades that we may ascend to heaven on the divine staircase not only in our dreams but also in truth.)

32. Sewall, *Diary*: vol. 1, p. 91, entry for January 2, 1685/6.

33. Sewall had been elected a member of the Court of Assistants, and as such became both a magistrate and an overseer of Harvard College.

34. Indeed, both the diary and the act of writing itself at times seem to function as means for controlling and moderating strong emotions.

35. Merle Curti, "The American Exploration of Dreams and Dreamers," *Journal of the History of Ideas* 27: 3 (1966), p. 395.

36. Cf. Charles L. Cohen, "Conversion Among Puritans and Amerindians: A Theological and Cultural Perspective," in *Puritanism: Transatlantic Perspectives on a Seventeenth-Century Anglo-American Faith*, ed. Frank Bremer (Boston: Massachusetts Historical Society, 1993), pp. 233–56.

37. Both the sumptuary laws and the apology are from Perry Miller, "Solomon Stoddard, 1643–1729," *Harvard Theological Review* 34: 4 (1941), pp. 281–82.

38. Sewall, *Diary*: vol. 1, pp. 518–19, entry for February 13, 1705.

39. Kathleen J. Bragdon, *Native People of Southern New England, 1500–1650* (Norman: University of Oklahoma Press, 1996), pp. 190–91; William S. Simmons, *Spirit of the New England Tribes: Indian History and Folklore, 1620–1984* (Hanover: University Press of New England, 1986), pp. 44–45. See also Ann Marie Plane, "Falling 'Into a Dreame': Native Americans, Colonization, and Consciousness in Early New England," pp. 84–105 in *Reinterpreting New England Indians and the Colonial Experience*, eds. Colin G. Calloway and Neal Salisbury (Boston: Colonial Society of Massachusetts, 2003).

40. Daniel Gookin, "Historical Collections of the Indians in New England," pp. 141–229 in *Collections of the Massachusetts Historical Society*, vol. 1 (1792 [rpt. 1968]), p. 154.

41. See William Cronon, *Changes in the Land: Indians, Colonists, and the Ecology of New England* (New York: Hill and Wang, 1983). Quotation from Dwight B. Heath, ed., *Mourt's Relation: A Journal of the Pilgrims at Plymouth* (Bedford, Mass.: Applewood Books, 1963), p. 84.

42. Edward Winslow, *Good News from New England, or a true Relation of things very remarkable at the Plantation of Plimoth in New England* (Bedford, Mass.: Applewood Books, n.d.), p. 49.

43. James Axtell, *The European and the Indian: Essays in the Ethnohistory of Colonial North America* (New York: Oxford University Press, 1981), pp. 54–56.

44. See Carol F. Karlsen, *The Devil in the Shape of a Woman: Witchcraft in Colonial New England* (1987; New York: Vintage Books, 1989).

45. The terminology is problematic here. Most Native Americans seem to prefer medicine man or medicine woman, rejecting the term shaman because of its potential misuse and "New Age" connotations. General religious studies and anthropology scholarship prefers the word shaman. I thank Neal Salisbury for alerting me to this controversy.

46. Thomas Mayhew, Jr., letter, October 16, 1651, to Mr. John Whitfield [sic.], pp. 23–27 in Henry Whitfield, *Strength out of Weakness, Or a Glorious Manifestation of the further Progresse of the Gospel amongst the Indians in New-England* (London: Printed by M. Simmons for John Blague and Samuel Howes, 1652), pp. 24–25.

47. Ibid.

48. Ibid.

49. Brown, "Anglo-Algonquian Gender Frontier," p. 27.

50. Goodwin, *The Mystery of Dreames*, pp. 41–43.

51. Ibid., pp. 43–44.

52. Gookin, "Historical Collections," p. 154.

53. John Eliot, letter, September 24, 1647, to Thomas Shepard, pp. 16–29 in Thomas Shepard, *The Clear Sun-Shine of the Gospel Breaking Forth upon the Indians in New-England* (London: Printed by R. Cotes for John Bellamy, 1648), p. 28. Yet on p. 25 he notes that some were concerned about how to heal the sick if they had given up pawwowing, "for they have no skill in Physick, though some of them understand the virtues of sundry things [i.e., plants], yet the state of mans body, and skill to apply them they have not: but all the refuge they have and relie upon in time of sicknesse is their *Powwaws*, who by antick, foolish and irrationall conceits delude the poore people."

54. William Wood, *New England's Prospect*, ed. and intro. Alden T. Vaughan (Amherst: University of Massachusetts Press, 1977), p. 101.

55. Shepard, *Clear Sun-Shine*, p. 32; Wood, *New England's Prospect*, pp. 101–2.

56. "Conclusions and Orders made and agreed upon by divers Sachims and other principall men amongst the Indians at Concord, in the end of the eleventh moneth, An[no]. 1646," pp. 4–5 in Shepard, *Clear Sun-Shine*, p. 4. And Gookin reports that pow-wowing was prohibited in "English jurisdictions" by a fine of five pounds each to both the shaman and the "procurer," and twenty pence from every person who was present. See Gookin, "Historical Collections," p. 154.

57. Gookin, "Historical Collections," p. 154.

58. [Thomas Shepard], *The Day-Breaking if Not the Sun-Rising of the Gospell with the Indians in New-England* (London: Richard Cotes for Fulk Clifton, 1647), pp. 21–22.

59. Ibid. Eliot could not resist making a further dig at shamans, who were, in his opinion, not only witches but also cheats. He notes that should the patient not recover, sometimes his "friends" would take vengeance on the shaman, "especially if they could not get their mony againe out of their hands, which they receive afterhand for their care."

60. Roger Williams, *A Key into the Language of America*, ed. and intro. John J. Teunissen and Evelyn J. Hinz (Detroit: Wayne State University Press, 1973), p. 108; on the related Iroquois phenomena, see Anthony F. C. Wallace, "Dreams and Wishes of the Soul: A Type of Psychoanalytic Theory Among the Seventeenth Century Iroquois," *American Anthropologist* 60, no. 2, part 1 (April 1958), 234–48.

61. Thomas Mayhew, Jr., letter, October 16, 1651, to Mr. John Whitfield [*sic.*], pp. 23–27 in Whitfield, *Strength out of Weakness*, p. 24.

62. Ibid., p. 25. The quote continues: "It was therefore the more to be acknowledged the work of God, that he should forsake this way, his friends, his gain, to follow the Lord, whose wayes are so despisable in the eyes of devilish minded men."

63. Winslow, *Good News*, p. 59.

64. Wood, *New England's Prospect*, pp. 101–2.

II

Warfare

3

"We are MEN"

Native American and Euroamerican Projections of Masculinity During the Seven Years' War

TYLER BOULWARE

"Your hands are like the hands of a child," declared a Cherokee warrior to a European prisoner. "They are unfit for the chace, or for war. In the winter's snow you must burn a fire; and in the summer's heat you faint in the shade." The Cherokee, on the other hand, "can always lift the hatchet: the snow does not freeze him; nor the sun make him faint. We are men." Thomas Percival, an eighteenth-century English physician and author, directed this account to the young readers of his work *A Father's Instructions*. Although intended as an allegory, the moral of the story was clear: the superior physical and martial capabilities of Native Americans meant they were real men, and thus the antithesis of Europeans and their colonists.[1]

The above encounter is not only a metaphor. During the Seven Years' War in North America (1754–63), in which Britain and France struggled for imperial supremacy, the British superintendent of Indian affairs in the southern district directed his deputy agent to respect the wishes of their Cherokee and Catawba allies, who had signified their dislike of provincial soldiers joining their expeditions against French-allied Indians. Since these colonists were not "used to that kind of service & therefore not fit for it," wrote Edmond Atkin, they "are a clog upon them and baulk them in their operations." As experience had shown from previous campaigns, colonists could not keep up with Indians "either in marching or running; nor endure hunger; and by making much noise and fire in the woods, make a discovery of them to the enemy." Atkin consequently instructed his commissary to prevent "any white men" from joining Indian scouting parties, "unless at the voluntary requests of those Indians."[2]

Thomas Percival and Edmond Atkin lived on opposite sides of the Atlantic, but their understandings of Native American and Euroamerican capabilities—or lack thereof—in woodland warfare were remarkably similar.

Where Percival differs from Atkin is his conspicuous association of proficiency in border warfare with masculinity, which can be explained by the nature of the two communications. Percival wrote to instruct English boys on how to become men, whereas Atkin's administrative advice conveyed the wishes of Cherokee and Catawba warriors. Recent scholarship has examined the connections between Anglo-Indian warfare and masculinity. Ann Little's *Abraham in Arms* is perhaps the most comprehensive account of the gendered dimensions of intercultural warfare between Native and newcomer in early America. Focusing on the northeastern borderlands primarily during the seventeenth century, Little demonstrates how European and Indian "ideas about gender and family life were central to the ways in which these people understood and explained their experience of cross-cultural warfare." But such notions were not limited to colonial New England. The mid-eighteenth-century Ohio country and southeast exhibited many similarities with the seventeenth-century northeastern borderlands. In fact, Little argues that much of the gendered language used in woodland warfare during the mid-eighteenth century had its origins in seventeenth-century New England. Although the literature has been slow to develop these connections, masculinity-laden discourse among Native Americans, Europeans, and colonists permeated intercultural communication during wartime in both regions.[3]

Nevertheless, the era of the Seven Years' War is distinctive for several reasons. First, warfare consumed a new region in North America and a new generation of borderland participants. In the second half of the eighteenth century, the mid-Atlantic and southern backcountries came to play a more decisive role in the shaping of British America, as tens of thousands of Euroamerican settlers surged west and south from Pennsylvania and Virginia, thereby engaging powerful Native American polities in the Ohio country and southeast. Most of these new arrivals had not been steeped in a "puritan warrior tradition," as in New England, which limited the influence of Christian piety on masculine discourse. The period also witnessed an imperial contest that made warfare a seemingly constant endeavor in the American hinterlands. British regulars, diverse Native American warriors, and provincial soldiers, militiamen, and rangers engaged one another in border warfare on a scale never before seen—even in seventeenth-century New England, where English troops were absent in both the Pequot War and King Philip's War. The Seven Years' War also marks a turning point in the history of the mid-Atlantic and southeastern borderlands because it ushered in a new era in Indian-white relations. Most notably, it brought to the region an exploding population sure of itself, bent on conquest, and distrustful of their Indian neighbors. These trends continued into and beyond the American Revolution, prompting some scholars to rightly envision this era as the "Long Seven Years' War." While the period between 1754 and 1815 witnessed much change, what proved remarkably consistent was that masculinity and masculine discourse remained an essential component to intercultural communication between Native and newcomer in the American borderlands.[4]

This chapter accordingly explores these projections of masculinity. It begins by describing the cultural background of warfare for Native Americans, before turning to their use of masculinity tropes in their dealings with the British during the Seven Years' War. For Indian men, references to masculinity were often cloaked in generational and gendered terms. Their status as warriors and headmen separated them from boys and women, and they consequently used manly language to assert individual power and identity. Native Americans also utilized masculine discourse to differentiate one's people from other indigenous groups as well as the British and their colonists. What did the British make of these masculinity tropes? Vast cultural differences divided Indians and Europeans, not only in their technologies, tactics, and motives in warfare, but also in a noticeably dissimilar gendered order of their respective societies. Despite these disparities, Native American expressions of masculinity were readily discernible to the British. Warfare was the near-exclusive domain of men for both peoples, which provided a common reference point for intercultural communication. Both Indian and British men used manly language to reinforce their own identity as warriors and to question the martial capabilities of each other. The British in particular used masculine discourse to project their power among a Native population far from convinced about English claims of conquest during and after the Seven Years' War.

Native Men and Warfare

> War has, for all the Indians, such singular attractions that they seem to be born and live for it.

Joseph-François Lafitau, a French Jesuit missionary among the Iroquois, was not alone in his assessment of the importance of war to Native American men. Fellow Frenchman Louis-Armand Lahontan likewise found among the Indians that "the true Qualifications of a Man are . . . to understand War." Although fishing, hunting, and other woodland activities were also the domain of Indian males, warfare held singular importance, for it was the cornerstone of Native American masculinity. War was "the noblest of all exercises," Lafitau continued, "and that on which the Indian prides himself most." Success in war satisfied the spirits of the deceased, weakened enemies, elevated one's standing in the community, and brought all the resulting benefits to a warrior's family, clan, and village.[5]

Native American men ritually performed their accomplishments to give proof of their manhood, which translated into greater respectability and standing in society. Attaining fame was especially important to acquiring status within the village and among outsiders. Individuals reached positions of authority based largely on their reputations, and since Native political leadership often rested on meritorious service, warriors gained greater influence as they advanced in rank. It was therefore a great insult to publicly defame a warrior.[6]

Defaming a warrior or headman could be accomplished by implying a man was a boy, which proved especially insulting because it signified a male without rank, one who was unskilled, untested, imprudent, and, at times, beyond authority. This generational aspect of Native American masculinity was rooted in the cultural foundations of indigenous societies, whereby Native peoples revered their elders, especially those who had proven themselves in battle. But Indian manhood was equally connected to gender. Among the many separate spheres of Indian men and women, war was perhaps the most distinct. Very few women participated in war, unlike other divisions of labor among Native peoples, such as farming and hunting. Men at times assisted women in farming just as some women joined hunting expeditions. Warfare, however, was an essentially male domain. It proved elemental to gendered identities and gendered constructions of power, which found clear expression in masculine discourse.[7]

Native Americans especially hurled gender-laden insults at outsiders. As Nancy Shoemaker skillfully argues, eastern Indians used gendered language to slight enemies and assert dominance. The Iroquois, for example, informed one Virginia trader that scalping a Cherokee "was not looked upon as a warlike Action," for the Cherokees were "but old Women" who allowed the Iroquois to "come into their Towns, eat and drink and take their Wives before their Face." Creek leaders continued to brand the Cherokees "old women" well into the revolutionary era, saying that "they had long ago obliged them to wear the petticoat"—"a most humiliating and degrading stroke," recalled the naturalist William Bartram. The British, too, could not escape the scathing attacks of headmen and warriors, who degraded the fighting abilities of the English and their colonists throughout the Seven Years' War. Two Ohio

Indians predicted the French and their Native allies would ultimately defeat the British because "the white people appeared to them like fools; they could neither guard against surprise, run, or fight." Cherokee leaders likewise believed they had little to fear from "the white People who they can kill like Fowls." Creek headmen also ridiculed the English, or "Dunghill Fowls," noting that "even the Looks of Indians were sufficient to kill them." Using gendered and generational language to carry the point home, the Creeks claimed that Cherokee "Boys and old Women" had "knocked many of the [British] Soldiers on the Head" during a failed invasion of Cherokee country in 1760.[8]

What did Native masculinity tropes, such as "old woman," mean to the British—a people who possessed a vastly different gendered order than their indigenous neighbors? The consensus is that European patriarchal societies encompassed a gender hierarchy that marginalized women, while egalitarian Native communities invested power in women, whose standing in society rivaled that of men. Indigenous women, for example, typically controlled the production of food, reproduction, the preservation of lineages, and the ownership of household property. With Native women held in such high esteem by their men, it seems surprising that headmen and warriors would belittle their wartime adversaries by labeling them women. Perhaps Indian men used such language specifically for their European audience, who readily understood the weakened position of women in their own societies. Or perhaps certain European gender structures did not deviate significantly from those of their Native American counterparts.[9]

Recent reinterpretations of Indian-white exchange, especially within the confines of warfare, suggest the latter. While Native American and European cultures differed markedly, and Native and newcomer brought varying cultural assumptions to their encounters with each other, Ann Little reminds us there existed "large areas of agreement in the gender ideologies of Native Americans and the English, in particular in politics and war." Challenging older assumptions that stressed gender equality in Native cultures, Little finds instead that both Indians and Europeans constructed "a gendered hierarchy that privileged manhood and reserved politics and war for men almost exclusively." Masculine discourse therefore provided a common language that Indian and European men could comprehend, despite their cultural differences. Calling a man a "woman," for instance, was not solely a Native American epithet, since it was, according to Little, "a universally understood insult throughout the early modern Atlantic world."[10]

British Views of Woodland Warfare

Similar gender roles and a shared understanding of manhood allowed European and Indian men to compare their martial abilities and methods of warfare. Headmen and warriors respected European technological power even as they questioned their military competence. Correspondingly, Europeans and their colonists expressed ambivalence about Native American warriors and their skills in woodland warfare. On the one hand, a streak of admiration ran throughout Euroamerican discourse concerning Indian men and their fighting capabilities. Observations typically began with physical descriptions of leading warriors. They "are tall, of a build superior to ours, well proportioned, of a good constitution, strong and skilful," wrote Lafitau. In "physical qualities," he concluded, "they are, in no sense, inferior to us." Others agreed that notable warriors were "of a majestic stature" with countenances "strongly expressive of energy and fortitude." Such appreciation of Indian bodies extended to war. Europeans often extolled the prowess Native men displayed in the woods. "None but the Savages can skip from Rock to Rock," recalled an impressed Lahontan, "and scour thro' the Thickets, as if 'twere an open Field." John Norton perhaps best encapsulated this admiration of warrior adroitness when he wrote, "so various are the stratagems that may be used according to the situations or talents of those engaged, that it would be endless to enumerate the whole."[11]

By the onset of the Seven Years' War, the British were thoroughly familiar with Indian proficiency in woodland warfare, but this did little to alter their inherent faith in the superiority of their own tactics, ordnance, and troops. The British brought their methods of war to North America, with which they planned to subdue the French and their Indian allies. Though more experienced officials recognized the necessity of securing Indian warriors for auxiliary services, some British commanders dismissed the idea. The most notable and often cited illustration is that of General Edward Braddock during his fatally flawed attempt to take Fort Duquesne in 1755. Braddock enraged potential recruits by bluntly rejecting their counsel and services. Scarouady, an Oneida leader with influence among the Shawnee and Delaware, later called the general "a bad man" who "looked upon us as Dogs, and would never hear any thing we said to him." Owing to "the Pride and Ignorance of that Great General that came from England," he added, "a great many of our Warriors left him and would not be under his Command." The consequences of this dissatisfaction and desertion are well-known: the British suffered a humiliating defeat at the Battle of the Monongahela, losing nearly one thousand men (killed or wounded), one of which was their commander.[12]

As seen in the Braddock campaign, the ethnocentrism and perceived haughtiness of British officers damaged Anglo-Indian relations in the Ohio country and eventually turned many Natives against them. Farther to the south, Lieutenant Henry Timberlake of Virginia similarly found the Cherokees disaffected, in part because "the pride of our officers often disgusts them." British Indian agent John Stuart agreed with this assessment. Unlike the French, Stuart wrote, the English failed to "put on a solemn and grave air, [and] at the same time to appear open and without reserve. This the Indians look on as respectful and treating them like men, but the least levity they interpret as proceeding from contempt." Such low opinions of Indians were not limited to a few officers, but were instead endemic throughout the British Army, even extending to the highest ranks. General Jeffery Amherst, who eventually became commander in chief of His Majesty's forces in North America, repeatedly referred to their prospective allies as "that fickle & vile crew."[13]

A relevant question, then, is why this disdain, especially since many Europeans considered Native men adept in woodland warfare? Part of the answer lies in the Indians' particular style of war. The "art of war consists in ambushing and surprizing our enemies," explained a Caughnawaga Mohawk leader, "and in preventing them from ambushing and surprizing us." This tenet guided indigenous men throughout their martial endeavors. Accordingly, some eyewitnesses, such as the English adventurer and trader John Long, were quick to admit "the Indians are superior to us in the woods." But the key issue here concerns that part of the phrase "in the woods." Europeans might appreciate the effectiveness of Indian warfare in the forests of America, but this did not translate into acceptance of Indian men as superior fighters and soldiers in conventional warfare. Europeans instead expressed their utter distaste for the Indians' "savage" way of fighting. Warriors "skulked" in the woods like animals, using stealth and cunning to ambush an enemy. "Their warfare is, properly speaking, nothing but surprises and treachery," wrote one early visitor to Indian country. Such tactics appeared all the more unpalatable when war parties indiscriminately targeted noncombatants. One British officer chided the French and their Indian allies for attacking a New England border town, "which was settled with plowman, Women, & Children who knew nothing of the War." A later account from the Carolinas similarly apprehended that "merciless savages" planned to "mix men, women, and children, in one common carnage." Attacking civilians may have been acceptable to Indians, so the thinking went, but it was considered dishonorable and, more important, undisciplined in eighteenth-century European warfare.[14]

Many officers believed warriors were unable or unwilling to follow orders and, even worse, prone to desert the army in the middle of a campaign. Braddock perceived this in 1755, as did his successor, General John Forbes, who led a successful drive against Fort Duquesne in 1758. Forbes initially sided with colonial officials in recognizing the need for Indian allies to not only conduct offensive operations but also protect Anglo-American settlements from Delaware and Shawnee incursions. Since the loyalties of the Ohio Indians were in doubt, leaders in Virginia and Pennsylvania recruited the Cherokees—a longtime British ally—to provide assistance. Hundreds of Cherokees answered the call and served in the British interest between 1756 and 1758. But Anglo-Cherokee relations withered as both peoples found each other intractable and hostile. When Cherokee warriors abandoned the British during their march against Fort Duquesne, Forbes derided "their natural fickle disposition," denouncing them as "a very great plague" for "putting us, to a very great expence and doing of nothing for it." The desertion of the Cherokees and other Native allies convinced the British that warriors made poor soldiers. Colonel Henry Bouquet lashed out against these "Rascals" in 1758, fuming to George Washington that "it would be easier to make Indians of our White men, than to cox that damned Tanny Race." This view of Indians as undisciplined and cowardly fighters contrasted the archetypical British soldier who was expected to maintain strict discipline, stand his ground, and hold the field when the guns fell silent.[15]

The British may have also denigrated Indian warriors to alleviate their own insecurities in woodland warfare, which had become painfully evident in the opening stages of the Seven Years' War. British and colonial forces suffered humiliating setbacks at Forts Necessity, Duquesne, Oswego, William Henry, and Carillon (Ticonderoga). Contingents of Delawares, Shawnees, and Mingos added to the misery with devastating raids against the western settlements of Pennsylvania and Virginia. Pennsylvania turned to the Iroquois Confederacy for assistance, but headmen representing the Six Nations expressed their disbelief at British inaction. Scarouady informed acting governor Robert Morris he was "amazed to find you still sitting with your Hands between your Knees . . . while Numbers of your People have been and are now Murthered." Hoping to shame the British into action, Scarouady cautioned the governor that his "Enemies have got great Advantage by your Inactivity; Show them you are Men." The Oneida leader then advised Morris to avoid the mistakes of Braddock and other officers by accepting Indian council and military support. Highlighting British ineptitude in woodland warfare, Scarouady noted the English were "extreamly heavy, move Slow, and are liable to Surprizes if you go by your selves." By contrast, the Indians were "a light Body" who traveled "Nimbly thro' the Woods" to ensure "no Enemy [is] lying concealed to cut you off"—a conspicuous reference, no doubt, to the Braddock expedition.[16]

British Projections of Power

To offset Indian understandings of British ineptitude in woodland warfare, the British repeatedly projected their power through masculine discourse. They did this by emphasizing their economic mastery over Indians, trumpeting their wartime successes, and proclaiming their invasions of Indian country as crowning military achievements. Trade was often the trump card British leaders played to manage Indian affairs. Nancy Shoemaker convincingly argues that English power rested on their capacity to provision their native clients. Due to their reliance on Indian allies in woodland warfare, she writes, the English "risked appearing unmanly," and thus "English claims to power in North America instead came to rest entirely on their ability to manufacture and supply Indian allies with trade goods." The evidence bears this out, as British officials attempted to offset their own dependency on Indian auxiliaries by stressing the Indians' dependency on English goods. A "Modern Indian cannot subsist without Europeans," wrote John Stuart, due to "their incapacity of subsisting without European Commodities." Lieutenant Governor William Bull of South Carolina agreed, reminding Attakullakulla in 1761 that the "English can live without the Cherokee Skins," but, he added, the Cherokees could not live without the English trade. In a world where Indian and European men viewed dependency as incompatible with manhood, masculine rhetoric helped to allay—or at the very least to disguise—a sense of vulnerability that both peoples felt about their economic and military interconnectedness.[17]

While trade was a serious concern for Native leaders, it was not the only concern. Lieutenant Governor Francis Fauquier of Virginia astutely noted the Indians "must be friends to those who could possess the Country and supply them." Indeed, village security rested on both trade and protection. As France and Britain struggled for control of the continent, village headmen were forced to engage the contending empires. An unchecked imperial power could prove dangerous, but an even greater threat could come from allying with the weaker side. It was "a known Practice" among the Indians, wrote one officer stationed in Cherokee country, "to join those they have Reason to dread or think the strongest Party." Teedyuscung, an influential Delaware headman from the Wyoming Valley, summed up the issue in this manner: "Strong Men are [on] both Sides; Hatchets on both Sides, whoever gives the best Assurances, him I will join."[18]

The British consequently projected their power by emphasizing recent wartime achievements. Officials were especially concerned about how British military operations in Canada and the Ohio country would reverberate among the southeastern Indians. The Cherokees in particular seemed on the brink of defection as a result of trader abuses, land encroachments, and frontier hostility. British and colonial leaders accordingly attached great weight to how the northern theater of war affected their Indian affairs to the south. If "God does not bless our arms, in the northern expedition," wrote one Indian trader, "Carolina shou'd stand on the strongest guard." A Carolina officer agreed that Cherokee neutrality seemed contingent "on the news, that we shall hear from the North"—a sentiment echoed by another officer, who believed the Cherokees would remain idle "till they see the issue of the Armies to the Northward."[19]

Of particular importance were the two campaigns aimed at dislodging the French from Canada and the Ohio country. British forces proved successful at Fort Niagara, Louisbourg, and Quebec in 1758–59, and they lost no time in linking these victories to their standing among the Cherokees. The "News of the glorious success of his Majesty's Arms," read one account from Charleston, "will soon reduce" the Cherokees "to Reason; and . . . induce these Barbarians to consider their real Interest." Fauquier felt the Cherokees posed little threat, for "they have had opportunities of seeing our Strength and the Forces the King of Great Britain can march against them." While the fall of Quebec (and later Montreal) was the decisive blow to New France, the fate of the Ohio country appeared more important to Cherokee neutrality. Edmond Atkin welcomed the news from Canada, but he believed the destruction of Fort Duquesne "would be of more moment with the Southern Nations." Fellow Indian agent George Croghan added, "Nothing in my opinion could prevent a War with the Southern Indians but our Success at Ohio." When Forbes's Army took the Forks of the Ohio in 1758, the British used their victories in the Ohio country and Canada to convince the Cherokees of the changing balance of power in North America. Apparently, the Cherokees were little impressed by these projections of power, for they warred against the British and their colonists for much of 1760 and 1761. In the latter stages of the conflict, William Bull attempted to end Cherokee hostilities by warning Attakullakulla, "You know we have Men enough; and we can bring more over the Sea, if we want more. You know that all Canada is now conquered." Realizing the threat of British force might not be enough, Bull and other officials warned Cherokee leaders of an even greater danger to their people: "our Friends the Mohawks" who, along with other "great bodies of Northward Indians," intended to "war against their Towns."[20]

If British victories in the north and repeated claims of military superiority failed to sway southeastern Indians, the English had recourse to another claim to power: their invasions of Indian country. The Anglo-Cherokee War illustrates this well. In 1760 and 1761, the British launched two expeditions against the Cherokees. Colonial troops joined British Regulars in performing a "severe military execution on their Towns & Plantations," as they burnt hundreds of houses, uprooted thousands of acres of cornfields, and reportedly destroyed nearly "every eatable thing in the Country." The British subsequently declared these incursions crowning achievements in woodland warfare. "Heaven has blest us with the greatest success," exulted one soldier, for no "body of troops was ever known to stay so long in an Indian country before; the dread of his Majesty's arms has been shewn to advantage." Eliza Pinckney, the famed lowcountry agriculturalist, likewise expressed pride in the campaigns, noting that the Cherokees never "expected white men would have resolution enough to march up their Mountains." Such manly resolution projected a clear and forceful message to the Cherokees and other Indians: the British were capable at any time "in bridling and reducing a savage and ferocious Enemy."[21]

British and colonial soldiers could feel secure in their manhood because they not only decimated Cherokee towns but also drove warriors from the field. Your "Young Men think themselves great Warriors, and make great Boasts to the Creeks of their Manhood," Bull told Attakullakulla prior to the war, but "they will not be able to withstand our Force and maintain their Ground." Cherokee men did in fact join their families in fleeing from the British, which was a typical strategy of village retreat. Although warriors engaged British forces during the campaigns—sometimes in large numbers and sometimes to great effect—British troops usually met little resistance upon entering a Cherokee village. One of the expedition's commanders, Colonel Archibald Montgomery, lamented that he could not "Extirpate" the Cherokees because "they had abandoned their Towns and taken Refuge in the Mountains & Woods." Others charged Cherokee men with cowardice. They have an "unknown courage," wrote Charleston merchant and militia officer Christopher Gadsden, for "no people under the sun are more remarkable than Indians, especially the cowardly Cherokees, for never rallying again, in a large body, if once routed."[22]

The flight of the Cherokees reinforced the belief that Indian warriors were undisciplined, cowardly, and unmanly. But it also forced them to confront the fact that woodland warfare was not real war, at least in the conventional European sense. The British did not rout a sizeable army in the open field, which prompted Lieutenant Governor Bull to empathize with Colonel Montgomery, who wished to return to "*actual* Service, into more open, tho' more Dangerous Fields of Glory." Bull later voiced similar sentiments to Montgomery's successor, Colonel James Grant. "But whatever contemptible idea the European warrior may form of your Campaign," Bull wrote, he hoped the colonel would attain "true Glory . . . in surmounting difficulties" against "a Savage Country & a Savage Enemy."[23]

Bull's comments allude to the ways in which the British constructed different meanings of "glory" in this peculiar manner of war. British troops had to conquer a "savage enemy," as Bull noted, but Cherokee warriors often fled and thus robbed them of their rightful claims to victory. British men therefore sought other ways to confirm their manhood. In doing so, they looked no further than "the Woods." British and colonial correspondence is filled with praise for the soldiers' fortitude in overcoming exhausting marches, impossible terrain, and extreme heat. Following an earlier expedition against the Cherokees led by South Carolina governor William Henry Lyttelton in 1759, the Presbyterian clergy praised the governor's "Firmness, and unshaken Resolution" after leading his men "thro' a long and fatiguing March, to an Enemy's Country." During the two British-led expeditions, Lieutenant Governor Bull transferred this praise to the troops' commanders. Bull wrote to Grant in July 1761, "The fatigue, which in this sultry season during 35 days duty, without Tents or Baggage in that rough & wild Country must have been severely felt by the most robust." Grant concurred, noting that his army encountered "the most difficult Country that can be imagined." Reduced to marching "Indian File" up the "the highest Mountain I have seen in America," Grant added, "our men were so much fatigued that they could hardly crawl—numbers of them were mounted on the Rangers horses, *even our Indians were knocked up.*" If Grant's Indian allies were "knocked up," then the campaign—though void of open warfare—certainly remained a valid test of British manhood.[24]

A Masculine Conquest?

Claiming victory against the elements or the Indians, however, rang hollow among some detractors. A few colonists questioned the destruction of Cherokee villages as evidence of military success. When "you consider what Indian Towns are, and how soon rebuilt," wrote Eliza Pinckney, "you will think we need not be too much elated with the success we have had." The Cherokees likewise contested British claims to masculinity and conquest from their invasions. Attakullakulla mocked Colonel Grant's nickname, "the dreadful Warrior . . . for my part I call him the Corn Puller." Attakullakulla derided Grant's supposed "warrior" identity and notoriety, because he and other Native leaders did not consider an attack on their crops as evidence of manly fighting. Nor did they consider it proof of conquest. One Cherokee headman later testified to the inconsequentiality of these campaigns when it came to British land claims by right of conquest. He asked his adversaries:

> What did you do? You marched into our towns with a superior force. Your numbers far exceeded us, and we fled to the stronghold of our woods, there to secure our women and children. Our towns were left to your mercy. You killed a few scattered and defenceless individuals, spread fire and desolation wherever you pleased, and returned to your own habitations. If you term this a conquest, you have overlooked the most essential point.[25]

Reference to that "most essential point" reflected differences in, and the interconnectedness of, Native American and Euroamerican understandings of warfare, masculinity, and power. The destruction of Indian villages, as noted above, meant little to Native conceptions of victory in war (a point not lost on the more astute colonists). This was especially the case if incursions were temporary, which negated any claims to conquest by force of arms. Anglo-American troops, for example, burned Cherokee towns in 1760–61 but then returned to their "own habitations." Neither the permanent occupancy of their villages by the enemy nor the permanent displacement of Cherokee peoples had occurred. The headman also asserted that British troops failed to engage and defeat Cherokee warriors, instead killing only "a few scattered and defenceless individuals." In a cultural tradition wherein killing or capturing the enemy was key to disabling a foe, Cherokee leaders remained unimpressed by the "corn pullers." Protecting village populations was in fact more important to Cherokee manhood than safeguarding village infrastructures. In many ways it was a numbers game. As Lafitau had written years earlier, "It is in their number that their main force and chief wealth consist. The loss of a single person is a great one" that can only be repaired "by replacing the person." Native men therefore took great pains to secure their women and children and to safeguard the strength of their clans and village populations. Evacuating the village when confronted by a superior force was one such method.[26]

This rationale also prompted headmen to protect their warriors. Accordingly, Native leaders did not consider strategies of village retreat, which included the male population, cowardly or unmanly behavior. Headmen and leading warriors typically avoided large-scale engagements, especially if it exposed their men to needless risks. Failing to do so could result in lost status and their position as village or war leaders. James Smith of Pennsylvania, who became intimate with Delaware modes of war as an adopted relation, defended Native leaders' efforts to preserve their men. They retreat if "their men are falling fast" in battle, he noted, for "they will not stand cutting, like the Highlanders, or other British troops." This partly explains the reticence of certain headmen to entrust their warriors to British officers who were untested in woodland warfare. This is not to say that Indian men shied away from confronting a superior force, for attacking or defeating an enemy was the duty of men as warriors. The Cherokees, for example, collected an army to counter the two British invasions. At the Battle of Etchoe in 1760, Cherokee resistance brought a quick end to Montgomery's expedition, thus prompting the mountain villagers to claim they "had beat the English."[27]

Nevertheless, Native men could not ignore the destruction of their villages by the enemy. In order to cope with these potential challenges to their capabilities as warriors and thus their manhood, some Indian men attributed their losses to the power of demography. "Your numbers far exceeded us," declared the headman who had disputed British claims to Cherokee lands. John Norton likewise agreed that the "Natives of America . . . have suffered in war from having to contend with superior numbers." Other Native leaders provided more detailed explanations by comparing "the English Army to Be Like the Leaves In the fall of the year on the Trees[.] In one Night a hard frost and a Great wind will Blow them all Down, and In the Spring there will Be Rather more than was Before[;] they say If the English Loose Ever so many In one Battle there will Be Rather more the Next Day."[28]

Conclusion: The American Experience

The numbers predicament for eastern Indians not only concerned large armies, but also exploding enemy populations. Euroamerican settlers poured into the mid-Atlantic and southeastern borderlands after mid-century, forever altering the demographic balance between Native and newcomer. These shifts may have appeared at first to be less ominous for Indians, who found many settlers wanting in the art of war. Indeed, the beginning of the Seven Years' War found a panicked population in the western settlements. Indian methods of woodland warfare—chiefly their "surprising the enemy as the cat does the mouse"—resulted in "the Inhabitants terrified every where." Threats both real and imagined typically generated two responses: flight and fortification. Both strategies were defensive in nature and won them little sympathy from either the enemy or eastern officials, who believed backcountry settlers were inordinately paralyzed by their fears. Even those settlers involved in more active measures against Indians, such as rangers and militiamen, encountered skepticism about their soldiery and bravery.[29]

Some colonists contested these challenges to their manhood. British and colonial armies had driven the French out of North America and successfully engaged their Indian enemies. Although many settlers in the region began the war as "Foreignors, and Strangers to the Method of Indians," many of them had overcome this fear of the unknown by war's end. As one Virginia officer related to his Cherokee counterpart, "my Men have beat all the Indians to the Northward, and are not to be frightened by your Yells." Europeans and their colonists, of course, had long been familiar with the Indians' "skulking way of war," but the Seven Years' War, replete with its discourses of masculinity and intercultural warfare, provided novel experiences for a new generation of settlers in a region that had never witnessed imperial contestation to this scale.[30]

NOTES

I would like to thank the Huntington Library, William L. Clements Library, American Philosophical Society, and West Virginia University for their generous financial support of my research on the eighteenth-century Cherokees. I would also like to thank Brian Luskey for reviewing portions of this work, and Tom Foster and the readers of this volume for their editorial acumen.

1. Thomas Percival, *A Father's Instructions; Consisting of Moral Tales, Fables, and Reflections; Designed to Promote the Love of Virtue, a Taste for Knowledge, and an Early Acquaintance with the Works of Nature*, 7th edition (Warrington, 1788), 249–50. Percival appropriated this statement, supposedly made by a Cherokee speaker, from John Bruce, *Elements of the Science of Ethics, on the Principles of Natural Philosophy* (London, 1786), 188.

2. Instructions to Christopher Gist, Esq., November 16, 1757, ed. Edith Mays, *Amherst Papers, 1756–1763: The Southern Sector* (Bowie, Md.: Heritage Books, 1999), 44.

3. Ann Little, *Abraham in Arms: War and Gender in Colonial New England* (Philadelphia: University of Pennsylvania Press, 2007), 2–3, 10, 60. For a gendered examination of Anglo-Indian warfare beyond New England, see Michelle Marie LeMaster, "'Thorough-paced girls' and 'cowardly bad men': Gender and Family in Indian-White Relations in the Colonial Southeast, 1660–1783" (Ph.D. diss., Johns Hopkins University, 2001), particularly chapter 3. For recent gender-centered studies of Europeans or Indians in early America, see Kathleen Brown, *Good Wives, Nasty Wenches, and Anxious Patriarchs: Gender, Race, and Power in Colonial Virginia* (Chapel Hill: University of North Carolina Press, 1996); Nancy Shoemaker, *A Strange Likeness: Becoming Red and White in Eighteenth-Century North America* (New York: Oxford University Press, 2004); Nancy Shoemaker, "An Alliance Between Men: Gender Metaphors in Eighteenth-Century American Indian Diplomacy East of the Mississippi," *Ethnohistory* 46:2 (1999): 239–63; Karen Kupperman, *Indians and English: Facing Off in Early America* (Ithaca: Cornell University Press, 2000); Theda Perdue, *Cherokee Women: Gender and Culture Change, 1700–1835* (Lincoln: University of Nebraska Press, 1998); Claudio Saunt, *A New Order of Things: Property, Power, and the Transformation of the Creek Indians, 1733–1816* (Cambridge: Cambridge University Press, 1999); Claudio Saunt, "'Domestick . . . Quiet being broke': Gender Conflict Among Creek Indians in the Eighteenth Century," eds. Andrew Cayton and Fredrika Teute, *Contact Points: American Frontiers from the Mohawk Valley to the Mississippi, 1750–1830* (Chapel Hill: University of North Carolina Press, 1998), 151–74; Susan Sleeper-Smith, *Indian Women and French Men: Rethinking Cultural Encounter in the Western Great Lakes* (Amherst: University of Massachusetts Press, 2001); Greg O'Brien, *Choctaws in a Revolutionary Age, 1750–1830* (Lincoln: University of Nebraska Press, 2002).

4. Little finds that a de-emphasis in Christian piety also extended to New Englanders during the mid-eighteenth century, as they embraced a "new masculinity" based on Anglo-American nationalism and anti-Catholicism rather than household headship and Christian piety. See Little, *Abraham in Arms*, 167, 172. On the use of the "Long Seven Years' War," see François Furstenberg, "The Significance of the Trans-Appalachian Frontier in Atlantic History," *American Historical Review* 113:3 (2008): 650, n3. I use the term British throughout this chapter to denote both the English and their colonists in North America.

5. Joseph François Lafitau, *Customs of the American Indians Compared with the Customs of Primitive Times*, ed. and trans. William N. Fenton and Elizabeth L. Moore, Volume I (Toronto: Champlain Society, 1974), 39; Baron de Lahontan, *New Voyages to North America*, ed. Reuben Gold Thwaites, Volume I (Chicago: A. C. McClurg, 1905), 421–22; Joseph François Lafitau, *Customs of the American Indians Compared with the Customs of Primitive Times*, ed. and trans. William N. Fenton and Elizabeth L. Moore, Volume II (Toronto: Champlain Society, 1977), 187. Michelle LeMaster rightly notes that the key determinant of identity and status for Native American men was their role as warriors. Although hunting was an equally important occupation for Native men, she continues, it rarely entered their discourse when projecting their manhood to Europeans or other Indians. See LeMaster, "Gender and Family in Indian-White Relations," 30, 161–62. For a brief discussion of hunting and masculinity among the Cherokees, see Nathaniel Sheidley, "Hunting and the Politics of Masculinity in Cherokee Treaty-Making, 1763–75," eds. Martin Daunton and Rick Halpern, *Empire and Others: British Encounters with Indigenous Peoples, 1600–1850* (Philadelphia: University of Pennsylvania Press, 1999), 167–85.

6. See, for example, Raymond D. Fogelson, "The Cherokee Ball Game: A Study in Southeastern Ethnology" (Ph.D. diss., University of Pennsylvania, 1962), 39–43; Warren Halliday Jackson, "Sketch of the Manners, Customs, Religion, and Government of the Senecas in 1800," Wallace Family Papers, American Philosophical Society, 30; John Stuart to William Henry Lyttelton, November 22, 1759, William Lyttelton Papers, William L. Clements Library, University of Michigan, Ann Arbor (hereafter cited as WLP).

7. See, for example, Alexander Hewat, *An Historical Account of the Rise and Progress of the Colonies of South Carolina and Georgia*, Volume I (London, 1779), 243–44; Shoemaker, "An Alliance Between Men," 255. Theda Perdue finds that some Cherokee women did perform war-related functions; these women were anomalies, however, for they never became "full-time" warriors. See Perdue, *Cherokee Women*, 37–39.

8. Caleb Swan, "Report to Henry Knox on Creek Indians, 1791," Series III, no. 32, Benjamin Smith Barton Papers, American Philosophical Society (hereafter cited as APS); Lud Grant to Governor Glen, April 29, 1755, ed. William L. McDowell, Jr., *The Colonial Records of South Carolina: Documents Relating to Indian Affairs, 1754–1765* (Columbia: South Carolina Department of Archives and History, 1992), 53 (hereafter cited as DRIA, II); James Adair, *The History of the American Indians* . . . (London, 1775), 258; William Bartram, *Travels Through North and South Carolina, Georgia, East and West Florida* . . . (Philadelphia: Printed by James and Johnson, 1791), 485–86; James Smith, *An Account of the Remarkable Occurrences in the Life and Travels of Col. James Smith*, ed. William Darlington (Cincinnati: Robert Clarke, 1870), 46–48; Richard Coytmore to William Henry Lyttelton, August 23, 1759, WLP; *Pennsylvania Gazette*, July 24, August 7, 1760. "White people" was a common expression used by eastern Indians to identify the British and their American colonists. A rich discussion of gender metaphors can be found in Shoemaker, "An Alliance Between Men," 239–63.

9. Perdue, *Cherokee Women*, 62.

10. Little, *Abraham in Arms*, 2–3, 14; see also Michelle LeMaster, "Gender and Family in Indian-White Relations," 60, 198.

11. Lafitau, *Customs of the American Indians*, I, 89; Carl F. Klinck and James J. Talman, eds., *The Journal of Major John Norton* (Toronto: Champlain Society, 1970), 116–17, 128–30; Lahontan, *New Voyages to North America*, 70.

12. Council held at the [Pennsylvania] State House, August 22, 1755, Material Pertaining to Pennsylvania Indian Affairs, 1755–58, APS. Ann Little notes that Native American men associated dogs with servility. Little, *Abraham in Arms*, 36. For more on the linkages between Indian discontent and British disrespect during the Seven Years' War and Pontiac's War, see Gregory Evans Dowd, *War Under Heaven: Pontiac, the Indian Nations, and the British Empire* (Baltimore: Johns Hopkins University Press, 2002).

13. Duane King, ed., *The Memoirs of Lt. Henry Timberlake: The Story of Soldier, Adventurer, and Emissary to the Cherokees, 1756–1765* (Chapel Hill: University of North Carolina Press, 2007), 37; John Stuart, "Of Indians in General," 265, quoted in Tom Hatley, *The Dividing Paths: Cherokees and South Carolinians Through the Revolutionary Era* (New York: Oxford University Press, 1995), 11; Jeffery Amherst to Col. Byrd, March 5, 1761, ed. Mays, *Amherst Papers*, 206.

14. Smith, *An Account of the Remarkable Occurrences*, 104–5, 150–54; John Long, *Voyages and Travels in the Years 1768–1788*, ed. Milo Milton Quaife (Chicago: Lakeside Press, 1922), 37–38; Gabriel Sagard, *The Long Journey to the Country of the Hurons*, ed. George M. Wrong (Toronto: Champlain Society, 1939), 152–53; Daniel Horsmanden, papers pertain-

ing to the Six Nations, ed. Henry C. Van Schaack, Provincial History of New York, 1714 to 1747: Collected, arranged, & presented to the New York Historical Society (1845), 83 (microfilm at the APS); *Pennsylvania Gazette*, August 7, 1776. Nancy Shoemaker argues that fears concerning Indian warfare might explain the appeal of animal metaphors among the English, who by "analogizing Indian warriors to wolves, transformed an apparent excess of masculinity into a deplorable lack of civility." Shoemaker, "An Alliance Between Men," 249. For more on the Indians' "skulking way of war" in seventeenth-century New England, see Patrick Malone, *The Skulking Way of War: Technology and Tactics Among the New England Indians* (Lanham, Md.: Madison Books, 1991).

15. Forbes to Bouquet, June 10, 1758, Forbes to Pitt, June 17, 1758, Forbes to Abercrombie, July 18, 1758, ed. Alfred P. James, *The Writings of General John Forbes Relating to His Service in North America* (Menasha, Wis.: Collegiate, 1938), 112, 117–18, 151; John Oliphant, *Peace and War on the Anglo-Cherokee Frontier* (Baton Rouge: Louisiana State University Press, 2001), 67; John P. Brown, *Old Frontiers: The Story of the Cherokee Indians from Earliest Times to the Date of Their Removal to the West, 1838* (Kingsport, Tenn.: Southern Publishers, 1938), 89; Bouquet to Washington, July 14, 1758, George Washington Papers at the Library of Congress, 1741–1799: Series 4, General Correspondence (1697–1799). Views of incapable Indian warriors and superior European soldiery likewise influenced some French officers in North America, perhaps most notably General Louis-Joseph de Montcalm, the failed defender of Quebec against British forces in 1759. As Fred Anderson argues, Montcalm dismissed long-held strategies of officers and officials in New France, who favored the use of Indian allies to wage a guerilla-style war against the British settlements. The general instead mistakenly believed a conventional defense managed by professional soldiers and militiamen would prevent the fall of Quebec. See Fred Anderson, *The War That Made America: A Short History of the French and Indian War* (New York: Viking, 2005), 195.

16. Council held at the [Pennsylvania] State House, April 8, 1756, Material Pertaining to Pennsylvania Indian Affairs, 1755–58, APS. For other examples of Indian shaming practices to influence English policy, see Shoemaker, "An Alliance Between Men," 247.

17. Shoemaker, "An Alliance Between Men," 239, 248, 254; John Stuart to the Board of Trade, March 9, 1764, British Public Record Office, Colonial Office 323/17/240 (microfilm at Hunter Library, Western Carolina University, Cullowhee, North Carolina); William Bull to Attakullakulla, March 30, 1761, James Grant of Ballindalloch Papers, Reel 32 (microfilm at the David Library of the American Revolution, Washington Crossing, Pennsylvania) (hereafter cited as James Grant of Ballindalloch Papers). See also Little, *Abraham in Arms*, 198.

18. Fauquier to the Board of Trade, January 30, 1759, ed. George Reese, *The Official Papers of Francis Fauquier Lieutenant Governor of Virginia, 1758–1768*, Volume I (Charlottesville: University Press of Virginia, 1980), 165; Captain Raymd. Demere to Governor Lyttelton, November 18, 1756, DRIA, II, 249; Council at Easton, July 28, 1756, Material Pertaining to Pennsylvania Indian Affairs, 1755–58, APS.

19. Lachland McGillivray to William Henry Lyttelton, July 15, 1758, WLP; Paul Demere to William Henry Lyttelton, July 30, 1758, WLP; Robert Dinwiddie to William Henry Lyttelton, November 20, 1756, WLP. Cherokee leaders did not depend solely on British intelligence for news about the northern campaigns, as they often sent runners to the Six Nations, Shawnees, Delawares, and others to gather information. Old Hopp to

Captain Rayd. Demere, DRIA, II, 234; White Outerbridge to William Henry Lyttelton, December 8, 1758, WLP; John Stuart to Allan Stuart, May 15, 1760, 31, James Grant of Ballindalloch Papers, Reel 31.

20. *Pennsylvania Gazette*, November 8, 1759; Francis Fauquier to William Henry Lyttelton, October 13, 1758, WLP; Edmond Atkin to William Henry Lyttelton, October 15, 1758, WLP; George Croghan to William Johnson, January 30, 1759, ed. Milton W. Hamilton, *The Papers of Sir William Johnson*, Volume X (Albany: University of the State of New York Press, 1951), 90; William Bull to Attakullakulla, March 30, 1761, James Grant of Ballindalloch Papers, Reel 32; John Stuart to Allan Stuart, May 15, 1760, James Grant of Ballindalloch Papers, Reel 31.

21. William Bull to James Grant, July 17, 1761, James Grant of Ballindalloch Papers, Reel 32; Journal of March and Operations Under Grant, James Grant of Ballindalloch Papers, Reel 32; *Pennsylvania Gazette*, August 6, 1761; Eliza Lucas Pinckney, *The Letterbook of Eliza Lucas Pinckney, 1739-1762*, ed. Elise Pinckney (Columbia: University of South Carolina Press, 1997), 138. Pinckney alluded to an earlier expedition led by South Carolina governor William Henry Lyttelton in 1759. The attempted invasion, however, never materialized, and the Carolinians and Cherokees brokered a temporary peace. See *Pennsylvania Gazette*, February 14, 1760.

22. William Bull to Attakullakulla, March 30, 1761, 32, Grant Papers; Archibald Montgomery to William Bull, July 19, 1760, 31, Grant Papers; Christopher Gadsden, *Some Observations on the Two Campaigns Against the Cherokee Indians, in 1760 and 1761: In a Second Letter from Philopatrios* (Charles-Town: Peter Timothy, 1762), 33.

23. William Bull to Archibald Montgomery, July 12, 1760, James Grant of Ballindalloch Papers, Reel 31;; William Bull to James Grant, June 18, 1761, James Grant of Ballindalloch Papers, Reel 32;. Italics mine.

24. *Pennsylvania Gazette*, February 14, 1760; Bull to Grant, July 17, 1761, James Grant of Ballindalloch Papers, Reel 32; Journal of March and Operations Under Grant, James Grant of Ballindalloch Papers, Reel 32; James Merrell, *Into the American Woods: Negotiators on the Pennsylvania Frontier* (New York: Norton, 1999). Italics mine.

25. Quoted from Brown, *Old Frontiers*, 166; Anthony Benezet, *Some Observations on the Situation, Disposition, and Character of the Indian Natives of this Continent* (Philadelphia: Joseph Crukshank, 1784), 59; Pinckney, *Letterbook*, 173; A Talk from the Little Carpenter, November 15, 1761, James Grant of Ballindalloch Papers, Reel 32; Lafitau, *Customs of the American Indians*, II, 98-99.

26. Lafitau, *Customs of the American Indians*, II, 98-99.

27. Smith responded to British charges of Indian cowardice by calling warriors "the best disciplined troops in the known world," adding that "British discipline in the woods, is the way to have men slaughtered." Smith, *An Account of the Remarkable Occurrences*, 155, 158-61; *Pennsylvania Gazette*, September 4, September 25, 1760; Croghan to Johnson, July 25, 1761, prepared for publication by Milton W. Hamilton and Albert B. Corey, *The Papers of Sir William Johnson*, Volume X (Albany: The University of the State of New York Press, 1951), 316.

28. James Beamer to William Henry Lyttelton, January 10, 1759, WLP. The repeated destruction of Indian villages had a profound impact on Native peoples. The memory of these invasions, from both the Seven Years' War and American Revolution, lasted well after the fighting ended. Thomas Foster, ed., *The Collected Works of Benjamin Hawkins*,

1796–1810 (Tuscaloosa: University of Alabama Press, 2003), 23; William Fenton, *The Great Law and the Longhouse: A Political History of the Iroquois Confederacy* (Norman: University of Oklahoma Press, 1998), 632. The numbers rationale continued long after the Seven Years' War. See Klinck and Talman, eds., *The Journal of Major John Norton*, 42–43, 47–48.

29. Lafitau, *Customs of the American Indians*, II, 139; Edmond Atkin to George Croghan, June 8, 1757, Indian and Military Affairs of Pennsylvania, 1737–1775, APS; Jeffery Amherst to Lt. Col. Grant of His Majesty's 40th Regt. of Foot, December 15, 1760, James Grant to Jeffery Amherst, March 15, 1761, Grant to Amherst, April 25, 1761, ed. Mays, *Amherst Papers*, 154. For more on how the terror of Indian warfare unsettled Pennsylvanians during the Seven Years' War, see Peter Silver, *Our Savage Neighbors: How Indian War Transformed Early America* (New York: Norton, 2007).

30. Gadsden, *Some Observations*, 21–22, 28; Council held at the [Pennsylvania] State House, August 22, 1755, Material Pertaining to Pennsylvania Indian Affairs, 1755–58, APS; John Fairchild to Governor Glen, May 10, 1751, William L. McDowell, Jr., ed., *The Colonial Records of South Carolina: Documents Relating to Indian Affairs, May 21, 1750 – August 7, 1754* (Columbia: South Carolina Archives Department, 1958), 48; *Pennsylvania Gazette*, November 13, 1760. Regarding the racial legacies of the war among British colonists, particularly within the context of "Indian hating," see Jane T. Merritt, *At the Crossroads: Indians and Empires on a Mid-Atlantic Frontier, 1700–1763* (Chapel Hill: University of North Carolina Press, 2003); Matthew Ward, *Breaking the Backcountry: The Seven Years' War in Virginia and Pennsylvania, 1754–1765* (Pittsburgh: University of Pittsburgh Press, 2003); Silver, *Our Savage Neighbors*.

4

Real Men

*Masculinity, Spirituality, and Community in
Late Eighteenth-Century Cherokee Warfare*

SUSAN ABRAM

In 1761 the colonial soldier William Fyffe noted that war was the "principal study" or "beloved occupation" of Cherokee men from the southern Appalachian region.[1] As the historian John Phillip Reid noted, "Warfare to the Cherokees was a business, a grim, dangerous, exciting business so important to their way of life that its mores and values dominated their culture."[2] Indeed, the Cherokee "beloved occupation" was a complex institution with gendered expectations and values that promoted leadership, brotherhood, and communal solidarity, and also validated traditional Cherokee gender roles. Virtually without exception, Cherokee men, at one time or another, participated in a culture of warfare as an integral part of their lives, typically demonstrating their manliness through the scalping of enemies and later dancing in performative celebration.

In the eighteenth century, warfare in Cherokee culture was an institution that expressed spiritual power, honor, and communal and clan values.[3] This chapter examines Cherokee warrior culture and how it reflected many of the gendered beliefs, values, and traditions of the Indian nation's society. In particular, it considers war not only as a path to manhood but also discusses how it played a dominant role in the expression of masculinity. In addition, this chapter will explore the battles played out in the spiritual realm as Cherokee men sought enhancement of their masculine powers and the diminution of that in their enemies. Ultimately, warfare served to interconnect warriors with the political and communal realms of Cherokee society. Unlike Anglo-American warfare, Cherokee warfare did not serve a patriarchal culture. Cherokee warriors fought for the honor and protection of their clans, to secure their place as real men, and to enter a warrior brotherhood. All these are expressions of Cherokee masculinity.

In the mid to late eighteenth century, warfare touched the lives of everyone. Towns and tribes throughout the southeast were both perpetrators and victims of violent actions, with warfare occupying a central part of the larger Cherokee belief system based on models sanctioned by sacred myths. For the most part, this spiritual aspect of warfare and its effects on Cherokee society as depicted in eighteenth-century accounts reveals only a partial picture of warrior culture, since these were written by outsiders (largely European), such as traders, missionaries, soldiers, and travelers. This group generally spent a great deal of time within the native community, often taking Cherokee wives and rearing their children within Cherokee society. These informants often witnessed or at times even participated in the described activities connected to warfare. Nevertheless, these records provide a glimpse of individual and communal warfare actions in early America. Although some of these accounts recorded by non-Cherokee may be inaccurate, Cherokee informants later corroborated a great deal.[4] While it is important to remember that although not any one account totally expresses the complexities and variations of Cherokee war actions or rituals, the essence of their belief of the importance of war and its gendered responsibilities within their society remains evident.[5]

Within early American studies there has been a movement in the last few years to broaden our understanding of native North American warfare and how it compares to Anglo-American warfare.[6] Yet there is still a void. Recent works on gender serve to tell us a great deal about the roles of Cherokee women and just how very gendered Cherokee society was.[7] The seminal work on the subject is Theda Perdue's *Cherokee Women: Gender and Culture Change, 1700–1835*. Yet surprisingly there has been little written to date that specifically examines the role of masculinity in Cherokee warfare.[8]

This chapter utilizes an ethnohistorical approach to concentrate on Cherokee warfare and how this complex institution interwove gendered expectations, spiritual dimensions, and communal values. By employing Cherokee voices, legends, and formulas (prayers) as often as possible, along with recorded history by outsiders of Cherokee voices, this chapter argues that though war affected all, the military organization primarily involved Cherokee men and emphasized their masculine connections to the sacred, social, and political dimensions of Cherokee society. Warfare was a path to manhood, increased social status, and secured political influence. It especially expressed Cherokee masculinity by allowing warriors to prove their worth as real men.

Gender Roles and the Making of Men

Cherokee society defined real men as strong, successful, and stealthy in their manly roles as providers and protectors. Cherokee men expressed their masculinity in a variety of ways, particularly through hunting, displays of athletic prowess, and warfare, although most Cherokee men chose to earn and express their manhood through the latter.[9] It was the most dangerous yet most rapid path to achieve recognition of manhood and to become a worthy and manly community member. If a male did not succeed in any of these gendered activities, his community did not respect him and saw him as an embarrassing burden to his clan and family.

Of course, not everyone was adept at one of these activities. Cherokee men could hold a position of status when they became somewhat infirm with age but had been a warrior in their younger days. Other respected manly duties included expertise in crafting hunting or war weapons and associated paraphernalia, or as herbal or formulistic experts (doctors/medicine men or priests). Old men who were not shamans, craftsmen, or diplomats would find themselves sitting on a platform in the corn field scaring crows away along with the young boys—a useful but unmanly task.

Cherokee society was organized into seven matrilineal clans where children were born into the clan of their mother. Cherokee warrior deeds, as well as those entered into by the entire community, represented sacred gendered acts designed to protect the people and the honor of the seven clans.[10] The first duty of a Cherokee man was to his own clan members, especially to his mother, mother's sisters, mother's brothers, his own sisters, and their children. A Cherokee man retained his own clan upon entering marriage with someone from another clan. Cherokee society was also traditionally matrifocal, meaning that a man lived near his wife's clan family. These affinal associations tied the clans together and strengthened Cherokee solidarity.[11]

Society expected male youths to pass into manhood through prowess in hunting, games of stickball, or warfare. Success in any of these endeavors represented the proper expression of manliness and masculinity. Males who did not meet the proper standards were somewhat stigmatized by the community. Women and their clan mothers especially sought out marriage partners who could excel in these activities, which symbolized their success, their strength, and the presence of spiritual blessings. Cherokee men who failed to act boldly as providers and protectors of the seven Cherokee clans held a lower status in society and were deemed undesirable marriage partners, even though Cherokee women were not directly dependent on their husbands.[12]

Cherokee society was gendered. Women controlled the subsistence activities related to plants, including gathering, horticulture, and trade.[13] Thus the matrilineal clans controlled the fields and particular food gathering areas. A woman and her clan were responsible for child rearing, with the maternal uncle playing more of a role than even the biological father. The sphere of Cherokee men demanded that they provide and protect to ensure the continued existence of the people. These included actions of hunting, diplomacy with outsiders, civil order (through clan blood law), and, of course, warfare.[14]

Cherokee youths were inculcated in traditional gender roles. Boys, for example, grew up seeing many facets of warfare, and their elders easily taught them its secular and sacred ways. Clan relatives often apprenticed a young boy to a specialist. His training and esoteric instruction prepared him for success in life. A war priest would sometimes choose a young man to indoctrinate in the spiritual aspects of war. The process ended with a purifying going-to-water ritual and a sacrifice of deer tongue and corn mush to the sacred fire.[15] The youth now waited for a chance to become a man by protecting the living and honoring the dead, a necessary rite of passage.

War and Manhood: Expressions of Masculinity

Geopolitical conflicts between the Cherokees and their neighbors provided ample prospects for Cherokee youths to pass into manhood through the ultimate exhibition of masculinity—killing an enemy. The proper preparation was important to insure success in the endeavor. One observer noted that "nothing but war-songs and war-dances could please them, during this flattering period of becoming great warriors."[16] War rituals began with a call for volunteers by an esteemed warrior of great rank, such as the Mankiller or the Great Warrior, since there was no centralized government during this time.[17]

Cherokee blood law required that the nearest male clan relation avenge or reconcile the "crying blood" of kin stolen into captivity or killed.[18] Should the avenger fail, his relative's ghost was doomed to never rest. It would remain nearby, leaving the community vulnerable to sickness or bad luck. This "kindred duty of retaliation" resulted in a cyclic process because there was "no [other] sure method to reconcile their differences," except via this time-honored perpetual process of give-and-take with their enemies.[19]

The Irish trader James Adair, who wrote an account of his time in the mid-eighteenth century among the southeastern Indians, recorded that ritual preparation began when the leader marched, sang war songs, beat his war drum, and called the men to gather. This veteran warrior sang one mourning song for those who might die in combat and for any community members killed by the enemy.[20] Next, he passionately made his case and invoked the symbol of the white paths, detailing how the enemy had "changed their beloved colour" by spilling the blood of kin, tainting the white path of friendship and peace with red and black, the colors of war:[21]

> Then he strongly persuades his kindred warriors and others, who are not afraid of the enemies bullets and arrows, to come and join him with *manly* [emphasis mine] cheerful hearts: he assures them . . . so they are ready to hazard their lives to revenge the blood of their kindred and country-men.[22]

This was the time for real men or those who aspired to that designation to come forward. This call presented an opportunity to procure military titles, for "it is by scalps they get all their war-titles."[23] Thus war was not only a passage for Cherokee males into manhood, but also a way to gain status as a warrior and to publicly display the power of their masculine identity.

As geopolitical threats intensified with European colonization in the mid-eighteenth century, emphasis on Cherokee male activities increased. Historically, males controlled the gendered world of hunting in the important deerskin trade with the colonists. But as the web of debt to Anglo-American traders increased Cherokee dependence on colonists, the importance of hunting as a representation of masculine success decreased while success in warfare became even more important and society became more militarized. For example, war councils occasionally involved hundreds of men from many towns, as opposed to smaller groups with representatives from a single town. Messengers ran from settlement to settlement carrying red sticks or red-painted tobacco to signify a military threat to all. At these relatively rare events, huge numbers of warriors turned out.[24]

The Cherokees held large war deliberations in the central town house. In the early nineteenth century, older Cherokees reported to the author John Howard Payne that in the mid to late eighteenth century the Great Warrior or the Great Man, *A ska yv stu e qo*, would address the gathering through his speaker: "Let us consider however, that if we conquer our enemies it will be because God fights for us; and if we return in safety, it will be because God preserves us."[25] The war chief had publicly declared at the time of his ritual induction into the office:[26]

You have now put me in blood up to my knees. . . . But if I hear the war whoop in my path, and see our enemies with warlike weapons in their hands, I will fight and subdue them, or die in the conflict. You have made me *A ska yv gv ste qa,* and I shall take care of my young warriors, and never engage in war without sufficient cause.[27]

With this, the war chief became an uncle to the younger warriors and the yet unproven, linking himself to them as if by blood. They rushed toward the red war standard in an emotional display of support and began the war dance. Seven of the foremost warriors from each company of men presented their red war clubs before the sacred fire.

The Sacred Realm of War and Masculinity

The volunteers sequestered themselves from the community and underwent fasting, purging, and going-to-water purification in preparation to fulfill their sacred duty. This in itself served to physically and spiritually divide the masculine from the feminine. A portion of the going-to-water ritual involved divination with the *ulunsuti,* or the divining crystal.[28] At the first gathering of potential volunteers for war expeditions, the war priest conducted a divining session to predict each warrior's fate. If the future held failure for a warrior, the leader honorably discharged this person from martial participation. This act, as far as can be ascertained, did nothing to diminish his masculine status. On the other hand, this dismissal took away the opportunity to prove or enhance his masculinity through warfare.[29]

The leader and his right-hand man underwent even more rigorous purification than the rest, but all remained celibate during this period. Any sexual contact would ruin the sanctification process by draining masculine power and thus jeopardize the safety and success of all the participating warriors. They therefore severed contact with women for several days before leaving and again upon their return when they were especially vulnerable to feminine power, being still in a state of masculine blood spilling.[30]

Another sacred connection was the war fire ritual. When the warriors first gathered, the war leader kindled a new fire "to be their guide and helper in the war." The war leader recognized this special fire as the "principal chief," believing that he was merely serving as the war fire's right hand man. The men passed their weapons through the fire's smoke to sanctify them. The priest also offered a meat sacrifice to the fire and "prayed for instruction," watching for omens of success.[31] Before leaving on the war trail, the leader placed live coals into a red clay vessel set into a sacred ark. The war fire signified the party's worth. If it went out, the mission was doomed and so aborted. Cessation of the fire represented the withdrawal of divine blessing. Any attempt to continue could end only in disaster.[32]

Only the priest/war leader and his right-hand man could touch the holy chest and its sacred contents.[33] The medicine bundle contained numerous potent objects. Their presence could portend the success of the mission and required that all honor the interdictions associated with their care. If blessed, the warriors could fulfill the sacred mission by following all proscriptions and taboos. In the mid-eighteenth century, James Adair recounted a story about an incident between an outsider and the protector of a Cherokee war ark. Its keeper caught a profane stranger peering at its unwrapped contents and threatened to release an arrow at the curiosity seeker if he did not retreat.[34] Such irreverence could doom the Cherokee mission, leaving its members disgraced and humiliated or worse.

Many other things could cause the mission's termination. The war leader kept attuned to omens that portended disaster, especially dreams presaging an ill outcome. He was also wary of young, inexperienced males, who might disregard prescribed taboos, which would not be appropriate masculine behavior and would thereby jeopardize the entire party's safety. To ignore signs or to behave inappropriately were direct breaches of the sacred, whereas real men knew what was expected and ignored temptations, thereby exhibiting their masculine strength and fortitude. If a breach did occur, any blessings previously bestowed could disappear, and illness, bad luck, or death might await he who had behaved in an unmanly way. Yet if some indicators predicted doom and required turning away from a fight, this act did not adversely affect the Cherokee vision of the rest of the party's masculine honor.[35]

Though omens could potentially curtail a war party, this was not often the case. A war expedition sometimes lasted for weeks or months, with the men traveling quickly and lightly.[36] Necessary items in a warrior's personal kit included a mirror for application of sacred war paint, a gun or a bow, a shot pouch or quiver of arrows, knife, tomahawk, war club, and snakebite medicine. They journeyed over trails or down rivers by canoe in disciplined order. Many recited or sang protection formulas or prayers along the way.[37] These incantations were "to shield one from the ancient dangers of the trail—the enemy in ambuscade, wild beasts, and the unfriendly elements."[38] One such surviving *idi:gawé:sdi*, or formula, reads in part:[39]

> Listen! *Ha!* You have just come to hear, You Provider who rests Above.
> *Ha!* Now You have just come to place my feet upon the Brown Stone.
> *Ha!* Let them be keeping my fine attire out of sight.
> Listen! From the Sunland where You rest, You have just come to hear, Red Man.
> *Ha!* Arise now!
> *Ha!* He has just brought your soul as high as the treetops.⁴⁰

In this prayer, the warrior/traveler invokes sacred assistance to become invisible to enemies. The Cherokees believed in seven levels to heaven or the top of the sky vault. The first level was at the treetops where, if he could place his soul, a warrior was impervious to bullets or arrows. He only became vulnerable if the enemy knew to aim up in the treetops to pierce the out-of-body soul in order to kill its earthly vessel.⁴¹

As the Cherokee warrior sought to protect his soul, he might also invoke Thunder's power to defeat his opponent:

> Da:hl(a)! Da:hl(a)! Da:hl(a)! Da:hl(a)!
> Now! Blue Lightning!
> You have just come to slap the earth in front of the warring.
> Now Thunder has just come to stamp in front of the Seven Clan Districts and the Seven Peoples.
> Put their souls down upon the ground!⁴²

This call to Thunder and Blue Lightning brought an enemy's soul to earth, where the Cherokee warrior could destroy it. Some protection charms relate to meeting a rival:

> From the White Mountains I originated:
> I am a Little Man.
> On White Pathways I am making my footprints: the Blue Ones cannot do it.
> Let it be raining when they will be making their footprints in the Pathway.
> In the very middle of the Pathway their souls have just come to be cut into slices!⁴³

In this prayer, the references to the color white signify a peaceful relationship between place, self, and others. The rain wipes an enemy's unworthy footprints from the righteous path as their souls are "sliced," a spiritual action that results in the enemy's befuddlement.[44]

These formulas represent a deep connection between the masculine realm of the male warrior and its relationship to the spiritual world. The concept of spiritual warfare included ritual maiming. By disfiguring the physical body, the enemy became degraded, unworthy, emasculated men. This also replicated the damage inflicted on an opponent's soul. Scalping was a direct assault against the "soul of conscious life" that resided at the top of the head.[45] By preventing the enemy from reaching spiritual fulfillment, scalping allowed Cherokee warriors to prove and enhance their worth as real men through martial success.

War paint, or *wodi,* and personal medicine of protection were other items with sacred war power. Cherokee soldiers took great pains to apply war paint before battle. Its most valued ingredient was hematite, the Brown Stone referred to earlier in this chapter. Cherokees valued *wodi* because "one cannot shoot through stone," and it represented a transformation of an evil force into a positive power. The Cherokees had long ago defeated the evil supernatural Stone Coat, who then surrendered the *wodi* with instructions on how to properly use it to their benefit.[46] A revered painter also prepared the feathers worn by the war party by coloring them red, the color of blood and war. As they steeped in the dye pot containing specific plants, including one named "the Blood," he prayed "for a Divine influence to accompany the feathers" so the enemy's "strength might be taken away, and they rendered unable to fight."[47]

Though all omens might be favorable and powerful spiritual medicine accompanied the warriors, the war party took other precautions to prevent detection. They counted on stealth and the ark's power to keep their mission secret until they were ready to strike. Warriors would even "crawl through thickets and swamps in the manner of wolves" to find an enemy.[48] The war party posted four experienced scouts with martial titles—Raven, Owl, Wolf, and Fox—to prevent ambush and to locate the enemy. All communicated by mimicking the animals whose skins they wore. By linking themselves to the power of spirit animals, Cherokee warriors kept themselves open to receive communications from the animal kingdom. Bird chirps, especially those of the chickadee, alerted the men that enemies were near. Owls, though considered harbingers of death (being associated with evil conjuring and shape-shifting), were sometimes helpful in warfare. Screech owl hoots heard off to either flank foretold victory. Cries repeatedly emanating from the company's front or rear spelled doom, however, and would turn a war party homeward.[49]

Usually the war party confronted an opposition force within foreign territory. If the element of surprise was lost, they hastily sought the best defensible ground. Parties often challenged each other with belittling insults, reminding their opponent of previous successful acts and how they intended to avenge previous injuries, or by direct ridicule by questioning their masculinity. Throughout this taunting, each man prepared to fight and quickly applied his war paint. They might also hope to recite one more short, protective *idi:gawé:sdi,* calling on the sons of Kanati and Selu, the Thunder Boys, to shield them.[50]

War priests meanwhile used individual sanctified objects to protect the warriors. One recorded instance included such "congering [sic] implements" as medicine pouches filled with sacred war paint. They granted spiritual protection to their wearers, as the war priest/leader reminded the men "that not one of us could be shot for those things Would turn the Balls from us," and to "*fight like men* [emphasis mine] for nothing could hurt us."[51]

The warriors attacked the enemy when the war priest sounded the charge on his bone whistle or gourd trumpet; during battle the war priest continued communing with the spirit world.[52] The engagement was usually short-lived, as both parties emptied their guns straightaway and flew into hand-to-hand combat. As comrades fell, the battle quickly turned to a search-and-rescue operation as the party attempted to keep their casualties from succumbing to the mutilating scalping knife of their enemies, or the humiliation and emasculation of enslavement or torture. At the same time, a push to retrieve the scalps from the heads of any fallen foe dominated the group's actions. They spared no body from mutilation through slashing or dismemberment if they could safely do so. Scalps were the treasured "trophies of honor" that guaranteed war titles and served as proof of their competence as real men. As soon as it was expedient, they stretched these over a small hoop and painted the interior flesh red.[53]

The Culture of War, Gender, and the Community

Not all engagements took place in the wilderness, and not all raids happened in this manner. War parties carefully chose settlements against which to launch surprise hit-and-run attacks, often just to obtain prisoners. Cherokee warriors often targeted isolated women and young children working in the communal cornfields or otherwise unprotected. They usually killed enemy warriors or took them captive for the purpose of humiliation before inflicting a torturous ritualistic death, often involving mental as well as physical emasculation. Sometimes Cherokees spared captives through either enslavement or adoption. Prisoners would not know their fate until they reached the Cherokee settlements, where community members would help to determine what would be done with them.

Most multiple martial engagements were not part of a larger campaign. Once the party met its mission of vindication, there was no further need to prolong their journey. Mission accomplished, the leader's responsibility became to return his men to the safety of home for reintegration into society, both to claim their honors and to exhibit their successful completion of their sacred duty as real men. If losses were high, however, the war leader returned in disgrace, the town leaders publicly stripped him of his status, and the stricken warrior began his path toward establishing his manhood once again. If the mission was successful, the company arrived just outside the town with much flourish and bravado, often announcing their presence with gunfire and loud cries, while insulting and displaying captives. Despite this boisterous exhibition, the returning triumphant warriors could not yet enter the town.[54]

Because of their acts of violence and spilling of blood, the war party was careful not to bring any dangerous spiritual vengeance to their community. Remaining at a safe distance, the group once more underwent rituals of purification and sanctification, while respecting particular taboos.[55] The transformation of this masculine power was a serious business. Power existed in many forms, but that unleashed by the spilling of blood was one of the most dangerous. "Tradition," Adair noted, "dictates to them that man was not born in a state of war" and interpreted Cherokee actions of purification as meaning that they felt impure or polluted.[56] Many early Anglo observers of southeastern Indian cultures have correlated this with their own concept of being dirty or tainted.[57] The problem went deeper. Warfare had not ended at the battle site—the act of spilling blood only marked the beginning of spiritual warfare, and the goal became to negate any ghostly or spiritual enemy powers.

Fire and water were vehicles through which to transform the unpredictable and dangerous power of spilled blood. Cherokee beliefs revolved around the constant maneuvering of power—with potential for its use for either good or evil. Cherokee society, as a rule, attempted to stop any evil abuse of power. If possible, most Cherokees sought to transform power into a positive energy, a light or bright force.[58]

Therefore, it made sense that those warriors who had recently invoked spiritual power in order to spill blood now sought to become "brightened." Masculine power was potentially dangerous and could bring harm to the person or their loved ones. The war leader released this power with the help of the spirits of fire and water so the men might rejoin Cherokee society. The war fire, created at the beginning of mission, was an entity to which the war priest offered a thanksgiving sacrifice upon the party's return.[59] With this last action, there was a need to control the war fire—to transform it. Therefore, at the end of the four days of rituals, the head warrior took the war fire to the council house and fed it to the sacred fire, where Ancient Red (the war fire) and Ancient White (the sacred fire) became one.[60] Or one could interpret this action as the ritualistic sacrifice of blood through war when fed to the sacred flames.

The reintegration process took place at the square-ground just outside the council house. Throughout these transformative days, all captives also remained outside the town. The warriors tied their prisoners to the red-painted war pole, which stood in the middle of the square-ground. The fates of these unfortunates varied—enslavement, adoption, or torture ending in death, usually by fire.[61] The Cherokee community took an active part in this aspect of warfare.

Emasculating the Enemy

Prisoners became war offerings to the women from their clan's warriors, who had acted on behalf of the clan's honor. Prisoners belonged to their captor until presented to the women or individual Cherokees. Apparently, there was no one method of determining the fate of captives, and it was often "left to passion, chance, and luck."[62] On occasion, family members would adopt a captive to fill the void left by a family member who had been taken by an enemy. Cherokee slavery, though, was not yet comparable to that practiced in the European colonies. Since slaves were outside the clan system, the Cherokees did not perceive them as one of the principal people, but rather an *atsi nahsa'i*, a being without a clan. Some of these slaves led horrid existences, often receiving beatings. Others did not fare too badly, helping the women in the fields and at other chores. Male slaves lost their status as men when relegated to women's work.[63] The Cherokees had stripped their enemy of their masculinity and relegated them to a negative or powerless status, and they certainly did not receive the respected feminine status that Cherokee women held.

From time to time a Cherokee deemed that a slave held potential and therefore offered them protection and redemption through adoption. Sometimes an older, well-established warrior took a male prisoner under his wing.

These opportunities were rare but did happen. The prisoner could prove his worth by killing an enemy of the Cherokee people—he then became a person, a real man, once again. Upon returning to the town, the Cherokee warrior and his captive exchanged clothes and became brothers. At other times, warriors stepped in on behalf of a female relation to spare a prisoner's life. With adoption the ex-slave then became a Cherokee and a clansman.[64]

On the rare occasion when a prisoner escaped to a sacred peace town, no one could spill his blood within its borders. If, however, he ventured outside this refuge, he forfeited his life.[65] In most circumstances a captive's life was just not valued. Cherokee women who had lost husbands, brothers, and fathers in war, or children, sisters, or mothers stolen or killed in enemy raids, were not often in the mood to demonstrate kindness. They especially abused male slaves, if they allowed them to live at all. Women slaves sometimes married into Cherokee society, but that was not common. The children produced from these unions were not members of one of the seven Cherokee clans unless adopted. Families did often adopt captive children to fill voids suffered from the loss of kin and raise them as Cherokees.

Community Recognition of Real Men in Warfare

Death was another part of Cherokee warfare that was connected to the spiritual. It released the body's four souls, one of which could remain behind as a ghostlike entity. Close family were likely to become ill or fall into a state of despair because of the lonely ghost calling for company. The priest sought to protect his patrons through sacred rituals associated with handling the deceased and their possessions. When the mourners completed the grieving process and subsequent purification, the town accepted them as relieved of any sickness that a lingering ghost might have inflicted.[66]

While some relatives mourned, other Cherokees celebrated the returning warriors. After the four-day waiting period, a gallant procession of warriors dressed in their finest and covered in their war paint entered the sacred square-ground to partake in the festivities.[67] Any male who had not "successfully accompanied their sacred ark" was not allowed to participate, because this honor was reserved for real men.[68] The returning victors cut the scalps obtained during the last foray into pieces and distributed them throughout the community.[69] The warriors placed these trophies atop the winter-houses, or sweat houses (*osi*), of those killed by enemies. This physical display of satisfied revenge released the lingering souls or ghosts to complete their journey to the Darkening Land. As the men somberly went about this task, the

Cherokee women sang "a grateful song of triumph" to the Creator.[70] In this manner, the blood placated both the ghosts and the Cherokee women. They then feasted and danced to express their thanks and happiness in releasing the spirits of their deceased relatives.

This was a time for the warriors to boast and revel in the accolades of the community. Each warrior took his turn as the central dancer, reenacting his masculine feats of stealth and bravery through hyperbole, while brandishing his red-and-black-painted war club.[71] Adair vividly described the excitement surrounding an honoring ceremony:

> In the time of their rejoicings, they fix a certain day for the warriors to be crowned; for they cannot sleep sound or easy under an old title, while a new, or higher one is due. On that long-wished for day, they all appear on the field of parade, as fine and cheerful as the birds in spring. Their martial drums beat, their bloody colours are displayed, and most the young people are dancing and rejoicing, for the present success of their nation, and the safe return and preferment of their friends and relations.[72]

The head civil leader, or *Uku,* also the town's religious chief, then congratulated the war chief and his victorious warriors, reminding them that their success had rested with following the proper religious prescriptions. He then praised "their strict observance of the law of purity, while they accompanied the beloved ark of war, which induced the supreme chieftain to give them the victory," and hoped that their brave actions would "encourage the rest to continue to thirst after glory, in imitation of their brave ancestors, who died nobly in defence [*sic*] of their country."[73]

The eagle tail dance was another ritual performance related to war. Here Cherokee men moved from exhibitions of war to peace—a transfer from the red state to the white state.[74] This exhibition of male strength and the generosity of peace made quite an impression on visiting dignitaries when about a dozen warriors "painted all over" ran toward them, dancing and waving sacred eagle tail wands.

This performance represented the setting aside of war between equals—real men—for a state of peace and friendship, at least for the time being. The eagle tail feathers represented victory, power, and peace, while a string of beads, probably white in color, represented the offering of peace, acceptance of friendship, honor, and respect. The Great Warrior proclaimed peace with the symbolic burying of the "bloody tommahawke [*sic*]."[75]

Another occasion that warranted the performance of a war dance allowed the warriors within Cherokee society to provide relief to those in need. Timberlake observed this ritual, judging it as "among the most laudable of their religious ceremonies" because they performed it with generosity in mind.[76] He explained that the town's headmen determined when the need for aid among its populace had reached a high enough level and called for a public war dance. The performance served as a charitable performance and exhibition of masculinity.

The warriors assembled and each in turn danced a pantomime reminiscent of his first taking of an enemy's scalp. One by one, each man exhibited his masculine stealth in order to demonstrate his success as a Cherokee man. Once the instrumental accompaniment ceased, the soloist stood with tomahawk in hand and narrated his feat for all to hear and appreciate. He then placed something of value on a large hide spread on the ground to receive the objects. The other men followed this procedure repeatedly until all had performed and contributed to the growing pile of goods.[77]

This gifting ceremony performed several functions. Though participation was voluntary, the community deemed eligible men who did not join in as selfish individuals.[78] This dance strengthened communal solidarity as Cherokee warriors gave notice that they were committed to their people's welfare. In addition, it served as a vehicle for gaining public recognition and validating Cherokee manhood. The exhibitions of how they enthusiastically met danger expressed their willingness to sacrifice their lives to uphold the honor of their clan, town, and tribe. Cherokee warriors displayed their commitment through public performance to gain and express status and to allow the community to show their pride in their accomplishments as a people.

Conclusion

Cherokee males used warfare to become men and then to earn various martial titles over the years to become even greater men. The older, experienced warriors were held in more esteem than younger, less experienced men.[79] John Philip Reid once contended that "martial glory was not a guarantee of influence or office in town or tribe, war titles were largely honorary, with little political significance." He related this statement to his study of war, "or at least the declaration and commencement of war, [which] was a matter largely of international law."[80] This argument is not entirely correct or complete. Though he stated that the main reason Cherokee men went to war was for retaliation, he never related these actions in any way as connected to a sacred duty, a sense of honor, or religious beliefs.

Moreover, earlier studies trivialized the meaning of war titles or ranks. Cherokee men earned these titles through their martial accomplishments, and the leaders bestowed these laurels in the public sphere with the approval of the town membership. This communal and tribal acknowledgement of their deeds honored that individual as a real man, one who deserved honor, status, and elevation above other lesser warriors and non-military men.[81]

The Cherokee "beloved occupation" of war was a complex institution with gendered expectations, spiritual dimensions, and communal values. War made participants of all Cherokees and no community was exempt. Cherokee warriors were "ready always to sacrifice every pleasure and gratification, even their blood, and life itself, to defend their territory and maintain their rights."[82] The military connected Cherokees to the sacred, social, and political dimensions of their society. Warfare was not only a path to manhood, increased social status, and political influence; for Cherokee men, it served as a vehicle to express their masculinity by proving their worth as real men.

NOTES

1. William Fyffe to Brother John, 1 February 1761, Gilcrease Institute, Tulsa, OK; John Phillip Reid, *Law of Blood: The Primitive Law of the Cherokee Nation* (New York: New York University Press, 1970), 186.

2. Reid, *Law of Blood*, 185.

3. Greg O'Brien, *Choctaws in a Revolutionary Age, 1750–1830* (Lincoln: University of Nebraska Press, 2002), xxi–xxvii.

4. William Anderson, Anne Rogers, and Jane Brown, eds., *John Howard Payne Papers*, 6 vols. (Lincoln: University of Nebraska Press, in press), 4:75 (transcription taken from John Howard Payne Papers, 4:262 [285], Newberry Library, Edward E. Ayer Collection, Chicago). Hereafter cited as Anderson et al., "Payne Papers," with reference to original microfilm pagination in parentheses. I want to especially thank the editors of this forthcoming publication for access and permission to use their transcription.

5. Gender identity and roles have been an important focus in these analyses. For examples, see Ann M. Little, *Abraham in Arms: War and Gender in Colonial New England* (Philadelphia: University of Pennsylvania Press, 2007); Richard Trexler, *Sex and Conquest: Gendered Violence, Political Order, and the European Conquest of the Americas* (Ithaca, NY: Cornell University Press, 1995); R. Todd Romero, *Making War and Minting Christians: Masculinity, Religion, and Colonialism in Early New England* (Amherst: University of Massachusetts Press, forthcoming).

6. John Grenier, *First Way of War: American War Making on the Frontier, 1607–1814* (New York: Cambridge University Press, 2005); Guy Chet, *Conquering the American Wilderness: The Triumph of European Warfare in Colonial Northeast* (Amherst: University of Massachusetts Press, 2003); Geoffrey Plank, *Unsettled Conquest: British Campaign Against*

the Peoples of Acadia (Philadelphia: University of Pennsylvania Press, 2001); Fred Anderson, *Crucible of War: The Seven Years' War and the Fate of Empire in British North America, 1754-1766* (New York: Alfred A. Knopf, 2000); Armstrong Starkey, *European and Native American Warfare, 1675-1814* (Norman: University of Oklahoma Press, 1998); Jill Lepore, *The Name of War: King Philip's War and the Origins of American Identity* (New York: Knopf, 1998).

7. See Theda Perdue, *Cherokee Women: Gender and Culture Change, 1700-1835* (Lincoln: University of Nebraska Press, 1998); Carolyn Johnston, *Cherokee Women in Crisis: Trail of Tears, Civil War and Allotment, 1838-1907* (Tuscaloosa: University of Alabama Press, 2003); Virginia M. Carney, *Eastern Band Cherokee Women: Cultural Persistence in their Letters and Speeches* (Knoxville: University of Tennessee Press, 2005); Sarah H. Hill, *Weaving New Worlds: Southeastern Cherokee Women and Their Basketry* (Chapel Hill: University of North Carolina Press, 1997); Tom Hatley, "Cherokee Women Farmers Hold Their Ground," *Powhatan's Mantle: Indians in the Colonial Southeast*, ed. Gregory A. Waselkov, Peter H. Wood, and Tom Hatley, rvs. ed. (Lincoln: University of Nebraska Press, 2006), 305-35; M. Thomas Hatley, "The Three Lives of Keowee: Loss and Recovery in the Eighteenth-Century Cherokee Villages," *American Encounters: Natives and Newcomers from European Contact to Indian Removal, 1500-1850*, ed. Peter C. Mancall and James H. Merrell (New York: Routledge, 2000), 241-60; Alice Taylor-Colbert, "Cherokee Women and Cultural Change," *Women of the American South: A Multicultural Reader*, ed. Christie Anne Farnham (New York: New York University Press, 1997), 43-55.

8. Greg O'Brien, "Hunting and the Politics of Masculinity in Cherokee Treaty-Making, 1763-75," *Empire and Others: British Encounters with Indigenous Peoples, 1600-1850*, ed. Martin Daunton and Rick Halpern (Philadelphia: University of Pennsylvania Press, 1999), 167-85; Nathaniel J. Sheidley, "Unruly Men: Indians, Settlers, and the Ethos of Frontier Patriarchy in the Upper Tennessee Watershed, 1763-1815" (Ph.D. diss., Princeton University, 1999).

9. Anderson et al., "Payne Papers," 4:75 (82). See also Clifton B. Kroeber and Bernard L. Fontana, *Massacre on the Gila: An Account of the Last Major Battle Between American Indians, with Reflections on the Origins of War* (Tucson: University of Arizona Press, 1986), 164.

10. See also O'Brien, *Choctaws in a Revolutionary Age*, 27-49, where he discusses how warfare shaped Choctaw culture and its sacred connections to masculinity.

11. William H. Gilbert, "Eastern Cherokee Social Organization," *Social Anthropology of North American Tribes*, ed. Fred Eggan (Chicago: University of Chicago Press, 1955), 296-97; Taylor-Colbert, "Cherokee Women and Cultural Change," 45-46; Perdue, *Cherokee Women*, 42-43, 47.

12. This is illustrated through the Cherokee legend "The Owl Gets Married," and through the traditional marriage ceremony where the male delivers venison to his bride's family to prove he will be a good husband and provider. Other examples of unworthy husbands are the legends "The Huhu Gets Married" and "Two Lazy Hunters." See James Mooney, *Myths of the Cherokees: Extract from the 19th Annual Report of the Bureau of American Ethnology* (Washington, DC: GPO, 1902), 291-93, 397-99; Cephas Washburn, *Reminiscences of the Indians* (Richmond, VA: Presbyterian Committee on Publications, 1869), 206-7; Hatley, "Three Lives of Keowee," 241-60; Perdue, *Cherokee Women*, 19-20, 24-25. See also Taylor-Colbert, "Cherokee Women and Cultural Change," 46.

13. Taylor-Colbert, "Cherokee Women and Cultural Change," 47; Perdue, *Cherokee Women*, 17–23, 73, 85.

14. For more discussion of Cherokee gender roles, see Perdue, *Cherokee Women*.

15. Anderson et al., "Payne Papers," 4:205 (215).

16. James Adair, *The History of the American Indians*, ed. Kathryn E. Holland Braund (1775; reprint, Tuscaloosa: University of Alabama Press, 2005), 265.

17. Ibid., 380; Henry Timberlake, *Memoirs of Lieutenant Henry Timberlake*, ed. Samuel Cole Williams (1765; reprint, Marietta, GA: Continental Book Company, 1948), 113; Anderson et al., "Payne Papers," 4:59 (65). See William H. Gilbert, "The Eastern Cherokees," Bulletin 133, *Anthropological Papers*, no. 23, Bureau of American Ethnology (Washington, DC: GPO, 1943), 356–58, for a discussion of the white (peace) and red (war) town governments.

18. Adair, *History*, 376.

19. Reid, *Law of Blood*, 168; Adair, *History*, 186.

20. Anderson et al., "Payne Papers," 3:61 (46), 4:103 (107), 213 (225), 406 (551).

21. James Mooney, *Sacred Formulas of the Cherokees*, 19th Annual Report, Bureau of American Ethnology, Smithsonian Institute (Washington, DC: GPO, 1900), 342; John P. Brown, *Old Frontiers: The Story of the Cherokee Indians from the Earliest Times to the Date of Their Removal to the West, 1838* (Kingsport, TN: Southern Publishers, 1938), 528.

22. Adair, *History*, 193.

23. Ibid., 186.

24. Reid, *Law of Blood*, 175–77. See also John Norton, *Journal of Major John Norton, 1816*, ed. Carl F. Klinck and James J. Talman, Publications of the Champlain Society 46 (Toronto: Champlain Society, 1970), 129.

25. Anderson et al., "Payne Papers," 4:67 (70), 217 (226), 399 (535).

26. Gilbert, "Eastern Cherokees," 349–50, relates the ceremony inducting the Great Warrior to office.

27. Anderson et al., "Payne Papers," 4:174–75 (182), 67 (70), 3:17 (12).

28. See James Mooney, "The Cherokee River Cult," *Journal of Cherokee Studies* 7 (Spring 1982): 30–36, for further discussion regarding going-to-water rituals involving the river, whose symbolic name was the Long Man (*Yû'nwĭ Gûnahíta*). See also Timberlake, *Memoirs*, 74; Anderson et al., "Payne Papers," 1:48 (57); 4:184 (192), 208–9 (219), 3:55 (42).

29. Anderson et al., "Payne Papers," 4:36–37 (32–36), 216 (226).

30. Adair, *History*, 193, 196; Anderson et al., "Payne Papers," 4:36 (32), 68, (74), 40 (37), 104 (107), 397 (533); Alexander Longe, "A Small Postscript of Ways and Manners of the Indians Called Charikees" (1725), ed. David H. Corkran, *Southern Indian Studies* 21 (October 1969): 44–45.

31. Anderson et al., "Payne Papers," 4:104 (107), 184 (192), 215 (226), 406–7 (551–52), 413 (563). Smoke represented the messenger, which carried prayers to the spirit world and the upper world. See David H. Corkran, "The Sacred Fire of the Cherokees," *Southern Indian Studies* 5 (October 1953): 22.

32. Longe, "Small Postscript," 44; Anderson et al., "Payne Papers," 4:37 (36), 109 (112), 184 (192); Corkran, "Sacred Fire," 25.

33. Anderson et al., "Payne Papers," 3:71 (53), 4:61 (65), 70 (75), 104 (107); Adair, *History*, 194.

34. Adair, *History*, 195. See also p. 502, n. 159, for further explanation of the 1756 Cherokee expedition to Ohio.

35. Reid, *Law of Blood*, 178.

36. Arlene Fradkin, *Cherokee Folk Zoology: The Animal World of a Native American People, 1700-1838* (New York: Garland Publishing, 1990), 335; Adair, *History*, 77; Timberlake, *Memoirs*, 77-78; Anderson et al., "Payne Papers," 4:70-72 (75-78), 404-6 (547-49).

37. Timberlake, *Memoirs*, 84-85, 118; Anderson et al., "Payne Papers," 4:217 (229). Thomas Jefferson recalled one of the Great Warriors reciting such a protection formula before leaving on the hazardous sea journey to England. Thomas Jefferson to John Adams, June 11, 1812, *The Adams-Jefferson Letters: The Complete Correspondence Between Thomas Jefferson and Abigail and John Adams*, ed. Lester J. Cappon, 2 vols. (Chapel Hill: University of North Carolina Press, 1959), 2:307.

38. Jack Frederick Kilpatrick and Anna Gritts Kilpatrick, *Run Toward the Nightland: Magic of the Oklahoma Cherokees* (Dallas: Southern Methodist University Press, 1967), 43.

39. The formulas used in this study are selected from those that already appear in print. Thus they are dead, which means that the proper ritual would need to occur before they could be viable again.

40. Kilpatrick and Kilpatrick, *Run Toward the Nightland*, 43, 45-46.

41. Mooney, *Myths of the Cherokees*, 240, 394; Anderson et al., "Payne Papers," 4:97 (101), 361 (414).

42. Ibid., 134.

43. Kilpatrick and Kilpatrick, *Run Toward the Nightland*, 44-45.

44. Ibid., 45.

45. John Witthoft, "Cherokee Beliefs Concerning Death," *Journal of Cherokee Studies* 8 (Fall 1983): 68-69. For further information on the history of scalping, see James Axtell and William C. Sturtevant, "The Unkindest Cut, or Who Invented Scalping," *William and Mary Quarterly*, 3rd ser., 37 (July 1980): 451-72. These scholars agree that most tribes considered the scalplock to possess ancient religious significance.

46. Kilpatrick and Kilpatrick, *Run Toward the Nightland*, 132. See also Mooney, *Myths of the Cherokees*, 320; Speck and Broom, *Cherokee Dance and Drama*, 16; Mooney, *Sacred Formulas of the Cherokees*, 340.

47. Anderson et al., "Payne Papers," 4:258-60 (279-80).

48. Adair, *History*, 84, 380-81.

49. Fradkin, *Cherokee Folk Zoology*, 419; Longe, "Small Postscript," 44-47. See, also Mooney, *Myths of the Cherokees*, 285-86, 318-19.

50. Raymond David Fogelson, "The Cherokee Ball Game: A Study in Southeastern Ethnology" (Ph.D. diss., University of Pennsylvania, 1962), 55; Speck and Broom, *Cherokee Dance and Drama*, 58. Adair, *History*, 381; Kilpatrick and Kilpatrick, *Run Toward the Nightland*, 132-33.

51. Colbey Chew to Henry Bouquet, "Report on Road," August 21, 1758, *Papers of Henry Bouquet: The Forbes Expedition*, ed. Sylvester K. Stevens, Donald H. Kent, Autumn L. Leonard et al., 5 vols. (Harrisburg: Pennsylvania Historical and Museum Commission, 1951), 2:402.

52. Anderson et al., "Payne Papers," 4:40 (37), 69 (75), 170 (177).

53. Ibid., 4:425 (593); Adair, *History*, 183, 214, 382-83, Timberlake, *Memoirs*, 113.

54. Anderson et al., "Payne Papers," 4:72-73 (78).

55. Corkran, "Sacred Fire," 25-26.

56. Adair, *History*, 383.

57. For a thorough discussion rebuking this ethnocentric concept, see Mary C. Churchill, "The Oppositional Paradigm of Purity Versus Pollution in Charles Hudson's *The Southeastern Indians*," *American Quarterly*, special issue, "To Hear the Eagles Cry: Contemporary Themes in Native American Spirituality," pt. II: "Dialogical Relations," ed. Lee Irwin, 20:4 (Summer 1996): 563–93.

58. This type of power was associated with the color white and the south, representing peace, happiness, health, and longevity. The civil arm of traditional Cherokee town life revolved around the peace government or white seat, the white path, and the sacred fire or Ancient White. Mooney, *Sacred Formulas of the Cherokees*, 342, 493–94.

59. Anderson et al., "Payne Papers," 4:74 (79), 408 (553).

60. Kathryn E. Holland Braund and Gregory A. Waselkov, eds., *William Bartram on the Southeastern Indians* (Lincoln: University of Nebraska Press, 1995), 149; Mooney, *Sacred Formulas of the Cherokees*, 359.

61. In 1775, Bartram claimed that the Cherokees no longer used the war or slave posts. See Braund and Waselkov, eds., *William Bartram*, 155. But he was wrong. In 1776, Beloved Woman Nancy Ward spared one such prisoner, while leaving a male youth to die from the flames, at Toqua, an Overhill town that Bartram did not visit. See Reid, *Law of Blood*, 187–88; and John Haywood, *The Natural and Aboriginal History of Tennessee Up to the First Settlements Therein by the White People in the Year 1768*, ed. Mary U. Rothrock (1823; reprint, Jackson, TN: Mercer Press, 1959), 278.

62. Reid, *Law of Blood*, 130, 153, 189. For multiple supporting examples of various prisoner experiences, see pp. 187–95.

63. Alan Gallay, *Indian Slave Trade: The Rise of the English Empire in the American South, 1670–1717* (New Haven, CT: Yale University Press, 2002), 338; Theda Perdue, *Slavery and the Evolution of Cherokee Society, 1540–1866* (Knoxville: University of Tennessee Press, 1979), 12, 14–15, 16.

64. Timberlake, in *Memoirs*, 111, remembered that some white slaves accompanied their male Cherokee owners on hunting expeditions. Usually these men were young and considered controllable or redeemable by their captors. See Antoine Bonnefoy, "Journal of Antoine Bonnefoy," *Early Travels in the Tennessee Country, 1540–1800*, ed. Samuel Cole Williams(1928; reprint, Nashville: Blue and Gray Press, 1972), 152; John Frost, ed., "The Captivity of Jane Brown and Her Family," *Heroic Women of the West: Comprising Thrilling Examples of Courage, Fortitude, Devotedness, and Self-Sacrifice Among the Pioneer Mothers of the Western Country*, Garland Library of Narratives of North American Indian Captives, 66 (1854; reprint, New York: Garland Publishing, 1976), 138; Brown, *Old Frontiers*, 274, 361.

65. Anderson et al., "Payne Papers," 4:59 (65); Adair, *History*, 192–93, 384.

66. Witthoft, "Cherokee Beliefs Concerning Death," 68–69; Adair, *History*, 390; Anderson et al., "Payne Papers," 4:96 (100–101); 3:52–54 (38–40); Mooney, *Myths of the Cherokees*, 421, 426, 547; Mooney, "Cherokee River Cult," 31–32.

67. Anderson et al., "Payne Papers," 3:53–54 (40), 4:96 (101), 218–19 (229), 408 (553).

68. Adair, *History*, 100.

69. Anderson et al., "Payne Papers," 4:400 (537).

70. Adair, *History*, 390.

71. Braund and Waselkov, eds., *William Bartram*, 86. See also Adair, *History*, 390–91; Speck and Broom, *Cherokee Dance and Drama*, 63–64.

72. Adair, *History*, 391.

73. Ibid.; Anderson et al., "Payne Papers," 4:339 (353).

74. One of the best descriptions of this dance is found in Timberlake, *Memoirs*, 14. See also J. P. Evans, "Sketches of Cherokee Customs, Character, and Manners," in Anderson et al., "Payne Papers," 6:303–5 (32–35). Evans described an eagle dance performed during the 1830s when men reenacted their war exploits.

75. Timberlake, *Memoirs*, 59–60; Fradkin, *Cherokee Folk Zoology*, 394.

76. Timberlake, *Memoirs*, 92.

77. Ibid., 93–94. Raymond Fogelson, "Cherokee Notions of Power," *Anthropology of Power: Ethnographic Studies from Asia, Oceania, and the New World*, ed. Raymond D. Fogelson and Richard N. Adams, Studies in Anthropology Series (New York: Academic Press, 1977), 188.

78. Reid, *Law of Blood*, 64. Reid discussed the Cherokee value of "unbounded liberty."

79. Timberlake, *Memoirs*, 95, argued that two classes of military men existed, the warriors of rank and the fighting men who had yet to prove themselves through war deeds, such as returning with an enemy's scalp.

80. Reid, in *Law of Blood*, 153, noted that the practices associated with warfare were of extreme importance in Cherokee society and had a profound influence on their culture.

81. Timberlake, *Memoirs*, 55, 94, n. 55; Anderson et al., "Payne Papers," 4:379 (463). Some examples of war titles were the Slave Catcher, the Mankiller, and the Raven.

82. Braund and Waselkov, eds., *William Bartram*, 112.

III

Atlantic

—————— 5 ——————

"Blood and Lust"

Masculinity and Sexuality in Illustrated Print
Portrayals of Early Pirates of the Caribbean

—————— CAROLYN EASTMAN ——————

"Why is it that the pirate has, and always has had, a certain lurid glamour of the heroical enveloping him round about?" asked *Howard Pyle's Book of Pirates*, a large-scale, richly illustrated book for children published in 1921. "Would not every boy . . . rather be a pirate captain than a Member of Parliament?" To answer his own question, Pyle waxed lyrical. "What a life of adventure is his, to be sure! A life of constant alertness, constant danger, constant escape! . . . What a setting of blood and lust and flames and rapine for such a hero!"[1]

Pyle went out of his way to avoid detailed discussions of "lust" and "rapine" for his young readers, but the fact that he invoked them at all is telling—and representative of pirate tales over the decades. Gender and sexuality play primary roles in popular portrayals of piracy and seafaring in such wide-ranging performances as Johnny Depp's gender-bending Jack Sparrow, the courtship antics of *The Pirates of Penzance*, Errol Flynn's portrayal of Captain Blood as a "devil-may-care philanderer," and John Belushi's 1979 *Saturday Night Live* skit about "manly" life among seafarers aboard the *Raging Queen*.[2] Neither are these emphases unique to the modern era. Ubiquitous as they are now, conventions for depicting pirates as dangerous, lusty, gendered heroes have a long history, one that is rooted as much in the book trade as in the "man's life at sea." These representations were born during the "golden age of piracy" (from roughly 1670 to 1730) and were reworked and codified in numerous illustrated books published in Europe and circulated throughout the Atlantic world. These volumes developed, reiterated, and augmented stereotypes about pirates to attract and titillate European and American readers who could afford illustrated books and whose lives adhered to far more conventional standards of behavior than the ones exhibited by the fictional pirates. Early modern readers encountered pirates as a series of literary and pictorial conventions that emerged in the late seventeenth century—drawn swords, eccentric clothing, and glaring scowls at the viewer—that strongly enhanced the books' emphases on masculinity and sexuality. Books like Alexandre Exquemelin's *Bucaniers of America* (1678) and Captain Charles Johnson's *A General History of the Pyrates* (1724) earned their immense popularity at least in part by combining mesmerizing narration with vivid, full-page illustrations of pirates. Examining these texts and images in tandem—particularly for the innovations developed from one edition or engraver to the next—allows us to see the vital intersections between manliness and sexuality, the transnational history of book publishing, and the role of images in the imaginative construction of bourgeois European identity. To date, this is the first scholarly treatment of the subject of manliness in pirate literature; the only prior studies that incorporate gender have dealt either exclusively with female pirates or the subject of same-sex sexuality on ship.[3]

The creation of what became stereotypical images of pirates—images that would continue to inform artists like Howard Pyle and filmmakers in the twentieth century and beyond—was sealed early on with a complex interplay between text and image in early print culture. Looking closely at the recurrence and reiteration of gendered representations of pirates—how texts and images were copied and enhanced over many decades—allows us to see how writers and engravers played with sexualized masculinities to make their books increasingly appealing to readers. Gender and sexuality were at the heart of these portrayals, granting pirates an outsider masculinity all the more striking for the ways it permitted middling and elite readers to imagine manliness without constraint—a social world in which men did not need to exercise self-control.

Imagining the Hypermasculine Pirate: Bucaniers of America

In the late seventeenth and early eighteenth centuries, the pirates who disrupted trade in the Caribbean, West Africa, North America, and all points in between seemed to exemplify the dynamism and extra-national energy made possible by maritime movement across the Atlantic Ocean. These men (and, famously, some women) formed international crews so fearsome that they proved to be major impediments to orderly European economic exchange. Just as European powers sought to create orderly means of drawing goods from the New World to enrich the Old, pirate ships became more numerous and audacious in their attacks, looting 2,500 merchant vessels in the ten years between 1716 and 1726 alone.[4] One eighteenth-century commentator estimated that England lost as much to pirates as it did to Spain and France during the catastrophic War of Spanish Succession fought between 1701 and 1714. By the 1720s Parliament began to enact harsh new laws against piracy and to conduct well-publicized criminal trials and hangings to punish pirates for their misdeeds, seeking with this display of juridical force to discourage what had clearly become a highly lucrative line of work.

As important as piracy was to European and American political, economic, and maritime development, it also proved significant to the history of the book—and it was early modern print media that developed modes of describing and representing pirates to titillate readers' imaginations about manly action and adventure. The most significant early text to do so was Alexandre Exquemelin's *De Americaensche Zee-Rovers* (translated shortly thereafter as *Bucaniers of America*), an octavo volume with full-page illustrations that emerged from Jan ten Hoorn's Amsterdam press in 1678 to become an unexpectedly long-lasting success. Exquemelin had worked as a buccaneer himself in the Caribbean, giving him an insider's knowledge that made his breathless narrative all the more authoritative. His first-person experience with some of the most terrifying pirate leaders and his description of their lair on the tiny island of Tortuga did not merely provide European readers with new information, nor did it tell the tale from the perspective of an educated, elite European (as did so many travel volumes of the era). Rather, *Bucaniers* offered a narrative that featured an insider's view of dramatic sieges, torture of Spanish leaders, and freewheeling pirate life. Its action took place in the Caribbean, figuring the New World as a site of drama, individual agency, and decided lack of hierarchy—all contrasting markedly with European society. Together, the book's voice, location, and subjects seemed to indicate that new forms of masculine freedoms were available in piracy.

Sales of the initial edition were so strong that the book appeared shortly thereafter in German (Nuremberg, 1679), two Spanish editions (Cologne, 1681 and 1682), English (at least eight London editions between 1684 and 1704), and French (at least six Paris and Brussels editions between 1686 and 1713), as well as a second Dutch edition in 1700; it would be revived in the 1740s for continued publishing success through the end of the eighteenth century and into the nineteenth by presses on both sides of the Atlantic.[5] The book appeared in the libraries of Robert "King" Carter of Virginia and other wealthy American colonists as well as in the Social Library of Salem, Massachusetts, indicating that it had broad appeal far beyond the confines of England and northern Europe.[6] The fact that the Dutch printer included twelve full-page copperplate engravings in the book indicates his faith in the book's success, for the investments required for such work would have been considerable. Given the book's octavo size, the engravers likely took several weeks or more to cut each one; once completed, printing the images for a five hundred copy edition would have taken at least twenty-four days, according to Roger Gaskell's estimates; and altogether each print would have cost the printer as much in labor and supplies as his own printing of twenty-four pages of text in letterpress.[7] The investment of time and money was rewarded: by any standard for the day, the book was a best seller.

Printers were the first to advertise the book as a novel and thrilling read. A London printer confessed in the preface to his 1684 edition that he had never even heard the term "buccaneer" until reading this volume, nor had he been aware of the extent of Caribbean piracy. In recommending it, he stressed most of all that the book "informeth us (with huge novelty), of as great and bold attempts, in point of Military conduct and valour, as ever were performed by mankind; without excepting, here, either *Alexander* the Great, or *Julius Caesar,* or the rest of the *Nine Worthy's of Fame*."[8] In fact, he went so far as to describe them as English national heroes because they had so frequently outwitted the Spanish, who were cast as heavies in the London edition. Of course, this was a stretch to say the least: the term *buccaneer* originally referred to French and Dutch hunters in the Caribbean who had taken up piracy against the Spanish. More to the point, these men were so thoroughly nonnational figures that one of them, "Rock Brasiliano," who apparently originated in the Low Countries, obtained his name by means of a residence in Brazil.[9]

Even without the puffery, the book was an easy sell. Exquemelin used a breezy narrative style to describe his subjects' manly heroism. "After a fight of almost three hours, wherein they behaved themselves with desperate Courage, . . . they became Masters [of the city of Maracaibo, in Venezuela] having made use of no other Arms than their Swords and Pistols," he explained of François Lolonois's dramatic defeat of the Spanish.[10] Invariably outmanned and outgunned, his pirates managed to take Spanish ships and entire towns; they escaped from custody no matter how tight the security. Sustained by an insatiable appetite for riches, they were alarmingly careless with treasure once they gained it: they invariably gambled away vast sums or spent it on trifles. This occasioned no bitterness on the part of the pirates, who seemed to view such drastic reversals as incidental to their way of life. Lolonois and his men provide a case in point. After capturing Maracaibo, they stole "twenty thousand Peices of Eight, several Mules laden with Houshold-goods and Merchandize, and twenty Prisoners, between men, women, and children. Some of these Prisoners were put to the Rack, onely to made them confess where they had hidden the rest of their Goods."[11] Within weeks, the pirates threatened again to burn the town unless they received an additional ten thousand pieces of eight; this threat was followed up by yet another demand for thirty thousand or else the Spaniards' homes would "*be entirely sack'd anew and burnt.*"[12] Yet upon their triumphal return to Tortuga, "they made shift to lose and spend the Riches they had gotten, in much less time than they were purchased by robbing." How was the wealth redistributed? "The Taverns and Stews, according to the custom of Pirats, got the greatest part," Exquemelin remarks wryly.[13] What would such passages have meant to the book's readers? Considering that it likely was sold to elite and some middling readers involved in commerce or international politics, such readers probably read passages like these with at least some moralistic disapproval, even if it was mixed with a healthy amount of admiration or envy.[14]

To underscore the violent side of the pirates' caprice, Exquemelin liked to include extensive depictions of the grisly tortures they inflicted on unlucky victims. Indeed, the ubiquity of physical cruelty of all kinds threading through the pages of *Bucaniers of America* was unusual enough according to narrative conventions of the day that it stands out. The author explained that when the sadistic Henry Morgan and his men refrained from putting men to the rack, they liked "to stretch their limbs with Cords, and at the same time beat them with Sticks and other Instruments. Others had burning Matches placed betwixt their fingers, which were thus burnt alive. Others had slender Cords or Matches twisted about their heads, till their eyes bursted out of the skull." In a rare moralizing moment, he added, "Thus all sort of inhumane Cruelties were executed upon those innocent people." Exquemelin described sexual viciousness like "insolent actions of Rape and Adultery" of "very honest women" to evoke further the corporal horrors of Caribbean piracy.[15] Indeed, his depictions of somatic cruelty veered close to a certain vein of late seventeenth-century pornographic writing that emphasized the erotic nature of flogging and the brutal ravishing of women, among other perversions.[16]

Impulsive and volatile, brave and rapacious, the pirates who came to life on the pages of *Bucaniers of America* served up an alternative model of manliness for early modern readers. Neither did readers need to venture very far into Exquemelin's chapters to figure this out. Editors made sure to underscore the pirates' manliness and bravery when they composed prefaces advertising the book's pleasures. They invariably highlighted the buccaneers' "unparallel'd, if not unimitable, adventures and *Heroick* exploits," as the 1684 edition put it. "Our common *English* Highway-men . . . seem guilty of Pusillamity in comparison with those [actions] of our Buccaniers," the editor continued.[17] By 1695 the London publisher had added a second volume with "the dangerous Voyages and bold Attempts of Capt. *Cook,* and Cap. *Sharp,* in the South-Sea," and had expanded the number of images from twelve to nineteen.[18] And by 1704, the London printer heralded the book's "wondrous Actions, and daring Adventures," claiming that all but "the most stupid minds" could not help but admire them. Here the editor finessed the question of the pirates' sexual license and propensity for rape, conceding halfheartedly that these men lacked the "Justness and Regularity" that marked a Christian man, or even the "tolerable morals" of more run-of-the-mill citizens. Even taking their moral failings into account, the editor assured readers that "a bolder Race of Men both as to personal Valour and Conduct, certainly never yet appear'd" on land nor sea.[19] London and Dublin printers reiterated these themes (and even lifted some of the same sentences) when the book reappeared in print in 1741, telling readers yet again that they ought to admire and even emulate the buccaneers for their courage and daring, particularly because some of them were English. This seemingly contradictory group of repeated themes in the prefaces of various editions—the pirates' admirable courage and alleged Englishness, on the one hand; their rejection of conventional morality and hierarchy on the other—combined to depict a dangerous, exciting mode of masculine action and behavior. In none of these ways did pirates conform to prescribed models of European manliness of the time, ideals that tended to stress fiscal responsibility, sexual control, and judicious understanding of one's social place. Buccaneers did more than merely ignore such advice: they repudiated it and adopted the opposite behavior.

Visualizing the Pirates in Book Illustration

If Exquemelin took a certain glee in recounting pirate adventures, the book's images underscored the pirates' ferocity and masculine brazenness. These illustrations established a visual repertoire that would influence all subsequent representations of pirates. The first of these provides a key to the images' success. Bartholomeus de Portugees is an iconoclastic figure encompassing everything from menace to heroism. He glowers at the viewer as if annoyed, distracted from his real purpose of watching his crew destroy a harbor full of Spanish ships. His drawn sword suggests his imminent participation in the attack; his dispassionate expression and the resolute set of his jaw signals an utter disdain for the panicked men glimpsed drowning in the foreground. Indeed, the image even hints at a smile on his face, although

"Bartholomeus de Portugees" from the original Dutch edition of *De Americaenesche Zee-Rovers* (1678). Courtesy of the Library of Congress.

the viewer senses that one's eyes might be fooled by the turn of his tidy mustache. His appearance is a mix of contradictions: his lack of a wig, his matted hair, and his crudely heavy brow assure the viewer that this is no gentleman, yet he wears a rich, billowing damask coat with a generous sleeve. His posture is reminiscent of Titian's portrait *A Man with a Quilted Sleeve* (ca. 1510), an extraordinarily influential image that had already inspired Rembrandt's 1640 *Self Portrait at the Age of 34*, among others. Yet Bartholomeus's facial expression is radically different than Titian's and Rembrandt's figures, evoking a thoroughgoing malice and twitchy energy.

Despite the fact that most of the sheath of Bartholomeus's drawn sword is concealed by his body, numerous details remind the viewer of its presence. All the print's movement directs the viewer's gaze up the blade—beginning with the angle of his elbow and shoulders, and mirrored in the shape of his nose, the shadow of his cheekbone, and the set of his jaw. Even the clouds of smoke from the burning Spanish ships in the distance become darkest and most ominous near the sword's tip. Bartholomeus's exposed blade encapsulates the danger, ruthlessness, and prowess. Military portraiture of the period

"Blood and Lust" | 101

often featured men with swords and armor, but virtually never with their swords drawn and erect.[20] Each of *Bucaniers of America*'s subsequent portraits, including those of Rock. Brasiliano and François Lolonois, provided variations on these themes: the scowl and heavy brow, drawn sword, and a detached perspective on their victims' suffering.

The images must have been potent, for these copperplates were reused at considerable expense by a series of printers for nearly thirty years after their initial production. This recycling took place not simply to save money, as the costs of transport and repair of the fragile copper were high—suggesting that it was the high quality of the images that prompted their long use in several different cities. Shortly after the book's 1678 appearance in Amsterdam, the text was translated into German and issued by a Nuremberg press in 1679. The German printer purchased the original plates and transported them approximately 670 kilometers inland—potentially a very expensive undertaking, since transportation and escort costs, tolls, and border levies increased an item's cost considerably. Transport overland between Frankfurt and Nuremberg, for example—less than half the distance from Amsterdam—ballooned a book's cost on average by about 25%.[21] The German printer had to worry that the plates would be damaged in transit, for even the smallest scratch in the copper would appear in subsequent prints; then he had to contract out to an engraver's workshop to find someone with the skills and equipment to print the images, as copperplates required a special press with extraordinary weight to coax the ink out of the plates' tiny, subtle cuts. In addition, the pressure imposed by a copperplate press was so extreme that the plates wore out—depending on the quality of the copper, this could occur as quickly as after only 125 impressions. In such cases printers hired engravers to recut the plates by using a tool to carefully trace over their worn lines to deepen them and restore their ability to produce sharp images.[22]

The move to Nuremberg did not mark the end of the plates' travels. By 1681 the plates had been sold yet again to appear in a Spanish-language edition produced by Lorenzo Struikman, a Cologne printer (located some four hundred kilometers from Nuremberg). Struikman sought to take advantage of eager Spanish-reading audiences willing to pay for imported books, as Spanish printing of the day did not match the high quality of northern European prints. Struikman had an engraver rub out the original Dutch caption and re-calligraph it for Spanish readers. When his edition quickly sold out, Struikman reprinted it a year later, again reusing the plates.

When the plate was used for the fifth time in 1684, the London publisher arranged to have the caption recut, but the shadow of the Dutch text is easily apparent. Meanwhile, the plate shows wear and tear from frequent reuse. Courtesy of the John Carter Brown Library at Brown University.

It was the popularity of the Spanish-language edition that gained the attention of London printers.[23] When William Crooke produced his own edition, he too decided that the original engravings were so superior that he purchased them. Yet again, the plates traveled nearly six hundred kilometers from Cologne across the Channel to London. This time the printer did a poor job reproducing the engravings, which appear decidedly worn and display the shadow of the rubbed-out Dutch caption even more clearly. But the quality of its prints did not prevent the book from selling out such that Crooke produced another edition within the year. By 1704 the plates had changed hands twice more to appear in four more London editions. Considering that the Dutch plates were ultimately used to produce nine separate editions of a consistently popular book, we might conservatively guess that at least five thousand copies of the book contained these images—and, more liberally, perhaps as many as thirteen thousand—radically testing the capacity of copperplates to produce legible images.[24] As a result of this frequent reuse over decades, the images established a visual repertoire of piracy from which other engravers borrowed.

Illustrated title page of the original Dutch edition of Exquemelin's *De Americaensche Zee-Roovers* (1678). Courtesy of the Library of Congress.

As *Bucaniers of America* circulated through Europe, one engraver after the next embroidered on the same themes of ominous danger and masculine bravado. Take the Paris printer, Jacques Le Febvre, who produced four editions of Exquemelin between 1686 and 1705. With only three images in the book, he did not attempt to reproduce the visual richness of the original; but the images he commissioned nevertheless built on the themes laid out in the Dutch originals. The Dutch title page, for example, portrayed its two central pirate figures as prone to an almost whimsical violence: one jauntily keeps one hand at his waist while brandishing his sword at the prostrate Indian, while the other appears more concerned with verbally abusing his victim, who begs for mercy. In contrast, the French engraver opted for less peripheral detail in favor of a more focused center of action. The engraver's buccaneers are hidden by shadows, avoiding the viewer's gaze. The pirates' physical threats appear more intimidating: the swords appear imminently to slash throats and pierce breasts, and the pirates' visages are intent on inflicting harm and less inclined to ineffective posturing.

Illustrated title page of the Paris edition (1688). Note how the French engraver has innovated on the Dutch images on either side of the calligraphed text. Courtesy of the John Carter Brown Library at Brown University.

It is significant that the elegantly dressed Spaniard who looks hopelessly to the viewer for help is not merely about to lose his life, but also receive a serious kick to the groin—a mode of violence emblematic of how pirates emasculated their victims. Pirates did more than render their victims prostrate (and possibly rape their wives): they also stole their goods. In doing so, pirates exemplified a radical form of status upheaval as well as a chaotic masculine threat. According to Exquemelin, this lowly group of men rose from obscurity and the lowest social orders to target the wealthiest ships and cities for attack, thereby depriving Europeans of the expectation of orderly trade and shipping. And once they had gained treasure, they famously divided it among themselves in comparatively equal terms, cultivating a rough equality among crewmen and a strict loyalty to one another.²⁵ These class inversions did not truly pose an open threat to the social order, of course; indeed, editors continued to claim that readers ought to admire these men for being "English." Still, the conquest of the ragged over the refined would have stood out to readers as a sign of the inversions of status and alternative masculinities that could exist in the imagined locale of the Caribbean.²⁶ It signaled that not all men needed to follow the same path.

The fact that the French engraver figured the pirates laying their riches at the feet of the symbolic figure of America, the Indian princess, rendered them perhaps even more dangerously capricious. This artistic decision visually suggested that they were taking from Europe to give to no one in particular—or even worse, to savages. In doing so, the image displayed the extent to which they had stepped outside the norms of European manhood. Unlike the figure of Britannia, who represented the justice and law of England, the "naked" Indian princess evoked a cruder form of order. This image figured America as a place where riches could not be utilized in the rational fashion Europeans idealized. Exquemelin's descriptions of the pirates' propensity to steal and then lose vast riches further underlined their separation from the ideals of financial moderation and manly self-control. As Peter Linebaugh and Marcus Rediker have noted, "Pirates thus stood against the brutal injustices of the merchant shipping industry, with one crew's even claiming to be 'Robbin Hoods Men.'"²⁷

Enhancing Textual and Visual Portrayals of Pirates: Johnson's General History

When Captain Charles Johnson's even more popular *General History of the Pyrates* appeared in London in 1724, it adopted a far different tone than Exquemelin's volume of nearly fifty years earlier.²⁸ Early in the book, Johnson affected a tone of stern disapproval of the pirates who had so successfully upset British trade relations for more than two decades, and who had been the center of highly publicized criminal trials for several years; thus Johnson's moralism was likely calculated to play well to official readers. But his subsequent narrative and the book's illustrations undermined any clear moral lesson about pirates. *A General History of the Pyrates* ultimately enhanced the narrative and visual conventions for representing piracy, especially by expanding the already-existing tendency to emphasize manliness and sexuality.

The book's emphasis on sexuality reflected a growing sophistication in visual literacy by engravers and at least some of their readers, made possi-

"Capt. Edward England" from Charles Johnson's *History and Lives of All the Most Notorious Pirates, and Their Crews* (London, 1725). Courtesy of the Library of Congress.

ble by the rapid expansion of the trade in visual prints and illustrated books during the eighteenth century.[29] Take, for example, the increasingly sexualized portrayals of pirates' display of their weapons. As discussed earlier, Exquemelin's illustrators had invariably displayed pirates with their swords unsheathed in a manner that evoked the pirates' dangerous manliness and violent proclivities. But the English engraver for the *General History*, B. Cole, exaggerated the pirates' caches of weapons to such an extent that one cannot ignore the possibility that he called forth phallic imagery. As much as Cole borrowed aspects of earlier pirate images—fierce scowls, drawn weapons, aggressive postures, and dramatic background action—he set a new pattern with his strong emphasis on "erect" swords, pistols, and hatchets.

Such images fit neatly with Johnson's text, which likewise placed heavier emphasis on the pirates' sex lives. He explained that Edward "Blackbeard" Teach, for example, forced his "fourteenth wife" to "prostitute herself" to members of his own crew while he watched. Thus, to accompany these textual descriptions, Cole positioned Blackbeard with an extraordinary array of weapons: he holds one drawn sword "up," while no fewer than six holstered pistols are arrayed across his chest; most striking, a second sword hangs prominently between his legs.[30] Likewise, the author describes Edward England and his crew as forcing women "in a barbarous manner to their lusts, and to requite them, destroyed their cocoa trees and fired several of their houses and churches."[31] Invariably, England was depicted in a provocative pose, displaying his hatchet arrayed in a phallic position, a posture copied in dozens of cheap editions of the book throughout the eighteenth century. But it was not merely the hatchet that guaranteed his cocky virility and manly bravado. With his hand on his hip and his body positioned in an open, frontal position to the viewer, England seems to invite viewers to see him in sexual terms. Underscoring this point, the text below the image in this edition begins, "It is very surprizing, that Men of Understanding should engage in Murder, Theft, and Rapine; and yet such was *England*." Even in a pre-Freudian Atlantic world, many readers would have seen the imagery of erect swords and angled hatchets as yoking together sexual and physical violence.

Johnson underscored their manliness by lavishing attention on the pirates' marriages, interracial sexual liaisons, multiple children, and most of all their perverse or barbaric sexual violence against women. He left little doubt that a good number of the pirates' outrageous acts had been sexual in nature. Captain Henry Avery and his crew moved to Madagascar, where they "married the most beautiful of the Negro women, not one or two, but as many as they liked . . . so that every one of them had as great a Seraglio as the Grand Seignior at Constantinople." Meanwhile, less sedentary pirates settled for perpetual "whoring" with women throughout the Caribbean and elsewhere.[32] Johnson thereby established a canon of myths that would remain in print for over a century—many of which revolved around the pirates' sexuality and malevolent fearlessness. The pirates' proclivities for sexual violence called attention to their manly prowess and position as gender outsiders, characterizations that readers might experience simultaneously as both immoral and titillating. The sexually evocative subject matter of the text worked in tandem with the images to suggest that the pirates inhabited a masculine subject position that was explicitly sexualized.

At this point it is worth stepping back to ask, why would books have drawn such attention to the gendered and sexual lives of the pirates? Such portrayals specifically appealed to the bourgeois and elite male readers who made up the vast majority of the consumers for such books. Reading about the exotic sexual lives of "*Heroick*" pirates would have provided a fascinating counterpoint to the more staid lives of such readers—but they could also cultivate male readers' identifications with the pirates by inviting them to imagine abandoning sexual self-restraint during these decades, long noted as an era during which an ethic of male sexual irresponsibility flourished in popular print media.[33] Books like Exquemelin's and Johnson's constituted rich contributions to a growing range of books—novels, travel narratives, and conduct manuals—that called forth new imaginative male identities made possible by permissive environments like the pirate ship or the Caribbean.

Although scholars have invariably used Johnson's portrayals of female pirates Anne Bonny and Mary Read to speculate about responses by female readers, these chapters also contributed significantly to wealthy men's imaginative relations to the pirates overall. Indeed, depictions of Bonny and Read display in even clearer relief how male readers might have enjoyed these books. Scholarship on popular reception of Bonny and Read frequently argues that these cross-dressing characters offered female readers new models of rebellion and female agency in matters of economics, sex, and self-protection—thereby encouraging readers to imagine far-reaching forms of personal liberation.[34] Such interpretations appear strikingly idealistic if we focus on those readers most likely to own these books: comparatively wealthy men who were already the most "free" in society, and who possessed the disposable income to purchase expensive illustrated books or patronize social libraries. If such men imagined freedom by reading these accounts, we must see it far differently than that experienced by those men's female subordinates.

Above all, Johnson's book emphasizes the pleasurable titillation of Read's and Bonny's cross-dressing in a series of set pieces highlighting gender confusion and sexual behavior. In one almost Shakespearean passage, Read enters the army only to fall in love with one of her officers, leading her to risk life and limb to be near him. Distracted by her love, she neglects her duty: "It seems Mars and Venus could not be served at the same time," Johnson comments philosophically. She eventually lets her love "discover her sex" one night as they lie together in a tent. Even more risqué is the moment when Bonny and Read meet aboard the pirate ship, each in full disguise. Taking Read "for a handsome young fellow," Bonny takes "a particular liking to her" and secretly reveals that she is a woman—presumably to solicit sex. Johnson allows the sexual confusion of the scene to transpire for his readers' enjoyment, delaying its resolution. He even indicates that Read at least considers the possibility of playing the paramour to prolong her ruse. But "knowing what she would be at" if she did not come clean, "and being very sensible for her own incapacity" to play the

Anne Bonny op Jamaica Gevangen.

"Anne Bonny" from the 1725 Amsterdam edition of Johnson's *Historie der Engelsche Zee-Rovers*. Courtesy of the John Carter Brown Library at Brown University.

man for Bonny's sake, she reveals the truth—to Bonny's "great disappointment."[35] Replete with transvestism, sex (consummated and otherwise), and a disdain for gender propriety, these biographical vignettes enhanced the themes that appeared throughout *A General History of the Pyrates*: they portrayed pirates as rejecting gender conventions and sexual decorum. The book's images further invited male readers to see these women as pleasurably dangerous sex objects; the Dutch edition of 1725, for example, displayed them in breeches, heavily armed, and striking jaunty and mildly threatening poses, while their long tresses and full breasts confirm their sexual appeal and availability, as in this image of Anne Bonny. It is not hard to see that publishers intended such tales and images for male readers: their constructions of manliness via the figure of the pirate, and in cultivating male readers' enjoyment of the pirates' sexual peccadilloes, constituted a fundamental part of their subject matter.

"Captain Keitt" from Howard Pyle's *Book of Pirates* (1921), from the collection of the author.

If Exquemelin's and Johnson's books had been less popular or long-lived, we might be skeptical that they had hit on a formula for representing pirates that would remain influential. But during the following centuries, books, plays, and eventually films continued to build on motifs established in the 1670s that emphasized manly adventure, gender transgression, erotic violence, and moral ambivalence.[36] By the time Howard Pyle began retelling a softer version of those stories alongside his evocative illustrations in magazines like *Harper's Weekly* in the 1880s, conventions for pirate representations were so accepted that it seemed obvious to him that "every boy" would "rather be a pirate captain than a Member of Parliament."[37]

These conventions had three important components that render them significant for the history of manliness in the "long eighteenth century." First, the books explicitly touted the pirates as admirable men, describing them as "*Heroick*" and capable of "wondrous Actions, and daring Adventures." Of course, those descriptors were hardly obvious, considering the buccaneers' penchants for robbery, rape, and torture; but even if such hero-worship created a degree of cognitive dissonance, these portrayals contrasted with the more sober lives of the books' readers. Illustrations of the pirates as scowling figures set against background scenes of destruction and suffering further underscored their potential for violent, dramatic action. Authors and publishers seemed to herald the alternative masculinities exemplified by the pirates and urged their readers to do the same.

Second, books by Exquemelin, Johnson, and their followers made the pirates' transgressive sexual behavior a prominent component of their masculinity that vividly encapsulated their moral ambiguity and unpredictability. Whether by discussing their interracial unions or their propensity for rape and other sexual perversions, and eventually by enhancing those tales with images of weapons displayed in exaggerated phallic postures, these authors used sexuality to compound their expressed admiration of the pirates as *men*. The increasing emphasis on sexual volatility served up for male readers a titillating world of male privilege and lack of restraint, and paralleled more explicitly erotic or bawdy writing of the era.

Finally, these texts located sexualized pirate masculinity in the imagined setting of the Caribbean—an American site far from established social networks, family responsibilities, or business obligations. For European and Anglo-American readers alike, its very remoteness rendered such a setting all the more available for fantasy, while its mostly Spanish settlers demanded no sympathy from northern Europeans jealous of their control over the area. The unrelenting hard work, indentured servitude, and modest desires for economic competency of Britain's mainland colonies were wholly absent from these narratives; when pirates made and lost vast fortunes on these pages, readers might enjoy the daydream of such an existence. Situating those events far away in the Americas, where palm-treed harbor towns suffered the attacks of brutal buccaneers, characterized this locale as a site of dynamism, movement, and heroic action.

NOTES

For their assistance I thank Frances Clarke, Judy Coffin, Tom Foster, Lauren Hewes, Dian Kriz, Mary Katherine Matalon, Rebecca Plant, David Rickman, the students at the University of Texas's Plan II Honors "Voltaire's Salon," and the staffs at the John Carter Brown Library, the Massachusetts Historical Society, and Harvard's Houghton Library. I am particularly grateful to *Common-Place: The Interactive Journal of Early American Life*, where I published an earlier version of this essay, "Shivering Timbers: Sexing Up the Pirates in

Early Modern Print Culture," in October 2009. Images described but not displayed in the chapter can be seen at http://www.common-place.org/vol-10/no-01/eastman/. Finally, I thank Cathy Kelly: editor, mentor, friend.

1. Howard Pyle, *Howard Pyle's Book of Pirates: Fiction, Fact, and Fancy Concerning the Buccaneers and Marooners of the Spanish Main*, compiled by Merle Johnson (New York: Harper and Bros., 1921), xiii, xiv.

2. See, for example, the trailer for *Captain Blood* (1935), available online at http://www.imdb.com/video/screenplay/vi2119368729/, accessed 15 Dec. 2009; and "The Adventures of Miles Cowperthwaite" from *Saturday Night Live*, Season 4, Episode 18 (12 May 1979), the transcript of which is available at http://snltranscripts.jt.org/78/78rcowperthwaite.phtml, accessed 15 Dec. 2009. David Cordingly's *Under the Black Flag: The Romance and the Reality of Life Among the Pirates* (New York: Harcourt Brace, 1995) entertainingly contrasts the long-lasting popularity of pirate lore with the original literature.

3. See, for example, essays by Dianne Dugaw and Marcus Rediker in *Iron Men, Wooden Women: Gender and Seafaring in the Atlantic World*, eds. Margaret Creighton and Lisa Norling (Baltimore: Johns Hopkins University Press, 1996), chaps. 1 and 2; and Hans Turley, *Rum, Sodomy, and the Lash: Piracy, Sexuality, and Masculine Identity* (New York: New York University Press, 1999).

4. Peter T. Leeson, *The Invisible Hook: The Hidden Economics of Pirates* (Princeton, NJ: Princeton University Press, 2009), 45–81. See also Marcus Rediker, *Villains of All Nations: Atlantic Pirates in the Golden Age* (Boston: Beacon Press, 2004), 1–18; and Rediker, *Between the Devil and the Deep Blue Sea: Merchant Seamen, Pirates, and the Anglo-American Maritime World, 1700–1750* (Cambridge: Cambridge University Press, 1987), chap. 6.

5. The original translator claimed that it "was no sooner published in the *Dutch Original*, than it was snatch up for the most curious Library's of *Holland*" before making its way around northern Europe. Alexandre Exquemelin, *Bucaniers of America* (London: William Crooke, 1684), I: [i]. Subsequent textual citations come from this edition unless otherwise noted. Crooke had the book translated from the Spanish edition, which itself was a "faithful rendering of the Dutch" by Alonzo de Bonne-Maison. Clarence Henry Haring, *Buccaneers of the West Indies in the XVII Century* (New York: Methuen, 1910), 279; *A Transcript of the Registers of the Worshipful Company of Stationers; from 1640–1708 A. D.* (London: privately printed, 1914), III: 254.

6. Louis B. Wright, "The 'Gentleman's Library' in Early Virginia: The Literary Interests of the First Carters," *Huntington Library Quarterly* 1 (October 1937): 53; Salem Social Library, Record Book (1761), Curwen Family Manuscript Collection, Box 3, Folder 5, American Antiquarian Society Manuscript Collections, Worcester, MA.

7. Roger Gaskell, "Printing House and Engraving Shop: A Mysterious Collaboration," *Book Collector* 53 (Summer 2004): 221–24.

8. Exquemelin, *Bucaniers of America*, I: [ii].

9. Leeson, *Invisible Hook*, 7.

10. Exquemelin, *Bucaniers of America*, II: 18.

11. Ibid., II: 20. Errors in the original.

12. Ibid., II: 28–29.

13. Ibid., II: 32–33.

14. On this subject, see Robert D. Hume, "The Economics of Culture in London, 1660–1740," *Huntington Library Quarterly* 69 (Dec. 2006): 487–533.

15. Exquemelin, *Bucaniers of America*, II: 116–17, 98.

16. On early modern erotic writing, see Jean Marie Goulemot, *Forbidden Texts: Erotic Literature and Its Readers in Eighteenth-Century France*, trans. James Simpson (Philadelphia: University of Pennsylvania Press, 1994); Karen Harvey, *Reading Sex in the Eighteenth Century* (Cambridge: Cambridge University Press, 2004); *The Invention of Pornography*, ed. Lynn Hunt (New York: Zone Books, 1996); and *Eighteenth-Century British Erotica*, eds. Alexander Pettit and Patrick Spedding (London: Pickering and Chatto, 2002).

17. Exquemelin, *Bucaniers of America*, I: [ii].

18. "Advertisement: The *History of the Bucaniers of* America" (London: William Whitwood and Anthony Feltham, 1695).

19. Exquemelin, *Bucaniers of America* (London: Tho. Newborough, John Nicholson, and Benj. Tooke, 1704), II: [ii–iii].

20. See, for example, the military portraiture of the Dutch artist Anthony Van Dyck, such as his 1624 *Portrait of a Young General* and his *Portrait of a Commander in Armor, with a Red Scarf* (ca. 1625), both of which evoke masculine power but not the volatility of Exquemelin's pirate images.

21. John L. Flood, "'Omnium totius orbis emporiorum compendium': The Frankfurt Fair in the Early Modern Period," *Fairs, Markets, and the Itinerant Book Trade*, eds. Robin Myers, Michael Harris, and Giles Mandelbrote (New Castle, DE: Oak Knoll Press and the British Library, 2007), 3.

22. On the special requirements of copperplate printing, which include using a particularly heavy, viscous ink, dampening the paper, and meticulously wiping the plates before each impression, see Gaskell, "Printing House and Engraving Shop," 219–20.

23. The translator of the original London edition claims that English readers first learned about *Bucaniers of America* in *Weekly Memorials for the Ingenious: Or, An Account of Books Lately Set Forth in Several Languages*, a 1682–83 journal that described new books appearing from presses throughout northern Europe.

24. Printers may have been willing to foot the bill for transporting and maintaining the plates due to the superior reputation of Dutch engravings during this era. At the same time, English engravers had quite poor reputations. I have found other book illustrations that similarly traveled throughout the region, most notably some of the grand folio-sized copperplate cuts for Cornelis de Bruyn's *Reizen*, which appeared in editions produced in Delft, London, Amsterdam, and Paris between 1698 and 1759.

How many copies might be produced in a single late seventeenth-century edition is a notoriously vexed question, but it is reasonable to assume that a popular book like this one would have appeared in editions of at least five hundred copies.

25. Christopher Hill, "Radical Pirates?" in *The Origins of Anglo-American Radicalism*, eds. Margaret Jacob and James Jacob (London: Allen and Unwin, 1984), 20.

26. On this subject, see Peter Linebaugh and Marcus Rediker, *The Many-Headed Hydra: Sailors, Slaves, Commoners, and the Hidden History of the Revolutionary Atlantic* (Boston: Beacon Press, 2000), 156, 162–67.

27. Ibid., 163–64.

28. This book appeared in over one hundred editions between 1724 and 1794, in English, Dutch, German, and French, published in at least nine different European cities.

Untangling the exact number is made doubly difficult not merely due to the vast number of cheap editions with variant titles, but because beginning in the 1930s some scholars attributed the book to Daniel Defoe. Subsequently, this attribution has been viewed with considerable skepticism; on this subject, see Turley, *Rum, Sodomy, and the Lash*, 159–60, n. 8. More recently the scholar Arne Bialuschewski has persuasively argued that the author behind the pseudonym "Captain Charles Johnson" was the journalist Nathaniel Mist. See "Daniel Defoe, Nathaniel Mist, and the *General History of the Pyrates*," *Papers of the Bibliographical Society of America* 98 (March 2004): 21–38.

29. Sheila O'Connell, *The Popular Print in England, 1550–1800* (London: British Museum Press, 1999), 48–53, 109–19, and chaps. 7 and 8.

30. Even Howard Pyle's 1921 children's book insisted on making oblique reference to Blackbeard's unfortunate wife: "The life that he and his rum-crazy shipmates led her to was too terrible to be told." Pyle, *Howard Pyle's Book of Pirates*, 29.

31. Capt. Charles Johnson, *A General History of the Robberies and Murders of the Most Notorious Pirates* (1724; reprint, Guilford, CT: Lyons Press, 2002), 93, 60–61, 198.

32. Johnson, *General History*, 35.

33. The literature on this subject is vast; see especially Tim Hitchcock, *English Sexualities, 1700–1800* (London: Basingstoke, 1997), 112–14; for an overview of literature on sexuality in the eighteenth century, see Karen Harvey, "The Century of Sex? Gender, Bodies, and Sexuality in the Long Eighteenth Century," *Historical Journal* 45 (Dec. 2002): 899–916.

34. Rudolf M. Dekker and Lotte C. Van de Pol, *The Tradition of Female Transvestism in Early Modern Europe* (London: Macmillan, 1989); Alfred F. Young, *Masquerade: The Life and Times of Deborah Sampson, Continental Soldier* (New York: Random House, 2004).

35. Johnson, *General History*, 116, 119, 121–22.

36. The playwright John Gay would recycle these themes of sexuality, violence, and titillation when he composed *Polly: An Opera* (1729), the sequel to his wildly popular *Beggar's Opera* (1728). In it, Polly dresses as a boy to escape white slavery and prostitution in the West Indies; after a long series of misadventures, she marries the son of a Carib chief.

37. Pyle, *Howard Pyle's Book of Pirates*, xiii. This book collects articles and images that Pyle published in *Harper's Weekly*, *Harper's Magazine*, *Collier's Weekly*, and other sources between 1887 and 1911.

6

"Banes of Society" and "Gentlemen of Strong Natural Parts"

Attacking and Defending West Indian Creole Masculinity

NATALIE A. ZACEK

A text that sheds much light on the social life of the West Indian colonies at the height of plantation prosperity and that has received almost no attention from historians is "Account of Travels" by Henry Hulton (1731–1790), an autobiographical account of the life of a British customs official whose travels took him throughout Europe and the American colonies, and who spent several years resident in Antigua as deputy collector of the customs in the island's capital, St. John's.[1] Hulton's text—composed in the mid-1780s, when he had retired to England and wished to create a record of his experiences for the benefit, particularly in moral terms, of his five sons—deals extensively with his experiences in Antigua, and especially with his evaluation of the character of the island's white society. The text is particularly useful for the study of ideals and practices of masculinity in this context, as he was a metropolitan Englishman who spent enough time living on the island to make well-informed evaluations of this colonial community; moreover, he was a worldly, well-educated man who was already fairly well traveled by the time he arrived in the islands, and he appears to have approached Antiguan society with a relatively open mind.[2] Throughout his text, Hulton is concerned, perhaps even obsessed, with evaluating the characters of the island's white men, and although the concluding chapter of the "Account" includes some barbed comments regarding the evils of West Indian society and the great potential for even virtuous individuals to be corrupted by this environment, his actual descriptions in the chapters relating to his time in Antigua include some very favorable evaluations of the characters of individual island residents, as well as more negative depictions thereof. A careful reading of Hulton's text, then, complicates and contradicts long-held stereotypes, nearly as prevalent today as they were in Hulton's lifetime, of the West Indian planters as, variously, brutes, philistines, dullards, and voluptuaries, and allows them to be seen at least as much as representatives of, rather than as exceptions to, the norms of masculinity prevalent in the eighteenth-century British Atlantic world.[3]

In the past decade or so, the historiography of colonial British America, and of gender relations therein, has been enriched by an ever-increasing series of studies that have interrogated ideals and practices of masculinity and illuminated both individual and communal experiences of the formation and re-formation of masculine character and behavior.[4] As has largely been true of early American historiography, New England has thus far received the lion's share of attention.[5] Rather less attention, however, has thus far been paid to white manhood in Britain's West Indian colonies, including the vastly profitable sugar islands of Barbados, Jamaica, and Antigua.

As Trevor Burnard has noted, the prevalent metropolitan conception of the West Indian planter throughout the eighteenth century was that these men "found it difficult not to be tyrants in all of their relationships."[6] Men who were accustomed to holding absolute power of life and death over dozens or even hundreds of slaves would, presumably, have trouble modifying their behavior along the lines mandated by genteel society, particularly in the latter half of the eighteenth century, in which the rise of the "cult of sensibility" in Britain and, to a lesser extent, its North American colonies encouraged men of fortune to adopt a more self-consciously polite and restrained mode of public and private social interaction, and to emphasize persuasion rather than aggression as the basis of intimate relationships. Of course, the same type of criticism could plausibly have been made of slaveholders in, for example, colonial Virginia or South Carolina, but contemporaries and historians alike have generally conceived of this latter group of planters as having been socialized through regular attendance at Anglican or evangelical religious services and by frequent visits to Williamsburg or Charleston—where they might come into contact with "civil tongues and polite letters," and participate in such self-consciously genteel institutions as the Jockey Club or the St. Cecilia Society.[7] Moreover, plantation life in the southern colonies was more self-consciously paternalist in practice than in the West Indies, with men such as George Washington, Thomas Jefferson, Landon Carter, and Henry Laurens striving to convince themselves and others that it was possible to balance financial success as a planter with humane treatment of one's bondspeople. Although even the South's most cultivated planter-aristocrats might, should they visit the mother country, find themselves struggling against "the curse of provincialism" in metropolitan eyes, they did not find it nearly as difficult to convince Englishmen that they were "creole gentlemen" as did rich West Indians, who along with the East India Company "nabobs" were not merely "the most conspicuous rich men of their age," but were execrated as sham gentry—"cowskin heroes" who had gained their riches through brutal exploitation of their miserable slaves, whose ostentatious style of life was ludicrous in its lack of taste, and whose manners had been irredeemably coarsened by years spent only in the company of slaves and of white persons no more cultured or sensible than themselves.[8]

In fact, earlier metropolitan critiques of white society in the West Indies had primarily blamed women, rather than men, for the perceived social shortcomings of these colonies. In the seventeenth and early eighteenth centuries, when Englishmen and -women tended to view the Caribbean as a sort of "Wild West" primarily inhabited by "rogues, whores, and vagabonds," white women who made their way to the West Indies were depicted in pamphlets, travelogues, and novels as those "such as have been Scandalous in England to the utmost degree, either Transported by the State, or led by their Vicious Inclinations; where they may be Wicked without Shame, and Whore on without Punishment."[9] The physical and social environment of the islands was supposedly so corrupting, even to seemingly solid English stock, that, according to William Pittis, the author of *The Jamaica Lady* (1720), the very air of Jamaica "so changes the constitution of its inhabitants that if a woman land there chaste as a vestal, she becomes in forty-eight hours a perfect Messalina," referring to a Roman empress notorious for her sexual depravity.[10] By the latter decades of the eighteenth century, however, the islands' white populations had experienced a significant gender rebalancing caused by the end of their "frontier stage," in which immigrants were overwhelmingly single men, and by the ongoing tendency of men in the islands to die more rapidly than women. As marriage to a white woman became a possibility for the majority of white West Indian men, and as a result of the rise of the "culture of sensibility" in the metropole, these potential wives and mothers underwent a cultural reevaluation by locals and visitors alike; "creole" women were now described not as lustful strumpets, but as angelic figures whose immaculate characters upheld both the purity of the white race and the legitimacy of imperial authority. But for creole women's individual and communal reputations to be rehabilitated, those of creole men could only decline, as clearly one gender if not the other had to shoulder the blame for the seemingly aberrant nature of West Indian society: for the frequently inhumane treatment of slaves, the common occurrence of interracial sex, the settlers' general lack of interest in the development of religious, social, and educational institutions, and the perceived overall failure of the colonists to transform these tropical plantation colonies into "little Englands."

Hulton's "Account" is a document filled with paradoxes, and heavily informed by the specific experiences and prejudices of its writer. Yet it offers a valuable perspective on the reality and perception of white masculinity in the English West Indies. Although Hulton includes in his narrative a large number of negative depictions of West Indian settlers, he also praises more than a few creole men as possessing all the most praiseworthy virtues, thus implying that residence in the colonies did not inherently prevent a man from developing and maintaining a solid character. While lurid depictions of brutish, uncultured slaveholders were seized on by metropolitan readers before, during, and after the rise of abolition as a popular cause—and have remained the principal image of the West Indian creole man within a modern historiography, which continues to a large extent to see Britain's Caribbean colonies as marginal and even defective in relation to the North American settlements—it is important to keep in mind that the reality, as always, was rather more complicated.

"Banes of Society"

Although Antigua offered Hulton his first taste of the West Indies, and indeed of the world beyond Europe, what appears to have been most striking to him upon his arrival was not the tropical climate, flora, or fauna, or even the presence of huge numbers of enslaved Africans, but the nature of the white inhabitants' hospitality. Antiguans, like their fellow colonists elsewhere in the West Indies, and in the southern mainland colonies, prided themselves on maintaining a lavish and openhanded hospitality, and Hulton, arriving as an unmarried man of good family and education and holding a fairly prestigious post, found himself constantly invited to social gatherings. Though he appreciated this show of friendliness, Hulton simultaneously found it somewhat alarming; he had endured a bad fever shortly after his arrival, and in order to maintain his health he committed himself to a strict program of diet and exercise, aiming each day to "rise early, and be on horseback before the Sun appeared." After ninety minutes' ride, he bathed, drank saltwater, and sat down to a hearty meal; after riding another hour in the evening, he preferred to go "early to bed, without eating meat suppers."[11] He found it difficult to reconcile his abstemious routine with the demands of social life, particularly as he discovered that the white Antiguan ladies were especially fond of dancing, and keen to have him as a partner; fearing that such exercise would cause his fever to return, he "avoided it as much as possible, as a European runs great risk on his first arrival in the West Indies, from the hospitality of the Gentlemen, and the civility due to the Ladies."[12]

More troubling to Hulton, and more assiduously to be avoided, was the masculine sphere of sociability, with its emphasis not on dancing and gallantry to the ladies, but on alcohol and gambling. Hulton described the planter Colonel Blizard as "a very sensible man," but deplored the fact that this sixty-year-old "lived very freely, kept an hospitable table and seldom went to bed sober." Although Hulton admitted that Blizard's "sense and spirit seemed to shine forth the more as he grew in liquor," he nevertheless criticized Blizard for setting a bad example, as "it was scarce possible to avoid excess in his company." Hulton himself suffered after partaking of Blizard's "Punch of Arack," which left him "tortured with the most violent head and eye ache imaginable" to the extent that he "bound up [his] head and eyes and rolled around the bed in agony," and only a plaster of opium provided relief. Blizard's social rival was Mr. Ottley, who had been "bred in the Guards, where he had acquired a taste for gambling and luxury." Hulton claimed that "several young people of fortune were led in to play deep at [Ottley's] parties, and this Gent was said to have made a considerable fortune by his success at the dice." Hulton's observations of these "bane[s] of Society," "corruptors of morals," and "wasters of substance" emphasize that these men's actions could not be attributed to youthful folly. These were middle-aged and even elderly men, husbands and fathers, and proprietors of great estates, yet they seemed unable or unwilling to set a virtuous example to youth. Although Hulton occasionally felt obligated to put in an appearance at these gatherings, he "generally retired with a book to another room, and before I left the Island, my acquaintance with these Gentlemen decreased."[13]

Even hospitality that did not center on alcohol and games of chance could pose a moral hazard to West Indian individual and communal masculinity, as Antiguans, Hulton claimed, seemed to be unable to draw a line between simple enjoyment of social intercourse and wretched and dangerous excess. As an example, Hulton offered the history of an unnamed man on the island who by the middle of his life "had run thro' his fortune." In order to support his wife and children, he had to take a position as manager of another planter's estate, a signal humiliation, as managers, like overseers and bookkeepers, ranked considerably below planters in the social hierarchy, and were in most cases impoverished men who had come to the West Indies to make their fortunes, rather than formerly landed men who had lost their estates.

But, according to Hulton, this man of mature years, a husband and a father, had not learned his lesson following this reversal of fortune, but instead was "always seeking for company and entertaining them at his house." To Hulton, such conduct was not merely foolhardy, but downright dangerous; in his view, "this desire of shewing what may be called hospitality . . . so much of a self-gratification attends the exercise of this virtue, that in indulging it, people are led to do injustice to their families." While welcoming friends to one's home can be seen as a polite "virtue," incautious men fail to sense the appropriate limits of such social displays, and may soon find that "these marks of attention which gratify vanity . . . are often paid at the expense of family comfort, and the confidence of generous creditors."[14] A man may believe that he is living up to ideals of manly honor by offering unstinting hospitality to his community, but in reality, in Hulton's opinion, he can easily fall into self-indulgence, and end up disgracing himself by taking on debts that he cannot pay and by placing his family, who depend on his prudence and self-restraint, in a situation of dire need.

While excess was one way a man might forfeit his good character and his ability to provide both financial security and be an effective role model for his children, Hulton believed that even the best-intentioned father could fall into habits that threatened to damage not only his reputation but also the physical and emotional health of his offspring. He was troubled by the story of Colonel Leslie, president of the Antiguan council, whom he described as "an hospitable good kind of man," but one who was also "somewhat vain and talkative, with little education, and but poor abilities." In Hulton's view, such qualities were far from the best attributes for a father, and the experiences of Leslie's three sons appeared to have confirmed Hulton's judgment. The eldest married the daughter of Colonel Blizard, the chief justice of Antigua, thus making an excellent match to a woman from a wealthy and respected family, but young Mr. Leslie soon "proved a worthless wretch, and after wasting his father about eighteen thousand pounds, he became abandoned, and died miserably in the Isle of Man." Young Leslie's conduct was not only a source of suffering to his wife and shame to his family, but it created a significant rupture within the island's tiny, heavily intermarried white planter society, as "the unhappiness of this marriage caused a breach between the families of the President and Chief Justice; and it was difficult in so small a society, to maintain an intercourse with both of them."[15]

Two of Colonel Leslie's other sons fared little better than their elder brother. One "contracted a violent Passion for a young Lady of family in the Island, and she had an equal attachment to him." But the lovers' passion came to naught, as "his Parents in the day of their Prosperity wou'd not listen to the match," hoping to convince their son to reserve himself for a potentially wealthier bride. Following this enforced separation, Hulton claimed, both young Leslie and his intended died of grief. The youngest of the brothers was a "poor creature, who married the daughter of Mr. Dunbar," Hulton's supervisor in the St. John's customhouse, and "leads now the life of a wretch." Only the second youngest of the Leslie boys appears to have attained any degree of success or happiness, having become a captain in the British Navy, where, it can be conjectured, strict military discipline and the positive example provided by his superior officers might have remedied the defects of his upbringing.[16]

In Hulton's opinion, the unhappiness that the Leslie sons' actions brought on themselves and others could be directly attributed to the failings of their father, as "in the conduct of this Parent there seems to have been a want of good sense, and great vanity." Colonel Leslie, though apparently a well-intentioned man, failed to provide appropriate guidance to his children: "the giving full scope to the passions of the youth, bringing one early to act for himself, without knowledge, or capacity; and curbing another in a just passion, proved the ruin of each of them." Colonel Leslie had "erred in bringing his Children too forward in life, who without capacity, were early put into the management of business they were not able to conduct"—thus allowing them power without responsibility, resulting in bankruptcy, disgrace, the suffering of their wives and parents, and the creation of a social breach that was difficult to ignore or repair in such a small, interconnected community.[17]

Hulton deploys this gloomy picture of the aged Leslie as a way of emphasizing to his children that a man must remain at all times aware of the possibility of a reversal of fortune, and that, while no man can always prevent such unwelcome changes from taking place, he can at least anticipate the possibility of such misfortunes and develop strategies by which to cope with them. Colonel Leslie, after all, had earlier in his life been seemingly blessed by fortune: he had inherited a large estate, married and had a large family, been appointed to a position of influence and prestige in the government of the island, and enjoyed extending his hospitality to his community and receiving it from them. He most likely had never imagined that he would come to such an unhappy end, with his fortune greatly diminished, three of his four sons dead or disgraced, and his old friends among the West Indian absentee community apparently snubbing him. Hulton urged his own sons to avoid such unhappiness by making certain that each of them had "some business or profession, by which a man may be enabled to subsist when deprived of patrimony, or fortune." But, in Hulton's opinion, too much concern with financial security could in some cases be as personally and socially damaging as too little. Perhaps the most appalling portrait in the "Account" is that which Hulton paints of Mr. Dunbar, surveyor-general of the customs for the Leeward Islands, and therefore his boss. Upon arrival in Antigua, Hulton had considered taking up Dunbar's offer of rented accommodation, but was dissuaded from doing so when others warned him that, once he moved in, Dunbar was likely to try to extort a much higher rent from him, counting on what he hoped would be Hulton's unwillingness to move. This early exposure to Dunbar's greed and dishonesty was compounded by Hulton's having to spend so much time in close quarters with him, as the former not only worked in the customhouse at St. John's, but also lived in the rooms above it.

The lust for money appears, at least to Hulton, to have been the key to Dunbar's character, and to have irreparably spoiled all his relationships. He had allowed his daughter to marry Colonel Leslie's third son, believing that the young man's commercial activities would increase not only his own wealth but also that of his wife's family, but those plans, as described earlier, came only to disaster; the young man was "weak, entered into trade, which he did not understand; at length got into jail, and came to ruin," leaving his wife destitute and socially disgraced.[18] Hulton depicted Dunbar's own elder son as being as tightfisted as his father, which meant that the two men were in almost constant conflict with each other over financial issues. The elder Dunbar had made over his estates to his son, who was then expected to pay his father a thousand pounds per year for the remainder of the latter's life, but both men were intensely suspicious of each other and were constantly convinced that the other was trying to cheat him. Hulton describes one of these encounters, stating that one day he was "allarmed in the Custom House by the cry of one of Mr. Dunbar's negroes." When Hulton made his way to his supervisor's rooms upstairs, he found father and son locked in conflict: "there was the old man in his chair, in a great passion, with his long cane, in the attitude to strike his Son, whilst his Son held it, preventing the blow; but receiving the imprecations, and abuses of his father." Hulton pronounced himself to have been "greatly shocked" by the sight of such violent hostility between a father and son, but soon found that such was "no uncommon incident" within the Dunbar family.[19]

Predictably, a lifetime of greed and manipulation brought Dunbar to a miserable old age. He died before Hulton departed Antigua in October 1760, a "miserable old wretch" who was "a monument of his own crimes, for ever shewing the intentions of the knave, without the ability of executing his own designs, and lived to see himself abhorred by the good, contemned even by the wicked, neglected and hated by his own family."[20] As such, Hulton affords Dunbar no hint of a single redeeming quality. While Colonel Leslie's mistakes as a father at least seemed to Hulton to be based on good intentions, Dunbar's were exclusively motivated by his lust for money. While Hulton admired men who were parsimonious in their lifestyle, choosing not to fritter away their money on frivolity, Dunbar was no more than a miser, a quality he passed on to his eldest son. And while Hulton had censured Sir William Young for his self-indulgence, he respected Young's brilliant mind and cultivated persona, whereas he depicted Dunbar as doubly repulsive, a man who attempted to engage in trickery and self-aggrandizement worthy of a knave, but lacked the cleverness and subtlety necessary to such endeavors. In stark contrast stood his nephew, Mr. Halliday, who had been raised in London and used his contacts there to set himself as a "considerable Merchant in the Island, and had large consignments of Negroes to dispose of. . . . From this Office, and his business, he amassed a large fortune, and lived to purchase all the great estates of his Cozen Dunbar," a turn of events that Hulton considered a case of pure justice.[21]

Hulton's depiction of these several white West Indian men is vehement in its denunciation of them as examples of failed masculinity, but it would be a mistake to take these images entirely at face value. Several factors may have combined to encourage Hulton to inveigh so aggressively against the allegedly corrupting influence of West Indian society. First, it is crucial to keep in mind the fact that he composed his narrative for specifically didactic purposes, not for his own entertainment or that of a wider reading public. His stated goal in describing his adventures in the West Indies, and elsewhere, is to encourage his five sons to "act in all circumstances upon right principles," by presenting them with "a relation of the most interesting parts in my past life . . . the various scenes which I have passed thro', the many difficulties, trials, and temptations, to which I have been exposed."[22] Though by his own account Hulton did encounter some men in Antigua who were worthy of great praise, and some of the more problematic individuals nonetheless showed themselves possessed of at least some good qualities, in his view the very fundamentals of life in the West Indies—the tropical climate, the reliance on enslaved labor, the volatility of a plantation-centered economy, the ethos of lavish hospitality—rendered the tenor of existence in the islands a challenge to the maintenance of high moral standards. As his greatest desire in the "Account" is to instill those very standards into his children, it is perhaps not surprising that he would choose to depict West Indian society as a whole, if not all West Indians in particular, as threatening to the bodily and mental health of the virtuous Englishman.

It is also important to keep in mind the fact that, in the more than two decades that separated Hulton's experiences in Antigua from his discussion of them in the "Account," opinion in the mother country had hardened considerably against the West Indian colonies and their white residents. While the abolitionist movement was by the mid-1780s still very much a minority crusade associated with a small number of radicals, texts such as James Ramsay's *An Essay on the Treatment and Conversion of African Slaves in the British Sugar Colonies* (1784), a damning account of the iniquities of plantation society penned by a clergyman who had lived in the islands for nearly two decades, dovetailed with long-held metropolitan prejudices against West Indian "creoles." Added to that was resentment that some of these morally deficient "creoles" were rich enough to live in great luxury in England, building mansions in Mayfair or Marylebone, buying up great country estates, swarming around the fashionable resort of Bath, and using the power of the "West India lobby" to demand preferential treatment by Parliament. At no point in his text does Hulton oppose slavery, either in the abstract or as practiced in the British colonies. Nevertheless, Hulton was extremely likely to be aware of the fact that, at the time he wrote his memoir, public opinion in England was turning slowly but steadily against slavery, and he may at the very least have wanted to distance himself, textually as well as physically, from places and people who seemed to represent such a definitively un-English mode of life.

Finally, we are well advised to consider Hulton's more recent experiences in Britain's American colonies. In November 1767, almost seven years after his return to England from Antigua, Hulton; his wife, Elizabeth; their infant son, Thomas; and Hulton's sister, Ann, set sail for Boston, where Hulton had been appointed a commissioner of customs.[23] The Hultons were in for a very rough time, as public opinion in the American colonies had been inflamed by the recent imposition of the Townshend duties; Boston was the locus of anti-imperial feeling, and Hulton and his fellow commissioners immediately became extraordinarily unpopular and encountered great difficulty in enforcing the regulations. On three separate occasions between 1768 and 1773 the Hultons and the other commissioners and their families were forced to flee for their safety to Castle William, a fort in Boston Harbor. In July 1776, just days after the Continental Congress declared independence, the family boarded the ship *Aston Hall* and returned to England, where the following year Hulton purchased a thousand-acre farm and a "good and pleasant house" near Andover, Hampshire, where he was to spend the remainder of his life, and where he composed his "Account of Travels."[24]

Hulton had been profoundly shaken by his experiences in Boston, first by his seemingly instant unpopularity among the Bostonians, then by the various riots and disturbances that had caused him to fear for his family's safety, and finally by the seemingly bizarre claims of American independence emanating from Philadelphia. It seems reasonable to infer that Hulton's admittedly traumatic experiences in Boston might have soured him on the entire colonial British American project, encouraging him to think of the men of these settlements, mainland and island alike, not as "Englishmen transplanted," but as men who had proved themselves entirely unwilling or unable to accommodate themselves to what he considered to be the ideal of masculine character and behavior. They were, in his own words, "a most rude, depraved, and degenerate race, and it is a mortification to us that they speak English and can trace themselves from that Stock."[25] But because his "Account" limits itself, for reasons unknown, to his experiences prior to his North American sojourn, it is the West Indians, rather than the Bostonians, who are the principal subjects of his opprobrium. It is, however, also worth noting that back in 1761, while resident in Antigua, Hulton had written in a letter to Nicholson that human society in general was no more than "a good deal of rubbish" that included only a "few diamonds."[26] Once he became a father, though, Hulton was clearly determined to do whatever he needed to do to help his five sons number among those diamonds, and to attain the masculine virtues that Hulton found so lacking wherever he went in Britain and its colonies.

Clearly, a number of factors, both personal and historical, combined to encourage Hulton to depict white West Indian men as examples of defective masculinity. Not only was Hulton likely to have been influenced by contemporary discourses that vilified the nature of such men, but the more negative of his images of the men he encountered, though intended primarily for didactic purposes, have been taken by scholars essentially at face value as a thoroughgoing indictment of the moral character of men in the island colonies. But such an interpretation misses out on the larger picture Hulton labored to present; although the "Account of Travels" includes the stinging discussions of bad examples of manliness described above, it also contains a series of extremely laudatory and sympathetic portraits of Antiguan men who were not "rubbish" but rather "diamonds."

"Gentlemen of Strong Natural Parts"

Not surprisingly, the Antiguans with whom Hulton formed the closest relationships were those who were least interested in a giddy round of social life, and who were fiscally conservative without being miserly, both attributes associated with the positive performance of Anglo-American masculinity. No one whom Hulton encountered in the course of his four-year sojourn in Antigua impressed him as much as Samuel Martin, who in addition to owning of one of the island's largest and most profitable estates, had served as colonel of the Antiguan militia and as speaker of its House. According to Hulton, Antigua was "obliged to Colo. Martin for many of its best laws," and for the encouragement of the militia. To these public benefits was added Martin's authorship of "the best treatise on planting the Sugar Cane," the *Essay on Plantership*. Just as important, Martin tempered sociability with sobriety. Although he enjoyed welcoming visitors to Green Castle, his plantation in the Shekerley Hills on the island's southern end, he absented himself from the parties of men like Blizard and Ottley. To Hulton, Martin represented all the most positive aspects of planter masculinity:

> The Scholar, and the Gentleman, shewed themselves at all times in his conversation, and behavior. . . . [He was] courteous to all, humane to his Negroes . . . and lived in a regular performance of the divine, social, and personal duties. So many polite and liberal endowments, so much publick spirit, and manly exertion of his talents; so much strictness in moral conduct, so much of a Virtuous and Christian behavior, are seldom united in one Man.[27]

Hulton found it distressing that Martin, although greatly respected by his fellow Antiguans, was not a truly popular figure within island society; his probity, industry, and benevolence appear to have endeared him more to such serious-minded visitors as Hulton and the Scots traveler Janet Schaw than to the young men of his community. Although, according to Hulton, Martin was "extremely fond of young company," in Antigua, "to be popular, a man must not only keep an hospitable table, but be the jolly companion"—in other words, to be willing to entertain in a lavish and boisterous style, unlike the quiet sort of sociability preferred by Martin.

Hulton described George Thomas, the governor of the Leeward Islands, in a similar vein: Thomas was "a character rather respected, than beloved; very sensible and of strict integrity; but severe and proud, haughty and distant, with a turn for satire." While Hulton found much to admire in Thomas's character, and he was generally esteemed by Antiguans as one of their more honest and capable leaders, his was not the type of personality most liked by his neighbors, not least because "he was considered parsimonious, and not living equal to his rank, but he was sober and temperate, not fond of profusion."[28]

Despite his preference for the staid company of austere older men such as Martin and Thomas, Hulton was not immune to the charms of somewhat livelier company. He and the governor both greatly enjoyed socializing with Arthur Freeman, a member of the island's council. Hulton had first met Freeman during his travels in Germany in 1752, and deemed him "a very sensible, well accomplished man, with a great vein for raillery and satire," who was notable for his "liberal endowments and captivating talents."[29] These qualities endeared him not only to Hulton and Thomas (he "suited the Governor's taste and was his most intimate companion"), but also to Margaret, Thomas's nineteen-year-old daughter, so much that Freeman, then aged thirty-eight, soon "made a conquest" of her. Thomas was moved to fury by the fact that the man he considered his closest friend had "in defiance of the laws of Great Britain and of this Island, in contempt of the respect due to him as his Majesty's Governor . . . and in violation of the laws of hospitality [had] basely and treacherously seduced his daughter . . . by prevailing upon her to make a private elopement." So distraught was the governor that he not only punished Freeman by suspending him from the council, but he himself resigned his post and went to England, where he made an unsuccessful attempt to prevent the Privy Council from restoring Freeman to his seat.[30]

One might have expected that a man as self-consciously upright as Hulton would have sympathized with Thomas, and execrated Freeman, but in fact he continued to think well of the latter, and found it not at all surprising that the rather sheltered Margaret would have fallen in love with him, particularly as there were "not many amusements for a young Lady in so small a society." In Hulton's opinion, the blame for this turn of events rested entirely with Thomas, as "to imagine the Governor could not suspect such a circumstance taking place, must be to suppose him ignorant of human nature." Specifically, why should Thomas "resent so highly that preference shewn by his daughter to the character to which he had given the highest approbation?" Hulton pronounced himself disgusted that Thomas had "sacrificed his friendship and tenderness to his pride," but was happy to report that eventually the governor was reconciled with his son-in-law, and made him and Margaret a generous financial bequest.[31]

By overcoming his injured pride and making peace with Freeman, Thomas proved himself willing to jettison an excessively rigid style of fatherhood and to replace it with the one better suited to the emerging cultural style of sentiment and sensibility. Similarly, Samuel Martin won Hulton's praise by seeming to epitomize the ideal father, one who was simultaneously firm and gentle, who kept his children, servants, and slaves under strict scrutiny, yet treated them with warm affection, attempting to bring out their individual talents without pushing them to take on new responsibilities before they were ready to do so. Such men added greatly to the happiness and success not only of their families, but also that of their community and of society in general. Similarly worthy of praise, in Hulton's view, were families such as the Warners, descendants of Sir Thomas Warner, the first governor of the Leewards. This cohort of seven brothers and three sisters had clearly benefited from the positive example set by virtuous parents, as all ten siblings were "living, married, and settled on that spot [Antigua]. The Men filled the chief publick offices in the Island, and the Ladies were very sensible, well bred, agreeable Women," despite the fact that all ten Warners "had never been off the Island." Encountering individuals such as Martin, Thomas, Freeman, and the Warners should, it seem, have encouraged Hulton to believe that Antigua and the other British colonies in the West Indies were in no way inimical to the flourishing of recognizably English forms of virtuous manhood; he went so far as to assert that "there were many Gentlemen of strong natural parts, as well as of liberal endowments, in the Society, at the time I lived at Antigua."[32]

Conclusion

As we have seen, although Hulton's narrative includes plenty of examples of Antiguan men whose immaturity, frivolity, poor judgment, bad financial management, and downright meanness rendered them not only seriously deficient as husbands and fathers, but also "banes of society" in general, it also includes a number of depictions of men who merited the highest possible praise for their performance in all aspects of genteel masculinity. Even some of the men who are portrayed as setting a bad example earned from Hulton some praise for their high intellect or good nature, with only Mr. Dunbar coming across as entirely lacking in redeeming qualities. Moreover, evil attributes do not seem to run in families. Despite Mr. Dunbar's many failings as a businessman and a human being, his nephew Halliday reaped enormous and, to Hulton, deserved success. And while Halliday's predecessor as collector of customs was apparently "sordid and wretched," because his wife was a "very sensible, well accomplished woman," their two daughters, "no doubt from the Mother's instructions, and example . . . were formed to be very amiable, as they both married to honorable connections in England."[33] Why, then, does Hulton claim that he has "great reason to be thankful, for the wonderful preservation of my life, and morals, thro' the dangers of the climate, and contagion of vicious manners, in the West Indies, [and] that I was snatched away from thence, before my health was impaired, or my principles of piety, and humanity, effaced"?[34]

It is important to note that, while Hulton was unmarried and childless throughout his Antiguan sojourn, by the time he penned his narrative he was the father of five sons.[35] Becoming a father, particularly of sons to whom he was expected to serve as a role model, appears to have rendered the already rather straitlaced Hulton still more censorious, and his principal goal in writing down his experiences was to offer his boys "Sketches, with a View to Fix Right Principles in the Minds of Children, and Lead Them to Just Sentiments, and a Virtuous Conduct." With this aim in mind, he devoted much of his narrative to description of men whose character and behavior would provide illuminating negative examples, although he assured his sons, "You must not think my dear Children, that I mention any characters as a record of their crimes or misfortunes; but as a lesson to you."[36] Moreover, in the three decades that separated Hulton's time in Antigua from his composition of the "Account of Travels," metropolitan opinion had become increasingly critical of the practice of slavery, and of the supposedly morally debilitating effects slaveholding exerted on men's characters; the reading public of the 1780s was considerably more receptive to blistering critiques such as James Ramsay's *Essay on the Treatment and Conversion of African Slaves in the British Sugar Colonies* than toward treatises such as Samuel Martin's *Essay on Plantership*, which insisted that profit and humanity were not irreconcilable in the context of plantation slavery. Finally, Hulton's experiences, and those of his family, in revolutionary Boston had rendered him far more cynical, not only about American colonists, but about human morality in general, encouraging him to see society as far more typified by "rubbish" than by "diamonds." Under such circumstances, it is far from surprising that, in composing his didactic narrative, he was quick to heap opprobrium on the characters of many of his West Indian acquaintances, and even to claim that the islands were afflicted with a "contagion of vicious manners."

Yet Hulton's description of his life in Antigua shows clearly that "principles of piety and humanity" were not entirely lacking in West Indian society:

some individuals preserved spotless characters, and even the children of the most problematic parents could learn from the examples of better mentors to attain a high standard of personal morality. The same could be said of colonial West Indian society more generally: as newer scholarship has shown, people of enlightened sensibility were indeed to be found in these colonies, and while the common image of the creole planter as uncultured and brutal was not without basis in fact, to reduce all West Indian men to this stereotype represents a dramatic oversimplification of the lived experience of these small but financially and geopolitically crucial British settlements. Hulton's primary intention in his "Account of Travels" may have been to turn the minds of his sons toward "Right Principles," "Just Sentiments, and a Virtuous Conduct," and despite his often self-contradictory rhetoric, his narrative presents a strong argument that such virtues were far from absent from the minds of creole men.

NOTES

1. Hulton's "Account" is Codex Eng. 74 at the John Carter Brown Library, Providence, Rhode Island. The only historian whose published work draws on Hulton's narrative is Michal J. Rozbicki, in "The Curse of Provincialism: Negative Perceptions of Colonial American Plantation Gentry," *Journal of Southern History* 63 (1997): 727–752; and *The Complete Colonial Gentleman: Cultural Legitimacy in Plantation America* (Charlottesville: University Press of Virginia, 1998).

2. Hulton, born in 1731, was the son of an affluent mercantile family in Chester. Following his twentieth birthday, he spent some time living in Germany and in France, then moved to London in order to lobby the Duke of Newcastle for a government appointment. In January 1756 the Duke secured him the post of deputy comptroller of the customs at St. John's, and Hulton set sail for the islands at the end of April of the same year. See Hulton, "Account"; and Wallace Brown, "An Englishman Views the American Revolution: The Letters of Henry Hulton, 1769–1776," *Huntington Library Quarterly* 36 (1972): 2.

3. This chapter, however, builds on some recent scholarship that offers a more nuanced picture of white masculinity in the English West Indies. See Sarah M. S. Pearsall, "'The late flagrant instance of depravity in my Family': The Story of an Anglo-Jamaican Cuckold," *William and Mary Quarterly* s3:60 (2003): 549–582; April Shelford, "'Birds of a Feather': Natural History and Male Sociability in Eighteenth-Century Jamaica," unpublished paper presented to the Seventh Symposium of the Social History Project, University of the West Indies, Mona, Jamaica, March 2006; and Natalie Zacek, "Cultivating Virtue: Samuel Martin and the Paternal Ideal in the Eighteenth-Century English West Indies," *Wadabagei* 10 (2007): 8–31.

4. For a summary and evaluation of this emerging historiography, see Toby L. Ditz, "The New Men's History and the Peculiar Absence of Gendered Power: Remedies from Early American Gender History," *Gender and History* 16 (2004): 1–35.

5. On New England, see Thomas A. Foster, *Sex and the Eighteenth-Century Man: Massachusetts and the History of Sexuality in America* (Boston: Beacon Press, 2006); Foster, "Deficient Husbands: Manhood, Sexual Incapacity, and Male Marital Sexuality in Seventeenth-Century New England," *William and Mary Quarterly* s3:56 (1999): 723–744; Richard Godbeer, "The Cry of Sodom: Discourse, Intercourse, and Desire in Colonial New England," *William and Mary Quarterly* s3:52 (1995): 259–286; Anne S. Lombard, *Making Manhood: Growing Up Male in Colonial New England* (Cambridge: Harvard University Press, 2003); and Lisa Wilson, *Ye Heart of a Man: The Domestic Life of Men in Colonial New England* (New Haven: Yale University Press, 1999). Important recent work by, among others, Toby Ditz and Clare Lyons has explored the crafting of male occupational and sexual identities in eighteenth-century Philadelphia, and studies by scholars such as Janet Moore Lindman, Rhys Isaac, and Lorri Glover have added depth and nuance to our understanding of white masculinity in the slave societies of the southern mainland colonies. For Philadelphia, see Ditz, "Shipwrecked; or, Masculinity Imperiled: Mercantile Representations of Failure and the Gendered Self in Eighteenth-Century Philadelphia," *Journal of American History* 81 (1994): 51–80, and Lyons, "Mapping an Atlantic Sexual Culture: Homoeroticism in Eighteenth-Century Philadelphia," *William and Mary Quarterly* s3:60 (2003): 119–154. On the South, see Lindman, "Acting the Manly Christian: White Evangelical Masculinity in Revolutionary Virginia," *William and Mary Quarterly* s3:57 (2000): 393–416; Isaac, *Landon Carter's Uneasy Kingdom: Revolution and Rebellion on a Virginia Plantation* (New York: Oxford University Press, 2004); and Glover, *All Our Relations: Blood Ties and Emotional Bonds Among the Early South Carolina Gentry* (Baltimore: Johns Hopkins University Press, 2000).

6. Trevor Burnard, "Theater of Terror: Domestic Violence in Thomas Thistlewood's Jamaica," in Christine Daniels and Michael V. Kennedy, eds., *Over the Threshold: Intimate Violence in Early America* (New York: Routledge, 1999), 244.

7. David S. Shields, *Civil Tongues and Polite Letters in British America* (Chapel Hill: University of North Carolina Press, 1997).

8. Rozbicki, "Curse of Provincialism"; Burnard, *Creole Gentlemen: The Maryland Elite, 1691–1776* (New York: Routledge, 2002); Richard Pares, *A West-India Fortune* (London: Longmans, Green and Co., 1950), 108; and Burnard, *Mastery, Tyranny, and Desire: Thomas Thistlewood and His Slaves in the Anglo-Jamaican World* (Chapel Hill: University of North Carolina Press, 2004), 69.

9. Edward Ward, *A Trip to Jamaica: With a True Character of the People and the Island* (London: J. How, 1700), 16.

10. Pittis, *The Jamaica Lady, or, The Life of Bavia* (London: Thomas Bickerton, 1720), 35.
11. Hulton, "Account," 49.
12. Ibid., 51.
13. Ibid., 63–66.
14. Ibid., 77–78.
15. Ibid., 72. Chief Justice Blizard was a kinsman of the Mr. Blizard whom Hulton criticized for his partying ways. In the mid-eighteenth century, the white population of Antigua was approximately 3,500. See Franklin W. Knight, *The Slave Societies of the Caribbean* (New York: UNESCO, 1997), 48.
16. Hulton, "Account," 73, 74.
17. Ibid., 72.

18. Ibid., 57.

19. Ibid., 58. Dunbar's machinations extended beyond his own children to his other kin, whom he attempted to manipulate for his own financial benefit. Some years prior to Hulton's arrival in Antigua, Dunbar had developed a scheme by which he "contrived to marry" his nephew Thomas to Lucy Chester Parke, the natural daughter of the murdered Leeward governor Colonel Daniel Parke, in the hopes of getting access to the "considerable estate" that he believed Parke had left her. So keen was Dunbar to make this match that he readily accepted the humiliating demand presented in Colonel Parke's will that, should Lucy marry, her husband must take her surname if he wished to have any legal rights to the estate. Although Thomas proved himself willing to obey his uncle and rename himself Thomas Dunbar Parke, his death at a fairly young age frustrated his uncle's ambitions, as did the fact that Colonel Parke had left enormous debts over whose payment Dunbar and Lucy squabbled for decades with her father's legitimate daughters and their husbands in Virginia. See Hulton, "Account," 57. The Parke case was not resolved until 1757, when the Privy Council ruled that Daniel Parke Custis, Colonel Parke's grandson and the first husband of the future Martha Washington, was not liable for his grandfather's debts. See George Adrian Washburne, *Imperial Control of the Administration of Justice in the Thirteen American Colonies, 1684–1776* (New York: Columbia University Press, 1923), 140–142.

20. Hulton, "Account," 58.

21. Ibid., 62–63.

22. Ibid., 3. Engaging in "strict scrutiny" of a son's character and behavior, and emphasizing the "manifold faults" to which he might fall victim, was a common strategy among elite Anglo-American men of the later eighteenth century, as exemplified by the widely read letter of Philip Dormer Stanhope, Earl of Chesterfield, to his son. See Sarah M. S. Pearsall, *Atlantic Families: Lives and Letters in the Later Eighteenth Century* (New York: Oxford University Press, 2008), 124.

23. Ann Hulton's letters from Boston are reprinted as *Letters of a Loyalist Lady* (Cambridge: Harvard University Press, 1927).

24. Brown, "Englishman," 3–7.

25. Brown, "Englishman," part II, *Huntington Library Quarterly* 36 (1973): 147.

26. Brown, "Englishman," 10.

27. Hulton, "Account," 54. See also Zacek, "Cultivating Virtue."

28. Hulton, "Account," 69.

29. Ibid.

30. Janet Schaw, *The Journal of a Lady of Quality*, ed. Charles M. Andrews and Evangeline Walker Andrews (New Haven: Yale University Press, 1921), 102; and Andrew J. O'Shaughnessy, "The Stamp Act Crisis in the British Caribbean," *William and Mary Quarterly* s3:51 (1994), 220.

31. Hulton, "Account," 69.

32. Ibid., 55.

33. Ibid., 61–62.

34. Ibid., 140.

35. In 1766, Hulton married Elizabeth Preston, and the couple's children, born between 1766 and 1778, were Thomas, Henry, Edward, Preston, and George.

36. Brown, "Englishman," 2; and Hulton, "Account," 60.

7

"Impatient of Subordination" and "Liable to Sudden Transports of Anger"

*White Masculinity and
Homosocial Relations with Black Men
in Eighteenth-Century Jamaica*

TREVOR BURNARD

Jamaica in the middle of the eighteenth century was a very masculine society. Men outnumbered women in every sector of the population except in the free black population, where women slightly outnumbered men. The number of white men was much greater than the number of white women in the population at large, where 70 percent of whites were men, and especially in the countryside, where 76 percent of whites were men. The disproportion in the slave population between men and women was not so great, with slave men accounting for 53 percent of the slave population of just over two hundred thousand slaves. Men were numerous in the sector of the population aged between twenty and forty, especially in the white population of around twelve to fifteen thousand individuals. In Clarendon Parish in 1788, for example, nearly 80 percent of a white population of six hundred people aged between twenty-one and forty were men.[1]

Given these statistics, it is perhaps not surprising that eighteenth-century Jamaican culture had a distinctly masculinist cast. Patriarchal values were extremely strong, especially among whites. Jamaica was a place where white men (and white men alone) had a degree of freedom to do as they pleased that was unusual even by the standards of the time. Of course, patriarchy was dominant everywhere in British America as the prevailing ideology governing relations between blacks and whites. But patriarchy had a special tone in Jamaica. It was a raw kind of doctrine that was predicated on white male equality and the ability of white men to live in unconstrained ways. Unlike in

Britain or in British America, patriarchal authority as exercised by white men was not shaped by concepts of stewardship; rather, it was shaped by ideas that white men were unconstrained in their actions by social disapproval or by ordinary moral standards.² A white man was assumed to fornicate with black women, drink excessively, gamble and fight, and to cow dependents, not least black men, through the constant and arbitrary application of violence and terror.³ In the long run, of course, the freedom that white men had in Jamaica to do as they pleased and the particular character of male society on the island contributed to metropolitan disdain about the type of society and the type of Britons who flourished there. White men had such power over black dependents that it made them tyrants. To be a white man was to be pleasure-seeking, self-aggrandizing, sensuous, and violent.

Abolitionists believed in a different model of manhood to that espoused by eighteenth-century Jamaican planters. One of the reasons why early abolitionists campaigned against the Atlantic slave trade was that they found the society that slaveholders created morally objectionable. James Ramsay, an early abolitionist and ardent conservative, for example, denigrated planters as belonging to "the kingdom of I." His initial involvement in abolition arose from his revulsion at planters' self-involved and antireligious behavior.⁴ Ramsay's phrase suggests that the problem with the West Indies was that it was the home of excessive individualism, of self-expression and narcissistic indulgence run riot. But for most white men—the majority of the white population who were recently arrived migrants in their early adulthood, who sought their fortune on the island, and who wanted to have a good time while doing so—the patriarchal privileges they were afforded made living in a society full of brutalized black men and women, likely at any time to rise up and kill them, worthwhile.

Despite the dominance of men in the Jamaican population, and despite the masculinist cast of Jamaican culture, masculinity in early Jamaica remains largely hidden. We know a lot about what white men did, in part because it is through their words that we get an understanding of how Jamaican society operated. Yet we seldom look at white men through the prism of masculinity. We know even less about black men, as men, than we do about white men. Works on Jamaican slavery sometimes deal with women as a specific category of inquiry; virtually no book, however, lists slave men as a separate category in its index. The male slave is the generic slave, rather than a specific subject of scholarly investigation.⁵

Gender studies relating to the early Caribbean are still "first wave" studies that concentrate overwhelmingly on the relations between men and women, when they concentrate on men at all. Gender history and gender analysis have begun to transform how we look at West Indian history and literature in the seventeenth and eighteenth centuries.[6] Most emphasis, however, has been placed on recovering female experience in the past rather than looking at men and masculinity.[7]

This chapter explores one aspect of masculinity in early Jamaica. My contention is that white male identity was not only forged in relationship to race (their position as white people, superior to all people of African descent) but also in relation to gender (their position as men, with patriarchal privileges over women, both black and white, some of which were shared with black men). The special tone of patriarchal relations in Jamaica—predicated on white libertinism and white egalitarianism as well on the principle that all men had special rights over women, or at least black women, which they could exercise by right of their being men—gave white men a great deal of freedom to behave as they pleased. It also connected them, in ways that many white men occasionally found troubling, with the interests and desires of black men.

White men were not just white but were also men. This is an obvious truism but it is not often recognized. White male identity in Jamaica is often considered as being constructed out of white men's relations with either white women or black women, but is seldom seen within the context of their relationships with black men. In this respect, this chapter breaks new ground by examining white men's attitudes to black men within the context of gender rather than race. White men generally had a very low opinion of the character of black men: they characterized them as feckless, thieving, animalistic, and stupid. But they also recognized that black men had patriarchal privileges both in the workplace and in family life. They also recognized, sometimes reluctantly, that black men possessed some characteristics that they themselves applauded and thought also applied to themselves, notably great courage in the presence of physical pain. White men were forced to accept, usually unwillingly, that the common attribute of maleness united them with black men in a number of ideologically uncomfortable ways. In particular, they were aware, through metropolitan criticism of them as people undergoing significant "Africanization," that their shared participation, alongside black men, in a sexual culture that insisted on wide sexual access to black women undermined their insistent claims that they were Englishmen, entitled to all the rights and privileges given to Englishmen in Britain.

Nature of Patriarchy

How might we look at the issue of masculinity in early Jamaica? One way of understanding gender relations and masculinity during the eighteenth century is to examine what men did and compare it to what women did. Gender relations were sharply polarized in Jamaica, especially in the white population. White men were hypermasculine while white women were supposed to be ultrafeminine.[8] Both genders, however, were parasitical insofar as they depended on black people to do most of the hard work of plantation labor. On the plantations, men were the owners and managers. From the late seventeenth century, white men were removed from doing fieldwork alongside slaves. They became part of the plantation managerial class, where their main role was to provide the fierce discipline that kept the plantation world going.[9] White women were removed from working on the plantation even earlier than men.[10] Jennifer Morgan has shown how by the mid-seventeenth century in Barbados, Englishmen felt uncomfortable about allowing white women to work in the fields, as this was so alien to customary gender expectations derived from English experience. Indeed, their ambivalence to white female workers, Morgan posits, was one reason for the shift away from indentured servitude to African chattel slavery.[11]

By contrast, the differences between what black men did and what black women did were greater than is usually suggested in the literature on Caribbean slavery. Both genders, of course, worked mostly within the plantation economy. Initially, men and women were undifferentiated in what they did: both worked in the fields as ganged laborers. Over time, however, the proportion of men who worked in the field declined considerably. Planters increasingly tried to eliminate plantation expenses by training men into trades so that they could do plantation work in-house. Consequently, many men—perhaps 25 percent by the third quarter of the eighteenth century—were removed from the field to become tradesmen. In addition, planters delegated some of their authority in the field to slave drivers, who were almost universally male. The work options open to women were more limited. Apart from a few women who became domestic servants, most women labored in the field, in lowly positions. The result was that whereas over three-quarters of slave women in total and over 90 percent of women on sugar estates worked in the field, only two-thirds of men were field-workers. This meant that women made up the majority of any field gang. Race was more important than gender in determining slave experience, but gender was not unimportant. White men believed that authority should be in the hands of men and assumed that slave men would be leaders in the slave community. They gave them the best jobs and allowed them authority over slave women. As long as slave men's authority did not interfere with the ability of white men to do as they pleased on plantations, masters were happy to allow black men to exercise a degree of patriarchal dominance within slave communities.[12] The particular circumstances of enslavement made it impossible for traditional African men's assumptions about the role of women to be translated perfectly into Jamaican slave culture, as Michael Mullin points out.[13] One of the results of changed relations of power between the genders was marked domestic discord in slave communities. Nevertheless, black men were patriarchs of a sort within slave families and communities. Planters expected them to be dominant, and organized their workforces in such a way that slave men had more power than slave women. What little evidence we have from slaves directly about what the proper balance of power should be between men and women suggests that black men also expected to be bosses within their own patriarchal kingdoms.[14]

The problem we have, of course, in looking at what men did and what masculinity meant in early Jamaica is the problem of evidence. One way of approaching the question of the role black men played in the colonial white male imaginary in Jamaica has been put forward for neighboring Saint-Domingue by Doris Garraway, who sets this colony within the context of libertinism. Garraway in turn draws on work done by Joan Dayan, who argues that Saint-Domingue resembled in reality what the Marquis de Sade visualized only in the imaginary. She suggests that Sade's most horrific scenarios of terror and pleasure may have been inspired by what was known about French colonial slavery: "Sade brought the plantation hell and its excesses into enlightenment Europe. . . . The debauchery and unbridled tyranny of Sade's libertines have their sources in the emblematic Creole planters, dedicated to the heady interests of pleasure, greed and abandon."[15]

No direct link connects Sade to the colonies. But whether Sade had any experience of life in Saint-Domingue in developing his theory of libertinage is less significant than the fact that there were plentiful echoes of Sadean libertinism in West Indian plantation societies. Examples of white male psychopathic behavior on the Sadean model exist in both Saint-Domingue and Jamaica. The most notorious psychopath in Jamaica was Lewis Hutchinson, a Hanover planter who reputedly killed forty passing travelers in the 1760s and early 1770s. He was hanged in 1773 after killing a white man. Hutchinson was defiant even in death, leaving one hundred pounds in gold at the foot of the scaffold when he was executed for the erection of a monument inscribed with the following couplet:

Their sentence, pride, and malice, I defy;
Despise their power, and like a Roman, die.[16]

Garraway examines the roles of desire and sexuality in mediating colonial power relations through conceiving colonial Saint-Domingue as a "libertine colony." By libertinism, she means a society that was a space of immorality, religious heresy, violence, and sexual license, a place where French emigrants reacted to their absolute power over black slaves by fashioning new identities outside the bounds of traditional authority, morality, and social and sexual codes. She sets libertinism in relation to the oppression of black and brown women.[17] I prefer to see libertinism as the basis for a radical egalitarianism through which ordinary white men could act out their desires without moderating their appetites by deference to established authority.

When we talk of masculinity in this period, we really need to talk in the plural—masculinities—rather than in the singular. Tim Hitchcock and Michele Cohen argue that one of the noticeable features of models of masculinity in the early to mid-eighteenth century was their very multiplicity. It was this threatening multiplicity that helped provoke the late eighteenth-century emergence of the "separate spheres" ideology. The appeal of this ideology lay in binaries that simplified the daunting complexities of modern life.[18] Norbert Elias suggests that realizing there were multiple ideas of manhood in the early modern world helps us to understand how the "civilizing" process worked. He sees a growing conflict between a plebeian and a genteel masculine culture in this period.[19] Such conflict was less noticeable in Jamaica than in western Europe. In a society such as Jamaica, where racial divisions were so profound, white cultural homogeneity was an important means whereby white men could maintain white solidarity. Contemporary observers stressed the extent to which white men shared a common culture in Jamaica, and the extent to which divisions between whites were discouraged in favor of a remarkable degree of white solidarity. Edward Long—no fan of democracy but an astute observer of white society in Jamaica—argued that there were no distinctions among whites, save those between good and bad citizens.[20]

Male homosociality has not been a conspicuous topic in recent scholarship on white Jamaican men. What has fascinated scholars, which also fascinated contemporaries, is what Saidiya Hartman calls "the phantasmal ensnaring agency of the lascivious black."[21] Edward Long was one contemporary observer, for example, who was fixated on the subject of white men's relations with black and brown women. He despairingly lamented that white men preferred to "riot in these goatish embraces" of "scheming black Jezebels" than "share the pure and lawful bliss derived from matrimonial, mutual love."[22]

Homosociality

Two aspects of male culture, however, are seldom discussed in evaluations of Jamaican gender relations. First, how did shared white male assumptions tie white society together? Second, how did white men define their masculinity not just in opposition to women, both black and white, but also in opposition to black men? In important respects what defined white men most of all was that they were not black men. It is true that women, especially the free brown woman, were figures of tension in Jamaican society. But we can also learn much from examining how white men viewed themselves in light of how they viewed black men. One thing we learn is how central violence was in securing white rule on the island. Another thing we discover is that ideas of masculinity complicated white men's relations with black men in the same way their sexual urges complicated their relationship with black women. In particular, white men veered between wanting to create as much distance between themselves and black men as they could while accepting that both black men and white men were participants, albeit unequal ones, in a shared culture of patriarchy.

Violence and freedom were intimately tied for Jamaican white men. White men differentiated themselves from black men in being able to both give out beatings and also manfully to receive them. As William Dorrill told Thomas Thistlewood on Thistlewood's arrival to the island in 1750, "in this Country it is highly necessary for a Man to fight once or twice, to keep Cowards from putting upon him."[23] Being able to stand up for oneself was a crucial measure of masterfulness. White Jamaicans were a combative people, "liable to sudden transports of anger." That white men were naturally violent was not surprising in a society in which slavery imbued slave owners and all those who controlled slaves (in other words, almost all white men) with "something of a haughty Disposition." As Charles Leslie commented, a noticeable feature of the white male character was that white men "required Submission" from all around them. Moreover, every man insisted on being the "absolute master of himself and his actions."[24]

White men prided themselves on their egalitarianism, which manifested itself in positive ways. They venerated liberty and were impatient with subordination to the will of others, be that other imperial governments or fellow white Jamaicans. It also manifested itself in negative ways, such as in sensitivity to insults, an extreme narcissism, and, for conservatives, a regrettable tendency to "the levelling principle . . . that entrenches upon the duties of society."²⁵ But what all commentators noted was that white men insisted that other white men not treat them in a patronizing manner as subordinates. Bryan Edwards noted that "a marked and predominant character to all the white residents" was "an independent spirit and a display of conscious equality throughout all ranks and conditions" so that "the poorest white person . . . approaches his employer with an extended hand."²⁶

That all white men, whatever their wealth and social standing, were in important respects equal had its roots in material realities. High white mortality made white men a scarce commodity. Because planters always needed white managers to oversee their slave forces, white men were always able to find employment. Rich white men were so anxious to secure the services of white male workers that poor white men had significant economic bargaining power, especially if they were tough enough to be able to take on the daunting task of controlling, punishing, and terrorizing black men as plantation overseers. That economic bargaining power was transformed into social, if not political, power. Poor white men insisted that the legendary hospitality of planters be extended to all whites regardless of circumstance. White men were always entitled to free lodgings, free meals, and often admittance to planters' social entertainments if they turned up unannounced at a planter's house. In a society where only 5 percent of the population in rural areas was white, whiteness had an inestimable value. Bryan Edwards acknowledged as much when he attributed Jamaicans' sense of conscious equality to "the preeminence and distinction which are necessarily attached even to the complexion of a white Man, in a country where the complexion, generally speaking, distinguishes freedom from slavery."²⁷

Whiteness was attached very closely to mastery, a key eighteenth-century component of masculinity. What made a man a man was the ability to control other men. Most white men, whether owners of slaves or merely men in charge of other men's slaves, had that power. Mastery extended very far down into all white social ranks. When almost all whites commanded slaves, then mastery and whiteness went together. Being a "master" in eighteenth-century society allowed ordinary white men to appropriate the language and behavior of patriarchs, even when they themselves were ostensibly dependents. The ubiquity of white control over slaves contributed to an "impatience with subordination" and meant that "men accustomed to be looked upon as a superior race of beings to slaves submit with reluctance, if they submit at all, to be treated as if they enjoyed no will of their own."[28]

White equality had some attractive aspects. White men were lively, generous, hospitable, and fond of pleasure, but it was not an unalloyed blessing. It made for an exceptionally narcissistic society. What rampant individualism and devotion to the main chance meant for individual white character was that white men tended to be egalitarian tyrants. Descriptions of white men focused on how they were indolent, self-indulgent, and full of overbearing pride. If they were warm and effusive toward their friends, they were also proud and touchy about their prerogatives, a group of men who "gloried in being a turbulent people, impatient of subordination." The privileges that whiteness gave them made them little tyrants, "habituated by Precept and Example, to Sensuality and Despotism."[29]

That despotism could be seen in how they treated their slaves. "No Country excels them," Charles Leslie proclaimed in 1740, "in their barbarous treatment of Slaves, or in the cruel Methods they put them to death."[30] Their sensuality was most obviously manifested in their avid pursuit of black women, an avocation that was shared by men of all classes. Much of white men's interest in black women was as much about power as it was about sexual gratification. White men molested slave women because they could do so without fear of social consequence and because they constantly needed to show slaves the extent of their dominance. The institutional dominance of white men had to be translated into personal dominance. Slave owners needed to show black men in particular that they were strong, virile men who ruled the little kingdoms of white autocracy that were the Jamaican plantations. What better way was there for white men to show who was in control than for them to have the pick of black women whenever they chose?[31]

Of course, black women were the principal victims of white men's sexual adventurism. Black women were frequently forced to have sex with white men. What they got back financially and socially for these ordeals hardly sufficed for the degradation they were forced to endure.[32] But black men suffered too. As white men knew, their violation of slave women breached a common understanding held by both black men and white men that men had a measure of patriarchal dominance over women of their own color. Normally, patriarchal dominance had to be respected. Violations led to difficulties and tensions between white men and black men. But what white men's sexual fascination with black women also did was to align them more closely with the "savages" that they supposed black men to be. In the list of attributes commonly attached to black men that proved for white defenders of slavery the rightness of African enslavement, black men's inordinate desire for women was noted. When white men "rioted in the goatish embraces" of black women they became "goats" themselves, men close to Africans and hence men close to beasts. Fear of Africanization and reversion to barbarity competed always with a desire for Anglicization and an ascent to civility at the heart of white male visions of their cultural futures.[33]

White Patriarchy and Black Male Animality

How did white men avoid being aligned with black men given that both had intimate relationships with black women? They did so through denigration of black male character. For Edward Long, black men were worthless. They were not fit to be compared to the virile, upright specimens of white manhood that were the Jamaican planters, whom he eulogized as perfect in almost very way save their unfortunate infatuation with black women. Black men were "void of genius, and . . . incapable of making any progress in civility and science." Without religion or morality, they were barbarians who treated their children especially barbarously and had no taste "but for women, gormandising, and drinking to excess"—attributes, incidentally, that many white men had in abundance.[34]

Long spent an inordinate amount of time in his history on an ingenious if scientifically ludicrous attempt to place blacks in a Great Chain of Being hierarchy where they were closer to animals than to men. He compares, in more detail than was customary for quasi-scientific tracts on race, African men to orangutans. He meditates on how male orangutans desired black women and tried to take them from African men in the same way that black men desired white women and would take them away from white men if the possibility arose. One unexplored theme of his work, therefore, is how black women were a source of desire for all men, be they white men, black men, or great apes. Significantly, he concentrates on the male rather than on the female orangutan when detailing an experiment to test how close orangutans were to humans in intelligence and understanding. What Long thought was crucial was to deny black men any humanity or intelligence. His determination to think black men naturally stupid helps to explain his lengthy digression in his history where he tried to prove that the free black poet Francis Williams was merely a skilled mimicrist rather than an artist of any talent or originality.[35]

Reducing black men to the status of animals as a means of justifying one's unchristian behavior to them was a common strategy for white Jamaicans, as Philip Morgan attests in his analysis of how Thomas Thistlewood treated his slaves at Vineyard Pen between 1750 and 1751. As Morgan notes, white Jamaicans went further than any other Englishmen in reducing the customary chasm between the animal and human realms. They jettisoned, for example, old injunctions about never giving an animal a Christian name and, more commonly than elsewhere, gave slaves names intended to cast a difference between blacks and whites. Men, in particular, were given first names that were derived from the classics or that were place-names.[36] But even if white Jamaicans came perilously close to considering black men as nothing other than beasts—they singled out in highly pejorative ways the supposed animallike ways of their slaves, such as a willingness to eat inappropriate animals, poor habits and lack of table manners, extreme sexual promiscuity, offensive smell, and "bestial fleece"—they were never able to take away black men's humanity altogether.

White observers did not very often talk about black men as men, but when they did a number of common tropes kept reappearing. Some are unremarkable—black men were thieves, inordinately lazy, suited to be servants, carefree but stupid, and so on. But some say interesting things about the ways that whites were thinking abut the extremes of their own behavior. Significantly, white Jamaicans in the eighteenth century did not use all the stereotypes about black men that became common after slaves received their freedom. They did not, for example, characterize black men in overtly sexual ways, or at least did not do so very often, either as people who were unusually well-endowed or as men who were sexually avaricious for white women. There are a few asides that suggest that black men desired white women, primarily as a means of social mobility, in ways akin to how great apes might aspire to mate with African women. They also assumed that black men were sexual creatures who devoted a lot of their time to having sex or thinking about sex. But such musings were muted and bear only a passing resemblance to the obsessive interest in the sexually rapacious black man common after slaves got their freedom. Indeed, when black men are mentioned in regard to sexual avidity, they are depicted often as victims of overly confident white women who were sexual viragos. One such depiction of innocent black men duped by white women is by Monk Lewis. In a poem called "The Runaway," he described how a black boy called Peter was enticed by a "lily white girl" to run away. Lewis was pardoned by his master, who told him:

> Well, for this once I forgive you—but mind
> With the buckra girls you no more go away
> Though fair without, they're foul within
> Their heart is black, though white their skin.[37]

The Tortured Male Rebel

White writers concentrated more obsessively, however, on how black men coped with violence. What amazed writers most were how steadfast black rebels were when faced with horrific torture. Long and Edwards both noted how slaves executed as rebels in the aftermath of Tacky's Rebellion in 1760 faced death with extraordinary fortitude. In Long's account, it was one of the few times when we see some sneaking admiration for the black man creeping through, as he marvels at the poor man's courage. The nineteenth-century planter and Gothic writer Monk Lewis was similarly impressed by the courage of Plato, a legendary rebel. Plato was one of the few slaves of the eighteenth century to leave a lasting legacy, Lewis noted, as a "tall athletic fellow," good with the ladies, "courageous and a professor of obeah." When he died he mocked his captors, passing away "most heroically, keep[ing] up the terrors of his imposture to the last moment."[38]

The most notorious description of a slave's courage in the face of excruciating torment comes from John Stedman, who described the death of Neptune in Surinam in what Marcus Wood shows was a form of pornographic objectification. Neptune, whose death is imagined in a famous copper engraving by William Blake, was a handsome young carpenter who killed an overseer in a dispute over women. Stedman describes how he was broken alive on the rack, with his limbs severed one by one. What was remarkable was that he "never uttered a groan or a sigh," but cursed his tormentors as a "pack of barbarous rascals." Stedman marveled at how "human nature could go through so much torture, with so much fortitude." Such bravery was "truly astonishing, without it being a mixture of rage, contempt, pride and hopes of going to another place, or at least to be relieved from this, and worse than which I verily believe some Africans know no other Hell."[39]

For Stedman, such bravery brought into question the whole colonial project. If black men could "martyr" themselves without complaint, then what did it say about the men who butchered Neptune and other slave "wretches" so viciously? It is noticeable that Stedman follows his description of Neptune's horrific death by an out-of-place comment, at odds with much of the sentiments in his book, that he is pleased "Britain is the standard of humanity, by being the first nation . . . that attempted the abolition of the slave trade." Even darker thoughts, though, are at work here. Stedman's description of Neptune's dismemberment includes a disturbing scene when the mutilated man offers a soldier eating a piece of white bread some of his own body as meat to accompany his meal: "First pick my hand that was chopped off clean to the bones, Sir. Next begin to myself, till you be glutted, and you'll have both bread and meat which best becomes you." As Stedman would have known, such an invitation mirrored the Christian Eucharist. Such words coming from a brave, tortured slave brought to mind those of Christ on the cross and cast doubt on the whole enterprise of enslavement and racial subordination. In death, black men became not only men but also saints—a most disturbing prospect for sinners such as white planters.[40]

Of course, whites had ways of dispelling the unpleasant thoughts conjured up by black men's ability to appropriate one of the principal characteristics of men—unflinching courage in the face of death. Black men did not utter complaints when being tortured and executed because they were without feeling, writers asserted, and, oddly enough, they were also brave because they had no understanding or fear of the afterlife. Thus courage was a sign of barbarity and animality rather than innate human strength. This equation of courage with animality was easy to pull off in a culture that customarily anthropomorphized animals (e.g., to be brave as a lion was a common phrase). But it still raised questions about how different black men were from white men.

This is clear in Bryan Edwards's poem of the early 1760s imagining the laments of a slave executed for treason following Tacky's Rebellion. Edwards imagines the slave bidding farewell to his wife and imbues him with as much humanity as he can muster. The overall effect is to try and evoke in the reader sensitivity to the black man's plight based on the slave's humanity. In short, Edwards tried to achieve in his poem the usual project of an emotional identification between subject and reader. The dangers of this approach became clear to Edwards later on during his time in Jamaica. The particular culture of Jamaica only worked, he realized, if there was no identification between whites and blacks. Edwards quickly recanted his poem. In a later reprinting of his poems of the 1760s, he belittled his poem as the naive expressions of an innocent only recently removed to Jamaica. Edwards described himself as a newcomer so horrified at the savagery of slave punishments that he felt compelled to empathize with black men. By the 1790s he was a man experienced in West Indian ways. Writing as someone who was about to compose a firsthand testimony of the depredations of rebel slaves in Saint-Domingue, Edwards ruefully regretted that his younger self did not realize in 1760 that the slaves executed in Tacky's Rebellion were vile criminals who deserved all they had coming to them.[41]

The difficulty, of course, with imagining an emotional identification with slave rebels (men identifying with other men) is that it opened up a very real fear about black male violence directed against whites, as in the concluding stanza of an anonymous poem from 1776:

> Some Afric chief will rise who scorning chains
> Racks, tortures, flames, excruciating pains,
> Will lead his injur'd friends to bloody flight,
> And in the flooded carnage take delight,
> Then dear repay us in some vengeful war,
> And give us blood for blood, and scar for scar.[42]

When white men imagined what would push black men over the edge and impel them into rebellion, they focused on two things. One was the malign effect of obeah. Blacks rebelled because their spiritual leaders told them to rebel. Black men were also pushed into rebellion when white men infringed on their patriarchal and sexual rights. John Taylor, an early chronicler of life in Jamaica, argued as early as 1687 that while black men could only be controlled through violence, it was also necessary to ensure them access to black women. He argued, "After a planter hath purchased some twenty, thirty or more Negroa slaves, he first gives to each man a wife, without which they will not be contented, or worke. Then he gives to each man and his wife one half accre of land for them to cleare for themselves."[43]

The Problem with White Patriarchy

Here white men had a problem. While they acknowledged that while black men might have a real grievance as a result of white male sexual opportunism, they were unprepared to take any measures that might lessen white male access to slave women. Their sexual exploits could, in some instances, help white men assure their dominance over slaves, but it also played havoc with some of the principles that undergirded slave management. White men were hardly victims in these circumstances, but they tried to convince themselves that they were not responsible for what they did. Their common assumption was that black women were insatiable sexual enthusiasts. They argued that black women's desire for frequent sexual congress meant they couldn't be victims of rape. They convinced themselves, moreover, that black women were so eager for sex that they manipulated hapless white men (so powerful everywhere, except in the bedroom) through giving or denying sexual favors. Of course, such self-deception hid obvious truths about the effect of their sexual aggression on black people. It was also hardly unique to the Caribbean, as it was common in English dealings with Africans in Britain, Africa, and North America. The effects of white sexual aggression on black women are obvious and well-known. But black women were not the only victims in these sordid encounters. The other victims, at least as white men understood the matter, were black men, whom white men acknowledged had rights over their women that white men should usually acknowledge.

White men may have been scared of black men and may have tried to treat them as invisible units of labor, but they also recognized the universality of patriarchy. They made sure their plantations were roughly balanced in terms of men and women; gave men dominant positions within the slave hierarchy as drivers and tradesmen; and allowed male slaves to recreate as much as possible the sort of sociosexual dynamics of family life that pertained in Africa where, as Caroline Bledsoe argues, "the control of women was central to . . . [social] stratification and social order."[44] Sexual opportunism by white men weakened that modus vivendi by showing black men that there was no area of their lives, even their domestic lives, that was free from white interference. Just as important, it pointed out some worrying aspects of white male culture. It demonstrated that many of the things that could be said about black men—their lack of self-control, their sexual promiscuity, their inability to worry about the consequences of their actions, their lack of concern for others—could also be said about white men. One of the ties that linked white men to black men was that they often shared the same women, the same predatory bonds, the same sexist jokes, and the same patriarchal assumptions.

Masters were convinced that supporting male authority was the way to prevent discord in the slave quarters. They made men head of households and accepted that slave men had rights over their wives and children, analogous to what they considered to be their own rights over white women and children. Yet slave patriarchy was a tender fruit, always likely to be stamped out by masters' assertions of authority and by the overwhelming presumption white Jamaicans made in favor of white men indulging their every desire.

For whites, commonalities between their sexual behavior and the sexual activities of black men raised disturbing questions. As usual with whites in Jamaica, these questions revolved around what they considered the disaster of Africanization—a condition that whites also feared was overwhelming their precarious attachment to English values. One reason why white men might have wanted to keep black men at a distance was because, otherwise, they might realize that the similarities between them showed common connections where white men liked to pretend none existed. Whites needed to understand Africans and how Africans felt and behaved if they were to rule successfully over them. If blacks watched their white masters carefully, so too did white men pay attention to their black charges. If understanding, however, turned into identification, then they risked a much greater project, which was the transformation of Jamaica into a civilized and European country. The commonalities between black men and white men, especially their shared assumptions of rights over women, brought into question very serious issues for whites seeking to define themselves as proper men. Nevertheless, this was not a crisis over masculinity—few groups of men have ever been quite as assured about their masculine prowess as members of Ramsay's "Kingdom of I." This was a crisis over civilization and the possibilities of reverting to barbarism.

That white men and black men were both participants in a remarkably loose sexual culture was an open but dirty secret that white men tried to avoid thinking about. Central to how white men thought of themselves was that they were not just men, not just white people, but Englishmen, with the rights and privileges of liberty-loving Englishman and with the social characteristics that made the English the most upstanding members of western European culture. Englishness, however, was not just a political category; it was increasingly becoming a racial category as well. White Jamaicans were keenly aware that their intercourse—social and sexual—with Africans laid them open to charges that they were not "proper" Englishmen but rather a strange hybrid, transcultured "race" that was far too close, culturally as well as physically, to African peoples for comfort. What they needed to do, as the historian Edward Long urged, was to open up a gap between themselves and black people in order to allay metropolitan suspicions of them as being not quite Englishmen. The particular nature of patriarchy developed in Jamaica—egalitarian and libertine as well as racially tinctured—cast severe doubts on white men's ability to shake off those suspicions of their character.[45]

NOTES

1. Trevor Burnard, *Mastery, Tyranny, and Desire: Thomas Thistlewood and His Slaves in the Anglo-Jamaican World* (Chapel Hill: University of North Carolina Press, 2004), 16–18.

2. For a full description of the workings of patriarchy in the eighteenth-century British world, see Philip D. Morgan, "Three Planters and Thirty Slaves: Perspectives on Slavery in Virginia, South Carolina, and Jamaica, 1750–1790" in Winthrop D. Jordan and Sheila Skemp, eds., *Race and Family in the Colonial South* (Oxford: University of Mississippi Press, 1987), 37–79 . See also Sarah Pearsall, "'The late flagrant instance of depravity in my Family': The Story of an Anglo-Jamaican Cuckold," *William and Mary Quarterly*, 3rd ser., 60 (2003), 549–82, for a different view of eighteenth-century planter patriarchy.

3. Burnard, *Mastery, Tyranny, and Desire*, 83–84.

4. James Ramsay, "Motives for the Improvement of the Sugar Colonies," Additional MSS 27621, British Library, ff. 44, 69.

5. Take, for instance, Vincent Brown's book on the cultural history of death in Jamaica during the period of slavery. His index has a space for "slave women" but slave men are collapsed into slavery in general. Vincent Brown, *The Reaper's Garden: Death and Power in the World of Atlantic Slavery* (Cambridge, Mass.: Harvard University Press, 2008).

6. Hilary McD. Beckles, *Natural Rebels: A Social History of Enslaved Black Women in Barbados* (New Brunswick, N.J.: Rutgers University Press, 1989); Bernard Moitt, *Women and Slavery in the French Antilles, 1635–1848* (Bloomington: Indiana University Press, 2001); Jennifer Morgan, *Laboring Women: Reproduction and Gender in New World Slavery* (Philadelphia: University of Pennsylvania Press, 2004); Marietta Morrissey, *Slave Women in the New World: Gender Stratification in the Caribbean* (Lawrence: University of Kansas Press, 1988); Barbara Bush, *Slave Women in Caribbean Society, 1650–1838* (Bloomington: Indiana University Press, 1990).

7. For an example of the type of work much needed for Jamaica, see the treatment of masculinity in Kathleen M. Brown, *Good Wives, Nasty Wenches, and Anxious Patriarchs: Gender, Race, and Power in Colonial Virginia* (Chapel Hill: University of North Carolina Press, 1996). For Jamaica, see remarks on slave men in Michael Mullin, *Africa in America: Slave Acculturation and Resistance in the American South and the British Caribbean, 1736–1831* (Urbana: University of Illinois Press, 1992), 171–72; and Orlando Patterson, *The Sociology of Slavery: An Analysis of the Origins, Development, and Structure of Negro Slave Society in Jamaica* (London: MacGibbon and Kee, 1967).

8. See Kathleen Wilson, *The Island Race: Englishness, Empire, and Gender in the Eighteenth Century* (Routledge: New York, 2003); and Wilson, "The Performance of Freedom: Maroons and the Colonial Order in Eighteenth-Century Jamaica and the Atlantic Sound," *William and Mary Quarterly*, 3rd ser., 66 (2009), 45–86, for nuanced work on femininity and masculinity in eighteenth-century Jamaica.

9. Michael Craton and James Walvin, *A Jamaican Plantation: The History of Worthy Park, 1670–1970* (London: W. H. Allen, 1970), 47–49.

10. When I first looked at what this process of being removed from active involvement in the plantation economy meant, I concluded that women were largely irrelevant in the plantation economy and that their major role was less economic than ideological: they were the reproducers of whiteness as mothers of white children. Such a conclusion is too sweeping, works only for women in the countryside, and ignores a growing body of evidence that many white women were economically and sexually independent and similar in kind, if not in visibility, to the brown mulatresses whose place in Jamaican society has been the subject of considerable scholarly interest. See Trevor Burnard, "Inheritance and Independence: Women's Status in Early Colonial Jamaica," *William and Mary Quarterly*, 3rd. ser., 48 (1991), 112; Burnard, "'Gay and Agreeable Ladies': White Women in Mid-Eighteenth-Century Kingston, Jamaica," *Wadabagei* 9 (2006), 27–49; Kay Dian Kriz, *Slavery, Sugar, and the Culture of Refinement: Picturing the British West Indies, 1700–1840* (New Haven, Conn.: Yale University Press, 2008), 37–70; and Kathleen Wilson, *This Island Race: Englishmen, Empire, and Gender in the Eighteenth Century* (New York: Routledge, 2003). For masculinity within the free black population, see, inter alia, Carol Barash, "The Character of Difference: The Creole Woman as Cultural Mediator in Narratives About Jamaica," *Eighteenth-Century Studies*, 23 (1990), 406–24.

11. Morgan, *Laboring Women*, 73–74.

12. For empirical evidence on the differences between male work and female work on plantations, see B. W. Higman, *Slave Population and Economy in Jamaica, 1807–1834* (Cambridge: Cambridge University Press, 1976), 187–211; and Michael Craton, *Searching for the Invisible Man: Slaves and Plantation Life in Jamaica* (Cambridge, Mass.: Harvard University Press, 1978). See also Trevor Burnard, "Evaluating Gender in Early Jamaica, 1674–1784," *History of the Family*, 12 (2007), 81–91; and Burnard, "Collecting and Accounting: Representing Slaves as Commodities in Jamaica, 1674–1784," in Daniella Bleichmar and Peter C. Mancall, eds., *Collecting Across Cultures in the Early Modern World* (Philadelphia: University of Pennsylvania Press, forthcoming).

13. Mullin, *Africa in America*, 171–72.

14. For differences between slave men and slave women's experiences generally, see Burnard, *Mastery, Tyranny, and Desire*, 175–240.

15. Doris Garraway, *The Libertine Colony: Creolization in the Early French Caribbean* (Durham, N.C.: Duke University Press, 2005); Joan Dayan, *Haiti, History, and the Gods* (Berkeley: University of California Press, 1995), 213–14.

16. Clinton Black, *Tales of Old Jamaica* (London: Collins, 1952), 114–15.

17. Garraway, *Libertine Colony*, 194–239.

18. Tim Hitchcock and Michele Cohen, eds., *English Masculinities, 1660–1800* (London: Addison Wesley Longman, 1999).

19. Norbert Elias, *The History of Manners*. Vol. 1: *The Civilizing Process* (New York: Pantheon, 1982), 194–205.

20. Edward Long, *The History of Jamaica* . . . 3 vols. (London, 1774, reprint: London: Frank Cass, 1970), II: 294–95.

21. Saidiya Hartman, *Scenes of Subjection: Terror, Slavery, and Self-Making in Nineteenth-Century America* (New York: Oxford University Press, 1997), 87.

22. Long, *History of Jamaica*, II: 328. For an extended discussion of these themes, see Trevor Burnard, "'Rioting in Goatish Embraces': Marriage and Improvement in Early British Jamaica, 1660–1780," *History of the Family* 11 (2006), 185–97.

23. Burnard, *Mastery, Tyranny, and Desire*, 21.

24. Long, *History of Jamaica*, II: 262–65; Charles Leslie, *A New and Exact Account of Jamaica* (Edinburgh, ca. 1740), 319.

25. William Beckford, *A Descriptive Account of the Island of Jamaica*, 2 vols. (London, 1790), II: 348.

26. Bryan Edwards, *The History, Civil and Commercial, of the British Colonies in the West Indies*, 2nd ed., 3 vols. (London, 1793), III: 7.

27. Ibid.

28. Ibid; Patrick Browne, *The Civil and Natural History of Jamaica* (London, 1756), 22; Jack P. Greene, *Imperatives, Behaviors, and Identities: Essays in Early American Cultural History* (Charlottesville: University of Virginia Press, 1992), 2–12.

29. Jack P. Greene, "The Jamaica Privilege Controversy, 1764–1766: An Episode in the Process of Constitutional Definition in the Early Modern British Empire," *Journal of Imperial and Commonwealth History* 22 (1994): 22.

30. Leslie, *Account of Jamaica*, 41.

31. Burnard, *Mastery, Tyranny, and Desire*, 156–62.

32. Burnard, "Rioting in Goatish Embraces."

33. Ibid.

34. Long, *History of Jamaica*, II: 353-54. For English attitudes about race in the middle of the eighteenth century, see Roxann Wheeler, *The Complexion of Race: Categories of Difference in Eighteenth-Century British Culture* (Philadelphia: University of Pennsylvania Press, 2000).

35. Long, *History of Jamaica*, II: 352-77; Thomas W. Krise, *Caribbeana: An Anthology of English Literature of the West Indies 1657-1777* (Chicago: University of Chicago Press, 1999), 319-24.

36. Philip Morgan, "Slaves and Livestock in Eighteenth Century Jamaica: Vineyard Pen, 1750-1751," *William and Mary Quarterly*, 3rd ser., 52 (1995): 47-76.

37. Matthew Lewis, *Journal of a West Indian Proprietor*, ed. Judith Terry (Oxford: Oxford University Press, 1999), 6.

38. Ibid., 59; Long, *History of Jamaica*, II: 447-60; Edwards, *History, Civil and Commercial*, II: 64-70.

39. Richard and Sally Price, *Stedman's Surinam: Life in an Eighteenth-Century Slave Society* (Baltimore: Johns Hopkins University Press, 1992), 285-86; Marcus Wood, *Blind Memory: Visual Representations of Slavery in England and America, 1780-1865* (Manchester: Manchester University Press, 2000).

40. Price and Price, *Stedman's Surinam*, 285-88.

41. Bryan Edwards, *Poems, Written Chiefly in the West Indies* (Kingston, 1792), 37; Edwards, *Speech . . . on the Subject of Mr. Wilberforce's Proposition . . . Concerning the Slave Trade . . .* (Kingston, 1789), 67-68.

42. Krise, *Caribbeana*, 339. The source of the original poem is Richard Savage, who in 1737 wrote a poem about slavery, "Of Public Spirit in Regard to Public Works," from which this stanza was derived. See G. Basker, "'The Next Insurrection': Johnson, Race, and Rebellion," *Age of Johnson*, 11 (2000), 39, 45, 47.

43. David Buisseret, ed., *Jamaica in 1687: The Taylor Manuscript at the National Library of Jamaica* (Kingston: University of the West Indies Press, 2008), 267.

44. Caroline H. Bledsoe, *Women and Marriage in Kpelle Society* (Stanford, Calif.: Stanford University Press, 1980), 48.

45. For meditations on the relationship between English liberty and slavery, see Jack P. Greene, "Liberty and Slavery: The Transfer of British Liberty to the West Indies, 1627-1865," in Greene, ed., *Exclusionary: Empire: English Liberty Overseas, 1600-1900* (New York: Cambridge University Press, 2009), 50-64. For white West Indian identity as transcultured and the West Indies as a performative space of cultural heteroglossia, see Wilson, "Performance of Freedom," 51. See also Long, *History of Jamaica*, II: 353-54.

IV

Enactment

8

"Effective Men" and Early Voluntary Associations in Philadelphia, 1725–1775

JESSICA CHOPPIN RONEY

Moore Trotter found herself in dire straits by 1768. An impoverished and desperate immigrant in Philadelphia, she beseeched the help of two of the wealthiest women in the city, Miss Elizabeth Graeme and Mrs. Mary McCall Plumstead. It is unclear what (if any) actions Graeme and Plumstead took immediately to help her, but they did recommend her case to the St. Andrew's Society, a voluntary association set up for two major purposes: to celebrate Scottish heritage and to provide economic assistance to struggling Scottish immigrants. Moore Trotter qualified for their charity, and, thanks in part to the recommendations of Graeme and Plumstead, she was granted thirty shillings.[1]

Trotter's case sheds light on the distinctive ways men and women might contribute to charitable causes in the eighteenth century. Presumably Trotter approached Graeme and Plumstead because she hoped that as women they would be sympathetic to her plight. Graeme and Plumstead, however, were limited in what they could do to help her. They might give her some food, clothing, or money, but though they were wealthy their charity was limited by the will of their male relatives—in Elizabeth Graeme's case, her father, and for Mary Plumstead, her husband. Whatever they did privately, these women evidently concluded that the best help for Moore Trotter would come from an institution larger than their own resources. They turned to the St. Andrew's Society, where Graeme's father and Plumstead's brothers were influential founding members. Neither woman was herself a member.[2]

The St. Andrew's Society, named for the patron saint of Scotland, had been founded in Philadelphia in 1749 by a number of Scottish immigrants. The Scotsmen had found themselves "frequently" approached by their "Country people here in distress." Rather than continue to try to aid them individually, the Scotsmen decided "to form ourselves into a Society in order to provide for these Indigents whereby they may be more easily more regularly and more bountifully Supply'd than cou'd well be done in the common troublesome way of making Occasional collections for such purposes." In other words, rather than rely on ad hoc or individual measures, these men would pool their resources and their efforts. No longer would they give charity to applicants individually, but instead refer them to the St. Andrew's Society officers, who would decide who should get assistance.[3]

Charity in the eighteenth century was a laudable characteristic—indeed the St. Andrew's Society thought it was "one of the first-rate moral Virtues" an individual, male or female, might possess. But the plight of Moore Trotter demonstrated a divergence in the ways that men and women in Philadelphia might enact that virtue. Women like Graeme and Plumstead might give individual charity, but they were limited by their own economic circumstances and, unless they were widows, by the will of their male head of household. Men had greater leeway than women in their ability to give charity, but over the course of the eighteenth century they began to approach it differently—moving away from individual giving and more toward institutional forms. They began to favor public, corporate, and codified endeavors.[4]

This move coincided with a trend over the course of the eighteenth century in Philadelphia: the growth of voluntary associations. In the fifty years before the American Revolution, Philadelphians founded more than sixty organizations. They ranged considerably: the first subscription libraries of North America, the first volunteer fire companies, the first hospital, the first nonsectarian college, several scientific and medical societies, a dancing society, and a host of sociable and ethnic clubs. Through these organizations Philadelphia men began to engage differently with their community, introducing and indeed inventing a new collective form in American society and politics.

This form did not spring anew into the world; in Philadelphia, it drew on the models of British voluntary associations, Protestant and Quaker religious structures, English political traditions, and the needs and opportunities presented by a heterogeneous colonial population. The formal voluntary associations that Philadelphians developed were further shaped deeply by their status on the edge of the British Empire, where greater latitude existed for them to act than in England, which had much more comprehensive governmental and church structures to provide necessary services.

Men monopolized voluntary organizations. Women like Elizabeth Graeme and Mary Plumstead could and did operate on the margins of men's formal voluntary associations, sometimes participating in their activities as guests, at other times providing important support services, but they were never voting members, and they were barred from most activities and all decision making. The scope these organizations provided for Philadelphia men provided a catalyst through which they transformed their own engagement with civil society and the public sphere. Like the men of the St. Andrew's Society who decided to formalize and regularize their charity by pooling it together, men in Philadelphia's voluntary associations found a new way to participate in the public life of their city, collaborating on larger-scale projects than could be attempted individually. By working together, men hoped they could streamline, rationalize, and modernize approaches to societal problems like poverty, sickness, fire, and the need for education. Voluntary associations broadened the scope in which they thought about and addressed these issues, and opened exciting possibilities for men to move beyond merely voting for others to contributing actively to the decisions that affected their community.

The innovation of voluntary associations thus reinforced masculine dominance in public life. Virtuous manhood came to be associated with service; public service became doubly associated with men and masculinity. Women, like Graeme and Plumstead, might engage in individual acts of moral virtue, but for men the enactment of virtues like charity could now become collective and public. In the colonial period voluntary organizations created a powerful space for the performance of masculine public virtue, connected increasingly with political participation and manly civic service.[5]

Masculine Spaces

One of the most striking aspects of Philadelphia voluntary associations is that not one organization explicitly excluded women in their rules or felt the need to justify having an all-male membership. Men never saw the need to build official barriers to female participation for two reasons. First, it appears not to have occurred to them that women would want to or try to join. They could not imagine women straying into the world of voluntary associations and, apart from a handful of women who joined subscription libraries, women in the colonial period did not challenge this assumption. Second, men shaped their voluntary associations in ways that made them accessible to men and inaccessible to women. Simply put, they never had to write rules against women participating because they met in spaces women could not go, defined themselves in ways that did not appeal to women, and engaged in activities and behaviors that were off-limits to women.[6]

Most associations met in taverns, which in the eighteenth century were overwhelmingly male spaces. Aside from a few female tavern keepers and workers, women did not frequent taverns, and socialized and conducted their business elsewhere. The protected environment taverns provided, replete with food, alcohol, and a haze of pipe smoke, made the meetings social events and melded club sociability with the masculine rituals of tavern life. The decision to meet in taverns and to merge the stated business of the organization with the raucous carousing and the heavy eating and drinking promoted in taverns structured voluntary culture as masculine and closed to—and mostly hidden from—women.[7]

Eating and drinking were central to most organizations. At a single meeting of a Scottish ethnic group called the St. Andrew's Society, members consumed sixteen pounds of beef, twelve hams, six chickens, two ducks, two tongues, a quarter of a lamb, six and a half pounds of veal, four gallons of wine, one gallon of liquor (probably mixed with around ten pounds of sugar and one hundred limes to make punch), and one and a half gallons of beer. They topped off the evening with "pipes & Tobacco." The members of the Union Fire Company likewise intended their group to fight fires, but it was also a social organization. Their monthly meetings included supper and, by strictly enforced rule, no business could be transacted until the members had enjoyed a full hour of conversation, drinking, and eating. When it was proposed to do away with the suppers, the members immediately and unanimously voted against the measure. Their suppers were sacrosanct.[8]

All-male organizations meeting in predominantly male taverns provided members a double layer of separation that buffered them from frequent or widespread female observation. Presumably, this absence of women allowed club members an unrestrained conviviality not possible in mixed society. Unfortunately, no Philadelphia club records survive that reproduce social conversations that occurred at meetings, so it is impossible to know exactly what they discussed aside from recorded matters of business. In Annapolis, Maryland, just south of Philadelphia, Dr. Alexander Hamilton recorded the conversations of the Honorable Tuesday Club. From his notes it is clear that at least for the Honorable Tuesday Club, heavy drinking, play, and derogatory humor about women were all key elements of the group's sociability. Almost certainly their neighbors in Philadelphia engaged in similar humor and masculine bonding through drinking, singing, and play, creating an environment unreceptive to female participation. By meeting in taverns and making the heavy consumption of food and alcohol a central part of meetings, clubs prioritized masculine modes of conversation and interaction that provided an implicit barrier to women.[9]

Drinking and ribald humor were not the only activities in which men's voluntary associations engaged that limited women's participation. Physical pursuits such as hunting, fishing, and horse racing were deemed more appropriate to men than women. In point of fact, women did enjoy sporting culture too. One elite woman, for example, wrote back to England about how much she enjoyed fishing, and boasted of spending most of her summer in 1737 engaged in that activity. Meanwhile, women collected together the funds for a "Ladies Purse" to be run for by the Jockey Club, indicating an interest in watching horse racing. But women were never members of the fishing clubs, the Jockey Club, or the Gloucester Fox Hunting Club.[10]

Activities that protected the community, like firefighting and joining a militia, were especially seen as the province of men. Benjamin Franklin in his newspaper lauded "Brave Men at Fires," and helped found the first voluntary fire company in North America (the first of twenty fire companies in Philadelphia before the American Revolution). Women were involved in some aspects of firefighting: the wives and widows of fire company members were often responsible for maintaining firefighting equipment and making sure that it was sent to the scene when there was a fire. Further, women appear to have been involved in one of the more crucial tasks when there was a fire: removing and protecting goods from the burning house.

The image of the firefighter was connected entirely with men, whatever women's actual role. "See there a gallant Man who has rescu'd Children from the Flames!" Franklin wrote. "Another receives in his Arms a poor scorch'd Creature escaping out at a Window!" These men fulfilled the most important characteristic of a man: protecting and helping dependents. Surveying firefighters, Franklin concluded, "Here are Heroes and effective Men." [11]

Effective Men and the Culture of Improvement

By fighting fires, these "effective Men" demonstrated their bravery, their manliness, and above all, their virtue in putting the needs of others before their own, risking life and limb for their neighbors. This kind of virtue transcended individual merit and individual men; it affected and indeed undergirded the entire community. Eighteenth-century English political thought linked "virtue" with good government. Specifically, most commentators believed that history taught that government tended always toward corruption and the threat of being taken over by despots. The only defense against such tyranny was the virtue of the citizenry, who must remain ever-vigilant for encroachments on their liberty. Virtue was essential, and its hallmarks included economic independence, willingness to sacrifice for the community, and civic service. Only when private citizens remained virtuous could the government do so. Firefighting was one activity that demonstrated this brand of virtue. It involved "brave Men, Men of Spirit and Humanity, good Citizens," and showed that they were "capable and worthy of civil Society, and the Enjoyment of a happy Government." Their willingness to hazard their own safety to protect their neighbors demonstrated their masculinity, their virtue, and their very capacity and worthiness for participation in civil society and "the Enjoyment of a happy Government."[12]

But this kind of virtue was explicitly masculine. Women had no place in public performances of virtue like those enacted by the "Brave Men at Fires." Whatever role they played in fighting fires, or indeed in any kind of civic service, was rendered almost entirely invisible. Instead these activities were inflected as masculine. Individual women might be virtuous within the confines of domesticity and their roles as wives and mothers, but their virtue remained atomized, splintered among individuals, relegated to private arenas (even when they might in fact act in public ones). As men began to utilize and craft a new form of public engagement through voluntary associations, they made a new platform on which to proclaim and perform their own virtue, not only as individuals but also as a gender.[13]

Firefighting was only one activity that made Philadelphia men "capable and worthy of civil Society, and the Enjoyment of a happy Government." Civic service more generally demonstrated individual and collective virtue. Voluntary associations offered a popular route to performing such civic service—by the eve of the American Revolution at least one in five adult, white men participated in one or more of Philadelphia's voluntary associations. The majority of groups had some civic purpose—sometimes to better the circumstances for one subcommunity or another, but often, in their own words, to "improve" all of Philadelphia.

"When Colonies are in their Infancy, the Refinements of Life . . . cannot be much attended to," noted the directors of one of the earliest voluntary associations, the Library Company of Philadelphia. But writing fifty years after Pennsylvania had first been settled, the directors believed it was time for Pennsylvanians to expand their attention from government, trade, and agriculture, to some of the higher pursuits of life. The Library Company founders had formed two years previously "to propagate Knowledge, and improve the Minds of Men, by rendring useful Science and cheap and easy of Access." Such a project, they were confident, would set Philadelphia on the path toward refinement and greatness, one day becoming nothing less than "the future Athens of America." Philadelphians continually echoed the Library Company directors' lofty ambitions, aiming for nothing less than the most modern medical facilities, the first nonsectarian college in North America, the broadest access to books, the most enlightened approach to poverty, and the most comprehensive protection from fire.[14]

Though organizations did exist primarily for more sociable or pleasurable ends, the drive for improvement proved a strong impetus for most groups, and this fact speaks to the status of eighteenth-century Philadelphia as a settler society, one still establishing and elaborating the apparatus of political, economic, and social life. The voluntary culture in this developing city would therefore not focus primarily on personal enjoyment, but would play a role in transforming the city from a small outpost in the hinterland to a metropolis in its own right.

Of course, "improvement" is a subjective term, always defined by the eye of the beholder. The vision of what constituted improvement in Philadelphia voluntary culture consolidated and underscored a masculine vision of the world, one that prioritized productivity, economic self-sufficiency, and the protection of dependents. Two intertwined goals underscored ideas of what constituted "improvement" for most organizations: protecting property and enhancing the individual and collective productivity of Philadelphians. These goals were not necessarily shared by all Philadelphians, but they were fundamental to those men who joined and shaped voluntary associations.

Productivity and property were essential both to masculine republican virtue and to patriarchy. By eighteenth-century lights, a virtuous man had to be economically independent, for if he was beholden to anyone else—perhaps as a tenant on someone else's land, or a debtor owing money to a creditor—he might be manipulated. He could not exercise his own virtue because he was compromised by his dependence on someone else. The virtuous citizen owned his own land, his own shop, and was in debt to no man. As we have seen, eighteenth-century thinkers believed that good government relied on a virtuous citizenry. By the same token, all social order was believed to rest on patriarchy, specifically on men controlling the subordinates in their families (wives, children, servants, slaves). Being a good provider was an essential part of being a patriarch. A man who could not furnish his family with the necessities of life could not in turn command respect and obedience from them. Without that control, the fabric of social order began to fray. Integral to full manhood, then, was economic self-sufficiency and the ability to provide for a family. By helping protect property and boosting a man's ability to earn a living, voluntary associations reinforced a patriarchal culture with men at the apex of the economic and social hierarchy.[15]

The protection of property impelled one of the most popular forms of voluntary association: fire companies. When the Union Fire Company, the first voluntary fire company in North America, formed in 1736, it gave one and only one reason for its existence: "for the better preserving our Goods and Effects from Fire." The twenty men who joined said nothing about saving lives or even putting out fires; they stressed only the protection of their property. Indeed, much of firefighting in this era before large fire engines (they used small, hand-carried and hand-pumped fire engines) was not so much about trying to put out fires, but instead conveying to safety as many of the goods in burning buildings as possible and controlling the spread of the fire. All fire companies that formed in the colonial period stressed that each member must show up at fires not only with buckets for water, but also with bags or baskets in which to carry out the householder's property; two fire company members were assigned at each fire to watch over the goods and make sure no miscreant carried anything off. A similar desire to protect individual property inspired the two extralegal militias that formed to protect the city from the threat of attack in wartime.[16]

A desire to protect property also motivated the formation of the first insurance company in North America. We think of insurance as a for-profit endeavor, but in its earliest iteration in Philadelphia it was connected not with profit but with mutual assistance. The Philadelphia Contributionship, founded in 1752, pooled together the resources of many householders so that if one member lost property in a fire, all the members would share the cost of rebuilding or repairing the damaged structure.

Where these groups acted to protect property, other groups focused on enhancing the productivity of Philadelphia and its inhabitants. Organizations existed for carpenters, shoemakers, hatmakers, tailors, ship captains, ministers, and doctors. Meanwhile, a number of scientific organizations worked to improve the collective productivity of the community as a whole through a variety of means. These groups sought to introduce viniculture (wine making) and silk production to Pennsylvania, discussed agricultural improvements, and charted the course of Venus in the heavens, an important step toward the first charting of lines of longitude and the improvement of navigation and shipping. Whether by helping one another track down runaway apprentices, as the shoemakers group did, or by sketching out the cultivation of a new and profitable product like silk, these voluntary associations aimed at increasing economic productivity.

Most voluntary associations also provided crucial nodes for networking. The Junto, founded in 1727 by the twenty-one-year-old Benjamin Franklin, is perhaps one of the best examples. Franklin invited his most "ingenious Acquaintance into a Club for mutual Improvement," but they were almost all young men, just starting out in life and with few economic resources. The group met once a week ostensibly to discuss natural and moral philosophy. The members came up with a long list of "queries" to be asked at the opening of each meeting—and between discussing each individual query, the members were supposed to pause long enough that "one might fill and drink a Glass of Wine." (If they followed that rule to the letter, the members would have stopped for no fewer than twenty-five glasses!) Many of the queries were not philosophical but practical, intended to help members pursue personal and economic improvement. Each week they asked, among other things, whether the members had "lately heard of any Citizen thriving well," and if so, how he had come to be successful. They pondered how "any present Rich Man got his Estate," and dissected the business failings of their neighbors to see what practical knowledge they could draw from these life lessons. Further, they tried to help one another. "Hath any Body attack'd your Reputation lately," they asked at each meeting, "and what can the Junto do toward securing it?" One of the queries posed each week asked whether "there [is] any Man whose Friendship you want, and which the Junto can procure for you?" At each meeting they took time to put their heads together to proffer advice and service for "any weighty Affairs in Hand" of their fellow members.[17]

For these young men, the camaraderie and philosophical debate served as only part of the attraction to membership. Of great weight as well were the personal and business contacts that might be formed with other members, or with the friends of members ("is there any Man whose Friendship you want?"). All voluntary associations served a similar function of bringing together potential contacts; the Junto, composed of young, aspiring tradesmen eager to make their way in the world, was simply more barefaced about pursuing those connections. The club young Franklin and his friends formed was distinctive in that it codified and made explicit what for most voluntary associations was merely implicit: the facilitation of all-male networks of social and economic exchange that provided tangible benefits for members.

After 1750 a few voluntary associations began to offer even more palpable assistance toward economic advancement. En route to fulfilling their stated objectives, several voluntary associations amassed large amounts of capital through dues, fines, and contributions. Some of those organizations had acquired such substantial pools of money that they began to loan the funds out in order to earn interest on it, and in the process offered a vital service to aspiring artisans and merchants: credit. Four voluntary organizations acted as proto-banks, making loans that ranged from ten pounds to thousands—in all making available more than one hundred thousand pounds between 1750 and 1776. The provision of such a vast quantity of loans contributed a key service in Philadelphia, where financial services were minimal and no private banks existed. Private individuals made loans to one another, but in most cases they only loaned small amounts, spreading around the risk that a borrower might default. It was difficult, time-consuming, and therefore inefficient for a borrower to cobble together large funds for new investment or expansion in his business. The difficulty in getting large loans in turn had a dampening effect on economic expansion, which affected the larger community.

In contrast to individual lending, four Philadelphia organizations—the College of Philadelphia, Pennsylvania Hospital, Philadelphia Contributionship, and Presbyterian Ministers Fund—made loans in very large amounts, almost always one hundred pounds or more, and sometimes as high as three thousand pounds. The six percent interest they earned helped fund the activities of the lenders, insuring their long-term security, and pumped large sums of money into the local economy, making possible Atlantic mercantile ventures, trade with Indians to the west, iron manufacturing, agricultural improvements, and myriad other projects. The borrowers did not need to be members of the lending organizations, and most were not. Indeed, part of what is distinctive about this organizational lending is that, in contrast to borrowing from friends or family, borrowing from voluntary associations marked the beginning of the more impersonal lending associated with formal banks. Borrowers had to post some form of collateral, usually a mortgage on property, but otherwise they did not have to have a personal relationship with the board members of the lending institution in order to secure the loan.[18]

The vast majority of the borrowers were men. Eight women were named in the loans, most as the cosigners of property with their husbands. Only in two or three cases was a woman apparently the primary borrower. The borrowers tended to be well-established, middle-aged men—much like the men on the boards of the organizations from which they borrowed. They benefitted from the board members' decision to make only large loans since women and poorer men could not afford the collateral, thereby limiting competition. Had board managers decided to parcel out their loans in smaller units, a much wider variety of borrowers might have availed themselves of this line of credit. As it was, the loans merely buttressed the economic prospects of other men, reifying not only gender but class lines.

Voluntary associations thus worked to "improve" Philadelphia by protecting property and providing economic assistance to members through trade groups, networking, and even by making substantial loans. But they did not stop at helping their own members. Two of the largest organizations tried also to enforce improvements on others, making them productive contributors the economy. The city's two largest charities were both obsessed with increasing the productivity of the poor. The Pennsylvania Hospital, founded in 1751, intended to use the most modern, up-to-date medical techniques to care for the sick poor and "Restore them to a Capacity of becoming useful Members of Society"—that is to say, able-bodied and employable. Tellingly, their emphasis was not on health care for its own sake, but up returning sick individuals to work so they could be "useful to the community once more."[19]

The Contributors to the Relief of the Poor were even more adamant about transforming the poor into productive laborers. Philadelphia struggled with poverty more and more throughout the eighteenth century. By the 1760s the Philadelphia government became overwhelmed by the swelling ranks of the poor, but the members of the newly formed Contributors to the Relief of the Poor believed that they had the answer, and they took over all poor relief in the city. They abolished the old practice of giving direct financial support to the poor (also called "outdoor relief" because the recipients continued to live on their own), and instead build a "House of Employment" in which the poor would be housed and put to work to pay for the cost of their maintenance. The Contributors believed that placing the poor in an institution and overseeing all aspects of their lives would provide them with the food and shelter they needed, while at the same time instilling in them the industry and work habits that would prevent them from future impoverishment. The Contributors ignored larger societal factors that led to poverty, such as the terrible depression that gripped the city in the wake of the Seven Years' War, and instead blamed the poor themselves for their condition, casting them as lazy or feckless.[20]

The Contributors' approach did not work. The number of the poor only rose, and the attempt to care for them only became more expensive and difficult. But the Contributors could not change their tactics, for they were locked in a mentality that hard work was the basis on which men provided for their families. If a family was poor, it stood to reason that the father had been insufficiently hardworking, regardless of whether he was injured, sick, or unable to find work. In fact, many of the poor had no male head of household at all. Women then and now were more likely to be impoverished than men. They were limited in the work they could do to earn a living, and if they had no able-bodied husband to help share the burden, they found themselves the hardest hit by the vicissitudes of economic downturn. The men who dominated the city's approach to poor relief did not take into consideration these factors; they were blinkered by a reliance on productivity as the answer to all societal and individual needs. They failed to see the feminization of poverty, and instead saw a failure on the part of men to support their families. The House of Employment was intended to reform such men into the hardworking model of a patriarch that voluntary association members thought all men ought to be.[21]

Voluntary Associations and Governance

Voluntary associations like the Contributors to the Relief of the Poor were deeply entrenched in the daily operations of the city of Philadelphia. In the case of the Contributors, the men in this association were able to impose on other Philadelphians their own ideas of the causes and remedies of poverty because in 1766 the local government ceded all authority over poor relief—even the power to tax Philadelphians—to the organization. This cession proved to be one of the most extreme—government formally reneging on its responsibilities in favor of a voluntary association taking them over—but it was not unusual. In the colonial period, Philadelphia's voluntary associations took over many aspects of governance.[22]

In the context of weak or hands-off government and religious pluralism, many of the tasks that kept the city functional or improved it into a cosmopolitan center came to be overseen by voluntary associations. In 1731 the Library Company of Philadelphia became the first organization to take steps to address needs left unmet by formally constituted authority. Noting that "no manner of Provision [had been] made by the Government for public Education," the Library Company founders established the first subscription library in North America. Shortly thereafter, when the municipal government proved too stagnant to undertake effective fire protection, Philadelphians organized a voluntary fire company. This organization served as the model for at least nineteen more voluntary fire companies that formed before the revolution. In 1747–48, under threat from privateer attacks during King George's War, and with the Quaker Assembly refusing to place the city in a posture of defense, as many as half the adult men of the city joined together to form an extralegal militia that mustered through the streets of Philadelphia, negotiated with neighboring governors for cannons and supplies, raised money through multiple lotteries, and built two forts on the banks of the Delaware River. A second militia formed along similar lines during the French and Indian War, and once more, famously, in 1775, assuming governmental powers. Quakers in 1756 formed the Friendly Association and sought to shape the colony's Indian policy through mediation at treaty negotiations. The Academy in 1749, and the College of Philadelphia in 1755, continued the mission to provide education to the sons and daughters of the city. Concerned citizens founded the first hospital in North America in 1751, to address the problems of rising poverty and illness in the city. And as we have seen, the Contributors for the Relief of the Poor successfully petitioned the Assembly in 1766 to take over all public poor relief in Philadelphia and its suburbs. Over the course of the century, then, in the absence of government or church involvement, voluntary associations assumed some or all responsibility for education, fire protection, defense, Indian diplomacy, and the care and relief of the poor.[23]

Legal authorities allowed these groups to assume so much control quite simply because they could not stop them and because they needed the help. Fire protection was one of the earliest examples. Despite devastating fires and petitions from the populace to improve mechanisms for fighting fires, the municipal government could not muster the organization or the energy to do anything that effectively addressed the problem. When voluntary fire companies finally filled that void, the officials of the municipal government were happy to let the voluntary companies act as they saw fit. Likewise, when ordinary Philadelphians formed voluntary militias or involved themselves in Indian diplomacy (neither of which they had any legal mandate to do), government officials found that they had to rely on their help, and therefore had to overlook the illegality (or we might say the *extra*-legality) of their actions.

Voluntary associations thus assumed many responsibilities in the city, and gave wide scope for men of many different walks of life to participate in and shape their community. In this sense, Philadelphia's voluntary associations dramatically expanded the avenues for men's civic and political participation and reworked understandings of eighteenth-century manliness. Men in voluntary association did not only vote for others to represent them, they themselves decided what the community needed and then acted on their assessments. Not only did voluntary associations enhance men's individual virtue and productive capacity, they provided a vehicle through which to shape the larger community in ways that benefitted men. Moreover, the extent to which voluntary associations inserted themselves into the running of the city—taking over or contributing largely to its fire fighting, poor relief, education structures, and defense—meant that nonmembers (women, lower-class men, African Americans) found themselves doubly barred from expressing their own voice on those matters. First government and then voluntary associations gave expanded capacity to white men to form and control many aspects of the public sphere, reinforcing their political, social, and economic dominance.

In carving out a "city in the wilderness," eighteenth-century Philadelphians introduced to North America a new form of collaborative enterprise. Alongside churches, courts, legislatures, and local governments now would stand another formal mechanism for men to pool their collective energies, pursue particular ends, and shape the texture of their communities. Philadelphians and the inhabitants of other North American urban areas pioneered voluntary associations, and in so doing began a phenomenon that established deep roots in American political practice and social life. When French commentator Alexis de Tocqueville traveled through the United States in 1832, he marveled at the importance of American voluntary associations and contended that they were vital to American democracy. The fascination with and importance ascribed to Americans' penchant for voluntary association continues to the present day, often with controversy.[24]

The first iteration—indeed the very invention—of voluntary associations in British North America remained throughout the colonial period firmly and unapologetically masculine. Voluntary associations were established for and by men—and more specifically, mature white men of comfortable economic means. In glaring contrast to later nineteenth-century organizations, these organizations had no female members. Women operated on the periphery of colonial voluntary associations in supporting roles and occasionally as guests to particular events, but they were not members, and in the colonial period they created no formal organizations of their own. In the buildup to the American Revolution and the period just after, women would make use of the malleable form to engage in political protests, reform movements, abolitionism, and eventually women's suffrage, but they were allowed almost no role in colonial America's first genesis of voluntary associations.

Colonial-era voluntary associations pursued objectives that appealed to men and apparently did not resonate enough with women to inspire them to try to join in. On the eve of revolution, the situation began to change as Philadelphians began to protest what they saw as unjust taxation from Britain. In the late 1760s and early 1770s, consumer boycotts became a popular mechanism through which to resist taxation without representation. Committees of men were set up to write the rules of the boycott and to oversee enforcement. The leadership thus remained male, but for the first time a voluntary association needed the help of women, because mistresses made many of the consumption decisions for households. The boycott committees appealed directly to women and worked to mobilize them by speaking to their patriotism and giving them tangible ways to participate. They were not to buy certain products, and they were to increase domestic production of vital goods proscribed by the boycott (such as cloth). Women responded enthusiastically, moving for the first time into the sphere of voluntary associational life.[25]

In the colonial era, voluntary associations represented a new form in American public life and in turn helped shape new gendered identities for white men of means. Voluntary associations appealed to men, met in masculine spaces, relied on a masculine culture of heavy eating and drinking, spoke to masculine concerns of economic self-sufficiency and virtuous civic service, and took advantage of great latitude to shape the city in ways that served the vision and interests of men.

NOTES

1. December 2, 1768. Minute Book of the St. Andrew's Society, 1749–1776, Papers of the St. Andrew's Society of Philadelphia.

2. Sydney V. James, *A People Among Peoples: Quaker Benevolence in Eighteenth-Century America* (Cambridge, MA: Harvard University Press, 1963); Gary B. Nash. "Poverty and Poor Relief in Pre-revolutionary Philadelphia," *William and Mary Quarterly*, 3rd ser., 33 no. 1 (Jan. 1976): 3–30; John K. Alexander. *Render Them Submissive: Responses to Poverty in Philadelphia, 1760–1800* (Amherst: University of Massachusetts Press, 1980); Amanda Bowie Moniz, "'Labours in the Cause of Humanity in Every Part of the Globe': Transatlantic Philanthropic Collaboration and the Cosmopolitan Ideal, 1760–1815" (PhD diss., University of Michigan, 2008); "A List of the Members of the St. Andrews Society," 1749?, Minute Book of the St. Andrew's Society, 1749–1776.

3. "Rules for the St. Andrew's Society," December 7, 1749, Minute Book of the St. Andrew's Society, 1749–1776.

4. Ibid.

5. Anthony E. Rotundo, *American Manhood: Transformations in Masculinity from the Revolution to the Modern Era* (New York; Basic Books, 1993); Toby L. Ditz, "Shipwrecked; or, Masculinity Imperiled: Mercantile Representations of Failure and the Gendered Self in Eighteenth-Century Philadelphia," *Journal of American History* 81 no. 1 (June 1994): 51–80; Lisa Wilson, *Ye Heart of a Man: The Domestic Life of Men in Colonial New England* (New Haven: Yale University Press, 1999); Richard Godbeer, *The Overflowing of Friendship: Love Between Men and the Creation of the American Republic* (Baltimore: Johns Hopkins University Press, 2009); John Gilbert McCurdy, *Citizen Bachelors: Manhood and the Creation of the United States* (Ithaca: Cornell University Press, 2009).

6. As far as I can discover, there were only four women who were formal members of voluntary associations in Philadelphia, out of roughly two thousand known members total. All four subscribed to either the Library Company of Philadelphia or the Union Library Company (which was absorbed into the LCP in 1769). It is not clear whether any of them were allowed to vote, or only to borrow books. May 10, 1742, May 9, 1763, Library Company of Philadelphia Minute Book (LCPM); Library Company of Philadelphia Record Book A, April 6, 1769, Library Company of Philadelphia.

7. Carole Shammas, "The Female Social Structure of Philadelphia in 1775," *Pennsylvania Magazine of History and Biography* 107 no. 1 (1983): 78; Peter Thompson, *Rum Punch and Revolution: Taverngoing and Public Life in Eighteenth-Century Philadelphia* (Philadelphia: University of Pennsylvania Press, 1999).

8. Receipt, May 31, 1759, Series 1, Subseries 1, Box 1, Folder 4, Papers of the St. Andrew's Society of Philadelphia; December 27, 1742, August 29, 1743, October 25, 1756, Minutes of the Union Fire Company, 1736–1785, Historical Society of Pennsylvania (henceforth HSP).

9. Alexander Hamilton. *History of the Ancient and Honorable Tuesday Club*, Robert Micklus ed. (Chapel Hill: University of North Carolina Press, 1990). See also Ruth H. Bloch "Changing Conceptions of Sexuality and Romance in Eighteenth-Century America," *WMQ*, 3rd ser., 60 no. 1 (January 2003): 24; October 10, 1766, Minutes of the Junto and the American Society for Promoting Useful Knowledge, American Philosophical Society (henceforth APS), 12–13. On Philadelphia tavern life, see Thompson. *Rum, Punch, and Revolution*. David S. Shields argues for the centrality of play in constructing club sociability. See *Civil Tongues and Polite Letters in British America*. (Chapel Hill: University of North Carolina Press, 1997).

10. Margaret Freame to John Penn, n.d., but presumed August 1737, Penn Papers, Private Correspondence, Vol. 2, p. 193, HSP; "The Ladies Contributions Purse of Fifty Pounds for Three Years Old Colts and Fillies," 1767, Jockey Club Register Book, HSP.

11. For example, the servant woman Joan Donovan described her role helping to save clothing out of her master's house. "Copy of Joan Donovan's Affadavit, Sworn Before Ralph Asheton, Esq.," April 26, 1744, *American Weekly Mercury*. See also Benjamin Franklin, "Brave Men at Fires," December 20, 1733, *Pennsylvania Gazette*; Wilson, *Ye Heart of a Man*; Anne S. Lombard, *Making Manhood: Growing Up Male in Colonial New England* (Cambridge: Harvard University Press, 2003).

12. J. G. A. Pocock, *The Machiavellian Moment: Florentine Political Thought and the Atlantic Republican Tradition* (Princeton: Princeton University Press, 1975); Bernard Bailyn, *The Ideological Origins of the American Revolution* (Cambridge: Harvard University Press, 1967); Franklin, "Brave Men at Fires."

13. Ruth H. Bloch, "The Gendered Meanings of Virtue in Revolutionary America," in *Gender and Morality in Anglo-American Culture, 1650–1800* (Berkeley: University of California Press, 2003).

14. The Library Company of Philadelphia to Peter Collinson, November 7, 1732, and Address of Library Company to Thomas Penn, Proprietor, May 24, 1733, LCPM.

15. Ditz, "Shipwrecked"; Thomas M. Doerflinger. *A Vigorous Spirit of Enterprise: Merchants and Economic Development in Revolutionary Philadelphia*. (Chapel Hill: University of North Carolina Press, 1986).

16. Articles of Union Fire Company, December 7, 1736, Minutes of the Union Fire Company, 1736–1785, HSP.

17. Leonard W. Labaree et al ed., *The Autobiography of Benjamin Franklin*, 2nd Edition (New Haven: Yale University Press, 2003), 116; Benjamin Franklin, Commonplace Book, Dreer Collection, HSP.

18. One hundred thousand pounds represented a vast economic resource; to put it in perspective, a journeyman artisan could expect to earn fifty-four pounds in a year, a college professor two hundred pounds. J. A. Leo Lemay, *The Life of Benjamin Franklin*, Vol. 2 (Philadelphia: University of Pennsylvania Press, 2006), 567.

19. January 31, 1764, Pennsylvania Hospital Minutes, Pennsylvania Hospital Archive.

20. "An act for the Better Employment, Relief and Support of the Poor, Within the City of Philadelphia, the District of Southwark, the Townships of Moyamensing and Passyunk, and the Northern Liberties," *Anno Regni Georgii III: Regis . . . At a general assembly of the Province of pennyslvania . . .* (Philadelphia, 1766); June 15, 1769, Overseers of Poor Minutes, 1768–1774, Philadelphia City Archives; Nash, "Poverty and Poor Relief"; Alexander, *Render Them Submissive*; Michael Meranze, *Laboratories of Virtue: Punishment, Revolution, and Authority in Philadelphia, 1760–1835* (Chapel Hill: University of North Carolina Press, 1996).

21. Billy G. Smith, *The "Lower Sort": Philadelphia's Laboring People, 1750–1800* (Ithaca: Cornell University Press, 1990); Carole Shammas, "The Female Social Structure of Philadelphia in 1775," *Pennsylvania Magazine of History and Biography* 107 no. 1 (1983): 69–83; Karin Wulf, *Not All Wives: Women of Colonial Philadelphia* (Ithaca: Cornell University Press, 2000).

22. "An act for the Better Employment"; "An act for Amending the Act Intituled, 'An Act for the Better Employment, Relief and Support of the Poor Within the City of Philadelphia, the District of Southwark, the Townships of Moyamensing and Passyunk, and the Northern Liberties.'" *Anno Regni Georgii III: Regis . . . At a general assembly of the Province of pennysylvania . . .* (Philadelphia, 1767).

23. The Library Company of Philadelphia to Peter Collinson, November 7, 1732, LCPM; Articles of Union Fire Company, December 7, 1736; November 24, 1747, "Form of [Defense] Association," HSP; January 1, 1756, July 28, 1775, *Pennsylvania Gazette*; Benjamin Franklin, *Proposals Relating to the Education of Youth in Pennsylvania* (Philadelphia, 1749); Constitutions of the Publick Academy in the City of Philadelphia, Trustees of the University of Pennsylvania Minute Books, Volume 1, 1749–1768, University Archives and Records Center, University of Pennsylvania; "An act to Encourage the Establishing of an Hospital for the Relief of the Sick Poor of this Province, and for the Reception and Cure of Lunaticks," bound in with Pennsylvania Hospital Minutes. Volume 1, 1751–1757; "An act for the Better Employment."

24. Carl Bridenbaugh, *Cities in the Wilderness: The First Century of Urban Life in America, 1625–1742* (New York: Alfred A. Knopf, 1938); Alexis de Tocqueville, *Democracy in America*, Richard D. Heffner ed. (New York: Penguin Books, 1956), 95, 97.

25. T. H. Breen, *The Marketplace of the Revolution: How Consumer Politics Shaped American Independence* (Oxford: Oxford University Press, 2004).

9

"Strength of the Lion... Arms Like Polished Iron"

Embodying Black Masculinity in an Age of Slavery and Propertied Manhood

KATHLEEN M. BROWN

In 1681, a York County, Virginia, man named Frank turned his body into a potentially lethal weapon of defiance and anger. Two neighbors, John MacCarty and Edward Thomas, had slighted him by refusing to admit his company. Furious at the insult, Frank enlisted a friend to help fight the two in a brawl. But Frank's honor was not sufficiently restored. Frank "stript himself naked only to his Drawers and came running after Macartie with a great Clubb on his back," according to one witness. Another witness reported that Frank had pulled up a fence stake, vowing that he "would fight Macarty soe long as hee could stand." When he overtook MacCarty, he declared to him, "Now I will be for you," and threw down the club in challenge.

An angry man, his shame rising unbearably, resorts to acts of violent self-assertion to avoid losing face with other men. He makes a split-second decision to turn an easily accessible blunt object into a weapon. He issues a verbal challenge before the fight to give meaning to the ensuing violence. In a curious act that perhaps combined fastidious concern for his clothes—rips and blood from the fight would certainly ruin them—and conscious display of his body, primed for a fight, he takes the trouble to remove all his garments except his drawers before pursuing the man who insulted him.

All these are the stock ingredients of the culture of male assertion, varying greatly over time but displaying nonetheless familiar elements: an unanswered insult imperiling a man's standing within the community of men; a resort to violence to rectify the wrong; the centrality of the male body to the process of regaining lost respect and reputation. Does anything change if we know that Frank is enslaved? That the two neighbors are white and their alleged insult was to tell him "they were not company for negroes"? That the body poised with a cudgel is that of a black man, his dark skin burdening him with legal impediments and constraints no white man faced?

In this brief consideration of what masculinity might have meant to men of African descent in North America, most of whom were enslaved during the seventeenth, eighteenth, and early nineteenth centuries, I argue that the bodies of enslaved men—or, more precisely, the social persons rooted in those bodies—were more crucial to the meanings and experience of their manhood than was the case for other men. Shortages of labor in colonial North America precipitated some of this focus on male bodies; the great demand for male labor in a colonial setting, where land was plentiful and labor scarce, increased the value placed on strength and stamina for men of all ages and races. Such qualities were especially important for those of the laboring classes, whose livelihoods depended on them. But the bars to property ownership—legal in the case of slaves, economic in the case of working-class white men during the eighteenth and nineteenth centuries—made the value of the robust, laboring, male body even more important for those without property. The propertyless free laborer made his way in the world by virtue of his strength and his wits, but at least he owned his labor. His bound counterparts were not so lucky; although their only value might be calculated with reference to their bodies, even this most personal of resources was owned by another. Stealing oneself (known to the master class as "running away") was one of the most fundamental ways of refuting the basic assumptions of slavery's chattel principle—and, significantly, it was a refutation undertaken by men more often than by women. But the enslaved man also claimed possession of his own body in seemingly more innocuous ways, by expressing personhood through clothing, speech, dance, song, eating, lovemaking, and fighting. For men in slavery, then, the body was the most important resource for expressing manhood. The bitter irony of slavery, however, was that this precious and most personal of resources also bore the brunt of exhausting labor, discipline, and brutal punishment. This was the fate of all propertyless laborers throughout the Atlantic basin, but it was the peculiar burden of the enslaved. The bodies of enslaved men might have been the site of their most potent enactments of manhood, but they were also likely to be damaged, maimed, and disfigured by the brutalities of life in bondage.[1]

Examining masculinity for enslaved man as well as for free men of color forces us to confront yet another fundamental historical issue: the conflation of manhood and human dignity. Historically, those excluded from the benefits of propertied manhood have had to stake their claim to greater recognition by arguing that male privilege should be redefined as human rights and open to all. Subjected to a labor system and a legal context that attempted to strip them of their humanity, enslaved men struggled to find space to be men. In what instances was an enslaved man's assertion of manhood really an insistence on his own humanity? Is it even possible for a person to assert his or her humanity in a non-gendered idiom? To be recognized by others as fully human without having a gender?

The creative responses of black men to the constraints placed on their manhood was a key development in the history of masculinity—one that uniquely exposes how contemporaries came to understand the intertwined relationships among manhood, humanity, and property. Focusing on black masculinity between the first European expansion across the Atlantic and the U.S. antebellum period, this chapter reveals how the premises and expectations for manhood changed dramatically, triggering changes in conceptions of what it meant to be human that were at odds with slavery's chattel principle. Yet slavery did not die an inevitable death; rather it became more entrenched, protected by laws that safeguarded the master's claim to human property. In the space between these dramatic transformations in the meanings of manhood and the denial of humanity that was the essence of slavery, male slaves enacted manhood—stubbornly, defiantly, and sometimes violently—with their bodies. They created a culture of male performance that offered them some protections from violence, and opportunities to dominate fellow slaves, particularly women, in certain circumscribed contexts. Expressions of slave manhood also fueled the fears of white people, whose narrow comfort zone with slave conduct left almost no possibility for male self-determination and assertion—except in those cases where a man's sexual and reproductive claims on black women promised to increase the master's profit. Thus black masculinity took root and flourished in the performances of the black male body even as white masculinity was developing alternative foundations and expressions of male authority and self-assertion derived from landed property, literacy, emotional refinement, and evangelical religion.

West Africans caught up in the juggernaut of Atlantic slavery came from societies in which manhood derived from several sources. European merchant adventurers, interested in establishing ties with powerful leaders who could become lucrative trading partners, wrote of West African men who enjoyed the privileges of political, legal, and economic authority. These were men with the power and savvy to compel Europeans to trade on West African terms and to compete with European rivals for the privilege of doing so. Away from these centers of power, Europeans wrote of men in the company of other men, watching over cattle and drinking palm wine. In these communities, village elders presided over networks of kin and laborers who provided them with material goods, labor, and loyalty; their relationships with women, enslaved and free, gave them the opportunity to expand and secure this position by fathering children. Religious connections also bound some of these men to their fellows, whether in secret religious societies or in their shared respect for the priestly authority. Often the rules governing purity and danger that structured village life and the interactions of men and women were inflected by Islam if not actually Islamic. In some Muslim and Muslim-influenced regions, for example, we know that, much to the discomfort of English commentators, grown men underwent ritual circumcision to mark their passage to adulthood. The English traveler Richard Jobson thus commented with dismay in 1624 that his young Mandingo guide had "ruined" himself by being circumcised against the objections of his English visitors. In others, women lived in separate quarters from the men who fathered their children, and observed strict rules governing hand washing, meal consumption, menstrual seclusion, and mourning.[2]

West African men moved about the landscape with a confidence inspired by this sense of connection to and authority over others. But their confidence also derived from deeply rooted local knowledge—of waterways, grazing lands, and safe passages to the coast; of powerful personalities and religious beliefs in surrounding communities; and, as the Atlantic trade intensified during the eighteenth century, of the dangers of being attacked or kidnapped. What an aspiring European merchant needed, most of all, was a savvy male guide who could give him safe passage to a male leader interested in cultivating new commercial ties. Such a guide could help him avoid the crocodile-infested waters, village rivalries, hostility to outsiders, and political gaffes that potentially doomed his efforts.

In some of the West Central African regions that supplied the Atlantic world with its first slaves, as in many parts of the world, manhood was also a matter of military prowess and reputations for ferocity and bravery. Veterans of Kongo-Angola's near-constant wars of the sixteenth and seventeenth centuries entered the transatlantic trade as commodities after years of experience as warriors. These were the men, according to Ira Berlin, who had the skills and the hard-won resources for self-assertion that enabled many to stave off the burdens of enslavement that were potentially the most crushing to African manhood: the loss of geographic literacy and mobility; the lack of access to instruments of the law, familiar religious traditions, and ties to kin and village; and the absence of the comforts and privileges that came with sexual access to women. As historians Linda Heywood and John Thornton note, these men were not simply canny cosmopolitans, but had also been steeped in a particular regional culture of militarism and creatively adapted Portuguese Catholicism. From the late sixteenth century to the early eighteenth century, Kongo-Angola was wracked by wars, many of them stirred up by the presence of European traders and missionaries, that exposed generations of men and women to the dangers and hardships of battle. The Englishman Andrew Battell, caught up in one of these early conflicts, wrote of reputations for ferocity that enabled men and their leaders to survive. That most of the earliest Atlantic creoles can be traced to West Central Africa changes our understanding of the importance of martial discipline and combat to the ways the first slaves experienced their introduction to the Atlantic slave trade.[3]

Heywood and Thornton's important research into the origins of the first generations of Atlantic slaves in war-torn Kongo-Angola helps us to make sense of the pattern of fierce, if seemingly futile, rebellions throughout the early Atlantic by saltwater slaves: veterans of war who had survived the Middle Passage, the humiliations of being sold, and the rigors of laboring to create colonial economies out of New World fields, forests, and mineral deposits. From South America to the Caribbean to coastal Carolina and the Chesapeake, rebellions small and large burst forth when enslaved men with experience of the protracted wars of Kongo-Angola decided to take their fate into their own hands. Saltwater slaves fomented plots in Barbados in 1676, in Virginia in 1709 and 1710, in New York City in 1712, in St. John in 1733, and in Antigua in 1738.[4]

But the impact of Kongo-Angolan male military culture appeared most explicitly in 1739 in Stono, South Carolina. Led by Jemmy, newly imported from Angola and put to work on a rice plantation alongside his countrywomen, a group of two to three dozen men converged on Hutcheson's store to get supplies. When two white storekeepers refused their demands, the rebels decapitated them in a display of ferocity reminiscent of Kongo-Angolan military conflicts. They then set off south across St. Paul's parish until they came to a crossroads with a tavern and several houses. There they spared the life of the tavern keeper but killed several other inhabitants. As they continued their march across the island, they recruited new followers. Their progress was not stealthy but noisily celebratory; banners, drums, and (allegedly) chants of "Liberty" announced their movements across the countryside. When they paused at a field near a local ferry crossing to celebrate with drink, a hastily recruited militia attacked them. After a brief skirmish, several slaves lay dead and the others were forced to flee.[5]

• • •

The law and practice of slaveholding that spread throughout the Atlantic basin put a premium on the physical capacity of enslaved men to labor and gradually closed off their access to the institutional props that were beginning to define manhood for the English, both at home and in their Atlantic diaspora. The most important of these props was property, which had always been one source for the father's authority over his family and his clout within his local community. By the seventeenth century, however, property had emerged in England as newly important for defining political and economic manhood. A series of legal redefinitions known as enclosure enabled English aristocrats and gentry to expand their formal ownership of land that had by custom been available for use by local residents. Fencing and penalties for trespass curtailed many of these customary privileges of grazing, cultivating, and hunting on local lands. But it also had the effect of closing off the privileges of political and economic manhood that formerly had been available to those with little or no property, who made use of village commons to support their families. When in 1690 John Locke refuted Robert Filmer's anachronistic defense of patriarchy and absolute monarchy, written amid the constitutional crisis that precipitated the English Civil War and published only in 1680, he was articulating a vision of political authority and identity that was already beginning to spread throughout England. Property, he argued, was the rational and moral basis for citizenship—there was no longer any place for monarchs presiding over subjects with an authority rooted in divine right and patriarchal privilege. Indeed, he went so far as to claim that even within the household, a husband enjoyed no special power over his wife other than what common sense and convenience dictated to enable the household to speak with one voice. It was this need for one voice and the indisputably greater claim of men to assume this role that provided the only male domestic authority Locke would recognize. Having challenged patriarchal authority within the household, Locke proceeded to deny it as the basis for the citizen's existence in the political realm. Rather, that existence was firmly and rationally grounded in the ownership of property.

Locke's role in writing the constitution for the colony of Carolina, founded by Anthony Ashley Cooper in 1663, is a well-known instance of the connections between the transformations in European political theory and the unprecedented opportunities to create the world anew in North America. Although Locke's vision ultimately did not survive the first generation of infighting, he did lay the groundwork for slavery in the colony as one of the privileges of property ownership that would become enshrined in the colony's and subsequently the state's history. Most telling was the circular logic of the slave's lack of political manhood—he could be subjected to an older form of patriarchal authority because he was both ineligible to own property and was himself the property of another.[6]

In practice, logic like this underpinned most of the rationale for denying black men the privileges that some white men enjoyed. Property ownership was the basis for white men's ability to be known and recognized by their communities and under the law. If he owned landed property, a man stood a reasonable chance of marrying and forming a household. These were the prerequisites for success in an agricultural economy and his ticket into the community of adult men, the cohort eligible for the local offices that would gain them respect and remuneration. Moreover, his legal voice—often referred to as his "word"—was audible in his community so long as he had the backing of this property. With his property as his bond, a man became known to his neighbors and eligible to participate in a network of creditors and debtors. Backed by property, a man's legal word also made him known in the sense of being legally and economically more predictable. The advantages of being part of this community of men who could be trusted to pay off debts and fines in time, rather than on the spot, gave sheriffs, tax collectors, and courts some assurance that a property-owning man would not run away from his responsibilities or take up arms against local authorities.

Property's ability to make a man visible, knowable, and trustworthy was put to the test by the tiny cohort of black property owners who enjoyed reasonably equitable dealings with white neighbors during the seventeenth century in places like Dutch New York and Virginia's eastern shore. Property enabled them to "pass" as white men in the eyes of their neighbors and the law—a feat of racial transformation that is even more telling when one considers the growing constraints on their enslaved counterparts. For much of the seventeenth century, property ownership enabled men like Anthony Johnson and Edward Nicken to enjoy access to the economic, political, and legal networks their white neighbors enjoyed. By the eighteenth century, several North American colonies had taken steps to close down this access and to ostracize free black men—a move that baffled imperial officials in London. Imposing legal impediments on free male property holders simply on the basis of race contradicted the English recognition of property as the basis for membership in the body politic.[7]

If we consider property's ability to endow men with the characteristics of stability and predictability—to create the trust that underpinned the rules of civil society among men who might otherwise pose a danger to their communities or, in a larger sense, to the state—then a man without property remained unknown, a wild card. Without the privileges or responsibilities of property, he had a lower stake in the stability of his community and in the regular and predictable exchanges of money, goods, and labor that constituted local economies. A propertyless man was a man who did not enjoy the full benefits of presiding over a household, and thus would have little incentive to defend hearth and home. Having failed to achieve adult manhood according to the standards supported by property ownership, a man without property could not be counted on to be a man in any political, economic, or military sense of the term. Enslaved men, of course, were not the only men unlucky enough to lack property in an age in which property made the man. Their white counterparts—in service, under age, impoverished, or physically unable to labor—also lacked this all-important grounding for their civil existence. Yet only enslaved men could claim the distinction of having been deliberately and permanently disconnected from this foundation for manhood. As societies with slaves became slave societies at the end of the seventeenth century—Barbados, Virginia, Maryland, South Carolina—nearly all passed laws to prevent enslaved men from gaining access to the institutional trappings of adult manhood: the ownership of property, the authority over wife, children, and household, and the right to bear arms, bring suits, or testify in court. All these were privileges enjoyed by adult men with property—yet like most privileges, these also subjected the men in question to being bound by laws and reciprocal relationships that ultimately turned their manhood into a resource for, rather than a threat to, the state.

So what space remained for an enslaved man to be a man, in a sense that would have been meaningful to him and recognizable to his contemporaries? Despite the growing importance of propertied manhood in political tracts like Locke's and in laws like those created in the slave colonies of North America and the Caribbean, and despite the constraints imposed on slave mobility and sociability, we have abundant evidence that enslaved men managed to enact manhood with their bodies in ways that were both appealing and threatening to white people.

Much ink has been spilled by historians about an alleged rape case in early Virginia involving a white woman, Katherine Watkins, and a black man, Jack. In 1681, Katherine claimed she had been raped by Jack, and exhibited the bruised face and body and swollen lips that her contemporaries often read as evidence of a woman's refusal to consent to sex. Yet witnesses testified to Katherine's own desires for this man, unleashed with the help of too much alcohol, and to her boldness in reaching into his pants in front of others as she chided him for not calling on her more often. Like her contemporaries, we cannot be certain that her desire and his response resulted in a consensual sexual act; but what we can tell from this case is that no one thought it odd for a white woman to feel such desire for an enslaved man. No one thought it necessary to find explanations other than previous acquaintance and large quantities of alcohol for her sexual desire. In keeping with early modern attitudes toward female sexuality—that it was vital and voracious rather than faint and difficult to stir—Katherine appears to have suffered from witness assumptions that she was teeming with sexual desire for Jack. At this point in the seventeenth century, however, witnesses attached no unique racial meanings to Jack's sexual assertiveness or prowess—no one suggested that Jack was more prone than a white man to take advantage of Katherine's willingness.[8]

We also have evidence in the correspondence of numerous seventeenth- and eighteenth-century planters of their enslaved men's requests for wives. Clearly, it was in the best interest of a planter to keep his slaves focused on their work, and to provide the female companions who might increase the planter's wealth by bearing children. But in these appeals to their masters, and their masters' willingness to interpret these requests as reasonable and necessary for maintaining order on the plantation, white slaveholders recognized a common manhood with their bound laborers, rooted in their "need" for wives. Implicit in this notion of manhood was a recognition of seemingly universal male needs for sexual pleasure, companionship, and comfort that slaveholders found it convenient to meet with female slaves, rather than with white women or other men.[9] But more important is what the requests themselves tell us about enslaved men's desires for intimacy and connection with women. Despite the degradations of slavery—daily humiliations and reminders of how their wills, their persons, and their bodies were supposed to be subordinated to their masters—enslaved men sought sexual relationships that might affirm their essential humanity.

Enslaved men also seem to have confronted white men with physical acts of self-assertion, ranging from Jack's challenge to the white man who had insulted him, to drawing on experience as warriors to mobilize followers and throw off the chains of slavery. In all these acts, enslaved men relied on their bodies—specifically, their ability to fight, use weapons, and commit acts of violence—to respond to the coercion underpinning slavery. Men like Frank, who refused to defer to white counterparts, rejected the most galling of all privileges—whiteness—enjoyed by men like MacCarty, who could boast few other advantages over enslaved men. If they survived the reprisals against such acts of self-assertion, enslaved men communicated to the larger community of white and black men that there were limits to the humiliation a man, even an enslaved man, could endure. Whereas in the community of free men such acts might gain a man the respect and grudging admiration of peers—ironically serving to improve his safety among other violence-prone men—acts of physical self-assertion could result in an enslaved man's brutal corporal punishment, or worse.[10]

Other sources provide us with vivid pictures of enslaved men on the move, seizing their destinies by escaping from their masters. Ads written by masters of escaped slaves included details they believed would assist readers in identifying their chattel. What is striking as one reads these ads in colonial newspapers is the wild combinations of wigs and hats, of cravats and vests and coats, of fancy trousers and boots. Could an enslaved man really run away in eye-catching colors and styles and expect to not be detected? Such garb seems less an attempt at camouflage than of opportunistic theft, the need to wear one's possessions on one's back, and sartorial self-assertion. No one could mistake a man dressed in this fashion as a toiler of the earth. The cost of his finery, its bold refutation of the drab, coarse, brown, or blue linen garb that was an Atlantic plantation slave's allotment, allow us to glimpse the aesthetic sensibility and the consumer desires of the man within—and his vision of his own personhood through the clothes he chose to seize and wear.[11]

Perhaps the most visceral evidence of the palpable power of black manhood, enacted by enslaved men with their bodies, was its inadmissibility in white portrait art. From the sixteenth century on, Europeans often depicted the enslaved attending the male or female subject of a portrait or hovering in the background shadows, a dark counterpoint to the white skin of the subject. Yet surveying the depictions of the enslaved, one is struck by the predominance of women and children. No portrait of a European woman, to my knowledge, included a depiction of a well-muscled man of color in his prime. Most often, the female subjects of portraits were accompanied by children or female attendants. Even the portraits of adult men rarely depicted an adult male slave in the scene: when they did, he was shown in the background, as part of the owner's estate, or in manacles, a sign of his subordination to his owner's will. Black manhood simply could not be admitted intact to the realm of portrait art in a way that enhanced the prestige of the sitter. The few acceptable ways to depict slaves in portraiture consisted of showing the enslaved as a child, a woman, or a man whose manhood had been domesticated and contained.[12]

By the eighteenth century, as new emotional calibrations of white manhood emerged, both the options and the seeming deficiencies expanded for black men; yet the obstacles to achieving propertied manhood continued to limit enslaved men to expressing manhood with their bodies. Sensibility—the emerging value of emotional refinement, which had counterpoints in the cultures of intellectual and physical refinement—encouraged literate men of letters to demonstrate that they were also men of feeling. By this standard it was no longer sufficient simply to be a rake, a wit, or a man who ruled with an iron fist. Such men's anachronistic emotional styles revealed them to be only superficially civilized; to be truly civilized, a man had to be capable of sympathy, of intense feeling, and of measured but authentic emotional expression.[13]

Evangelical Protestantism also contributed its mite to manhood. After Methodists won a following on both sides of the Atlantic, to be followed soon after by the Baptists, manhood appeared to be as much a matter of restraint as of display. An evangelical man distinguished himself by reining in his baser passions. This cut him off from most of his male peers, whose male identities celebrated these passions in alcohol consumption, competitions to prove physical prowess and skill, the sexual exploitation of women, fights, and gambling. Evangelical men disavowed such rowdy, potentially explosive scenes of male rivalry, domination, and sociability. As an alternative, they sought out their male evangelical peers to create a pious community of brothers. Itinerant preachers also cultivated manly reputations for enduring hardship on the circuit, for steadfastness in the face of temptation, and for aloofness from popular cultural forms based on male self-assertion and physical display.[14]

Did any of these alternatives to mainstream manhood's reliance on physical culture and property ownership offer black men viable models for their own lives? Memoirs and autobiographies point to the difficulties of putting forth a credible performance of manhood when one was trading in alternative masculinities and already burdened by the stigma of slavery. Olaudah Equiano, a man of African descent who was also known as Gustavus Vassa, represented his manhood at the end of the eighteenth century in keeping with the trend toward sensibility and evangelical emotion. His narrative clearly revealed its author's belief that a black man's capacity for feeling might be a more useful weapon in the battle to end slavery than guns or knives. Claiming to have been captured as a youth in West Africa, Equiano narrated a life story that featured his empathy for other human beings, his sensitivity to the brutalities of slavery, maritime life, and war, and his embrace of learning and Christianity. Equiano miraculously emerged from slavery not as a primitive or savage man, as many of his contemporaries might have assumed, but as a pious gentleman, capable of all the finer feelings that educated white men claimed as their own. If an enslaved man could feel the degradation and the humiliations of slavery as much as any white man would—if he could aspire to the refined experiences of learning, cognizance of eternal life, and love of his fellow human beings—what could be the justification for keeping him a slave?[15]

Christian piety, however, especially in the way the Society for the Propagation of the Gospel presented it to the enslaved, created a dilemma for black manhood. It celebrated the combination of deference, dutifulness, and humility that was supposed to mark the character of the ideal slave, but left little room for slave manhood. As a tool of the master class, piety smacked of subordination and submission rather than masculine assertion. It was a poor resource for a man seeking license to physically resist slavery. Its call to avoid the temptations of the world, especially the vices of popularly enacted masculinity, were in many ways irrelevant for enslaved men, who had been systematically prohibited from indulging in these pleasures and did so at their peril, in a defiant refutation of their subordination.[16]

But piety could be interpreted differently. It could license a man to insist on the equality of his soul, his right to be seated in the main body of the congregation, or to time off to observe the Sabbath. It could also provide him with a speaking role at a time when there were few legitimate ways for a black man to be heard in public: he might voice an opinion about the Christian upbringing of his child or become a mouthpiece for the Lord through preaching. Efforts to save other souls and to testify to his own salvation, in other words, justified a black man's public speech. Black evangelicals, male and female, ignored the racial divide to reach souls in turmoil. Many listeners described black preachers as having a particular embodied charisma that enabled them to stir the hearts and spirits of their listeners. But such a gift was not the prerogative of men—black women's claims to mystical piety and ecstatic experience were taken seriously by white and black alike. Even if male preachers struggled to make their voices heard in a crowded field, however, enslaved men on nineteenth-century plantations seem to have enjoyed special prerogatives of spiritual and community leadership: accounts of plantation life include descriptions of men playing a prominent role in initiating songs, leading dances and ring shouts, and provoking ecstatic religious experiences. Within the slave communities of the nineteenth-century South, this was an empowering role filled mainly by men—and it is from this attendance to the spirits of the those within their communities that black men began to combine spiritual with political authority.[17]

The Atlantic revolutions—American, French, and Saint-Dominguan—and the rise of an international movement to abolish slavery had an enormous impact on the colonial period's dual legacy of masculinity—the rootedness of black masculinity in the body, and the venue opened up by evangelical religion for black men to claim a legitimate speaking role for themselves. British generals viewed slaves as potential contraband, yet they also recognized their ability to actively seize their freedom. Indeed, during the war, enslaved people in all regions of British North America took flight in unprecedented numbers. This threat to slave property made patriots out of southern slave owners. Although black men were initially defined as lacking the qualities of a trustworthy soldier, this barrier to service eventually fell during the war out of necessity. Despite their service, black men were written out of the community of male citizens defined by the Constitution. Many struggled well into the nineteenth century to secure veteran's pensions to compensate them for injuries that had added to the burdens of racial discrimination to keep them from gainful employment.[18]

The French Revolution and the Declaration of the Rights of Man and of the Citizen (1789) opened the door to abolishing slavery in France and in French territories on the principle of equality, but the subsequent political and economic crisis in the French slaveholding colonies undermined its promise. When slaves seized the moment in Saint-Domingue, they revived the African military traditions that had crossed the Atlantic to the Americas. Toussaint Louverture, in particular, did much to remake this tradition. A canny and cosmopolitan politician and a skilled general, he tried to craft his public authority by successfully navigating among imperial powers. Louverture anchored his political leadership in his military credentials, like his contemporary Napoleon, making patriarchal claims on the downtrodden slaves he had helped to liberate and whose labor was still the most valuable resource in Haiti, the first black republic.[19]

The stages on which black men performed their manhood during the antebellum period built on these antecedents and bore many similarities to the expressions of manhood by white men who lacked property and counted on their muscle to get through the world. With their path to property blocked by law and by custom, free black men viewed the maritime trades as a golden opportunity for advancement and a steady living. Older, more likely to be married, and often embarked on long-term maritime careers, free black sailors in the early decades of the nineteenth century explicitly described their lives at sea as fulfilling male ideals for hard work and provision for families. Yet long absences took their toll on black families and left sailors without the roots of established households and the benefits of property ownership. For many during the antebellum period, brothels became substitute households, providing sailors with an address, a roof over their heads, and a place to store personal belongings that could not be taken aboard ship. As opportunities for black seamen stagnated during the antebellum period, sailors attempted to distinguish themselves through bold and daring deeds at sea that there would have been little opportunity for on land.[20]

On shipboard, and at work on the wharves and docks of North America's port cities, black men became cosmopolitan in their knowledge of the world and their connections to news, commerce, and politics. No surprise that some of the most successful and enterprising enslaved and free men could claim some experience on shipboard or working on the waterfront: Equiano; Denmark Vesey, an ex-sailor who recruited followers from Charleston for an ill-fated rebellion in 1822; Gabriel Prosser, a boatman from Richmond whose rebellion in 1800 was also unsuccessful; Frederick Douglass, who made his escape from slavery by knowing the ways of the black maritime world; and Robert Smalls, a boat pilot who became famous for his exploits during the Civil War. Compared to white sailors, who were denigrated as crude, unpolished men on the margins of society, black men in the maritime trades were central to black leadership in the nineteenth century. Compared to sparse opportunities for free men of color on land, life at sea provided black men with opportunities for upward mobility as a consequence of their skill, contacts, confidence, and access. The political potential for networking and leadership among black maritime workers was recognized backhandedly by the Negro Seaman Acts of 1822 in South Carolina, a set of restrictions on the freedoms of black sailors that was adopted by several other southern states as well as Cuba. Historian Jeffrey Bolster estimates that close to ten thousand black seamen were incarcerated under these acts, a significant curtailment of black mobility but one that nonetheless appears to have done little to prevent black men from turning the experience of maritime labor into a sensibility about their own manhood that could become the basis for political consciousness and leadership.[21]

From the grog shops, taverns, and brothels of urban ports, black men joined black women in making the streets a vibrant place for black cultural expression. Whether traveling on their master's business or their own, hawking goods and services, or simply seeking company, black men attracted attention with their clothing, their voices, their hairstyles, their music, and their bodily comportment. White observers commented on black men's distinctive gait, which they described just as often with admiration for its grace and rhythm as with derision. Many white people described the discomfort they felt when black people gazed at them directly—with what they described as brazenness—but black men who looked at the ground and failed to make eye contact also elicited derogatory comments from white people. Black men's hairstyles seemed exotic compared to the coiffures common among white people. White people found them fascinating and occasionally even beautiful, but always somewhat confounding of conventions of grooming. And the clothing urban black men wore in the streets seemed inappropriate for laborers, according to the white observers who commented on it—a criticism many middle-class white women also leveled at working-class white women who dressed in expensive finery incongruous with what was supposed to be their station.[22]

For rural men, in contrast, roads connecting plantations, paths through the woods, and plantation quarters themselves were the setting for the vast majority of enslaved men to assert themselves as men. Geographic literacy—knowing how to get around from plantation to plantation, to navigate local rivers and creeks and shortcuts through the woods—to know how to escape for a few days respite as well as to run the master's errands to the next plantation—these were all the skills that distinguished enslaved men from their female counterparts, whose work and care for children resulted in more circumscribed lives. Rural enslaved men, along with enslaved women, also refuted slavery's chattel principle by owning property. Significantly, their property did not take the form of land, which would have conveyed political recognition, but livestock, tools, and the produce from plots allotted to them to work on their own time. In some districts of the southern United States, slave-owned livestock was substantial. Yet none of these forms of property made them men in the eyes of the law—and this is precisely why this form of property ownership could be tolerated.[23]

In addition to city streets, taverns, and rural spaces, enslaved and free people of color also claimed sacred space as their own during the antebellum period. There were very few separate black churches before 1865 in the South, but in the North, black churches became the anchors of black neighborhoods early in the century, supporting black aspirations to property ownership and education and fostering community. In these sacred spaces, preaching, song, music, food, and clothing nurtured a sense of soul equality for both men and women, although men provided much of the intellectual and publicly recognized leadership for these institutions.[24]

Feeling like a man, being seen as a man, was as much a matter of voice, gesture, posture, and physical culture for black men in the nineteenth century as it was about clothes and grooming. What the historian Stephanie Camp has described as "the pleasures of resistance" included the body's comportment as well as an enslaved person's quite deliberate efforts to refuse the soul-crushing realities of slavery.[25] Jaunty gaits, difficult dance moves, raucous laughter, songs that moaned and soared, displays of prideful anger, edgy combinations of clothes, labor-intensive hairstyles—all suggested an insistence on joy, sensuality, and vitality as the defiant response to slavery's destructive force. Yet these same bodies bore the scars from whippings, the disfigurements resulting from beatings and accidents, and the symptoms of chronic illness.

But the pleasures of resistance could take a more literal form, at least in the contemplation of it. David Walker's *Appeal* (1829) called on the simmering anger and unfulfilled desire of black men for open, violent resistance against white people who denied them liberty, livelihoods, and justice. His raw call to arms echoed centuries of black male efforts to stir their peers to collective violent engagement with white oppressors—and embarrassed his antislavery contacts, who found it all too difficult to circumvent white fears about black men whose anger was visceral and potentially explosive. Walker disseminated his call up and down the eastern seaboard, using the black maritime networks that supported black men economically, politically, and psychically and connected his Boston business to other Atlantic ports. His success was the specific spark for new laws restricting black sailors and preventing the circulation of antislavery pamphlets throughout the South.[26]

The disadvantages of asserting black manhood in such an embodied way were obvious to many nineteenth-century reformers, who brought Equiano's aspirations to a more genteel manhood to bear on their observations of all that was wrong with slavery. To depend so much on one's body to assert manhood was to reinforce white depictions of black men as potentially murderous and rebellious primitives, whose teeming physicality seemed to threaten the livelihoods of white working men, the lives of all slaveholders, and the virtue of white women. And yet the vigor and vitality of black men was clearly attractive to many—not simply to other black men and women, but to white men and women as well.

The response of black men to this dilemma is instructive of the limits of a manhood so dependent on bodily expression and performance. The Massachusetts butler and successful author Robert Roberts urged black men to leave the noisy attractions of male display on the streets for the quiet and dignified world of domestic labor in the parlors of the wealthy. Roberts provided explicit instructions in *The House Servant's Directory* (1828) for black men to attain professional dignity and secure employment by taming their physicality—the unpleasant smells and ungainly movements of a body used to the competitive and open spaces of city streets. Roberts tried to teach his readers to become aware of the way they walked, of how they looked after their clothing, and the jarring presence of their own laboring body in domestic spaces whose alchemy depended on effacing the traces of the labor needed to produce them. The manhood he recommended—one of quiet endurance and professional competence—was completely at odds with the ways white people described black men inhabiting city streets. But Roberts harked back to evangelical Christianity's potential to provide a resource for black men with a passage in the introduction that enjoined those of the servant class to remember but not to respond to the injuries more powerful people inflicted on them.[27]

Occasionally, a black man's skills and heroism drew the attention and praise of the white public. Early in the Civil War, Robert Smalls mobilized his considerable skills as a stevedore, ship rigger, deckhand, and pilot to score a blow for the Union. Born in South Carolina, Smalls was in charge of piloting the *Planter*, a Confederate vessel, despite being himself a slave. While in charge of navigating the ship, Smalls outwitted the captain and crew to turn the vessel over to Union forces in May 1862. Public citations of his heroism reveal how, for black men, achieving recognition as men in the eyes of their white counterparts required careful skirting of the physicality of manhood (which white people found so threatening in black men) without actually effacing it. The *New York Daily Tribune* placed the vexing question of manhood's relationship to the privileges of freedom front and center in its comment:

> Is he not also a man—and is he not fit for freedom, since he made such a hazardous dash to gain it? . . . Is he not a man and a hero—whose pluck has not been questioned by even *The Charleston Courier* or *The New York Herald*? What white man has made a bolder dash, or won a richer prize in the teeth of such perils during the war?[28]

Perhaps nothing spoke as poignantly to the dilemmas of black masculinity's rootedness in the black male body than Frederick Douglass's efforts to create an enslaved hero in his 1852 novel *The Heroic Slave*. Of his hero, Madison, the preeminent African American political leader of the nineteenth century wrote:

> Madison was of manly form, tall, symmetrical, round, and strong. In his movements he seemed to combine, with the strength of the lion, a lion's elasticity. His torn sleeves disclosed arms like polished iron.[29]

Douglass's depiction of Madison, provided by an admiring but only partially comprehending white narrator, harked to the seemingly primitive physical endowments of the slave by likening him to the king of the African savannahs, the lion. But Douglass salvaged and tamed this primitive masculine power, subjecting it to Madison's "head to conceive" and suggesting its relevance for the needs of the industrializing economy. With arms like polished iron, the substance that marked technological superiority over primitives as well as the achievements of the rapidly changing economy, Madison could not be mistaken for a savage. Rather, he was a man whose body reflected the potential of black men, as Douglass saw it, for free labor in the burgeoning industries of the North. More fully committed to women's rights than any other black male abolitionist, Douglass had nonetheless begun the process of staking the progress of his race on the rights of black men to be recognized as gendered human beings—as men.[30]

The physical being and potential value of the labor of black men dominated the thinking even of an abolitionist and political activist as prominent as Douglass. In his own well-known account of achieving manhood, recorded in *Narrative of the Life of Frederick Douglass* (1845) and *My Bondage and My Freedom* (1855), the necessary rite of passage was violent conflict with a white man. Douglass likely would have seen something of his own youthful self-assertion in Frank's seventeenth-century pursuit of MacCarty to revenge an insult. Black manhood remained a matter of the body throughout the antebellum period. A black man ultimately deflected violence and humiliation and rejected subjugation with the only resource he could count on, his body. Even if he could not protect his person from the violence embedded in slavery, and his body suffered injury, accident, and illness, he still had to rely on it to project dignity, integrity, and defiant pride during the worst moments of humiliation and subordination. Ultimately, for black men, manhood was not something one could merely think one's way to or accumulate like property. Rather, achieving it was a matter of constant performance aimed at a bodily aesthetic that defied subordination and stirred the admiration, the fear, and the mindfulness of observers, black and white, of the potential for male self-assertion.

NOTES

Thanks to Angus Corbett, Ted Pearson, and the University of Sydney American History reading group, especially Clare Corbould, Michael McDonnell, Stephen Robertson, Blanca Tovias, and Shane White, for their helpful suggestions.

1. Frantz Fanon, *Black Skin, White Masks*, trans. Charles Lam Martham (New York, 1967; orig. pub. 1952); Charles Rosenberg, "Sexuality, Class, and Role in Nineteenth Century America," in Elizabeth Pleck and Joseph E. Pleck, eds., *The American Man* (Englewood Cliffs, N.J., 1980), 219–257; Anthony Rotundo, *American Manhood: Transformations in Masculinity from the Revolution to the Modern Era* (New York, 1993); R. W. Connell, *Masculinities: Knowledge, Power, and Social Change* (Berkeley, Calif., 1995); John Saillant, "The Black Body Erotic and the Republican Body Politic, 1790–1820," *Journal of the History of Sexuality* 5, no. 3 (1995): 403–428; Michael Kimmel, *Manhood in America: A Cultural History* (New York, 1995, 2nd ed.); Walter Johnson, *Soul by Soul: Inside the Antebellum Slave Market* (Cambridge, Mass., 1999); Patricia Hill Collins, *Black Sexual Politics: African Americans, Gender, and the New Racism* (New York, 2004).

2. Richard Jobson, *The Golden Trade, or, a Discovery of the River Gambra* (London, 1623); P. E. H. Hair, Adam Jones, and Robin Law, eds., *Barbot on Guinea: The Writings of Jean Barbot on West Africa, 1678–1712*, 2 vols. (London, 1992); John Thornton, *Africa and Africans in the Making of the Atlantic World, 1400–1680* (New York, 1992).

3. Ira Berlin, *Many Thousands Gone: The First Two Centuries of Slavery in North America* (Cambridge, Mass., 1998); Linda Heywood and John Thornton, *Central Africans, Atlantic Creoles, and the Foundation of the Americas, 1585–1660* (New York, 2007).

4. Ira Berlin, *Generations of Captivity: A History of African American Slaves* (Cambridge, Mass., 2003); Stephanie E. Smallwood, *Saltwater Slavery: The Middle Passage from Africa to American Diaspora* (Cambridge, Mass., 2007).

5. Peter Wood, *Black Majority: Negroes in Colonial South Carolina from 1670 Through the Stono Rebellion* (New York, 1974); John Thornton "African Dimensions of the Stono Rebellion," *American Historical Review* 96, no. 4 (1991): 1101–1113; Edward Pearson, "'A Countryside Full of Flames': A Reconsideration of the Stono Rebellion and Slave Rebelliousness in the Early Eighteenth-Century South Carolina Lowcountry," *Slavery and Abolition* 17, no. 2 (1996): 22–50; Mark M. Smith, ed., *Stono: Documenting and Interpreting a Southern Slave Revolt* (Columbia, S.C., 2005), 73–86.

6. Stephanie McCurry, *Masters of Small Worlds: Yeoman Households and the Political Culture of the South Carolina Low Country* (New York, 1995).

7. T. H. Breen and Stephen Innes, *Myne Owne Ground: Race and Freedom on Virginia's Eastern Shore, 1640–1676* (New York, 1980); J. Douglas Deal, *Race and Class in Colonial Virginia: Indians, Englishmen, and Africans on the Eastern Shore in the Seventeenth Century* (New York, 1993); Kathleen M. Brown, *Good Wives, Nasty Wenches, and Nasty Patriarchs: Gender, Race, and Power in Colonial Virginia* (Chapel Hill, N.C., 1996).

8. Warren M. Billings, ed., *The Old Dominion in the Seventeenth Century* (Chapel Hill, N.C., 1975); Sharon Block, *Rape and Sexual Power in Early America* (Chapel Hill, N.C., 2006).

9. Brown, *Good Wives, Nasty Wenches*; Jennifer Morgan, *Laboring Women: Reproduction and Gender in New World Slavery* (Philadelphia, 2004).

10. See Shane White, *Somewhat More Independent: The End of Slavery in New York City, 1770–1810* (Athens, Ga., 1991), 181, for an enslaved New York man's response to a challenge to his manhood.

11. Philip D. Morgan, "Colonial South Carolina Runaways and Their Significance for Slave Culture," *Slavery and Abolition* 6, no. 3 (1985): 57–78; David Waldstreicher, "Reading the Runaways: Self-Fashioning, Print Culture, and Confidence in Slavery in the Eighteenth-Century Mid-Atlantic," *WMQ*, 3rd ser., 56 (1999): 243–272; David Waldstreicher, *Runaway America, Benjamin Franklin, Slavery, and the American Revolution* (New York, 2005), 7–8; White, *Somewhat More Independent*, 114–149, 185, 194–200.

12. Kim F. Hall, *Things of Darkness: Economies of Race and Gender in Early Modern England* (New York, 1995); Susan Amussen, *Caribbean Exchanges: Slavery and the Transformation of English Society, 1640–1700* (Chapel Hill, N.C., 2007).

13. G. J. Barker-Benfield, *The Culture of Sensibility: Sex and Society in Eighteenth-Century Britain* (Chicago, 1992); Kenneth Lockridge, *On the Sources of Patriarchal Rage: The Commonplace Books of William Byrd and Thomas Jefferson and the Gendering of Power in the Eighteenth Century* (New York, 1992); Andrew Burstein, *Sentimental Democracy: The Evolution of America's Romantic Self-Image* (New York, 1999); Sarah Knott, *Sensibility and the American Revolution* (Chapel Hill, N.C., 2009).

14. Janet Moore Lindman, *Bodies of Belief: Baptist Community in Early America* (Philadelphia, 2008).

15. Vincent Carretta, *Equiano, the African: Biography of a Self-Made Man* (Athens, Ga., 2005); Olaudah Equiano, *The Interesting Narrative, and Other Writings*, ed. Vincent Carretta (New York, 2003).

16. Sylvia R. Frey and Betty Wood, *Come Shouting to Zion: African American Protestantism in the American South and British Caribbean to 1830* (Chapel Hill, N.C., 1998), 63–83.

17. Ibid., 98–103, 114–117, 118–125; 143–148; Shane White and Graham J. White, *The Sounds of Slavery: Discovering African American History Through Songs, Sermons, and Speech* (Boston, 2005); Steven Hahn, *A Nation Under Our Feet: Black Political Struggles in the Rural South from Slavery to the Great Migration* (Cambridge, Mass., 2003).

18. James Sidbury, *Ploughshares into Swords: Race, Rebellion, and Identity in Gabriel's Virginia, 1730–1810* (New York, 1997); Sidbury, *Becoming African in America: Race and Nation in the Early Black Atlantic* (New York, 2007); Frey and Wood, *Come Shouting to Zion*; Woody Holton, *Forced Founders: Indians, Debtors, and Slaves and the Making of the American Revolution in Virginia* (Chapel Hill, N.C., 1999); Michael McDonnell, *The Politics of War: Race, Class, and Conflict in Revolutionary Virginia* (Chapel Hill, N.C., 2007); White, *Somewhat More Independent*.

19. Laurent Dubois, *Avengers of the New World: The Story of the Haitian Revolution* (Cambridge, Mass., 2004).

20. Jeffrey Bolster, *Black Jacks: African American Seamen in the Age of Sail* (Cambridge, Mass., 1997), 158–170, 180, 187–188.

21. Ibid., 206.

22. White, *Somewhat More Independent*, 195–197, 201–202.

23. Stephanie Camp, *Closer to Freedom: Enslaved Women and Everyday Resistance in the Plantation South* (Chapel Hill, N.C., 2004); Philip Morgan, "The Ownership of Property by Slaves in the Mid-Nineteenth Century Low Country," *Journal of Southern History* 49 (1983): 399–420.

24. Erica Dunbar, *A Fragile Freedom: African American Women and Emancipation in the Antebellum City* (New Haven, Conn., 2008).

25. Stephanie Camp, "The Pleasures of Resistance: Enslaved Women and Body Politics in the Plantation South, 1830–1861," *Journal of Southern History* 68, no. 3 (2002): 533–572.

26. David Walker, *David Walker's Appeal . . . to the Coloured Citizens of the World* (Boston, 1829); James Oliver Horton and Lois E. Horton, "Violence, Protest, and Identity: Black Manhood in Antebellum America," in James Oliver Horton, *Free People of Color: Inside the African American Community* (Washington, D.C., 1993), 80–96; Peter P. Hinks, *To Awaken My Afflicted Brethren: David Walker and the Problem of Antebellum Slave Resistance* (University Park, Pa., 1997); Bolster, *Black Jacks*, 197.

27. Graham Hodges, ed., Robert Roberts, *A House Servant's Directory* (Boston, 1827).

28. *New York Daily Tribune*, September 10, 1862.

29. Frederick Douglass, *The Heroic Slave* (Cleveland, 1853), 5.

30. Ibid.; Bruce Dorsey, *Reforming Men and Women: Gender in the Antebellum City* (Ithaca, N.Y., 2002); Martha Jones, *All Bound Up Together: The Woman Question in African American Public Culture, 1830–1900* (Chapel Hill, N.C., 2007); Judith Butler, *Undoing Gender* (New York, 2004).

V

Revolution

10

Of Eloquence "Manly" and "Monstrous"

The Henpecked Husband in Revolutionary Political Debate, 1774–1775

BENJAMIN H. IRVIN

> the henpect man rides behind his Wife and lets her wear the Spurs and govern the Reins. . . . He is but subordinate and ministerial to his Wife, who commands in chief, and he dares do nothing without her Order. . . . He and she make up a Kind of Hermaphrodite, a Monster.
> —Samuel Butler, *The Genuine Remains in Verse and Prose of Mr. Samuel Butler* (1759)

When, in the fall of 1774, the Continental Congress published the Articles of Association, announcing a scheme of non-importation, non-exportation, and non-consumption to be enforced by extralegal committees of local patriots, many British North Americans felt betrayed. Colonists who bristled at the prospect of economic resistance—either because they feared that aggressive political posturing would widen the breach between the colonies and Great Britain or simply because they dreaded the baneful financial consequences of yet another boycott—had expected the Continental Congress to embrace more conciliatory measures, much as had the Stamp Act Congress ten years before. "The hopes of all moderate and considerate persons among us . . . were long fixed upon the general *American Congress*," wrote the Reverend Thomas Bradbury Chandler, rector of St. John's Church in Elizabethtown, New Jersey. "But the poor *Americans*," he despondently concluded, "are doomed to disappointment."[1] Chandler and other "disappointed" Americans responded to news of Congress's boycott by publishing a flurry of condemnatory pamphlets in the winter of 1774–75. During the sixth-month adjournment between the First Continental Congress and the Second, nearly two dozen of these oppositional tracts appeared in print.

| 195

Their titles—*Pills for the Delegates, The Two Congresses Cut Up, What Think Ye of the Congress Now?*—announced their authors' aim to undermine the Continental Congress and thwart its Association.

Many of these writers tendered sound constitutional, political, and economic arguments against Congress and the Association. Chandler and his loyalist contemporaries claimed that colonial assemblies and provincial conventions did not possess the authority to appoint delegates to a general convention.[2] They asserted that Americans owed no obedience to such an irregularly assembled body. They challenged the legal right of local committees to monitor the business activities of merchants, traders, and other private persons. And they warned that a trade boycott would bring ruin to American farmers.

Yet, in addition to disputing the legality of Congress and the wisdom of its resolutions, these authors also poured a great deal of scorn on the delegates who had gathered in Philadelphia. Numerous writers inserted derogatory comments about congressmen into their pamphlets: contemptuous dicta amid more formal arguments against the Association. But a few went further, penning humorous and bounding satires wholly dedicated to smearing the members of Congress. These writers almost never singled out congressmen for attack; some, in fact, expressly denied any intention to do so. Chandler opened his *What Think Ye of the Congress Now?* by asserting, "I mean to avoid all personal reflexions upon the members of the Congress; for I never had any personal objections to any of them."[3] But though these writers rarely slurred particular individuals, they relentlessly assailed the Congress as a group or order of men.

One of the foremost strategies by which loyalist pamphleteers and poets attempted to delegitimize the Continental Congress was by attacking the masculinity of its members. Foes of Congress invoked an array of bigotries, including those of region and religion as well as of class and race. Quite often, though, they couched such attacks within, or yoked them to, equally or even more damning imputations of gender inadequacy or deviance. Most fundamentally, these authors challenged the congressmen's *mastery*—that is, their patriarchal dominion over selves and others. In eighteenth-century British North America, the attainment of full manhood depended, normatively speaking, on a man's physical and emotional maturation; his accumulation of wealth, if not through inheritance than by the pursuit of a respectable vocation or profession; his contraction of marriage; his governance of family, servants, or slaves; and his fulfillment of civic obligations such as militia service or the payment of taxes.[4]

Loyalist writers charged that members of Congress lacked these most basic attributes and achievements of adult white manhood. One author, for example, disparaged the congressmen's maturity and discernment, likening them to the unwhiskered pupils of Eton College: "Less fit for Senates, than for Toys, / in politicks, at best but Boys." He belittled the congressmen's professional stature, ranking the many lawyers in Congress mere "Scriv'ners," "[f]orm'd at most, to scrawl a Lease." And he scathingly insinuated that life on a "savage" continent had sullied the congressional delegates and rendered them insensible to their English liberties: "Men to Atlantic Empire born / Look down on Greece, and Rome with Scorn, / / Prefer their Mohawks, and their Creeks, / To Romans, Britons, Swiss, or Greeks." By portraying members of Congress as giddy schoolboys, dull notaries, and debased provincials, this loyalist critic characterized patriot leaders as flawed or incomplete men, unfit to govern and undeserving of the public's faith.[5]

Of all the unflattering representations by which loyalist critics maligned the Continental Congressman, perhaps none cast graver aspersion on his mastery or his manhood than their depiction of him as a henpecked husband. Recent scholarship on Anglo-American masculinity has demonstrated that the progression from bachelorhood into marriage was perhaps the most vital stage of adult manhood.[6] And yet, shrill and recurrent denunciations of the henpecked husband—the cowering sop who yielded patriarchal authority to his overbearing wife—reveal that marriage alone did not secure manliness.[7] A man not only had to take a wife, he had to keep her under his thumb. This obligation arose in substantial measure from the legal doctrine of *coverture*. Early American women's historians have compellingly demonstrated that coverture forcefully shaped gender relations within the institution of marriage.[8] At common law, a married woman's legal identity and property rights melded with those of her male spouse. As a consequence of marriage, the *feme covert* relinquished her rights to own or to alienate property, to sue or to be sued, or to stand trial for crimes committed in the presence of or with the permission of her husband. Legally and financially dependent on him, the married woman was not expected to exercise independent thought or will. As Linda K. Kerber has explained, "The husband's control of all property gave him such coercive power over the wife that she could not defy him."[9]

By vesting such coercive power in the husband, the doctrine of coverture established rigid constraints on married women, but it also imposed tremendous burdens on married men. These included not merely the obligation to provide shelter and material sustenance for their wives or to manage familial affairs, but far more invidiously, the obligation to speak for their wives, to discipline and to control their wives—in a word, to *cover* their wives. Henpeckery, the failure to meet such obligations, was considered a failure of manhood. It exposed the husband to the humiliating charge of weakness or impotency. It diminished his stature as a man. Further, because the subordination of wives remained a husbandly duty—a touchstone of masculine integrity—accusations of henpeckery bore the potential to embarrass or shame. As an assertion of gender aberrance, the charge of henpeckery was politically potent.[10] The henpecked husband, who could not govern his house, made for sharply barbed satire of men who aspired to govern the state.

This chapter examines the motif of henpeckery in two satirical publications. *A Dialogue Between a Southern Delegate and His Spouse on His Return from the Grand Continental Congress*—a romping verse printed as an octavo pamphlet in the late fall of 1774, presumably by the New York newspaperman James Rivington—invited readers to eavesdrop on one congressman's querulous homecoming. The loyalist author of this raucous poem heaped aspersions on patriot masculinity, but in so doing, he or she only treated Whig propagandists to a taste of their own medicine. For in support of their trade boycotts, American resistance leaders also exploited patriarchal gender norms. The creator of "Arabella's *Complaint of the* Congress," a short letter published in the *Pennsylvania Magazine, or American Monthly Museum* in September 1775, artfully utilized henpeckery to promote the cause of liberty.

A Dialogue and "Arabella's *Complaint*" represent a very small portion of the satire written during the American Revolution, and they may be the only two works that took henpeckery as their organizing themes. Together, however, *A Dialogue* and "Arabella's *Complaint*" help to illuminate the mobilizing power of gender in political debate—that is, the power of gendered rhetoric to rally individuals in support of, or in opposition to, political leaders and their platforms, in this case the Continental Congress and its Articles of Association.[11] In New York, where much of the prose and poetry denouncing patriot masculinity first appeared, the colonial assembly voted not to consider the proceedings of Congress, not to thank the merchants of New York City for abiding by the Association, and not to appoint delegates to the Second Continental Congress to be held the following May.[12] Writing from as a far away as Pennsylvania, Maryland, and Delaware, grateful loyalists credited Thomas Bradbury Chandler and his collaborative penmen with this "happy effect."[13] Meanwhile, the extraordinary acrimony with which American patriots greeted anti-congressional pamphlets further suggests that their authors had struck a nerve. In New York and Virginia, crowds of Associators made a ritual of burning loyalist publications.[14] In Monmouth County, New Jersey, a patriot crowd tarred and feathered one such tract and nailed it to the pillory, "there to remain as a monument to the indignation of a free and loyal people."[15] Whig leaders in New Jersey and Pennsylvania also organized boycotts of Rivington's press and swore not to conduct business with post riders who carried his publications.[16] By helping to mobilize these constituencies, the henpecked husband, for all his namby-pamby ways, might well be recognized as a forgotten foot soldier of the revolution.

Henpecked Husbands

As an exemplar of unmanly spousal behavior, the henpecked husband has an ancient heritage. A stock character in the fabliaux of medieval Europe, he made frequent appearances in the writings of Chaucer and Lydgate.[17] Reworked by Shakespeare and revived by Restoration dramatists, this well-established antihero captured the imagination of Augustan satirists, who by recounting the foibles of the henpecked husband simultaneously affirmed their commitment to companionate marriage and upheld the prerogative of the male head of house.[18] John Arbuthnot's pedantic Martinus Scriblerus, for example, informed readers that they might recognize the henpecked husband by his overdeveloped "*levatores Scapulae*," the so-called Muscle of Patience, which runs the length of the neck and enables men to shrug. More darkly, Drury Lane's Arthur Murphy, keeper of the *Gray's Inn Journal*, recounted the tragic self-murder of "John Henpeck," whose suicide note read in its entirety: "A frowning World and a scolding Wife, / Is the Cause of my putting an End to my Life." By the mid-eighteenth century, the henpecked husband was so fully entrenched in British literature and art that a unique vocabulary had emerged to describe his particular failings: the meacocke, the cat's foot, the grimalkined man, the subject of a petticoat judgment, and so forth.[19]

Britain's North American colonists knew the henpecked husband well. American consumers devoured British books and periodicals, circulating them among friends and acquaintances and reading them aloud in clubs, taverns, and coffeehouses.[20] American subscribers to the wildly popular *Spectator* thus shared in the amusement of the Whig playwrights and essayists Richard Steele and Joseph Addison, who offered comfort to the "*Fraternity of the Henpeck'd*" by celebrating Socrates, the notoriously wife-ridden philosopher whose "Virtue" owed in great part "to the Exercise which his useful Wife constantly gave it."[21] Readers of American newspapers, too, digested reports of English villagers who compelled submissive husbands and domineering wives to "ride the stang," a mode of public ridicule that one Boston newspaper characterized as late as 1752 as "the usual Burlesque when the Female gains the Breeches."[22] American sailors, meanwhile, perhaps heard or spun their own yarns of an English privateer, outfitted during the War of the Austrian Succession and christened the *Henpeck* to torment enemy shipping as ever a cruel wife did her husband.[23] More recently, the English playwright Samuel Foote had vividly depicted the follies of the man who too cravenly yielded to the will of a domineering spouse. In his 1763 comedy *The Mayor of Garratt*—a play that delighted American audiences until the eve of the Civil War—Foote introduced Jerry Sneak, "a paltry, puddling, puppy" of a husband who, though farcically elected mayor by a whimsical mob, proved unable to govern his scolding and adulterous wife.[24] Perhaps hoping to capitalize on the popularity of Jerry Sneak, one London engraver published a work titled "The Hen Peck'd Grocer" in 1778. Capturing the submissive husband's many faults, this etching depicts a diminutive, shrug-shouldered grocer fleeing the cudgel of his blustering wife. No submissive helpmeet she, this menacing woman usurps her husband's mastery. Driving him from his shop, presumably so that she might assert control over his prominently displayed goods and wares, this "hoarse grown" wife claims all of the prerogatives that coverture reserved for men.

By mocking the peculiar anguish of the henpecked husband, eighteenth-century British engravers, playwrights, and shipowners, too, sculpted in bas-relief a model of the virtuous and masterly man. Compassionate and loving, the idealized husband was nevertheless self-willed, quick to attend and to please his wife, but slow to bend to her command. As the antithesis of these commendable masculine qualities, the henpecked husband came to delineate the boundaries of respectable domesticity for a nascent middle class. In his many cautionary tales was preserved some measure of masculine authority against the egalitarian implications of emergent notions of romantic love. Precisely because the revolution threatened to destabilize gender relations, patriot and loyalist writers employed conventionalized gender imagery and metaphors, including the henpecked husband, to mobilize their constituencies and to police the boundaries of their respective communities.

Arabella's Complaint

"Arabella's *Complaint*" appeared in the *Pennsylvania Magazine*—a new, radical periodical printed under the editorial care and contributing authorship of Thomas Paine—in September 1775, nine or ten months *after* the publication of *A Dialogue Between a Southern Delegate and His Spouse*. But it is useful

"The Hen Peck'd Grocer" (1778), from the Colonial Williamsburg Foundation. The verse reads:
> Bred in the Learn'd Schools of Billingsgate
> Behold this Beauty Cudgeling her Mate
> Hoarse Grown with Rhetorick, she now Assists
> The want of that, by Potent use of Fists;
> Fierce as a Tygress, to his Back she Flies
> & at his head the well known Cudgel Plys.

to examine "Arabella's *Complaint*" first, for timed as it was to reinvigorate American patriots after nearly a full year of non-importation and to steel them for the non-exportation campaign scheduled to commence that fall, this patriot satire exposes the gendered moral economy that undergirded the Continental Congress's program of trade boycotts. Penned by a henpecking housewife, "Arabella's *Complaint*" was intended to shame a particularly abominable sort of unpatriotic behavior. Juxtaposing masculine virtue with feminine vice, "Arabella's *Complaint*" conjured a spendthrift wife, farcically habituated to consumer fashion, as she whittled away at the patriarchal authority of her patriot husband. To fully appreciate the gendered ideology in which Arabella trafficked, we must examine more carefully the Continental Congress and its platform of economic resistance.

The Continental Congress adopted the Articles of Association, a series of trade boycotts, in October 1774. Effective that December, the Association called on merchants to refrain from importing British goods and foodstuffs and from participating in the Atlantic slave trade. Effective as of September 1775, the same month that "Arabella's *Complaint*" appeared, the Association bound planters, farmers, fishermen, distillers, lumbermen, and other producers from exporting their yields to Great Britain, Ireland, and the West Indies. The Association also urged colonists to forego the consumption of East India tea and to abstain from the purchase of imported "goods, wares, or merchandise." Finally, the Association beseeched Americans to relinquish popular leisure activities and social customs, including "every species of extravagance and dissipation, especially all horse-racing, and all kinds of games, cock fighting, exhibitions of shews, plays, and other expensive diversions and entertainments."

Premised on a profoundly gendered political economy, the Articles of Association embodied a patriarchal faith in male superiority. By imploring Americans to surrender their livelihoods, to renounce playful amusements, and to abstain from luxuries and even certain necessities of life, the Continental Congress consciously endeavored to promote civic *virtue*. The Articles of Association expressly bound Congress's constituents by virtue's "sacred ties." Imagining virtue as a masculine attribute, republican and Christian thinkers conceptualized virtue's opposites—indulgence, weakness, and dependency—as feminine.[25] Both classical and Protestant tradition envisioned luxury as a female seductress whose beguiling charms softened the political will. During the 1760s and 1770s, the gendered rhetoric of virtue and luxury suffused debates over the worsening imperial crisis. Whig writers at home and in the colonies asserted that the English constitution had fallen into decrepitude. Luxury, they alleged, had corrupted Britain's ruling elites, given rise to a tyrannical ministry, and ultimately imperiled the cherished rights and liberties of English*men*.[26] As a remedy for womanly vice, Congress prescribed manly virtue, and it did so in a proud, manful voice. On the day that Congress voted its support for the inflammatory Suffolk County Resolves—by which the people of Boston proclaimed the stoutest opposition to British government—John Adams declared, "This was one of the happiest days of my life. In Congress We had generous, noble Sentiments, and manly Eloquence."[27]

As a strategy of economic resistance, the Articles of Association compounded Whig ideologies of virtue and luxury with an equally masculinist ethos of the burgeoning world of goods and of the place of women within it. Several decades earlier, around the 1740s, Britain's North American colonists began to import and consume increasing quantities of European merchandise and commodities, including furniture, silver and plate, fabric and clothing, and global foodstuffs such as tea and chocolate. The Consumer Revolution refashioned the material landscape of British North America, while at the same time instilling in its participants a vigorous market sensibility.[28] But it also piqued anxieties about women's frailty. Cautioning against women's participation in the marketplace, ministers, editorialists, and the writers of prescriptive literature invoked ancient suppositions of female sensuality, the classical and biblical notion that women are more vulnerable to temptation and less capable of rational self-control than men.[29] Heightening such masculinist apprehensions was the power of the Consumer Revolution to mobilize women's spending: many of the goods and comestibles that flooded American ports had been marketed specifically for female consumption. Fabrics, for example, such as silk, fine linen, and lace largely appealed to women of fashion; likewise, the accoutrements of tea consumption—tea service, tea tables, tablecloths, napkins, china, and silverware—marked the increasingly feminized space of the private tea salon (gender and class norms having mostly excluded elite women from the public space of the coffeehouse).[30] This rise in female purchasing posed a threat to male privilege. As consumers, women exercised control over household finances; they exerted authority over property that, under the doctrine of coverture, legally belonged to their husbands. The spendthrift wife might even "ruin" her husband by driving him to an unmanly dependency.[31] Such dangers provoked a variety of misogynistic discourses against women's consumption and female power. To return to the examples of fabrics and tea, fretful social commentators denounced women's vain pursuit of fashion and disparaged the salon as a site of gossip and social pretense.[32]

Patriot organizers grasped the magnitude of female purchasing power and actively encouraged American women to participate in colonial trade boycotts.[33] But they also comprehended, far less sanguinely, the potential of female political activity to transform gender relations in Revolutionary America. As Mary Beth Norton has observed, "Never before had female Americans formally shouldered the responsibility of a public role, never before had they claimed a voice—even a compliant one—in public policy."[34] Reflecting deep-seated ambivalence toward women's political behavior,

Whig preconceptions about female fragility persisted, even shaping public discourse about Congress and its Articles of Association, as for example in "Arabella's *Complaint of the* Congress."

Epitomizing womanly indulgence and dissolution, the fictitious Arabella writes to the *Pennsylvania Magazine* to describe the "distressed situation" of American ladies and to beg relief from—that is, to complain of—Congress's onerous boycott. In the process, Arabella embarrasses her husband—a zealous Whig who would "not suffer a single rule of the Congress to be violated in his family"—both by defying his patriotic wishes and by seeking relief, not in private consultation with him, but rather in this humiliating remonstrance to the press. Disavowing her husband's will in this scandalously public way, Arabella thus "gains the breeches," to borrow the metaphorical language of henpeckery. In short, she disgraces her husband by contesting his rightful authority over their domestic realm. Firm and manly husbands—readers of this farce can only conclude—must exercise patriarchal dominion to safeguard American rights against profligate wives.[35]

Non-importation and non-consumption had placed Arabella in an unfamiliar and preposterously uncomfortable condition of material want: "If you'll believe me Mr. Printer," Arabella huffily protests, "there is scarce a tolerable piece of gause or Paris-net, or lawn, or lace to be had in the city: and as for silks and chintzes and such things, they are all as old fashioned as the north star.—In short we are in great danger of suffering." Arabella's pining for the finest, *au courant* fabrics identifies her as a woman of fashion; indeed, she professes to have embraced Congress's Association when *it* was a fashionable thing: "[The boycott] was to be sure well enough at first: It was something *new*: It afforded a good deal of agreeable conversation, and gave an opportunity of much entertaining scandal." But, for Arabella, the boycott had dragged on too long: "[A]re we forever to be debarred the use of *India Teas*!" she laments. "[A]re we to have no more new fashions; no more fine things from *England?* are we to have no more plays, nor balls, nor feasts, nor parties of pleasure, nor concerts of music?"[36] From her lament for expensive prohibited goods and costly proscribed activities, readers may readily deduce what a drain Arabella represents on her husband's wealth. Only the enforced abstemiousness of Congress's Association preserves him.

The author of this parody—whose true identity we may only surmise—inscribed reprehensible effeteness on the female gender, not only by writing in the character of a silly woman, but by further imputing to Arabella a host of blameworthy and stereotypically womanly vices. As the letter's title suggests and as its text amply confirms, Arabella is a carper: at best a whiner, at worst a shrew. Presumably, she has only turned to the press after first giving her husband an earful. No less contemptibly, Arabella is a reprobate gossip. Insensible of her own impropriety, she confesses, "I myself had once the pleasure of whispering to a select company of ten or a dozen particular friends, that my servant had told me that she was acquainted with *Mrs. Filpot's* servant, who told her that her mistress pretended to breakfast with her family on Coffee; but retired immediately after to her closet, where she had a snug dish of Tea by herself."[37] In her very grousing and gossiping talkativeness, Arabella drones out her husband's voice. Scarcely are his patriotic murmurs audible above her chattery din. By appropriating the masculine privilege of political discourse, Arabella literally silences her husband's speech.[38]

Arabella also possesses the harpy's power to enfeeble and emasculate men.[39] As proof of her patriotism, Arabella recounts how she crafted her son Billy's regimental sword knot with her own hands. But rather than aiding and encouraging Billy's military service, the very bedrock of masculine virtue, as many Revolutionary women did, Arabella merely reduces his to a foppish effeminacy. "I spent a whole morning," she preens, "in going from shop to shop to choose a feather for his hat and the gold *thing-um-bobs* for his shoulders." In a postscript, she adds, "Our *Billy* looks exceedingly well in his regimentals." Arabella has thus made a macaroni, or extravagant dandy, of her son at the expense of his martial virility.[40] By publishing her *Complaint*, Arabella has worked a similar diminishment on her husband, reducing him from staunch Whig to impotent fool.

Contrary to its title, "Arabella's *Complaint*" actually celebrated Congress and its scheme of economic resistance. This bit of lampoonery sought to define the American community by distinguishing selflessness, a masculine virtue, from self-indulgence, an effeminate vice. By the logic of its satire, and in spite of Arabella's ridiculous prattle, the *Complaint* represented Congress's Association as a commendable, even salutary response to British tyranny. Only laughable persons, only the vain and frivolous, refused to comply with the Association or resented its impositions. The *Complaint* actually *invited* women to participate in Congress's boycotts. In the voice of Arabella, the author lampooned the assertion that women, as the economic and political dependents of men, had no concern with parliamentary taxation and thus ought not be asked to sacrifice. In so doing, the author acknowledged that women had a meaningful role to play in the resistance movement.[41]

But to achieve its rhetorical purposes—that is, to foster support for Congress and to promote compliance with the Association—"Arabella's *Complaint*" invoked gendered beliefs about female extravagance and infidelity.

Presuming a readership sympathetic both to patriotism and to patriarchy, "Arabella's *Complaint*" attributed to all who chaffed under Congress's boycotts a womanly infatuation with baubles and fripperies. It disavowed such persons' ability to sacrifice for the sake of American rights. It portrayed femininity as a threat both to family and to state. In sum, it perpetuated the misogynistic pretense at the heart of Whig ideology: that the preservation of liberty depended on firm, masculine resistance to soft, feminine luxuriance. In doing all of these things, "Arabella's *Complaint*" implicitly called on henpecked patriots to reassert their authority over spoiled and domineering wives, for the cause of liberty depended on it.

A Dialogue Between a Southern Delegate and His Spouse

Desperate for reconciliation with Great Britain and disquieted by Congress's aggressive strategy of economic resistance, loyalists responded by slinging mud, much of it filled with gendered calumny. No sooner had Congress published its Articles of Association in the autumn of 1774 than embittered opponents mounted a furious campaign to suppress it. The most vociferous of Congress's foes were Anglican clergymen from New York and New Jersey. In addition to Thomas Bradbury Chandler, these included Samuel Seabury, rector of St. Peter's Church in Westchester, and Myles Cooper, president of King's College in New York.

For ten years now, these clerics had watched with alarm as the American resistance movement gathered momentum. Deeply devoted to the Church of England and to the crown that sustained it, these clergymen blamed much of the era's political agitation on dissenting sects, which they believed threatened monarchy and bred civil discord. During the Stamp Act Crisis of 1765, this Episcopal trio championed the Anglican Church as a bulwark against "Clamour & Discontent." At decade's end, they began to lobby for the appointment of an American bishop, provoking the ire of Congregationalists and Presbyterians, and clashing in the pamphlet war that ensued with a number of strident Whigs, including a few who would later serve as delegates to the Continental Congress.[42] In 1772, Chandler, Seabury, and Cooper entered a pact: fearing that republican dissenters would dash their hopes for a bishopric, or worse, that they would overwhelm royal administration in America, these clergymen agreed "to watch and confute all publications that threatened mischief to the Church of England and the British government."[43] After the Continental Congress circulated its Articles of Association, they and other loyalists sprang to action.

In December 1774, shortly after the First Continental Congress adjourned, the loyalist newspaperman James Rivington published *A Dialogue Between a Southern Delegate and His Spouse on His Return from the Grand Continental Congress*, written by the pseudonymous Mary V. V.[44] An overt attack on the masculinity of congressional delegates, this satire offered readers a glimpse of marital discord in one southern congressman's household. Across fourteen pages of versified dialogue, the delegate's wife chides Congress and its radical measures. The wife accuses Congress of usurping the powers of government; she proclaims that Congress's Articles of Association fall "little short" of high treason; and she protests that the committees Congress had empowered to enforce the Association would have shamed a Roman inquisitor or a Moroccan despot.[45]

The rhetorical power of *A Dialogue Between a Southern Delegate and His Spouse*, however, derived less from its allegations of *political* malfeasance than from its allegations of *gender* malfeasance—that is, from its central assertion that this frail and irresolute congressman has surrendered his rightful domestic authority to his bride. The very action that shapes the *Dialogue*'s dramatic structure—a wife rebuking her husband—fundamentally challenges the southern delegate's command over his own household. From the first page, the author makes apparent that this "dialogue" is no mere conversation, and certainly no welcome-home greeting. Rather, the dialogue is a contentious dispute, and the congressman-husband is getting the worst of it. Futilely urging his wife to pipe down, to "be a little discreet" lest she "alarm the whole Street," the delegate reveals himself to be an emasculated husband whose scolding wife has publicly repudiated his claim to the head of their house.

Neighbors already know that the congressman's wife wears the pants in his family. They call him "Jerry Sneak," after Foote's submissive and cuckolded title character. But though the neighbors consider his wife's bossiness "Sport," the congressman moans that to him, "[I]t is Death."[46] By this lament, the congressman acknowledges that his patriarchal command, especially as performed in the community eye, is the essence of his life. His wife's usurpation thus amounts to murder, a figurative petit treason, abhorrent both to the family and the state.[47] And yet she refuses to relent. She expresses mock concern that her husband had been bitten by a mad dog, he so "foam[s] and slaver[s]." When her husband commands her not to "dabble" in politics, she laughs in his face.[48]

The lesson for readers was clear: the congressman is an impotent man who could not control his wife. Such would have been an unflattering accusation for any male head of house in early modern Anglo-America. But in singling out a southern delegate, the *Dialogue* offered an especially ruinous critique. As many scholars have demonstrated, the reputation and social cachet of the southern planter derived not only from his wealth, but in large part too from his mastery over dependents, namely his family, servants, and slaves.[49] Perhaps for this reason, Virginia almanacs of the 1770s repeatedly ranted against henpeckery. "He who marries a wife whose tongue rings like a bell," admonished the *Virginia Almanack* in 1770, "had better have his brains knocked out with the clapper. To such a henpecked fellow his wife's tongue is as terrible as thunder; her presence shakes the house like an earthquake."[50] The *Dialogue*'s southern congressman has married just such a bell ringer. Sounding throughout the neighborhood, her "clapper" has rattled the very foundations of his social stature. Just as disparagingly, the wife asserts that her planter-husband's supposed dominion over his dependents is not equal to that which will be required of him in Congress:

> Thou born! thou! the Machine of an Empire to wield?
> Art thou wise in Debate? Should'st feel bold in the Field?
> If thou'st Wisdom to manage Tobacco, and Slave,
> It's as much as God ever design'd thee to have.[51]

The author thus contended that not even the great planters of Virginia and the Carolinas, for all their wealth and power, were qualified to represent the American colonies in their controversy with Parliament.[52]

Humiliated by his powerlessness, the southern delegate becomes angry. As the *Dialogue* progresses, the delegate reveals himself to be not merely a weak husband, but also a more despicable gender deviant, a would-be tyrant. Like Jerry Sneak, the character in Foote's play, the congressman attempts to reassert his authority over his wife. Though in the past he has suffered her to lead him "by the Nose," he now insists, "[F]or once I will speak." Reminding his wife of her place as a "Woman of Fashion," he chastises her "indecent" behavior. When his wife expresses her dread that the Association will bring not redress, but rather "Perdition and Murder," the delegate dismisses her fears as "Rant" and "Bombast." He belittlingly accuses his wife of "heating" her brain by reading "Romances, and Plays."[53] At last fed up with his wife's harangue, he admonishes her not to interfere in affairs of state, but rather to return to her proper confinement within the domestic sphere: "Mind thy Household-Affairs, teach thy Children to read, / And never, Dear, with Politics, trouble thy Head." Making a bitter mockery of his wife's meddling in politics, the husband exclaims, "You're so patient, so cool, so monstrous eloquent / Next Congress, my Empress, shall be made President."[54]

This oxymoronic epithet, "monstrous eloquent," suggests that the delegate-husband sees something grotesque in his wife's oratorical abilities. A woman who can speak articulately and persuasively on political subjects represents, for the husband, a perversion of the proper gender order, much as would a female president of Congress. But for contemporary readers of the *Dialogue*, it was the congressman-husband, more so than his spouse, who transgressed gender norms. The author of the *Dialogue* portrayed the southern delegate as both unmasculine and hypermasculine. The delegate veers wildly from one extreme of immoderate husbandly behavior, his piteous submission to his wife, to another, his despotic lording over her. At either end, he deviated from the eighteenth-century norm of a firm and assertive, but not domineering, husband. His very lack of restraint ran afoul of the ideal of well-tempered manhood.[55] Through the delegate's efforts to dominate his wife, no less than the condescension with which he speaks to her, the author of the *Dialogue* suggested that members of Congress were cruel and oppressive men. That the *Dialogue* represented congressmen simultaneously as both servile and overbearing need not be read as a contradiction, for both of those attributes signified an aberration from normative masculinity.

By accentuating the congressman's domestic tyranny, the author of *A Dialogue Between a Southern Delegate and His Spouse* artfully rehabilitates the character of the wife. Casting the delegate as an object of contempt and disdain, the author renders his spouse an object of sympathy. At the *Dialogue*'s end, the wife emerges not as an obnoxious, overbearing nag, as does Arabella or Jerry Sneak's wife, but rather as a dedicated helpmeet who feels a strong concern both for her family and for the welfare of her country. She also stakes her ground as an admirable advocate for the rights of women. In response to her husband's insistence that she butt out of state affairs, the wife challenges the patriarchal underpinnings of his gendered-sphere ideology. "Because Men are Males, are they all Politicians?" the wife asks. "Why then I presume they're Divines and Physicians." The wife further asserts that the women of America could have done a much better job in Congress than did the men. "Wou'd! instead of Delegates, they'd sent Delegates Wives; / Heavens! we cou'dn't have bungled it so for our Lives!"[56]

The wife's retort served as a strong commentary against masculinist assumptions about women's roles in eighteenth-century society. It will be recalled that the author of this *Dialogue* adopted a female pseudonym, Mary V. V. In so doing, the author signaled his or her sympathy for the feminist or proto-feminist views expressed by the southern wife. Notably, Mary V. V. dedicated her *Dialogue* "To the Married Ladies of *America*," thus inviting female readers to critically reflect on the gendered balance of power within their own households. But this dedication also served as a call to arms in the imperial dispute. The author of the *Dialogue* beckoned women readers to dissuade their "patriotic" husbands from rushing hastily into war. For, as becomes increasingly apparent through the *Dialogue*'s progression, the congressman's wife is not such a carp after all. She confesses that she "may be sometimes too pert," but she maintains that she has always spoken and acted with sincere regard for her husband's "true Interest," "Health," and "ease." She deplores Congress's measures in large part because she does not wish to see her husband imprisoned or hanged.[57] With this display of affectionate concern for her husband's happiness and safety, the wife redeems herself for the reader. The author thus enables the audience to value her counsel rather than to dismiss it as mere caterwauling. At the *Dialogue*'s end, the wife proclaims, "Let Fools, Pedants, and Husbands, continue to hate / The Advice of us Women, and call it all Prate." Wise persons, the reader must conclude, will hear, and heed, her somber warning: "Make your Peace:—Fear the King:— The Parliament fear. / / Repent! or you are forever, forever undone."[58]

With this note of caution, the congressman's wife literally gets the last word. Unlike his more fortunate spouse, the delegate-husband does not regain the reader's affection as the poem progresses. Rather, by his tyrannical outburst the congressman squanders whatever sympathy he might have won as the victim of his berating wife. And here was the dilemma for husbands in an era of companionate marriage. The persistence of patriarchy, as manifest for instance in the legal doctrine of coverture, demanded that husbands govern and subjugate their wives. But burgeoning ideals of romantic love insisted that husbands treat their wives with tenderness and esteem. To err too greatly on one side was to incur the stigma of viciousness or cruelty. To err too greatly on the other was to risk the odium of henpeckery. Respectable marital manhood thus compelled men to walk a fine and rigidly self-regulated line.

At the height of the imperial crisis, when resistance began to turn toward revolution, patriot and loyalist writers alike invoked gender norms to discredit their adversaries. The patriot author of "Arabella's *Complaint*" urged women not to nag their virtuous husbands with frivolous demands for luxurious fabrics and tea. The loyalist poet of *A Dialogue Between a Southern Delegate and His Spouse* counseled Americans not to put their trust in a

Congress of "puddling" Jerry Sneaks. That in this urgent moment writers on both sides of the Revolutionary conflict resorted to the mobilizing power of gender in political debate suggests just how elemental a constituent of individual identity gender was in eighteenth-century British North America. These invocations of the henpecked husband further illustrate the ways in which Revolutionary political rhetoric reaffirmed traditional norms of masculine deportment. By smearing the manhood of their political adversaries, even in lampoon or patent jest, patriot and loyalist writers occasionally challenged, but more often validated, long-standing conventions of manly behavior in the home and in the statehouse. Both wits reinforced the notion that a man's worth and reputation depend in large measure on his primacy over his wife. In so doing, both exhorted husbands to command their wives, if only gently so.

The American Revolution imperiled neither the doctrine of coverture nor the ideal of companionate marriage; indeed, the cause of liberty depended on both. As Linda K. Kerber has observed, "There was a direct relationship between the developing egalitarian democracy among men and the expectation of continued deferential behavior among women."[59] By exalting republican mothers, the nascent American political order sought to channel women's energies not toward individual equality or personal autonomy but rather toward the sustenance of husband and children. It endeavored to confine women to the home and to subordinate them within a marriage premised on romantic love. But in circumscribing the roles of women, this domestic ideology continued to exact a price from men. Obliging husbands to regulate and to constrain their wives, it predicated the individual's masculine identity on his unwillingness to yield up the spurs or to turn over the reins. The shame of henpeckery compelled husbands to maintain their upper hand.

NOTES

For their generous and helpful critiques of this chapter, the author thanks Thomas A. Foster, Brian P. Luskey, Anne S. Lombard, Martha Few, members of the Group for Early Modern Studies at the University of Arizona, and participants in the Rocky Mountain Seminar in Early American History.

    1. Thomas Bradbury Chandler, *A Friendly Address to All Reasonable Americans* (New York, 1774), 31–32.

    2. Throughout this chapter, I use the term "patriot" to describe individuals who supported radical economic resistance, Congress, or the Association. Similarly, I use "loyalist" to refer to individuals who opposed the Continental Congress and the Articles of Association. Though somewhat anachronistic before independence, "loyalist" carries less opprobrium than the term "Tory."

3. Thomas Bradbury Chandler, *What Think Ye of the* Congress *Now? Or, An Enquiry, How Far the Americans Are Bound to Abide by and Execute the Decisions of the Late* Congress? (New York, 1774), 5.

4. See generally Lisa Wilson, *Ye Heart of a Man: The Domestic Life of Men in Colonial New England* (New Haven: Yale University Press, 1999); Anne S. Lombard, *Making Manhood: Growing Up Male in Colonial New England* (Cambridge: Harvard University Press, 2003); and John Gilbert McCurdy, *Citizen Bachelors: Manhood and the Creation of the United States* (Ithaca: Cornell University Press, 2009), esp. 6–9.

5. Myles Cooper, *The Patriots of North America: A Sketch* (New York, 1775), 8, 12–16.

6. See Wilson, *Ye Heart of a Man*, chaps. 2–4; Lombard, *Making Manhood*, esp. chap. 5; and McCurdy, *Citizen Bachelors*.

7. The henpecked husband was thus one of many gender malcontents and villains—including the fop, the bachelor, the rake, the libertine, the sodomite, and the cuckold—against whose negative examples boys and men were socialized to reputable manhood in the early modern period. See Thomas A. Foster, "Antimasonic Satire, Sodomy, and Eighteenth-Century Masculinity in the *Boston Evening-Post*," *William and Mary Quarterly* 60 (2003): 171–84; and more generally, Foster, *Sex and the Eighteenth-Century Man: Massachusetts and the History of Sexuality in America* (Boston: Beacon Press, 2006); Clare Lyons, *Sex Among the Rabble: An Intimate History of Gender and Power in the Age of Revolution, Philadelphia, 1730–1830* (Chapel Hill: University of North Carolina Press, 2006); McCurdy, *Citizen Bachelors*; and Sarah M. S. Pearsall, "'The late flagrant instance of depravity in my Family': The Story of an Anglo-Jamaican Cuckold," *William and Mary Quarterly* 60 (2003): 549–82. See also Randolph Trumbach, *Sex and the Gender Revolution*, Vol. 1: *Heterosexuality and the Third Gender in Enlightenment London* (Chicago: University of Chicago Press, 1998).

8. Linda K. Kerber, *Women of the Republic: Intellect and Ideology in Revolutionary America* (Chapel Hill: University of North Carolina Press, 1980), 120–36; Mary Beth Norton, *Liberty's Daughters: The Revolutionary Experience of American Women, 1750–1800* (Boston: Little, Brown, 1980), 44–51; Mark A. Kann, *The Gendering of American Politics: Founding Mothers, Founding Fathers, and Political Patriarchy* (Westport, Conn.: Praeger, 1999), 4–8.

9. Linda K. Kerber, *No Constitutional Right to Be Ladies: Women and the Obligations of Citizenship* (New York: Hill and Wang, 1998), 14.

10. In this regard, the charge of henpeckery might be fruitfully compared to that of transvestism, as leveled against the governor of New York, Edward Hyde, Lord Cornbury, in the early eighteenth century. See Patricia U. Bonomi, *The Lord Cornbury Scandal: The Politics of Reputation in British America* (Chapel Hill: University of North Carolina Press, 1998).

11. This notion of the *mobilizing* power of gender takes inspiration from Kristin L. Hoganson's insightful analysis of the *coercive* power of gender in political debate. See Hoganson, *Fighting for American Manhood: How Gender Politics Provoked the Spanish-American and Philippine-American Wars* (New Haven: Yale University Press, 1998), esp. chap 4.

12. On the history of colonial and Revolutionary New York, see Carl L. Becker, "The History of Political Parties in the Province of New York, 1760–1776" (Ph.D. diss., University of Wisconsin, 1909); Virginia D. Harrington, *The New York Merchant on the Eve of the Revolution* (Gloucester, Mass.: P. Smith, 1964); Patricia U. Bonomi, *A Factious People: Politics and Society in Colonial New York* (New York: Columbia University Press, 1971);

Milton M. Klein, *The Politics of Diversity: Essays in the History of Colonial New York* (Port Washington, N.Y.: Kennikat Press, 1974); Michael G. Kammen, *Colonial New York: A History* (New York: Scribner, 1975); and Judith L. Van Buskirk, *Generous Enemies: Patriots and Loyalists in Revolutionary New York* (Philadelphia: University of Pennsylvania Press, 2002).

13. Bruce E. Steiner, *Samuel Seabury, 1729–1796: A Study in High Church Tradition* (Athens: Ohio University Press, 1971), 154; William H. Nelson, *The American Tory* (1961; reprint, Westport, Conn.: Greenwood Press, 1980), 83.

14. Steiner, *Samuel Seabury*, 144–46.

15. Peter Force, comp., *American Archives*, 4th ser., 6 vols. (Washington, D.C., 1837–1853), 2:35–36.

16. Steiner, *Samuel Seabury*, 159–60.

17. Lesley Johnson, "Women on Top: Antifeminism in the Fabliaux?" *Modern Language Review* 78 (1983): 298–307; Barbara Page, "Concerning the Host," *Chaucer Review* 4 (1969): 1–13; Martin Stevens, "'And Venus Laugheth': An Interpretation of the Merchant's Tale," *Chaucer Review* 7 (1972): 118–31; Beverly Boyd, "Chaucer's Audience and the Henpecked Husband," *Florilegium* 12 (1993): 177–80; Nicole Nolan Sidhu, "Henpecked Husbands, Unruly Wives, and Royal Authority in Lydgate's *Mumming At Hertford*," *Chaucer Review* 42 (2008): 431–60.

18. On companionate marriage in Britain, see generally Lawrence Stone, *The Family, Sex and Marriage in England, 1500–1800* (New York: Harper and Row, 1977); and Stone, *Uncertain Unions: Marriage in England, 1660–1753* (New York: Oxford University Press, 1992). See also Stephanie Coontz, *Marriage, a History: From Obedience to Intimacy, or How Love Conquered Marriage* (New York: Viking, 2005).

19. Though attributed chiefly to Arbuthnot, the musings of Martinus Scriblerus were published in the works of Alexander Pope. See *The Works of Alexander Pope, Esq.* 9 vols. (London, 1760), 6: 171. For John Henpeck, see Murphy, *The Gray's-Inn Journal* 2 vols. (Dublin, 1756), 2:189–90. For a lexicon of henpeckery, see James Caulfield, *Blackguardiana: Or, a Dictionary of Rogues, Bawds, Pimps, Whores, Pickpockets, Shoplifters* (London, 1793). See also Marie L. C. Linthicum, "Shakespeare's Meacocke," *Modern Language Notes* 40 (1925): 96–98.

20. See generally Michael Warner, *Letters of the Republic: Publication and the Public Sphere in Eighteenth-Century America* (Cambridge: Harvard University Press, 1990); and David S. Shields, *Civil Tongues and Polite Letters in British America* (Chapel Hill: University of North Carolina Press, 1997).

21. *Spectator*, 9, 12 September 1712. On the circulation of the *Spectator* in British North America, see Richard Beale Davis, *A Colonial Southern Bookshelf: Reading in the Eighteenth Century* (Athens: University of Georgia Press, 1979), 114; Ned C. Landsman, *From Colonials to Provincials: American Thought and Culture, 1680–1760* (New York: Twayne Publishers, 1997), 38–39.

22. *Boston Post-Boy*, 20 July 1752. On henpeckery and skimmington, see B. Howard Cunnington, "'A Skimmington' in 1618," *Folklore* 41 (1930): 287–90; Martin Ingram, "Ridings, Rough Music, and the 'Reform of Popular Culture' in Early Modern England," *Past and Present* 105 (1984): 79–113. On the transmission of English folk practices to North America, see Alfred F. Young, "English Plebian Culture and Eighteenth-Century American Radicalism," in *The Origins of Anglo-American Radicalism*, ed. Margaret Jacob and James Jacob (London: Allen and Unwin, 1984), 185–212.

23. *Daily Gazetteer* (London), 25 April 1745. On the transatlantic exchange of sexual and gender norms, see Clare Lyons, "Mapping an Atlantic Sexual Culture: Homoeroticism in Eighteenth-Century Philadelphia," *William and Mary Quarterly* 60 (2003): 119–54.

24. Samuel Foote, *Mayor of Garratt* (London, 1794), 41.

25. Ruth H. Bloch, "The Gendered Meanings of Virtue in Revolutionary America," *Signs* 13 (1987): 37–58.

26. Bloch, "Gendered Meanings of Virtue in Revolutionary America." See also T. H. Breen, *The Marketplace of Revolution: How Consumer Politics Shaped American Independence* (New York: Oxford University Press, 2004), 172–82; and Michal J. Rozbicki, *The Complete Colonial Gentleman: Cultural Legitimacy in Plantation America* (Charlottesville: University Press of Virginia, 1998), esp. chap. 5.

27. John Adams's diary, Philadelphia, 17 September 1774, in Paul H. Smith, ed., *Letters of Delegates to Congress, 1774–1789*, 26 vols. (Washington, D.C.: Library of Congress, 1976–), 1:75.

28. On the origins and history of the Consumer Revolution, see generally Richard L. Bushman, *The Refinement of America: Persons, Houses, Cities* (New York: Alfred A. Knopf, 1992); Cary Carson, Ronald Hoffman, and Peter J. Albert, eds., *Of Consuming Interests: The Style of Life in the Eighteenth Century* (Charlottesville: University Press of Virginia, 1994); Shields, *Civil Tongues and Polite Letters in British America*; Breen, *Marketplace of Revolution*; and Rozbicki, *Complete Colonial Gentleman*.

29. On classical and biblical notions of women's sensuality, see Bloch, "Gendered Meanings of Virtue in Revolutionary America," 41–42. See also Bloch, "Untangling the Roots of Modern Sex Roles: A Survey of Four Centuries of Change," *Signs* 4 (1978): 237–52. For Consumer Revolution discourses about the frailty of female purchasers, see Breen, *Marketplace of Revolution*, 172–82.

30. Breen, *Marketplace of Revolution*, 130; Shields, *Civil Tongues and Polite Letters in British America*, 55–140.

31. On men's financial failure as a gendered experience, see Toby L. Ditz, "Shipwrecked; or, Masculinity Imperiled: Mercantile Representations of Failure and the Gendered Self in Eighteenth-Century Philadelphia," *Journal of American History* 81 (1994), 51–80, esp. 60–61.

32. Breen, *Marketplace of Revolution*, 281–83; Shields, *Civil Tongues and Polite Letters in British America*, 107–8.

33. "Arabella's *Complaint of the* Congress," *Pennsylvania Magazine, or American Monthly Museum* 1 (Sept. 1775): 407–8.

34. Joan R. Gundersen, *To Be Useful to the World: Women in Revolutionary America, 1740–1790*, rev. ed. (Chapel Hill: University of North Carolina Press, 2006), 174. On the participation of women in the American resistance movement, see generally Kerber, *Women of the Republic*; and Kerber, *No Constitutional Right to Be Ladies*, esp. chap. 1; Norton, *Liberty's Daughters*; Holly A. Mayer, *Belonging to the Army: Camp Followers and Community During the American Revolution* (Columbia: University of South Carolina Press, 1999); Breen, *Marketplace of Revolution*, 231–34; Carol Berkin, *Revolutionary Mothers: Women in the Struggle for America's Independence* (New York: Alfred A. Knopf, 2005); and Rosemarie Zagarri, *Revolutionary Backlash: Women and Politics in the Early American Republic* (Philadelphia: University of Pennsylvania Press, 2007).

35. Norton, *Liberty's Daughters*, 161.

36. "Arabella's *Complaint of the* Congress," 407.

37. Ibid.

38. On public speech as a male prerogative in early America, see Jane Kamensky, "Talk Like a Man: Speech, Power, and Masculinity in Early New England," in *A Shared Experience: Men, Women and the History of Gender*, ed. Laura McCall and Donald Yacavone (New York: New York University Press, 1998), 19–50.

39. On the figure of the harpy in eighteenth-century British merchants' letters, see Ditz, "Shipwrecked," 60–61.

40. "Arabella's *Complaint of the* Congress," 407–8.

41. Ibid.

42. Steiner, *Samuel Seabury*, 109, 122. On the bishop's controversy, see Nancy L. Rhoden, *Revolutionary Anglicanism: The Colonial Church of England Clergy During the American Revolution* (Basingstoke: Macmillan, 1999), chap. 3; Carl Bridenbaugh, *Mitre and Sceptre: Transatlantic Faiths, Ideas, Personalities, and Politics, 1689–1775* (New York: Oxford University Press, 1962); and Bernard Bailyn, *The Ideological Origins of the American Revolution* (1967; reprint, Cambridge: Belknap Press of Harvard University Press, 1976), 96–98.

43. Quoted in Nelson, *American Tory*, 73. See also Thomas Bradbury Chandler to Daniel Burton, 15 January 1766, quoted in Judith Sumner Hanson, "For Church and State: Thomas Bradbury Chandler and the Coming of the American Revolution" (master's thesis, University of Utah, 1977), 34. Charles Inglis, curate of Trinity Church, New York, was also a party to this pact. Inglis wrote a handful of pamphlets in opposition to Paine's *Common Sense* and in opposition to Congress after it declared independence.

44. The authorship of the *Dialogue* has not been established. Earlier in life, Myles Cooper published a book of poems, including some that used a similar dialogic format and others that explored themes of cuckoldry, but the evidence is too slim to extrapolate his authorship of this particular piece. See Cooper, *Poems on Several Occasions* (Oxford, 1761).

45. Mary V. V., *A Dialogue Between a Southern Delegate and His Spouse* (New York, 1774), 11, 13. On Anglo-American representations of despotism in the Muslim world, see Robert J. Allison, *The Crescent Obscured: The United States and the Muslim World, 1776–1815* (New York: Oxford University Press, 1995).

46. Mary V. V., *A Dialogue Between a Southern Delegate and His Spouse*, 3, 6.

47. On a wife's murder of her husband as petit treason, see Kerber, *Women of the Republic*, 119–120; and Kerber, *No Constitutional Right to Be Ladies*, 13.

48. Mary V. V., *A Dialogue Between a Southern Delegate and His Spouse*, 4, 6.

49. Rhys Isaac, *The Transformation of Virginia, 1740–1790* (Chapel Hill: University of North Carolina Press, 1982), 132–35; Rozbicki, *Complete Colonial Gentleman*, 118–19; Kenneth Lockridge, *On the Sources of Patriarchal Rage: The Commonplace Books of William Byrd and Thomas Jefferson and the Gendering of Power in the Eighteenth Century* (New York: New York University Press, 1993), 96; Kathleen Brown, *Good Wives, Nasty Wenches, and Anxious Patriarchs: Gender, Race, and Power in Colonial Virginia* (Chapel Hill: University of North Carolina Press, 1996), chaps. 8, 10.

50. *The Virginia Almanack for the Year of Our Lord God 1770* (Williamsburg, 1769), np. See also *The Virginia Almanack for the Year of Our Lord God 1772* (Williamsburg, 1771), np.

51. Mary V. V., *A Dialogue Between a Southern Delegate and His Spouse*, 7.

52. If the pseudonymous author of the *Dialogue* was in fact one of the three prolific loyalist clerics—Chandler, Seabury, or Cooper—he may have chosen to portray the southern delegate as a milksop husband so as to castigate southern Anglicans for their refusal to back the New Yorkers' campaign for an episcopacy several years earlier. On Virginia's failure to support an American bishopric, see Rhoden, *Revolutionary Anglicanism*, 41–42.

53. Mary V. V., *A Dialogue Between a Southern Delegate and His Spouse*, 4, 6, 12. On the deleterious effects on women ascribed to romance novels in the eighteenth century, see Cathy N. Davidson, *Revolution and the Word: The Rise of the Novel in America* (New York: Oxford University Press, 1986), chap. 3.

54. Mary V. V., *A Dialogue Between a Southern Delegate and His Spouse*, 7, 8. On the ideology of gendered spheres, see Nancy Cott, *The Bonds of Womanhood: "Woman's Sphere" in New England, 1780–1835* (New Haven: Yale University Press, 1977).

55. Brown, *Good Wives, Nasty Wenches, and Anxious Patriarchs*, 324–28; Wilson, *Ye Heart of a Man*, chap. 3; Lombard, *Making Manhood*, chap. 2, esp. 114–19.

56. Mary V. V., *Dialogue Between a Southern Delegate and his Spouse*, 7–8. The fictional southern wife's assertion that the colonies should have "sent Delegates Wives" may be understood as a sort of literary counterpart to Abigail Adams's near-contemporary appeal to her husband that Congress "Remember the Ladies." John's reply to Abigail, "I cannot but laugh.... We know better than to repeal our Masculine systems," offers an unfortunate historical counterpart to the southern delegate's dismissive responses. John Adams to Abigail Adams, Philadelphia, 14 April 1776, *Letters of Delegates to Congress*, 3:519–20 and n. 2.

57. Mary V. V., *A Dialogue Between a Southern Delegate and His Spouse*, 9.

58. Ibid., 14. Notwithstanding the many ways in which Mary V. V. challenged eighteenth-century assumptions about gender, it must also be recognized that the character of the southern delegate's wife, as a champion of lawfulness and deference to British authorities, also served to reinforce traditional, patriarchal associations of women with order and harmony. I am grateful to Ruth Bloch and Sarah Knott for this insight.

59. Kerber, *Women of the Republic*, 285.

11

John Adams and the Choice of Hercules

Manliness and Sexual Virtue in Eighteenth-Century British America

THOMAS A. FOSTER

In August 1776 John Adams wrote to his wife, Abigail, that he had proposed that the image for the seal of the new nation be the "Choice of Hercules." Referencing the classical allegory of choosing virtue over vice, Adams selected a particularly masculine, heroic figure to represent public and private virtue. He believed individuals should choose to lead moral personal lives and devote themselves to civic duty; for him, the image captured both the heart of the nation and also, as we shall see, his view of manhood. That Adams chose a decidedly manly figure to illustrate what was increasingly becoming associated with womanhood—private virtue—indicates his view that manliness included so-called feminine traits, including chastity and self-restraint.

In eighteenth-century British America, proper manhood was secured by success in two main areas of a man's life: his position as head-of-household and his "calling" or career.[1] Sex mattered in these two most important areas of a man's life. As head-of-household, a man ideally sired children and developed and maintained intimacy with his wife. (He was, of course, also ultimately responsible for the sexual conduct, or misconduct, of his dependents—his wife, children, and any servants or slaves.) His self-mastery could also deeply affect his public reputation, which could in turn affect his and his family's economic affairs. In both respects he was to follow the three M's of eighteenth-century sexual manhood—marriage, monogamy, and moderation. Family was not yet the idealized exclusive domain of women as it would be by the nineteenth-century, when home, hearth, and familial love were considered primarily female concerns, whereas business and politics were desexualized and male.[2] Simply put, sexuality was one important and dynamic component of manliness in eighteenth-century British America.

Of course many men espoused or lived one of many counter-norms that also flourished—especially in the later eighteenth century.[3] In print culture, for example, the rake, an antiheroic type known for his sexual conquests, was often celebrated as swaggering and virile, a hypermasculine model of manliness. But like most eighteenth-century Americans, Adams did not view self-retrained manliness as weak or effeminate. Indeed, he saw moral manliness as more masculine than the excesses of the uncontained rake. The personal writings of John Adams reveal a masculine identity predicated on sexual virtue and moral restraint. This chapter demonstrates that Adams utilized the mythic figure of Hercules to embody his notion of masculine virtue; I pay close attention to the sexual component of Adams's beliefs. Relatively few early modern American men left sustained commentary about their sexual behaviors and identities, and John Adams is no exception. Yet his voluminous surviving letters, personal diaries, and unpublished autobiography reveal glimpses of his views of masculine sexual identity—much of which was articulated both explicitly and implicitly via the figure of Hercules. Historians of both the eighteenth and nineteenth centuries have shown an enduring Christian evangelical model of manliness that emphasized chastity and self-restraint for men.[4] Given the eighteenth-century resonance of republican notions of virtue, it should come as no surprise that from time to time, Adams invoked in his writings not a biblical or Christian reference to illustrate proper masculine sexual restraint, but rather the classical heroic figure of Hercules, a man notable for extraordinary masculine strength and physical power.[5]

Virtue and morality were broadly construed in early America, of course, encompassing much more than sexual conduct—but for Adams and others it notably also included specific sexual morality and linked it to a host of other concerns more typically associated with masculine comportment. As historian Ruth Bloch has shown, the meaning of "virtue" in early America drew on older meanings of "sexual purity and personal sacrifice" and newer "early modern republican forms" that focused on "male public spirit"—the "willingness of citizens to engage actively in civic life and to sacrifice individual interests for the common good."[6] As Bloch argued, the concept of virtue changed through the eighteenth century as the culture blended older and newer interpretations, drawing on religious, Enlightenment, and "literary sentimentalism" influences. The concept of private virtue became increasingly seen as an inherently feminine trait, while public virtue remained decidedly masculine.[7] According to Bloch, neither public nor private virtue was the exclusive domain of one sex or the other, and

Adams's selection of the Choice of Hercules underscores his own blending of feminine and masculine traits. That he selected a figure of extraordinary physical stature, however, suggests that overall he viewed the nature of both the choice itself and its implications for the nation as decidedly masculine. Arguably, Adams's interest in the image of Hercules represents a certain visual compensation for the "feminization of ideas about public virtue" that Bloch identifies—a kind of pushing back against the emerging notion that virtue, with its increased association with sexual morality, was feminine.[8] That virtue became feminized and associated with chastity did not mean, however, that it no longer applied to manliness. Popular literature, such as the best-selling novel *The Coquette*, published at the end of the eighteenth century, could therefore include a condemnation of the rake, Major Sanford, which described him as a man "deficient in one of the great essentials of character, and that is, *virtue*," and explained that this characterization was entirely about his sexual misconduct, his "having but too successfully practiced the arts of seduction; by triumphing in the destruction of innocence and the peace of families!"[9]

Adams certainly fit the bill for manly achievement in his establishment of household and in his calling. Born in 1735 to a Braintree, Massachusetts, farmer, he graduated from Harvard in 1755. After briefly considering the ministry, he taught for a few years before becoming a lawyer in 1758 at the age of twenty-three. Just shy of thirty years old, he married Abigail Smith, with whom he had five children, three boys and two girls. During the 1760s, as the colonies and Great Britain faced off over questions of taxation and representation, Adams emerged as a leader of the patriot movement in Massachusetts, serving as the Massachusetts delegate to the first and second Continental Congresses. During the revolution and for several years after he served as a diplomat in Europe, and he eventually became the new nation's first vice president and second president.

Adams has long enjoyed a reputation for his moral uprightness.[10] Biographers of the "founding fathers" consistently tell us he was "priggish," something of a prude.[11] As one biographer in 1884 wrote, John was "like the better men of the day" in New England; unlike those who wrestled with "hard drinking" and "carnal sins" in the face of strict Puritan teachings, Adams succeeded at being "rigid in every point of morals."[12] This characterization has only deepened through the years. One recent biographer argued that Adams was an ineffective European diplomat because he wouldn't "flirt with the ladies."[13]

Biographers routinely point out that Adams certainly saw himself as more moral than his fellow revolutionaries and often wrote scathing commentary about his peers' sexual dispositions and behaviors, positioning himself as a standard bearer of moral manhood. Biographer Judith St. George explains, "John especially objected to Franklin's constant partying, his open flirtations with women."[14] Others have noted his personal barbs lobbed at his political enemy, Alexander Hamilton, whom Adams famously referred to as a "bastard brat," drawing attention to his birth out of wedlock. Adams claimed that Hamilton had a "superabundance of secretions" and "could not find whores enough to draw off," and he vilified Hamilton for the "profligacy of his life—his fornications, adulteries, and his incests."[15]

Throughout his life, his biographers have told us, Adams would shake his head with disapproval and then pat himself on the back for doing so. All of this created an image of him as a man who held true to a particularly stereotyped view of Adams's Puritan ancestors. As an eighteenth-century Massachusetts denizen, Adams was certainly the product of an enduring seventeenth-century Puritan culture, but that culture was not necessarily the one of popular memory. Indeed, as historians have shown, by the eighteenth century it was dynamic and increasingly connected to the emerging sexual subcultures of the Atlantic world. He was exposed to broader Atlantic influences, moral codes, and ways of structuring sexual lives and identities that were prevalent in other parts of the globe—and even simply other colonies.

Within this changing context, Adams saw utility in the story of Hercules as a model for a manly life. The figure is a classical one whose various interpretations and meanings have changed over the centuries. In today's culture, Hercules is reduced to one singular ancient understanding of him as a figure of strength. The term *herculean* is currently used to denote a task requiring much energy and force.[16] The mythic hero Hercules is a figure who embodies that force with muscular manhood. To a large extent he has also become eroticized in contemporary culture. Our relatively recent portrayals of Hercules have tended to the beefcake sort, played by leading actors noted for their bodies.[17]

Early modern English society viewed Hercules' physique with less awe and a little concern. Indeed, as scholar Chloe Chard brilliantly argues, representations of Hercules indicate a "tension" between celebrating his "large brawny limbs" and the emerging view that such a body was an indicator of dangerously "unrestrained masculinity," a negative in a world that emphasized moderation and self-control. She finds emerging in this period images and sculpture of Hercules that present him as less muscled and more slender than in his classical representations.[18]

Early modern Atlantic culture embraced Hercules and focused less on his body than we do today, and more on his capabilities via the story of his twelve labors, with the slaying of the many-headed hydra as his most famous one. As Peter Linebaugh and Marcus Rediker argue, the many-headed hydra was for early modern Atlantic society a "symbol of disorder and resistance."[19] By destroying it, Hercules underscored his symbolic stature for "power and order." In England this was explicitly linked to the economy and empirical designs of the era. In seventeenth-century England, a full-blown "cult of Hercules" focused on him as a "model for exploration, trade, conquest, and plantation of English mercantilism."[20] To provide another example, as Lynn Hunt has argued, in late eighteenth-century France the "giant male" figure of Hercules, "representing the French people [having] used its club to smash the hydra of federalism," came to replace the "feminine statue of Liberty" precisely at the moment that revolutionaries wished to underscore the radicalism of their movement and the end of the more "moderate republic," initially represented by her image.[21]

In early America as elsewhere in the Atlantic world, Hercules certainly stood for "power and order" and enjoyed a cultural presence. As the historian Gordon Wood and others have argued, "the mid-eighteenth century was truly a neo-classical age" and "classical references and allusions run through much of the colonists' writings, both public and private."[22] Through the eighteenth century, the name Hercules was a favored one for strong ships. It was also used for male slaves, as a "kind of cosmic jest." As Ira Berlin and others have explained, "The more insignificant the person in the eyes of the planters, the greater the name."[23] At the time of the revolution, the political leaders of the new nation looked to the Greco-Roman world in broad political and cultural reference.

But when Adams invoked Hercules, he did so only using the particular story of the Choice of Hercules. The story focused narrowly on young Hercules' confrontation with two women or goddesses, Virtue and Pleasure. Hercules must decide between taking the proper path for his life. Pleasure unsuccessfully attempted to seduce Hercules from the hard path of virtue. The story thus emphasized a moment in the life of young Hercules when he chose virtue and a moral path over a life of pleasure and indulgence.

Adams did not select an obscure cultural reference in his focus on the Choice of Hercules, and it was, alongside the stories of his twelve labors, well-known in early America. Both word and song celebrated the tale as one with a larger resonance. The focus on a choice between good and evil lent itself to various interpretations, and its political import would only increase through the developments of the American Revolution. But even before those specific political concerns, the story was being celebrated as a hallmark of republican virtue. In the early eighteenth century it was published in texts that found a broad reading audience in early America, including via the popular London magazine the *Tatler* as well as Shaftesbury's *Judgment of Hercules*, which appeared in numerous imported editions.[24] As scholars have argued, for authors such as Shaftesbury, the Enlightenment emphasis on educated, rational virtue made the story one of great appeal.[25] The story was also celebrated in music. By mid-century, Handel composed an oratorio titled "The Choice of Hercules," which was soon thereafter performed in Philadelphia.[26] Booksellers in early America frequently advertised in newspapers other published accounts of the tale, including Xenophon's *Memoirs of Socrates*, which circulated in the colonies and was a popular text for educating young boys in England.[27] The *Judgment of Hercules* also reprinted the tale and was advertised in colonial newspapers in the 1760s.[28] Adams left for us an unusually well-chronicled record of his views of the story—but he was not unique in his regard for the tale and its moral lesson, which was so applicable to early Americans in personal and political meaning.

That Adams linked sexual and romantic virtue to the broader lesson of choosing a moral life did not make him unusual. In eighteenth-century America the story certainly carried sexual overtones. In Xenophon's *Memoirs of Socrates*, Pleasure suggestively explains to Hercules that she has been wrongly "brand[ed] with the Name of *Sensuality*."[29] Yet the text makes it clear to the reader that she is worthy of her reputation and she is described as a Goddess for whom "the Blush of Modesty she was a Stranger to,—And her Dress was contrived not to *conceal*, but *display* those Beauties she supposed herself possessed of."[30]

Similarly, in Handel's oratorio her beckoning carries a particular depiction of sexual and physical allures:

> While for thy arms that beauty glows,
> That love awakes its purest fire,
> And to each ravish'd sense bestows
> All that can raise or sate desire.

When Virtue rebuffs her, in her appeal to Hercules, she specifically links a resistance to superficial "beauty" and "love" to masculine traits of strength and fortitude:

> This manly youth's exalted mind,
> Above thy grov'lling taste refin'd,
> Shall listen to my awful voice.
> His childhood, in its earliest rise,
> Bespoke him gen'rous, brave and wise,
> And manhood shall confirm his choice.[31]

For Adams the defining moment for Hercules was just this—when he chose the path toward virtue and rejected the seductive allure of vice. Although the moral lesson had wide applicability, the figures suggest a gendered interpretation that would have had appeal in Adams's time. Drawing on a view of women as temptresses and seducers that men needed to guard against, the story spoke of both the specific danger of immoral women (and desires for them) and the general loss of moral productivity.

In his writings Adams underscored the importance of masculine self-restraint in the area of love and romance. Although he did not explicitly reference the story of Hercules, in the following examples his portrayal of wrestling with youthful desires and ultimately choosing the proper pathway strikingly mirrors the Choice of Hercules. Indeed, as there was no singular moment for Adams when he chose the proper pathway, but rather something he wrote about as a process, it is perhaps not surprising that he did not explicitly reference Hercules. In his unpublished autobiography, written when he was in his late sixties and early seventies, John Adams reflected that as a boy he wrestled with youthful urges as he established a moral code that would guide his life. Indicating his belief in the significance of controlling romance and sexuality for proper manhood, he recalled about himself:

> I was of an amorous disposition and very early from ten or eleven Years of Age, was very fond of the Society of females. I had my favorites among the young Women and spent many of my Evenings in their Company and this disposition although controlled for seven Years after my Entrance into College returned and engaged me too much till I was married.

Having established that he did indeed have desires to keep in check, he then proceeded to outline his successes in doing so. Of the women he courted, he declared: "they were all modest and virtuous Girls and always maintained this Character through Life. No Wife or Virgin or Matron ever had cause to blush at the sight of me, or to regret her Acquaintance with me." His declaration of chastity protected not only himself and the young woman; it had implications for a masculine brotherhood of men as well. He continued: "No Father, Brother, Son or Friend ever had cause of Grief or Resentment for any Intercourse between me and any Daughter, Sister, Mother, or any other Relation of the female Sex." And, of course, his youthful restraint would have implications for his immediate family: "My Children may be assured that no illegitimate Brother or Sister exists or ever existed."[32]

Sexual restraint had wide social ramifications. And for Adams it also affected personal "Happiness." "I have seen enough of the Effects of a different practice," he continued. "Corroding Reflections through Life are the never failing consequence of illicit amours." "Happiness is lost forever if Innocence is lost," he went on, "at least untill a Repentance is undergone [?] so severe as to be an overballance to all the gratifications of Licentiousness. Repentance itself cannot restore the Happiness of Innocence, at least in this Life."[33] Notably the "Happiness" referenced then, in the story of Hercules as Pleasure attempts to seduce him away from the path of Virtue, was for Adams a misnomer—reflecting instead "Grief," as true happiness came only from virtue and moral conduct.

Adams was not simply fashioning his life story to mirror a Herculean tale. At the age of twenty, he wrote in his diary about his view of the "great World"—that it was populated by "Kings, Politicians . . . Fops, Buffoons, Fidlers, Sychophants, Fools, Coxcombs . . . and every other Character." But he believed that one should only "bestow the proper applause upon virtuous and generous Actions, to blame and punish every vicious and contracted Trick." "Let others waste the bloom of Life," he wrote, "at the Card or biliard Table, among rakes and fools, and when their minds are sufficiently fretted with losses, and inflamed by Wine, ramble through the Streets, assaulting innocent People, breaking Windows or debauching young Girls." Adams boasted, "I envy not their exalted happiness."[34]

He was motivated to write about this subject in his diary because of a story that had distressed him:

> About 4, months since a poor Girl in this neighbourhood walking by the meeting H. [House] upon some Ocasion, in the evening, met a fine Gentleman with laced hat and wast coat, and a sword who sollicited her to turn aside with him into the horse Stable. The Girl reluctd a little, upon which he gave her 3 Guineas, and wished he might be damned if he did not have her in 3 months. Into the horse Stable they went. The 3 Guineas proved 3 farthings-and the Girl proves with Child, without a Friend upon Earth that will own her, or knowing the father of her 3 farthing Bastard.[35]

The story of a man who seduced and impregnated a "poor Girl," whether truly local or one he copied from the newspaper, resonated for Adams. In life he positioned himself in contrast to the "fine Gentleman" who violated not only the girl's chastity but also his own.

Adams's diary entries attest to his attempts to avoid becoming like the men who thought "exalted happiness" could be found "debauching young Girls" and to control his desires and stay focused on virtuous and productive tasks. "I never spent a whole Day upon one Book in my Life," he complained to his diary in 1759. "What is the Reason that I cant remove all Papers and Books from my Table, take one Volume into my Hands, and read it, and then reflect upon it, till night, without wishing for my Pen and Ink to write a Letter, or taking down any other Book, or thinking of the Girls? Because I cant command my attention. My Thoughts are roving from Girls to friends."[36] If his mind was distracted, however, his behavior remained in check.

As a young man, Adams wrote in his diary that he found himself facing temptation. An early intrigue with a young woman tested his powers of self-control but also his will to stay focused on what he considered the most important tasks at hand. In his commonplace book he reflected: "I found a Passion growing in my heart and a consequent Habit [*illegible*] of thinking, forming and strengthening in my Mind, that would have eat out every seed of ambition, in the first, and every wise Design or Plan in the last." He berated himself for not being more on guard against the young woman's apparent insincerity. "[I] Should have drawn a Confession from her," he wrote, "(by shewing the Imprudence, Danger, Cruelty, and Wickedness of her Conduct without that supposition) that she loved me, and was determined to run all Hazards with me, to run the chance of Business, and success. Should have tryed, what the [*illegible*] Imputation of Jilting, and Wheedling, and hinting, for a Courtship, in order to Torment, or at least to secure one for fear another should fail, would have produced." He continued, lamenting that he did not confront her directly: "[I] Should have said . . . you was dissatisfied with your situation and desirous of a Husband. In order to get one, you Wheedled Wibirt; you wheedled Lincoln. You gave each of them hints and Encouragement to Court you. But especially you wheedled me. For 6 months past you and I have never been alone together but you have given me broad Hints, that you desired I should court you."[37] This young woman whom he disapproved of had tempted him, and he had narrowly escaped being unmanned by losing control of his passions and desires for her love. That his escape came by chance and not from his own

John Adams and the Choice of Hercules | 225

self-control must have prompted the extended self-scrutiny and the wish to learn from his own mistakes.

To understand how Adams's proposal for the seal of the new nation captured his views on the necessary blending of both public and private virtue, we can turn to the handful of moments in his private writings when he explicitly referenced the Choice of Hercules. In these instances, sexual and private morality was linked to public good. The above story of near heartbreak caused Adams to look inward, but his judgment also focused on the behavior of others.

The first explicit reference that he made to Hercules comes this same year from a diary entry: "Met Mr. Wibirt . . . went with him to his Lodgings, slept with him and spent all the next day with him, reading."[38] The time he spent presented him with an opportunity for self-inspection as well as his customary evaluation of those around him. During his visit he read *Reflections on Courtship and Marriage* while at the home of Parson Anthony Wibirt, the minister for the Braintree church. The popular text "expressed similar sentiments about the importance of marriage for both individuals and for communities. "The Conjugal Tie" was the "sacred Cement of all Societies," according to the author."[39] But the time spent reading and relaxing left the twenty-four year-old John Adams with a bad taste in his mouth, and he explicitly referenced the story of the Choice of Hercules to illustrate his error:

> Here are 2 nights, and one day and an half, spent in a softening, enervating, dissipating, series of hustling, pratling, Poetry, Love, Courtship, Marriage. During all this Time, I was seduced into the Course of unmanly Pleasures, that Vice describes to Hercules, forgetful of the glorious Promises of Fame, Immortality, and a good Conscience, which Virtue, makes to the same Hero, as Rewards of a hardy, toilsome, watchful Life, in the service of Mankind.[40]

Having thought about the Choice of Hercules, he wrote in his diary that he interpreted the story to mean: "Which, dear Youth, will you prefer? a Life of Effeminacy, Indolence and obscurity, or a Life of Industry, Temperance, and Honour?" "Let no trifling Diversion or amuzement or Company decoy you from your Books, i.e. let no Girl, no Gun, no Cards, no flutes, no Violins, no Dress, no Tobacco, no Laziness, decoy you from your Books." "My mind is liable to be called off from Law, by a Girl, a Pipe, a Poem, a Love Letter, a Spectator, &c. &c. &c. a Play, &c."[41] The very days that he spent visiting and reading and contemplating on his own moral fiber and the writings of philosophers brought him distress. Adams castigated himself for letting "unmanly Pleasures" take him away from "Industry, Temperance, and Honour." And he saw in the Choice of Hercules the masculine nature of the moral dilemma.

He concluded that his visit with Wibirt could be a productive one simply by negative example: As a minister he clearly had a wealth of knowledge about what Adams called "human nature." "Something is to be learned, of human Nature, human Life, Love, Court Ship, Marriage. He has spent much of his Life, from his Youth, in Conversation with young and old Persons of both sexes, maried and unmaried, and therefore has his Mind stuffed with Remarks and stories of human Virtues, and Vices, Wisdom and folly, &c." His own life, however, did not serve as an example to Adams. "But his Opinion, out of Poetry, Love, Court ship, Mariage, Politicks, War, Beauty, Grace, Decency &c. is not very valuable. His Soul is lost, in a dronish effeminacy. Ide rather be lost in a Whirlwind of Activity, Study, Business, great and good Designs of promoting the Honour, Grandeur, Wealth, Happiness of Mankind."

Adams may have gleaned a great deal from his friend's knowledge, but he remained skeptical of Wibirt's choices and behavior. Wibirt was a bachelor and would remain so throughout his life. "He says he has not Resolution enough to court a Woman. He wants to find one that will charm, conquer him and rouse his spirit. He is like a Turkey, retiring to Roost," Adams wrote disapprovingly. Wibirt "exposes very freely to me his Disposition, the past and present state of his mind, his susceptibility of Impressions from Beauty &c., [*illegible*] his Being amourous, and inclined to love, his Want of Resolution to Court, his Regard, fondness, for O., his Intimacy [*illegible*] and dalliance with her &c. He has if I mistake not a good many [*illegible*] half born Thoughts, of courting O."[42]

Here his critique fit well with what he was reading at Wibirt's. *Reflections on Courtship and Marriage* specified that loneliness was a chief affliction of remaining unmarried: "Old batchelours in general, may see their unconnected, unrelative State in Society, tottering to their Graves in a gloomy Solitude," warned the author. Bachelors, according to that text, suffered without wives. What every man needed was:

> [a] tender affectionate Companion, of similar Mind and Manners, whose *constant* Sunshine of Love, warm'd the Spring and Summer of his Days, and now with an *unalterable* Friendship and Fellow-feeling, accompanies him Arm-in Arm thro' the dreary Wilds of Winter, with the Guard of a Son or Sons, whose filial Piety and manly Vigour, is ever ready to protect him from the Insolence of others or to defend him from those Calamities to which our feeble Age exposes us.

Contributing to the developing norm of companionate marriage, the author highlighted the "tender affectionate Companion" and the "*unalterable Friendship and Fellow-feeling*" that he believed accompanied good marriages. He also emphasized that such marriages made possible the nurturing of a "manly" "Guard of a Son or Sons" who could protect their fathers' reputations and watch over them when elderly.[43]

As a young man Adams cultivated a personal self that took part in the emerging world of eighteenth-century sexuality—with its move away from strict Puritan morality. Yet at the same time he lauded himself for being a man who stood above that developing culture. And he modeled himself after masculine, courageous, and moral Hercules in his choice of Virtue over Vice.

Mentioned at the outset of this chapter, the specific reference to Hercules and remaining firm would find its expression in Adams's proposed vision of the design of the "Great Seal of the confederated States." Writing to Abigail he explained: "I proposed the Choice of Hercules." Adams had been serving on a committee with Thomas Jefferson and Benjamin Franklin to develop a seal for the new nation. In consultation with an artist, Eugène Pierre du Simitière, the three men put forth their own suggestions—none of which were accepted by the designer, whose own first attempt was also unacceptable to the Congress.[44] It would take years and several more committees before Congress would approve the final design, still in use today, of an American bald eagle clutching thirteen arrows in one talon and an olive branch in the other. Only the motto "E Pluribus Unum" survived from the committee on which Adams served. Adams's idea came from one that he shared with his wife, Abigail, of an image "engraved by Gribeline in some Editions of Lord Shaftsburys Works."[45]

The image itself featured a young Hercules at the moment of his decision. On the right side of the image, one female figure, with legs exposed, gazes up at him. On the left a sterner female figure points over his shoulder to the path he should select. Adams's description of Virtue was curt and focused on her action, "pointing to her rugged Mountain, on one Hand, and perswading him to ascend." Vice, or "Sloth," as he called her here, was described by Adams in greater detail: "glancing at her flowery Paths of Pleasure, wantonly reclining on the Ground, displaying the Charms both of her Eloquence and Person, to seduce him into Vice." For Adams, sexual immorality was evident in the image of "Sloth" despite her more general-sounding name.[46]

For Adams, the Choice of Hercules neatly captured the critical fortitude needed for individual happiness and the avoidance of being "unmanly." Yet it could also expand and have equal applicability for the new nation. As

In a letter to Abigail, John Adams referenced this image of "Hercules at the Crossroads." Engraving by Simon Gribelin, 1713. Anthony Ashley Cooper Shaftesbury, *Characteristicks of Men, Manners, Opinions, Times*, vol. 3 (London, 1714), 345. Photo courtesy of the Newberry Library, Chicago.

Mark Kann and others have argued, the political leaders of the new nation viewed the polity in gendered terms, as a fraternal order of virtuous men. For Adams, the Choice of Hercules applied to men and women, of course, but the specific focus on the strength to choose the right path gave it a distinctly masculine quality. A nation of men choosing as did Hercules then could be illustrated by his image for the seal of the United States.[47]

As a statesman abroad, Adams confronted a sexually charged European cultural atmosphere that would serve as more fodder for his moral opining. He would eventually sum up his view of the moral challenge facing European society using the story of the Choice of Hercules. In his diary—even after nearly ten years in Europe—he would comment while in London: "The

Temples to Bacchus and Venus, are quite unnecessary as Mankind have no need of artificial Incitements, to such Amuzements."[48] For Adams the society had far too many social settings that encouraged rather than kept in check natural desires for indulgences, including sexual ones ("Venus"). Paris would also provide him with much to shake his head over. In one letter he wrote to Abigail a typical assessment of Parisian morals that included indulging in all pleasures of the flesh: "Luxury, dissipation, and Effeminacy, are pretty nearly at the same degree of Excess here, and in every other Part of Europe."[49]

Some of Adams's comments were highly critical of the social and sexual world of elite Parisian life. Later in his life, for example, Adams wrote in his autobiography about his astonishment at learning that monogamous marriage was not held in high esteem in Paris. Reflecting on one couple's openly kept extramarital affairs, he wrote:

> When I afterwards learned both from Dr. Franklin and his Grandson, and from many other Persons, that this Woman was the Amie of Mr. Brillion and that Madam Brillion consoled herself by the Amitie of Mr. Le Vailliant, I was astonished that these People could live together in such apparent Friendship and indeed without cutting each others throats. But I did not know the World. I soon saw and heard so much of these Things in other Families and among allmost all the great People of the Kingdom that I found it was a thing of course. It was universally understood and Nobody lost any reputation by it.[50]

For Adams the custom was widespread among elite society—but he also took pains to point out that he was previously unfamiliar with such a thing, quipping, "I did not know the World."

Despite recognizing that no one "lost any reputation," Adams was quick to note that he saw in non-monogamy no real happiness. He continued:

> Yet I must say that I never knew an Instance of it, without perceiving that all their Complaisancy was [*illegible*] external and ostensible only: a mere conformity to the fashion: and that internally there was so far from being any real friendship or conjugal Affection that their minds and hearts were full of jealousy, Envy, revenge and rancour. In short that it was deadly poison to all the calm felicity of Life. There were none of the delightful Enjoyments of conscious Innocence and mutual Confidence. It was mere brutal pleasure.[51]

Adams found the "fashion" and elite society's "conformity" to it not simply to defy Christian moral teachings (a muted reference point here) but rather a thing that inhibited "Enjoyments." Positioning non-monogamy as giving in to "brutal pleasure," he suggested the participants operated at the level of beasts indulging in sexual desires.

By 1780, after observing all this for several years, Adams would once again turn to the story of the Choice of Hercules to sum up for his wife what he had witnessed. Writing to Abigail from Paris, he praised the rich culture that he found: "There is every Thing here that can inform the Understanding, or refine the Taste, and indeed one would think that could purify the Heart." But he noted that it was not without an immoral lining. "Yet it must be remembered," he told his wife, "there is every thing here too, which can seduce, betray, deceive, deprave, corrupt and debauch it." "Hercules marches here in full View of the Steeps of Virtue on one hand, and the flowery Paths of Pleasure on the other" he referenced, "and there are few who make the Choice of Hercules." Adams saw in the lesson a story of moral gravity, and he continued by expressing concern for his loved ones: "That my Children may follow his Example, is my earnest Prayer: but I sometimes tremble, when I hear the syren songs of sloth, least they should be captivated with her bewitching Charms and her soft, insinuating Musick."[52] The particular visual of Hercules as he "marches here in full View" may well have also been intended to assure his wife that amid all the "flowery Paths of Pleasure" Adams remained steadfast and true to her, a Hercules himself.

Adams viewed proper manhood as marked by possessing the capability to make a masculine choice to eschew the pitfalls of immorality and embrace the true path to happiness, marked by virtue. He may have appeared prudish by some standards, but for him this choice to be sexually virtuous was to exemplify masculinity. It had implications for not only personal "happiness" but also for the stability and success of the nation as a whole. John Adams followed a model of Hercules throughout his life. His priggishness was part of his masculine identity, as much as Ben Franklin's flirtations or George Washington's self-control. This reminds us of the multiple models of sexual masculinity in eighteenth-century America, and the variety of ways that sex could inform manliness in the founding era.

Adams's understanding of the masculine fortitude required to enact moral manhood did not make him simply an "old-fashioned" man. Instead, he was arguably a new man—in part a reactionary one, in response to an increasingly sexually liberal and secular society. As historians tell us, by the mid-eighteenth century America was in the throes of something of a "sexual revolution," marked by increased diversity of sexual subcultures and behaviors.[53] Adams should not be seen simply as an outdated model of manhood informed by seventeenth-century (read: static) religious morality—but as a *new* manly identity that drew on traditional models of sexual manhood and asserted their superiority in the face of shifting sexual mores and masculine comportment in an increasingly heterogeneous late eighteenth-century America. Adams also reminds us that as virtue became increasingly associated with femininity and chastity, it would remain for many a trait to also be embraced by masculine men in the new nation. Adams invoked the image of Hercules as a model of masculine virtue and did so to indicate morality broadly but also linked specifically to sex and sexuality. For Adams, the Choice of Hercules was an old one that had new connotations and significance for his personal identity, but also for his family, society, and ultimately, nation.

NOTES

1. See Anne S. Lombard, *Making Manhood: Growing Up Male in Colonial New England* (Cambridge: Harvard University Press, 2003); Lisa Wilson, *Ye Heart of a Man: The Domestic Life of Men in Colonial New England* (New Haven: Yale University Press, 1999).

2. See, for example, Thomas A. Foster, *Sex and the Eighteenth-Century Man: Massachusetts and the History of Sexuality in America* (Boston: Beacon Press, 2006).

3. Richard Godbeer, *Sexual Revolution in Early America* (Baltimore: Johns Hopkins University Press, 2002); and Clare Lyons, *Sex Among the Rabble: An Intimate History of Gender and Power in the Age of Revolution, Philadelphia, 1730–1830* (Chapel Hill: University of North Carolina Press, 2006).

4. See, for example, Brian D. Carroll, "'I indulged my desire too freely': Sexuality, Spirituality, and the Sin of Self-Pollution in the Diary of Joseph Moody, 1720–1724," *William and Mary Quarterly* 60 (January 2003): 155–70; Janet Moore Lindman, "Acting the Manly Christian: White Evangelical Masculinity in Revolutionary Virginia," *William and Mary Quarterly* 57 (April 2000): 393–416; and E. Anthony Rotundo, *American Manhood: Transformations in Masculinity from the Revolution to the Modern Era* (New York: Basic Books, 1993).

5. Bernard Bailyn, *The Ideological Origins of the American Revolution* (Cambridge: Belknap, 1992). On Adams and virtue, see also Andy Trees, "John Adams and the Problem of Virtue," *Journal of the Early Republic* 21 (Autumn 2001): 393–412.

6. Ruth H. Bloch, *Gender and Morality in Anglo-American Culture, 1650–1800* (Berkeley: University of California Press, 2003), 136–153.

7. Ibid..

8. Ibid., 149.

9. Cathy N. Davidson, ed., Hanna W. Foster, *The Coquette* (1797; New York: Oxford University Press, 1986), 20.

10. Recent biographies include John E. Ferling, *John Adams: A Life* (Newton, CT: American Political Biography Press, 1997); Edith B. Gelles, *Portia: The World of Abigail Adams* (Bloomington: Indiana University Press, 1992); Margaret A. Hogan and C. James Taylor, *My Dearest Friend: Letters of John and Abigail Adams* (Cambridge, MA: Belknap Press, 2007); David McCullough, *John Adams* (New York: Simon & Schuster, 2008); Judith St. George, *John and Abigail Adams: An American Love Story* (New York: Holiday House, 2001); Gore Vidal, *Inventing a Nation: Washington, Adams, Jefferson* (New Haven: Yale University Press, 2003).

11. Ferling, *John Adams*, 3, 53.

12. John T. Morse, Jr., *John Adams* (Boston: Houghton Mifflin, 1884), 6–7.

13. Walter Stahr, *John Jay: Founding Father* (New York: Hambledon and London, 2005), 162.

14. St. George, *John and Abigail Adams*, 46.

15. On the rivalry and comment, see Vidal, *Inventing a Nation*, 17; and Arnold A. Rogow, *A Fatal Friendship: Alexander Hamilton and Aaron Burr* (New York: Hill and Wang, 1998), 76, 150.

16. He is widely referenced in this manner—from popular cultural reference in films such as Eddie Murphy's hit movie *The Nutty Professor* (1996), in which a doting mother praises her rotund son for his biceps by exclaiming "Hercules! Hercules!" to products such as the Hercules Hook, so named to tout its holding power. On Hercules in Western literature "from Homer to our time," see G. Karl Galinsky, *The Herakles Theme: The Adaptations of the Hero in Literature from Homer to the Twentieth Century* (Totowa, NJ: Rowman and Littlefield Publishers, 1972).

17. A 1970 movie starring Arnold Schwarzenegger in his professional bodybuilding prime and a popular 1998 television show highlight Hercules as a man of great physique. In 1997 Disney animators likewise fashioned Hercules as a muscle-bound hunk, with promotional materials in particular focusing with almost pornographic detail on his physique, a standard pose showing a flexed bulging bicep.

18. Chloe Chard, "Effeminacy, Pleasure, and the Classical Body," in Gill Perry and Michael Rossington, eds., *Femininity and Masculinity in Eighteenth-Century Art and Culture* (Manchester: Manchester University Press, 1994), 142–61.

19. Peter Linebaugh and Marcus Rediker, *The Many-Headed Hydra: Sailors, Slaves, Commoners, and the Hidden History of the Revolutionary Atlantic* (Boston: Beacon Press, 2000), 2.

20. Ibid., 36.

21. Lynn Hunt, "Hercules and the Radical Image in the French Revolution," *Representations* 2 (Spring 1983): 100, 103.

22. Gordon S. Wood, *The Creation of the American Republic, 1776–1787* (1969; Chapel Hill: University of North Carolina Press for the Omohundro Institute of Early American History and Culture, 1998), 49.

23. Ira Berlin, *Many Thousands Gone: The First Two Centuries of Slavery in North America* (Cambridge, MA: Belknap Press, 1998), 95.

24. "Choice of Hercules" in *Tatler*, no. 97, November 22, 1709; Anthony Ashley Cooper Shaftesbury, *A Notion of the Historical Draught of Tablature of the Judgment of Hercules* (London, 1723).

25. David Mannings, "Reynolds, Garrick, and the Choice of Hercules," *Eighteenth-Century Studies* 17 (Spring 1984): 263.

26. See, for example, advertisement for one such performance in the *Pennsylvania Gazette*, November 30, 1769.

27. Mannings, "Reynolds, Garrick, and the Choice of Hercules," 263. Ayers Bagley finds in Hercules a "durable hero" "associated with moral education" in books and manuals favored by seventeenth-century English "schoolmasters and tutors." See Bagley, "Hercules in Emblem Books and Schools," in Ayers L. Bagley, Edward M. Griffin, and Austin J. McLean, eds., *The Telling Image: Explorations in the Emblem* (New York: AMS Press, 1996), 69.

28. See, for example, booksellers' advertisements in the *Pennsylvania Gazette*, August 10, 1758; October 6, 1763.

29. Sara Fielding, trans., *Xenophon's Memoirs of Socrates*, 3rd ed. (London, 1787), 116.

30. Fielding, *Xenophon's Memoirs of Socrates*, 118.

31. George Frideric Handel, "The Choice of Hercules" (1751). See http://opera.stanford.edu/iu/libretti/choice.htm.

32. John Adams autobiography, part 1, "John Adams," through 1776, sheet 3 of 53 (electronic edition), *Adams Family Papers: An Electronic Archive* (Boston: Massachusetts Historical Society), http://www.masshist.org/digitaladams/.

33. Ibid.

34. March 15, 1756, John Adams diary 1, 18 November 1755–29 August 1756, *Adams Family Papers: An Electronic Archive*.

35. Ibid.

36. John Adams diary 3, 1759, *Adams Family Papers: An Electronic Archive*.

37. Ibid.

38. "Tuesday January 1759," John Adams diary 2, 5 October 1758–9 April 1759, *Adams Family Papers: An Electronic Archive*.

39. *Reflections on Courtship and Marriage* (Philadelphia, 1746), v. See also Foster, *Sex and the Eighteenth-Century Man*.

40. "Tuesday January 1759," John Adams diary 2.

41. Ibid.

42. Ibid.

43. *Reflections on Courtship and Marriage*, vi. On bachelors in early America, see John McCurdy, *Citizen Bachelors: Manhood and the Creation of the United States* (Ithaca: Cornell University Press, 2009). See also Foster, *Sex and the Eighteenth-Century Man*.

44. Gaillard Hunt, *The History of the Seal of the United States* (Washington, DC: Department of State, 1909).

45. Here Adams refers to Anthony Ashley Cooper Shaftesbury, *Characteristicks of Men, Manners, Opinions, Times*, vol. 3 (London, 1714), 345.

46. His design differed from that put forth by Benjamin Franklin, who proposed "Moses lifting up his Wand, and dividing the Red Sea, and Pharaoh, in his Chariot overwhelmed with the Waters.—This Motto. Rebellion to Tyrants is Obedience to God." It was also unlike that of Thomas Jefferson, who envisioned "The Children of Israel in the Wilderness, led by a Cloud by day, and a Pillar of Fire by night, and on the other Side Hengist and Horsa, the Saxon Chiefs, from whom We claim the Honour of being descended and whose Political Principles and Form of Government We have assumed." Letter from John Adams to Abigail Adams, August 14, 1776, *Adams Family Papers: An Electronic Archive*.

47. Mark Kann, *A Republic of Men: The American Founders, Gendered Language, and Patriarchal Politics* (New York: New York University Press, 1998).

48. John Adams diary 44, 27 March–21 July 1786, *Adams Family Papers: An Electronic Archive.*

49. Letter from John Adams to Abigail Adams, June 3 1778, *Adams Family Papers: An Electronic Archive.*

50. John Adams autobiography, part 2, "Travels, and Negotiations," 1777–1778, sheet 11 of 37, *Adams Family Papers: An Electronic Archive.*

51. Ibid.

52. Letter from John Adams to Abigail Adams, April–May 1780, *Adams Family Papers: An Electronic Archive.*

53. See, for example, Godbeer, *Sexual Revolution in Early America*; and Lyons, *Sex Among the Rabble.*

12

"Play the Man... for Your Bleeding Country"

Military Chaplains as Gender Brokers During the American Revolutionary War

JANET MOORE LINDMAN

In December 1783, the Presbyterian cleric George Duffield preached a sermon before Congress to celebrate the American triumph in war and the return of peace. His oration lauded the heroic action of American colonists against the tyranny of Britain. Though America had "contributed her liberal share" to the empire and never withheld "her blood or her treasure when requisitions were made," England still wished to keep her under "servile submission." To obviate this possibility, American men reacted with a militant spirit in 1775:

> The peaceful husband forsook his farm; the merchant relinquished his trade; the compassionate physician forgot his daily round; the mariner laid aside his compass and quadrant; and the mechanic resigned his implements of employment... all prepared for war, and eagerly flew to the field.[1]

Anxious to serve, American men willingly left their livelihoods to take up arms. As "faithful watchmen," American soldiers "blew the trumpet on the walls of our Zion" to defend their native country—gendered female—with military aggression—gendered male—against a common enemy. Duffield's sermon weaves together gender, religion, and politics to commemorate the American victory. His seamless history, however, omits the civil upheaval caused by the American Revolution, as white men fought against England as well as among themselves to realize national independence. Nor does it allude to the changing nature of manhood as the revolutionary era instigated a new level of political engagement for white men of lower and middling status.[2] By the 1770s, a white man's rank was not only based on his role as head of household, master, husband, father, or property owner, but also on his position relative to British imperial policy and the onset of war. Men were judged by their political position; even the most retiring and pacifist had to take a public stand. Not participating in debates or policies to protest English legislation, such as the non-importation agreements, impugned many men's reputation. Once the war broke out, American men were expected to partake in the manly exercise of military service.[3]

Though Duffield contends that American men were quick to respond to the threat of subjection with martial commitment, his conception of masculinity did not fit all white men. Though traditional manhood was based on property, mastery, and dominance, these were not the only ways for white men to enact male identity in eighteenth-century America. Beginning in the middle of the century, the emergence of evangelical revivalism led to a new form of manhood, one based on Christian concepts of humility, piety, and sobriety. This evangelical masculinity stood in stark contrast to a traditional one that valued economic autonomy, political power, physical strength, and military expertise. American evangelicals counseled withdrawal from secular society in favor of prayer, contemplation, and circumspect behavior, as male converts to evangelical Christianity trod a new path toward manhood. The exemplar of this ideal was the minister, who provided male leadership within the church but also endorsed and acted out Christian principles of prudence, temperance, and meditation as well as abstention from sinful activities and worldly pursuits.

When the war against Britain began, this exemplary role was taken on by military chaplains, pious believers who abhorred violence and dissension and yet wished to serve their country as men. Their participation in the war comprised both a negation and affirmation of traditional manhood. Two different modes of white masculinity came together in the role of the military chaplain during the American Revolutionary War. Clergy who served as chaplains with the American forces censored the customs of military life at the same time that they bolstered traditional manliness through religious leadership and rhetoric.[4] They melded republican ideology with holy text to support the patriot cause. Drawing on biblical and contemporary concepts of manhood, the American chaplain acted as a conduit of white male aspirations for political freedom and military success, as well as a morally justified war against their British enemy.[5] Chaplains functioned as gender brokers in this military context, fusing the seeming contradiction of traditional male traits, such as contention and combativeness, with the female characteristics of clerical service: nurturing the sick, consoling the dying, and tending to the dead.⁶ As moral guides and intimate counselors, chaplains personified the tensions between a traditional and evangelical model of manhood. Clergy joined the American cause as military men to live in male communities based on camaraderie, competition, violence, and deprivation. As chaplains embodying "feminine" values, they participated in a "masculine" world, and in the process, mediated the shifting nature of gender roles for white men in late eighteenth-century America.

Chaplains and Christian Manhood

The role of chaplains as gender brokers within the American military came through their ministerial role to model spiritual behavior, to sermonize Christian values, and to nurture soldiers when sick and dying. Their role as negotiator was evident in their intermediate status within the American military. Chaplains were considered adjutants but did not share in the perils of warfare; they were noncombatants. Their religious role mitigated involvement in military activities, and most chaplains were present but not active on the battlefield. During the Battle of Bunker Hill, David Avery watched from a neighboring hill and prayed for "divine blessings to succeed." Likewise, "Mr. Ellis" imparted "friendship and esteem" to officers and enlisted men alike during battle but did not join in. By not engaging in military action, chaplains served as an auxiliary force similar to women, who took care of others and during the war served as camp followers to provide for soldiers' material and physical needs.⁷ Many soldiers had a low opinion of chaplains because they were paid but did not participate in military operations. Some clerics were aware of their reputation among the men. John Gano, who took part in the fierce fighting at Chatterton's Hill, noticed the pressure he felt to live up to the men's ideals of manly behavior while under fire: "somehow I got in front of the regiment, yet I durst not quit my place for fear of dampening the spirits of the soldiers or of bringing on me an imputation of cowardice."⁸ Thomas Allen's heroic stand at Bennington garnered praise from his men. Such actions gave some chaplains increased legitimacy because of their performance on the battlefield.

The chaplaincy offered clergymen an opportunity to serve their country and their brethren. Dissenting ministers were especially eager to tend to their fellow believers in the Continental Army and state militias. Chaplains preached to men of various faiths, heard sermons by other denominational divines, and experienced the challenges of camp life. This included not only exposure to disease, such as smallpox, but the bad food, poor sanitation, and moral dangers posed by military living. Chaplains were anxious to boost morale and forestall sinful behavior among the men. They offered solace and support to soldiers wearied by difficult battles and long service. They not only comforted those ailing and dying and provided clerical leadership, they wanted to spur soldiers on in their mission. Ammi Robbins sought to encourage soldiers when "doing their duty, to pray for and with them when sick, and bury them when they died." Besides traditional pastoral duties, they officiated at parades, public fasts, marriages, funerals, and baptisms. They were present at executions of court-martialed soldiers. Some chaplains served as quartermasters, surgeons, intelligence officers, and commanders.[9] Chaplains performed their duties whenever and wherever: in the hospital, while on parade, or on the move. While marching to Quebec, Ammi Robbins held worship services at the edge of Lake George, with exhortation, prayer, and singing. When Samuel Spring was on the road to Canada, he preached every morning from a pile of knapsacks before leaving camp.

The primary activity of chaplains was to be moral and physical caretakers, and some specialized as hospital chaplains. James Sproat rode a medical circuit visiting several hospitals on a regular basis. He would typically meet with the wounded first and then preach in the afternoon at a local church or barn. Many chaplains spent a great deal of their time counseling the sick and wounded, usually before the onset of death. Caring for the physical health of others was traditionally a female occupation, one that some clergy found difficult to master. Philip Vickers Fithian initially found this work onerous. Unused to this supplemental service, he was revolted by the sicknesses plaguing his charges. But he felt it his duty as a soldier and patriot to "hazard and suffer equally" with his countrymen. Ammi Robbins declared that his poor constitution left him unfit for the rigors of clerical work in military hospitals. After "inhaling such diseased breath," he felt sick and faint as well as depressed by the invalids' sorrows. Chaplains worked to balance the needs of the military with their form of Christian masculinity. Ammi Robbins ensured that pressing military concerns did not keep him from commemorating the Sabbath. When he was unable to preach one Sunday because there was "no time or leisure for any thing," he took a book into the woods by himself and spent two hours in a "sweet season." While in camp, services were typically conducted on Sundays in both the morning and afternoon; the first was often held in conjunction with parading of the troops. Officers supported religious activity in their military camps. General Anthony Wayne issued divisional orders requiring every officer to arrive punctually with his corps for the delivery of sermons by two chaplains. Ministerial work was meshed with military activities as prayers and exhortations accompanied musters and parades as well as victory celebrations. After the British surrender at Saratoga, one American brigade marked the event with religious discourses followed by cannon fire and a *feu de joie*. William Van Horne held that this combination of parading and prayer was a right and privilege of all soldiers; it was also a way for clergy to marry military triumph with religious faith.[10]

Ministers hoped to model appropriate behavior among the men by espousing Christian ideals to their martial audience. When Ammi Robbins visited some soldiers and officers in camp, he found they took his "reproofs well." While he had "profitable conversations" with some men, most soldiers indulged in "very chaffy and light" talk. American men "seemed possessed of an heroic spirit," while they were "careless of their precious souls." Chaplains complained about the low level of morality among their new congregants. James Armstrong disproved of the disreputable conduct in military camps: "rioting and drunkenness, what chambering and wantonness, what pride, luxury, and sensuality; what neglect and contempt of the Gospel and Gospel ordinances!" He claimed that such activity carried the "seeds of destruction," and would bring "brimstone upon our habitations, . . . from ever-burning, unconsumed sulphurious beds."[11] Chaplains were horrified by the immorality of soldiers and their interactions with the locals. Robbins was shocked by the wicked behavior of the inhabitants of Albany, who made Sunday "a high play day" with many social diversions. Isaac Bangs was repulsed by the "impudence and immodesty" of the prostitutes who congregated at "Holy Ground" in New York City and the soldiers who frequented them. He condemned those who made use of their services: "it seems strange that any man can divest himself of manhood as to desire a connexion with these worse than brutal creatures." Such actions not only endangered soldiers' souls, it could unman them for their primary purpose in the American military.[12]

Chaplains lamented the use of profane language among American soldiers. Ammi Robbins reproved men for swearing and "needless disregard of the Sabbath." Hezekiah Smith preached a whole sermon on the evils of swearing, while Ebenezer David wrote that "the profanity of our camps is very great." Thomas Allen stated that his "camp was full of blasphemers, and resounds with the language of the infernal regions." James Armstrong found swearing to be the most common sin practiced in the American military. While "luxury, avarice, and prodigality are here circumscribed by the times," this was only a "partial virtue and partial virtue had never yet saved a people from destruction." Defining swearing as a "shameful intemperance of words,"

Armstrong found "this practice of profane cursing and swearing equally reprobated by the soldier, gentleman and Christian [and] certainly never discovered itself with such daring effrontery." This was especially troubling among military men because they were the most likely to experience death, and yet they "cast off every obligation to him who can kill both soul and body in hell." He predicted a dark end for the "profane swearer," who "will be banished from the comfortable presence of his maker to those dreary abodes where hope never comes."

The penchant for swearing and profanity among officers and soldiers alike continued despite military and religious prohibitions. As Royster notes, "curses were marks of toughness and bravado" and a means of demonstrating fearlessness; no one could constrain this manly behavior even when blaspheming God. Soldiers readily embraced a camp life composed of jocularity, ribaldry, drinking, and gambling. The "swaggering, cavalier manner" of many soldiers opposed that of the sober and circumspect Christian, and military camps were not conducive to a saintly life. Despite an early interest in religion, Daniel Trabue entered the army, neglected prayer, and adopted deism. He soon began to "frolick, carouse, and dance, and curse and swear" like other soldiers. His reaction to camp life was common. Some military men charged that too much religion could have an adverse impact on the soldiery. When a group of enlisted men came under the influence of evangelicalism on the Virginia frontier, they were "despised by their officers." Their heartfelt displays of religious emotionalism were ridiculed; the officers supposed that their new faith "disqualified them for fighting." Defining spirituality as a feminizing influence, these converts had unmanned themselves for military service.[13]

As soldiers, chaplains became part of a masculine world steeped in martial attributes of strength, violence, and sacrifice. The harshness of military life and camp conditions within this male community affirmed traditional concepts of manhood. At the same time, chaplains sought to exemplify Christian ideals of tenderness, subservience, and piety, and convert others to the faith. Chaplains tried to bring about a spiritual awakening in their men. Hezekiah Smith used his position as chaplain to ensure his commanding officer, General Sullivan, adopted evangelical religion: "a soul like yours, possessed with so many superior amiable qualifications, viewed in a military or civil light, would shine the sphere of Christianity, were it to be deeply impressed with the glorious religion of a meek and lovely Jesus." Chaplains urged soldiers to "repent lest the Lord come and smite you with a curse." By converting soldiers, chaplains hoped to instill habits of devoutness and abstinence and combat traditional attributes of camp life, such as swearing, drinking, gaming, and whoring. Such wanton behavior was not only injurious to individual souls, it also affected American war aims. According to one pastor, "many by their wickedness do more hurt a thousand fold than they themselves do good in the cause." Another wrote that if "Christ was honoured more, if his venerable name was profaned less, we might expect a more effectual blessing of our arms."[14]

Despite their best efforts, chaplains bemoaned the prevalent disinterest in all things religious among the American forces. As one cleric recorded in the fall of 1775, "there is no disposition here to religious duties. We have not had one Day of Thanksgiving or publick prayer ordered for all the victories of this season. I hate such company and ardently wish for the return of seasons of domestic and public worship." The vagaries of warfare meant that Sunday was often a workday: "All are busy, men, carts, even the women are all busy washing, no signs of a Sabbath of rest. Everything is a continual whirl, all noise." This was especially true when men and materiel were moved for battle. During the march to White Plains on a Sunday in October 1776, Thomas Allen admitted that he had never seen "such a confused Sabbath." In Philip Vickers Fithian's experience, "The Sabbath is scarcely known in the Army," and he feared the consequences of such neglect: "Dreadful is the thought that men who expect an engagement every day with an obstinate, wise, and powerful enemy, should be so ungodly."[15]

Holy Warfare

When the war broke out, some clerics wrote sermons justifying the use of force against Britain. Ministers who came out early in support of the patriots found moral justification for political rebellion. Oliver Hart believed the American cause to be a "righteous" one: "[I] have not a doubt but that America will yet be delivered from all her troubles, and become the greatest, and most flourishing empire in the universe." David Jones preached a sermon in summer of 1775 called "Defensive War Is a Just Cause Sinless." Hezekiah Smith prepared a patriotic homily at the same time titled "The Soldier's Spiritual Armor." Smith took Ephesians 6:13 for his text: "Wherefore take unto the whole armor of God[,] that ye may be able to withstand in the evil day, and having done all to stand." He acknowledged that this passage was "suitable" for "the meditation, attention and practice of those who are in the army." Noting that there are both "spiritual" and "natural" battles to be fought, he asserted:

> Three things are to be attended to in this war. First. Whether the cause is just and good. Second. Whether we are able with a common blessing to conquer. Third. Whether it be duty to actually engage our enemies.—I trust these particulars have been thoroughly weighted by you who are here ready upon the spot to engage in the defence of your just rights and privileges and of our injured land.

Though Smith came out in favor of the war, he wanted his fellow believers to "thoroughly" weigh the moral questions posed by this conflict.[16]

In a sermon titled "A Self-Defensive War Lawful," John Carmichael observed the biblical prohibitions against killing others. Though war was "a very great evil," he reasoned it was unavoidable in certain circumstances. At such times, duty demanded Christians to engage in warfare. He wished soldiers "to serve" their military calling as well as "a plowman or preacher" did his. Like Smith, he argued that the war against Britain was just. He insisted that God had given men the ability to fight, and since in this time "when we are not to expect miracles," it was logical "to arm ourselves and use our arms for our own preservation against an invading army." He assured his hearers that "every one that draws the sword, should be well satisfied in his conscience, that he is called of God to do so." He declared that to fight successfully, the individual soldier should believe in Jesus Christ and not be in "a state of enmity and rebellion" against God. Only by fearing God and having faith in salvation could a soldier meet the dangers of warfare. Through "becoming boldness and Christian serenity, accompanied with true courage," the soldier would "put his life in God's hands." Carmichael closed his sermon by encouraging men to connect religious belief to military action:

> Put on, gentlemen, the gospel armoury—have your feet shod with its preparation—for your helmet salvation—for your shield, faith—and be girt with truth—This, sirs is a gospel uniform, that becomes the Christian soldier.[17]

Jacob Duché made a similar argument by stating that American colonists were fighting for both their "temporal rights" and their "spiritual privileges," which needed preserving as much as political ones. He saw the conflict with Britain as evidence of God's unhappiness with the colonists by bringing the "flames of unnatural war" into the "very bowels of our native land." He called on all Americans to return to their savior's favor through prayer, supplication, and repentance. The people would be led by "the chosen band of Christian soldiers," who would fight "vice and slavery" and return the country to God's favor. Despite the need for warfare, Duché still counseled soldiers to remember that loss occurred on both sides. He called on participants to follow the biblical directive to give food to the hungry, care of the poor, cover the naked, and weep with mourners. As Christian soldiers, they had a duty not only to vanquish their enemy but also to demonstrate charity and nurturance to those who suffered in wartime.[18]

Chaplains consciously associated the war against Britain with God's plan for America. By their sermonizing, they coupled the religious cause to the political battle for independence. General Burgoyne's surrender at Saratoga was defined as a "signal success," made possible by "the supreme disposer of all human events." When the American forces were victorious, this was due to God's beneficence; when they were in retreat, it was because they were "a sinful nation" that hoped for God's mercy. Military service had a religious component for many soldiers, and chaplains linked individual spiritual destinies to national political outcomes in their sermons. By defeating those who would enslave Americans, soldiers would serve divine goals.[19]

Chaplains crafted sermons to fit the circumstances of the men in their regiments and brigades. Abiel Leonard was adept at explaining to soldiers why they were fighting and how they were defending their nation. Sometimes officers suggested passages for use in sermons that related to the current military situation. On the eve of the battle of Brandywine, John Trout took as his text "they that take the sword, shall perish by the sword." He promised American soldiers that they had taken up the sword "for truth, for justice and for right" compared to their foes, who had taken up in "the spirit of wrong and revenge," which they will punished for with death. In the fall of 1776, William McKay Tennent preached from Nehemiah 4:14: "Be not ye afraid of them." He confirmed for his hearers that these words came from "the voice of heaven, the voice of your bleeding country, the voice of the Church, and the voice of all who are dear to you."[20]

Chaplains played on gender ideals to encourage soldiers into battle. Many clerics used the biblical concepts of manhood to embolden soldiers to continue the fight. The books of the Old Testament proffered popular texts for chaplains. Thomas Allen paraphrased II Samuel 10:2 to persuade soldiers to be "valiant" and to "play the man. Let no danger appear too great—let no suffering appear too severe for you to encounter for your bleeding country." Abiel Leonard did the same, telling his listeners "be of good courage, and let us play men for our people." David Jones voiced a similar message: "If you will only acquit yourselves like men, and with firmness of mind go forth against your enemies, resolving either to return with victory or to die gloriously." William McKay Tennent remarked on the natural response of fear to the dangers of military warfare. He advised his military hearers to "keep guard upon this passion lest, in its excess, it should prove ruinous." Ministers reiterated the need for courage and bravery in warfare and obedience to their superior officers; such discourses inculcated ideals of traditional manhood while they maintained military discipline.[21]

Hezekiah Smith referred to soldiers' paternal role within civilian society as husbands and fathers by reminding them of "the defenceless children, the helpless women, the superannuated men" who have suffered at the hands of the British. As a "band of brothers," American soldiers would be part of a "great and respectable" army that would be "brave, hardy, patient in sufferings, determined in action, well disciplined, and a terror to the most veteran troops in the world." These skills would come from a God "who teacheth our hands to war and our fingers to fight" and who inspired "the brave sons of America with martial zeal and courage." David Jones spoke of dire consequences for American women if American men did not do their military duty: "see the dear wives of your bosoms forced from their peaceful habitations, and perhaps used with such indecency that modesty would forbid the description. Behold the fair virgins of your land, whose benevolent souls are now filled with a thousand good wishes and hopes of seeing their admirers return home crowned with victory." John Trout also emphasized this theme, telling soldiers to fight "the good fight" for their homes, wives, and children. He invoked the obligation men felt toward their families and communities. To encourage soldiers to "take up sword," Trout reminded his listeners of the violence done to their fellow Americans: "let the blood-stained valley—the desolated homes—the burned farm home—the murdered farmer—the whitening bones of our own countrymen answer!" He used the ideal of male protectiveness and female vulnerability to engender a swift response to British brutality: "Let the starving mother with the babe clinging to her withered breast, let her answer—with the death rattle mingling with the murmuring tones that mark the last struggle for life; let the dying mother and her babe answer!"[22]

Gender was a salient element of revolutionary discourse. By assigning a feminine identity to the new nation, soldiers were told to fight for "her defense," to "do her honor" by a military response, to exhibit the "heroism, firmness, and magnanimity which this cause requires." American men were to defend women, children, and the aged from British belligerence and treachery. Gender was applied to political ideology to strengthen the American cause. Defining cosmopolitan influences as feminizing to manly citizens, American soldiers were to "banish the syren [sic] luxury, with all her train of fascinating pleasures, idle dissipation and expensive amusements." By rejecting the enervating effeminacy induced by dependency on Britain, American soldiers could assert their national sovereignty and political identity as men. With the manly determination of its soldiers, "America shall blast her fiercest foes . . . and shine sole empress of the Western world!"[23]

Religious and Political Dissent

The contours of white manhood underwent significant change before the onset of the American Revolution. In the decades preceding the outbreak of colonial protests, American colonists had experienced religious revivalism up and down the eastern seaboard from the 1740s into the 1770s. The growth of the Baptist, Methodist, and Presbyterian denominations presented new opportunities for spiritual expression. Evangelical religion required an emotional conversion experience before admittance to church membership. Along with conversion went a radical change in personal behavior to adhere to an evangelical ideal of being in the world but not of the world. For men who converted to the new faith, this change in spiritual status provoked a gender crisis, as they had to alter their traditional beliefs and behaviors. Early American society supported the belief that women were more pious than men and more in need of religion because of their maternal role and secondary status in society. Perceived as feminine, evangelical Christianity required the wholesale withdrawal of white men from traditional forms of masculinity and provided an alternative avenue to manhood.[24]

The differences between these two modes of manhood were compounded by the outbreak of the American Revolution. The participation of evangelicals, such Baptists, Methodists, and Presbyterians, in the American Revolution varied. Evangelical religion recommended withdrawal from a sinful world and interaction with like-minded believers. Initially, many denominations were reluctant to support the patriot cause. Backcountry settlers, among them Lutherans, German Reformed, and Presbyterians, questioned the call for revolution. As Jon Butler argues, religious persecution at the hands of their colonial governments factored into their alleged loyalism. Clergymen of all kinds feared that talk of politics and warfare would take people away from the church and religion. Radical groups, such as Quakers and Mennonites, were pacifists and only desired to stay out of this worldly event. But their nonparticipation led to ostracism by the wider society; they disguised their Toryism as pacifism. By professing religious beliefs, such men could harbor subversive political convictions.[25]

A continuum of participation in the political and military events of the revolutionary era emerged among religious denominations. Methodists were at one end of the continuum. John Wesley's directive to remain neutral during the conflict lessened the Methodist presence in the American Revolution.[26] This meant many American Methodist men became pacifists during the war. State officials viewed their pacifism as a convenient cover for closet loyalism, and some Methodist men were harassed, fined, and imprisoned for refusing to participate in the draft. The persecution of Methodist ministers in Maryland coincided with the outbreak of war. Methodist pacifists confronted the political binary of loyalist versus patriot at the same time they repudiated traditional expectations and activities of white manhood: participation in musters, militias, and armed combat. The Methodist Freeborn Garrettson embodied this ideal of evangelical masculinity, one that eschewed traditional elements of white manliness. He disputed the traditional role of men as masters and property owners by freeing his slaves. For his beliefs, Garrettson narrowly escaped being lynched by a Maryland mob. He refused to take the oath of allegiance as a matter of conscience. He staunchly opposed the war: "I was determined I would have nothing to do with the unhappy war; it was contrary to my mind, and grievous to my conscience, to have any hand in shedding human blood." These positions made him suspect and liable to persecution. Other Methodists wished to avoid the war and focus on their godly duty. Francis Asbury wrote in 1775 in response to the Battle of Lexington, "surely the Lord will overrule, and make all these things subservient to the spiritual welfare of his Church." Asbury made a conscious decision to become a nonjuror and moved to Delaware to continue his pastorate. Ministers navigated an arduous course between spiritual demands and worldly concerns, between being sufficiently pious yet loyal to their country. Serving God and the state was not always easy. Jesse Lee, a Methodist preacher, refused to take the oath of loyalty, and when recruited into the army, refused to fight. Because he was not ordained, he could not serve as a chaplain. Placed under guard for refusing to take up a gun, Lee served as a wagon driver and engineer, while also preaching and tending the sick.[27]

Several Baptist men served in the Continental Army as chaplains.[28] The difficulty was how to participate in this secular venture yet preserve their spiritual identity. Many Baptist clergymen augmented their chaplain duties with sermonizing at local meetinghouses. William Van Horne joined General Glover's brigade of Massachusetts and arranged for others to serve his congregation in the Delaware Valley. As an army chaplain, he preached three sermons on Sundays before a religiously mixed audience; David Jones of Pennsylvania serviced his church in the Great Valley when he was home on leave. Hezekiah Smith of Massachusetts attended Baptist meetings in New Jersey while stationed in New York, preached at others' meetinghouses, and officiated at funerals and weddings. He remarked on military activities and held daily prayers with the men. John Pitman went to the services of other clergy and commented on the "lame discourse" of an Anglican minister and the Arminian sermon of an Indian preacher.[29]

Service in the army displaced many men from their regular schedule of preaching assignments at the same time that it extended their ministry. While in the army during the year 1775, William Rogers ministered to the Philadelphia Baptist church and traveled to Rhode Island and Maryland on itinerant trips. He made the circuit of Baptist meetings in New Jersey and preached repeatedly in Baltimore and the outlying area. He sermonized for other denominations, including Seventh Day Baptists, Presbyterians, and Anglicans when they were bereft of clergy. He attended and spoke at association meetings. When Hezekiah Smith traveled from Massachusetts to New York as an army chaplain, he visited friends and family members and ministered at Baptist and Presbyterian meetings in Massachusetts, Connecticut, and New Jersey. When Oliver Hart left Charleston after the British assault in 1780, he toured North Carolina, Virginia, and Pennsylvania and preached at Baptist and Presbyterian churches.[30]

Some clergy provided political leadership for their new governments, who used the geographic mobility and oratory skill of ministers to state advantage. This was especially crucial when the war turned south, where there were large pockets of loyalists. Oliver Hart remained a civilian but served the revolutionary cause when he was appointed by the South Carolina Committee of Safety to persuade western inhabitants to back the new regime. He investigated "disaffected" inhabitants and ministered to soldiers sentenced to death for desertion. William Tennent and William Henry Drayton journeyed into the Carolina backcountry to whip up support for the American cause. Two New Jersey Presbyterian clergymen, Elihu Spencer and Alexander McWhorter, traveled throughout North Carolina during 1776 for the same purpose.[31] Ministerial talents were used by the state for political reasons; this political service afforded clerics a new means to exercise secular power as men.

Pursuing both the military and ministry were incompatible occupations for some clerics, who decided to leave their pulpits to join the service. John Cleaveland, a Congregationalist, preached to members of his church to support the war and then enlisted. The Methodist John Littlejohn eventually sanctioned the American cause and averred that it was "every Christ[ia]n's duty to fight for his country." Jedidiah Chapman gave up his ministry to become a soldier. The German Lutheran Peter Gabriel Muhlenberg did the same; his dramatic exit from church galvanized support among his congregants. But his choice earned criticism from one of his brothers, who was also a cleric. Muhlenberg defended his decision against his sibling's complaint:

> You say, as a clergyman nothing can excuse my conduct. I am a clergyman, it is true, but I am a member of society as well as the poorest laymen, and my liberty is as dear to me as to any man. . . . Were I a bishop, even a Lutheran one, I should obey without hesitation.

The call for warfare was a responsibility he owed to God and his country, and yet one that demanded he leave behind his spiritual vocation.[32]

As a soldier and minister, John Pitman straddled these two worlds of pious duty and secular manliness. He served in the military but preferred to follow his religious calling. When Pitman's enlistment came to end in 1777, he began a yearlong tour. He traveled repeatedly throughout New Jersey and Pennsylvania, north to Rhode Island and Massachusetts, and back again. He preached at established Baptist meetings and filled in at Presbyterian churches, all the while keeping abreast of the progress of the war. In September, he heard that American troops "had killed 4000 of the enemy at Pennsylvania & wholly routed ye army of the northward." Pitman's travels often paralleled that of the Continental Army, at times causing him inconvenience (e.g., the army delayed his crossing at a ferry in New Jersey). He had trouble finding lodging, food, and supplies for his horse because of wartime shortages and relied on Baptist friends as well as strangers to assist him. Though Pitman preached to sick soldiers, heard of protracted battles, and saw the destruction by "British robbers" in New Jersey, he kept a busy schedule as an itinerant and did not reenlist; he opted out of the military role to follow his spiritual mission as a pastor.[33]

Conversely, John Gano decided to remain in the army after his enlistment ended. He believed providence had put him in the Continental Army for a reason. Though he loathed army life because there was "little Christian conversation, no retirement or study, discouraging prospects for convening or converting sinners or quickening and edifying God's children," he valued American war aims. Gano turned down an offer to take over the pastorate of the Philadelphia church because he thought the patriot cause to be "just and of so much importance to my country both in a civil and religious sense as to render me incapable of refusing any services or suffering I might be called to in it." Though Gano fully intended to resume the ministry once the war was over, he wished to serve his country during the conflict with Britain. Unlike John Pitman, John Gano continued in his role as minister and soldier to reconcile the confluence of spiritual and military needs during the war.[34]

The participation of chaplains in the American Revolutionary War injected a spiritual component into this military conflict. Chaplains joined biblical text with contemporary events to sustain American soldiers' prolonged warfare against the British army. Their involvement in the military allowed them to serve political and religious ends—for their nation and their brethren. They utilized biblical and martial concepts of manhood in their sermons to motivate their congregants. They sought the adoption of social behavior consistent with Christian beliefs, and they both critiqued and affirmed traditional ideals of white manliness. Being too pious (to officers) or too sinful (for clergy) could endanger the manly performance of American soldiers. Both extremes could make white men unfit for duty and imperil their manhood, which in turn could threaten the American war effort. Acting as an intermediary between two modes of masculinity, chaplains bridged the gap between the militarism necessary for political revolution and the devotion required by religious vocation.[35] Chaplains advocated the model of a Christian soldier, who in his "gospel uniform" merged deep piety with military violence to defeat a formidable adversary.

NOTES

1. George Duffield, A.M., *A Sermon Preached in the Third Presbyterian Church in the City of Philadelphia* (Boston: Fleets, 1784), 10, American Antiquarian Society. This article focuses on the experience of white men during the American Revolutionary War.

2. For one example, see Alfred Young, *The Shoemaker and the Tea Party: Memory and the American Revolution* (Boston: Beacon Press, 1999).

3. On white manhood during colonial era, see Lisa Wilson, *Ye Heart of a Man: The Domestic Life of Men in Colonial New England* (New Haven, CT: Yale University Press, 1999); Anne S. Lombard, *Growing Up Male in Colonial New England* (Cambridge, MA: Harvard University Press, 2003); Kenneth Lockridge, *On the Sources of Patriarchal Rage: The Commonplace Books of William Byrd and Thomas Jefferson and the Gendering of Power in Eighteenth-Century America* (New York: New York University Press, 1992); Toby Ditz, "Shipwrecked; or, Masculinity Imperiled: Mercantile Representations of Failure and the Gendered Self in Eighteenth-Century Philadelphia," *JAH* 81, 1 (1994): 51–80; Janet Moore Lindman, "Acting the Manly Christian: White Evangelical Masculinity in Revolutionary Virginia," *WMQ* 3rd Ser., 57, 2 (2000): 393–416; Craig Thompson Friend and Lori Glover, *Southern Manhood: Perspectives on Masculinity in the Old South* (Athens: University of Georgia Press, 2004).

4. More than 280 American men served as chaplains with the American forces. For those whose religious affiliation is known, the majority were Congregational (74), Presbyterian (58), Baptist (30), and Anglican (20) ministers (12 men were coded as "other" [German Reformed, Lutheran, Roman Catholic, and Universalist]; this data is a compilation of men who served as Continental, state, naval, and auxiliary chaplains). Most of the men served in New England, followed by the Mid-Atlantic, Chesapeake, and the Lower South. There is great variance in length of service. A majority of chaplains either served one year or less (72%) or three years or more (51%), with only 12 men serving two years. Among those whose birth dates are known, 52 were born before 1730, 147 were born after 1730. Data compiled from C. Rogers McLane, ed., *American Chaplains of the Revolution* (Louisville, KY: National Society of Sons of the American Revolution, 1991). See also Eugene Franklin Williams, "Soldiers of God: The Chaplains of the Revolutionary War" (PhD dissertation, Texas Christian University, 1972). Chaplains were initially paid $20 a month; this was increased to $33.33 by the end of 1775; it was later raised to $40 per month. Some hospital chaplains earned $60 per month. Charles H. Metzger, "Chaplains in the American Revolution," *Catholic Historical Review* 31, 1 (1945): 45.

5. In 1775, the Continental Congress recognized the importance of religion when it advised soldiers and officers to attend public worship. George Washington requested the presence of chaplains in the Continental Army not only to perform clerical duties but also to maintain order among the ranks. Each regiment was to have a chaplain because "the blessing and protection of heaven are at all times necessary, but especially so in times of public distress and danger." He hoped men of pious outlook would help "remedy the evil" of camp life. July 7, 1776, Orderly Book of George Washington, reprinted in Reuben Aldrich Guild, *Chaplain Smith and the Baptists, Or Life, Journals, Letters, and Address of the Rev. Hezekiah Smith, D.D.* (Philadelphia: American Baptist Publication Society, 1885), 190. Karen O'Brien argues that the religious toleration within the Continental Army was a critical factor in forging political allegiance and national identity among a disparate group of soldiers. O'Brien, "Pragmatic Toleration: Lived Religion, Obligation, and Political Identity in the American Revolution" (PhD dissertation, Northwestern University, 2005), 1.

6. Little of the historical literature on American soldiers during the Revolutionary War provides a gender analysis of chaplains or examines their role as liaisons between the secular and sacred worlds. On chaplains, see Fred Anderson, *The People's Army: Massachusetts Soldiers in the Seven Years' War* (Chapel Hill: University of North Carolina Press, 1984); and Charles Royster, *A Revolutionary People at War: The Continental Army and American Character, 1775–1783* (New York: Norton, 1979). On military conditions, see John Resch, *Suffering Soldiers: Revolutionary War Veterans, Moral Sentiment, Politics, and Culture in the Early Republic* (Amherst: University of Massachusetts Press, 1999); and Robert Gross, *The Minutemen and Their World* (New York: Hill and Wang, 1976). For soldiers' experience, see Thomas Fleming, intro., *A Narrative of Revolutionary Soldier: Some of the Adventures, Dangers, and Sufferings of Joseph Plumb Martin* (New York: Penguin, 2001); and John Shy, ed., *Winding Down: The Revolutionary War Letters of Lieutenant Benjamin Gilbert of Massachusetts, 1780–1783* (Ann Arbor: University of Michigan Press, 1989).

7. J. T. Headley, *The Chaplains and Clergy of the Revolution* (Springfield, MA, 1861), 295; "Mr. Ellis" cited in O'Brien, "Pragmatic Toleration," 145. On camp followers, see Holly A. Mayer, *Belonging to the Army: Camp Followers and Community During the American Revolution* (Columbia: University of South Carolina Press, 1996).

8. Metzger, "Chaplains in the American Revolution," 171–72; Headley, *Chaplains and Clergy of the Revolution*, 255; O'Brien, "Pragmatic Toleration," 152; Peter Thompson, *From Its European Antecedents to 1791: The United States Army Chaplaincy* (Washington, DC: Office of the Chief Chaplain, Department of the Army, 1978), 197, 279.

9. [Ammi Robbins], *Journal of the Rev. Ammi Robbins, a Chaplain in the American Army in the Northern Campaign of 1776* (New Haven, CT: B. L. Hamlen, 1850), 4; Thompson, *From Its European Antecedents to 1791*, 95, 153, 171; W. H. W. Sabine, ed., *The New York Diary of Jabez Fitch* (New York: New York Public Library, 1954), 71.

10. [Robbins], *Journal of Rev. Ammi Robbins*, 7, 33; Robert Greenhalgh Albion and Leonidas Dodson, eds., *Philip Vickers Fithian: Journal, 1775–1776, Written on the Virginia-Pennsylvania Frontier and in the Army Around New York* (Princeton, NJ: Princeton University Press, 1934), 203; John W. Jordan, "Extracts from the Journal of the Rev. James Sproat, Hospital Chaplain of the Middle Department, 1778," *PMHB* 27, 4 (1903): 441; John W. Jordan, ed., "Orderly Book of the Secondary Pennsylvania Continental Line, Col. Henry Bicker," *PMHB* 36, 1 (1912): 39; [John Peter Gabriel Muhlenberg], "Orderly Book of John Peter Gabriel Muhlenberg, March 26–December 20, 1777," *PMHB* 35, 1 (1911): 85; O'Brien, "Pragmatic Toleration," 183.

11. [Robbins], *Journal of Rev. Ammi Robbins*, 5; 43; Albion and Dodson, *Philip Vickers Fithian*, 204; James Armstrong, "Righteousness Exalteth a Nation," in Marian D. McLeod, ed., *Light to My Path: Sermons by the Rev. James F. Armstrong, Revolutionary Chaplain* (Trenton, NJ: First Presbyterian Church of Trenton, 1976), 15.

12. Thompson, *From Its European Antecedents to 1791*, 157, 282. George Washington had a particular dislike for profanity, which he thought not only undermined "decency and order," but also led to rebellion and mutiny. Royster, *Revolutionary People at War*, 76–77. One captain offered a prayer for his men asking God to keep them from "profaneness and blasphemy, the lewdness and debauchery, the rudeness and violence that are most incident to men of our profession." "Diary of Captain Barnard Elliott," reprinted in Thompson, *From Its European Antecedents to 1791*, 276; Edward Barngs, ed., *Journal of Lieutenant Isaac Bangs, April 1 to July 29, 1776* (Cambridge: John Wilson and Sons, 1890), 29; *Journal of the Rev. Ammi Robbins*, 5, 10. Smith's sermon on swearing was delivered to Colonel Nixon's regiment in July 1779. Guild, *Chaplain Smith*, 256–58.

13. Armstrong claimed swearing in military camps would only end when it became "as infamous as cowardice or as dangerous as for a sentinel to sleep on his post." "Righteousness Exalteth a Nation," 14–15; Royster, *Revolutionary People at War*, 77, 164; Raymond Chester Young, ed., *Baptists on the American Frontier: A History of Ten Baptist Churches of Which the Author Has Been Alternately a Member by John Taylor* (Macon, GA: Mercer University Press, 1995), 131.

14. May 24, 1776, letter, Hezekiah Smith to General Sullivan, in Guild, *Chaplain Smith*, 177–78. On Trabue, see Chester Raymond Young, ed., *Westward into Kentucky: The Narrative of Daniel Trabue* (Lexington, KY: University Press of Kentucky, 1981), 5; Thompson, *From Its European Antecedents to 1791*, 282; [Robbins], *Journal of Rev. Ammi Robbins*, 39; Albion and Dodson, *Philip Vickers Fithian*, 194.

15. Albion and Dodson, *Philip Vickers Fithian*, 207–8, 227; Thompson, *From Its European Antecedents to 1791*, 124, 146.

16. February 26, 1777, letter, Oliver Hart to Isaac Backus, Simon Gratz Collection, Historical Society of Pennsylvania; Guild, *Chaplain Smith*, 163. David Jones moved out of

Freehold, New Jersey, because of all the "Tories who abounded in that part of the state," to fill the pastorate at the Great Valley church. William B. Sprague, *Annals of the American Pulpit* (New York: Robert Carter and Brothers, 1860), 86.

17. John Carmichael, *A Self-Defensive War Lawful, Proven in a Sermon, Preached at Lancaster Before Captain Ross's Company of Militia, in the Presbyterian Church, on Sabbath Morning, June 4, 1775* (Philadelphia: John Dean, 1775), 9, 15, 21–22, 32–33.

18. Jacob Duché, *The American View, a Sermon, Preached in Christ-Church, Philadelphia, Before the Honourable Continental Congress, July 20th, 1775, Being the Day Recommended by Them for a General Fast Throughout the United English Colonies of America* (Philadelphia: James Humphreys, Jr., 1775), 21, 24, 31–33. Hezekiah Smith preached a similar sermon from Isaiah 3:14, to "share with [the] poor." Guild, *Chaplain Smith*, 187.

19. [Muhlenberg], "Orderly Book of John Peter Gabriel Muhlenberg," 84; Albion and Dodson, *Philip Vickers Fithian*, 234; Royster, *Revolutionary People at War*, 16.

20. Metzger, "Chaplains in the American Revolution," 73; Royster, *Revolutionary People at War*, 167; Thompson, *From Its European Antecedents to 1791*, 281, Headley, *Chaplains and Clergy of the Revolution*, 377.

21. Royster, *Revolutionary People at War*, 171–72; Headley, *Chaplains and Clergy of the Revolution*, 377.

22. David Jones, "Address to General St. Clair's Brigade at Fort Ticonderoga, When the Enemy Were Hourly Expected, October 20 1776," reprinted in Thompson, *From Its European Antecedents to 1791*, 278; Thompson, *From Its European Antecedents to 1791*, 286–87; Headley, *Chaplains and Clergy of the Revolution*, 399, 401.

23. Headley, *Chaplains and Clergy of the Revolution*, 377; Duché, *American View*, 27; John Hurt, "Sermon Delivered at Valley Forge on May 6, 1778, to Remember of the 1st and 2nd Virginia Brigade, in Celebration of France's Entry into the War," reprinted in Thompson, *From Its European Antecedents to 1791*, 290.

24. See Janet Moore Lindman, *Bodies of Belief: Baptist Community in Early America* (Philadelphia: University of Pennsylvania Press, 2008), 64–65, and chapter 8.

25. Jon Butler, *Awash in a Sea of Faith: Christianizing the American People* (Cambridge, MA: Harvard University Press, 1990), 204–5, 209. On Quakers and the Revolutionary War, see Arthur J. Mekeel, *The Relation of the Quakers to the American Revolution* (Washington, DC, 1979); Richard Alan Ryerson, *The Revolution Has Now Begun: The Radical Committees of Philadelphia, 1765–1776* (Philadelphia: University of Pennsylvania Press, 1978); and Richard Bauman, *For the Reputation of Truth: Politics, Religion, and Conflict Among the Pennsylvania Quakers, 1750–1800* (Baltimore: Johns Hopkins University Press, 1971).

26. On Methodists, see Russell E. Richey, *Early American Methodism* (Bloomington: University of Indiana Press, 1991); Cynthia Lynn Lyerly, *Methodism and the Southern Mind, 1779–1810* (New York: Oxford University Press, 1998); A. Gregory Schneider, *The Way of the Cross Leads Home: The Domestication of American Methodism* (Bloomington: University of Indiana Press, 1993); John H. Wigger, *Taking Heaven by Storm: Methodism and the Rise of Popular Christianity in America* (New York: Oxford University Press, 1998); and Dee E. Andrews, *The Methodists and Revolutionary America: The Shaping of an Evangelical Culture* (Princeton, NJ: Princeton University Press, 2000). The disestablishment of the Anglican church focused more attention on the British background of Methodist preachers. Andrews, *Methodists and Revolutionary America*, 51.

27. Robert Drew Simpson, ed., *American Methodist Pioneer: The Life and Journals of The Rev. Freeborn Garrettson, 1752–1827* (Rutland, VT: Academic Books, 1984), 50; Elmer T. Clark, ed., *The Journal and Letters of Francis Asbury*, vol. 1, *1773–1793* (Nashville, TN: Abingdon Press, 1958), 155. Andrews argues that Methodist ministers distinguished themselves from "conventionally masculine displays of ribaldry and local mastery." *Methodists and Revolutionary America*, 58–59; Thompson, *From Its European Antecedents to 1791*, 198–99.

28. On Baptists, see William McLoughlin, *New England Dissent: 1630–1833: The Baptists and the Separation of Church and State* (Cambridge, MA: Harvard University Press, 1971); Susan Juster, *Disorderly Women: Sexual Politics and Evangelicalism in Revolutionary New England* (Ithaca, NY: Cornell University Press, 1994); Rhys Isaac, *The Transformation of Virginia, 1740–1790* (Chapel Hill: University of North Carolina Press, 1982); Richard Beeman, *The Transformation of the Backcountry: A Case Study of Lunenburg County, Virginia, 1740–1832* (Philadelphia: University of Pennsylvania Press, 1983); Christine Leigh Heyrman, *Southern Cross: The Beginnings of the Bible Belt* (New York: Knopf, 1998); Gregory A. Wills, *Democratic Religion, Freedom, Authority, and Church Discipline in the Baptist South, 1758–1900* (New York: Oxford University Press, 1997); and Jewel Spangler, *Virginians Reborn: Anglican Monopoly, Evangelical Dissent, and the Rise of Baptists in the Late Eighteenth Century* (Charlottesville: University of Virginia Press, 2008).

29. John Pitman Journals, 1776 and 1777, Rhode Island Historical Society (hereafter RIHS); Guild, *Chaplain Smith*, 252–54; August 27, 1779, letter, William Van Horne to Nicholas Brown, Nicholas Brown and Co., Miscellaneous Papers, John Carter Brown Library (hereafter JCBL).

30. Pocket Account Book of William Rogers, 1775; September 11, 16, and 23, 1781; October 6 and 7, 1781, Journal of William Rogers, 1776 and 1781, Papers of Williams Rogers, JCBL. Hezekiah Smith preached eight sermons as he traveled from Winter Hill Camp to New York City over the course of twenty-seven days. See Guild, *Chaplain Smith*, 175–76. A Fragment of the Oliver Hart Diary, August 4, 1754, to October 27, 1754, American Baptist Historical Society (hereafter ABHS). On Presbyterian ministers, see Patricia Bonomi, *Under the Cope of Heaven: Religion, Society, and Politics in Colonial America* (New York: Oxford University Press, 1986), 211.

31. On Hart, see William Rogers, *A Sermon Occasioned by the Death of the Rev. Oliver Hart, A.M.* (Philadelphia, 1796), 23, Library Company of Philadelphia. July 31, 1775, and July 22, 1778, "a copy of the original diary of the Rev. Oliver Hart of Charlestown, Pastor of the Baptist Church of Charlestown" (attached to A Fragment of the Diary of Oliver Hart, 1754), AHBS. Some clerics were taken captive by the English. When the British landed at Warren, Rhode Island, they occupied the meetinghouse and parsonage and took the minister, Charles Thompson, prisoner. Robert G. Torbet, *A Social History of the Philadelphia Baptist Association, 1707–1940* (PhD dissertation, University of Pennsylvania, 1944), 48.

32. On ministers who served as soldiers, see McLane, *American Chaplains of the Revolution* 31–39; August 20, 1777, Journal of John Littlejohn, vol. 3, ABHS; Christopher M. Jedry, *The World of John Cleaveland: Family and Community in Eighteenth-Century New England* (New York: Norton, 1979), 135; Headley, *Chaplains and Clergy of the Revolution*, 126.

33. July 31, 1777, September 23, 1777, October 3, 1777, Journal of John Pitman, 1777; April 27, 1778, Journal of John Pitman, 1778, RIHS. Pitman was excused from service in the militia by applying to the Court of Appeals. July 6, 1781, Journal of John Pitman, 1781, RIHS.

34. 1780 letter, John Gano to the Philadelphia Baptist Church, reprinted in William Keen, *The Bicentennial Celebration of the Founding of the First Baptist Church of the City of Philadelphia, 1698-1898* (Philadelphia: American Baptist Society, 1898), 65. Though he never served in the army, James Manning maintained friendships and exchanged correspondence with several American military men. He visited General Washington's camp, where he met Baron von Steuben and secretaries of the French ambassador. August 1, 1779 to September 17, 1779, Journal of James Manning, excerpted in Reuben Aldridge Guild, *Early History of Brown University, Including the Life, Times, and Correspondence of President Manning, 1756-1791* (Providence: Snow and Farnham, 1897), 325-28. Ambrose Dudley served in the military during the war; he was stationed at Williamsburg, where he underwent conversion. After his discharge, he became a minister. Young, *Baptists on the American Frontier*, 245, fn278.

35. New England Baptist clergy gained a new level of political maturity by participating in the American Revolution. See Juster, *Disorderly Women*, 7.

Afterword

Contending Masculinities in Early America

───── TOBY L. DITZ ─────

Until recently, scholars and laypeople thought of early America as a world in which aristocratic ideals of manhood anchored in the claims of blood and honor dominated the cultural landscape. We even said that these ideals were "hegemonic." By this we meant that other social groups deferred to elites, granting their superiority as men and their entitlement to a disproportionate share of economic and political resources. Nonaristocratic standards of manliness were at best culturally marginal and associated with less powerful social groups and individuals. In this view, the American Revolution and its rupture with the "Old World" broke the grip of aristocratic standards of manhood and unleashed the potential of new democratic manhood ideals.

This collection of essays drives home the point that historians of gender and manhood have been making for some time now: several models of masculinity competed with one another throughout the colonial era and would continue to do so after the revolution. What is most striking about early America is the sheer variety of manhood ideals and their associated practices.[1] This variety creates a triple challenge for historians. The first is to identify the conditions that fostered this variety. The second is to trace the strands of competition and mutual influence among them and how they helped to structure disparities of wealth and power among men along racial and class lines. And there is a third task too: to show how these standards of manhood structured men's relationship to women. The essays in this volume collectively rise to this threefold challenge.

Two features of early America were especially important in shaping standards of manhood and their associated practices. The first is that the American colonies were highly militarized societies located at the periphery of the European empires that were responsible for the conquest of the Americas. European settlers in the Americas were located far from metropolitan centers of political and military administration in an era when travel and communications were slow and dangerous. The requirements of conquest, the unending rivalries among the European powers for colonial possessions, and the persisting presence of powerful native American groups also ensured that the British American colonies would be highly militarized and nearly continuously at war.[2]

These conditions created unusual opportunities for new standards of masculinity to proliferate as men jockeyed for material and social resources in the era of first settlement and later. Take the men who settled at Jamestown. They had, according to John McCurdy, not one, but at least two models of "military masculinity" available to them: an older aristocratic ideal that rested claims to high military office on noble birth ratified by competent command, and a newer ideal supported by men like John Smith that put a premium on "dedication," "physical prowess," and a proven record of bravery on the battlefield. These competing standards signaled a struggle for recognition among men of different classes. The older ideal confirmed the high social status of men who were already wellborn; Smith's hypermasculine ideal suited men whose social origins were more obscure and who sought to enhance their social standing by rising through the military ranks on their merits. In this setting, aristocratic ideals were certainly not hegemonic; rather, they were under considerable pressure. The stakes are not trivial: McCurdy argues that these competing models of military masculinity can help us better understand political rivalries among Jamestown's early leaders, and thus the notorious instability of the Jamestown settlement in the early seventeenth century.

Turning to the American Revolution, we also find that competing models of manhood structured military life. Janet Lindman points out that evangelical military chaplains were "gender brokers" who bridged the tensions between two different styles of masculinity: the violence, physical strength, and courage inhering in contemporary martial masculinity, and a new style of evangelical Christian manhood, which incorporated virtues such as humility, service, and piety that were elsewhere coded as feminine. When these chaplains promoted their own brand of patriotic Christian manhood, they were also attempting to carve out positions of cultural authority for themselves in an era when neither elite officers nor the rank and file automatically deferred any longer (if they ever did) to ministers.

These and other essays also confirm that the military is an important location for examining how European state builders and imperial officials developed new techniques for disciplining and securing the loyalty of their citizen-subjects. John Smith's version of militarized hypermasculinity was yoked to the attempt to build a more disciplined army—one that put a premium on obedience and that deprived the plebian rank and file of the standard rewards of war: the booty and women that signified manly privilege for the ordinary soldier. The pious chaplains of the revolutionary era, who somewhat quixotically wished to rid the military camps of drinking, prostitution, and cursing, might seem like unlikely minions of a new American empire. But they pursued their moral cleanup campaign in the name of a crusading, martial Christianity of their own, and they were enthusiastic promoters of military order. Promising the ordinary recruit that he fought under the banner of divine sanction, they exhorted the rank and file to be disciplined and courageous on the battlefield.

The long-term fate of the pirate and our changing stories about him also tell us a lot about state formation, the creation of good citizen-subjects, and ideals of manhood. In the sixteenth and early seventeenth centuries, as England at first tentatively and then with greater confidence tested its mettle against rival European powers in America and elsewhere, pirates could be much admired, although covert emissaries of their sovereign. They embodied manly virtues that echoed those of their ancestor, the late medieval knight: physical courage, tenacity, and fidelity. The pirate was, in short, a hero, whose manly virtues redounded to the glory of his monarch, especially when he harassed the English Crown's main rivals overseas. But as England and other European states consolidated their military authority, enhanced their oceangoing capacities, and improved the efficiency of their colonial administrations, the pirate's status gradually changed. During the eighteenth century, he was demoted in official accounting from a hero to a despised and feared criminal: a kidnapper and scavenger, a mere marauder who operated outside the bounds of law and civilized norms of manly conduct. But as Carolyn Eastman tellingly points out, eighteenth-century European and American readers continued to gobble up best-selling "texts that cheerfully retailed the violence" and "sexual exploits" of buccaneers and pirate adventurers like Henry Morgan. Exiled beyond the laws and conventions of civilized nations, the renegade pirate remains in our legends and stories a fascinating antihero, registering the covert protest of readers against the disciplining and domestication of men.[3]

The different peoples and cultures that populated North America were in constant interaction. And this is the second feature of the political and cultural landscape that is crucial for understanding the proliferation and co-articulation of standards of manhood in early America. These interactions were often antagonistic and violent, as was true of warfare, captivity, and slavery, but they also included trade, intermarriage, and other forms of cultural exchange. As different cultural groups came into contact in borderland areas, manhood ideals and their associated practices underwent transformation on both sides of what Kathleen Brown has called the "gender frontier." These colliding and interpenetrating ideals of masculinity were deeply implicated in the growing power differentials between European settlers, Native Americans, and Africans.

Consider, for example, the highly gendered language that seventeenth-century Puritans used to differentiate their own practices of dream interpretation from those of Native Americans. As Ann Marie Plane informs us, Puritans thought of dream interpretation as a difficult art. They attributed success to the interpreter's piety and moral self-control—to his rectitude as a man. By the same token, the Puritans heaped scorn on the "elegant and intricate system of dreaming" practiced by their Algonquin neighbors. Puritans castigated Native American dream work as the product of a disordered masculinity—a too "credulous," "undisciplined," and "wildly effeminate" abandonment to passion and fancy. They also repudiated in similar terms the ranting of unorthodox religious enthusiasts such as Quakers and Baptists. From the Puritans' perspective, these racial and cultural outsiders lacked the capacity to properly order their emotional and spiritual lives. This incapacity rendered them uncivilized and less than men.

The interplay and competition among standards of manliness in the borderlands show up starkly on the battlefield, as the essays by Tyler Boulware and Susan Abram show so clearly. Native Americans and Anglo-Americans alike regarded defeat and captivity with loathing because it meant loss of masculine honor and standing. It feminized men. The Iroquois and the Creeks called defeated Cherokees "old Women," who were forced by their victorious enemies "to wear the petticoat." And everyone castigated their enemies for using unmanly tactics in battle. Europeans grudgingly admired Indians' skills in woodland warfare, but repeatedly dismissed their hit-and-run tactics and their willingness to abandon villages and fortified installations as signs of their irresolute, "undisciplined" natures. And Anglo-Americans who fought during the Seven Years' War accused their French enemies of using the Indians' cowardly tactics of decoy and ambush and of deliberately encouraging their Native American allies' savage violence.

The Anglo-Americans' professed disdain for Indian tactics of war is arguably a classic instance of willful cultural misunderstanding. For Europeans, taking enemy ground and forcing enemies to flee was a sign of "manly resolution." The failure of Native Americans to stand their ground or fight openly was from this perspective the essence of cowardice: a "skulking way of war." But the main aim of warfare for the Native American groups discussed by Boulware and Abrams was not the taking and holding of territory. What disgraced the Native American warrior and stripped him of manhood was not the loss of ground, but the failure to exact revenge for loss of life. An honored warrior redeemed prior deaths by killing enemies or taking them as captives, while minimizing further losses. Hit-and-run tactics and defensive retreat were in alignment with those goals. Regardless of whether willful misunderstanding was at work, Anglo-Americans used their ideals of martial valor and discipline to array themselves and their Indian neighbors along an axis of civilized Christian manhood and pagan savagery. As they did so, they racialized and hardened the cultural boundaries between Europeans and Native Americans.

Interactions along the "gender frontier" involved not only cultural repudiation and distancing, but also cultural borrowing and cross-identifications. To continue with the case of woodland fighting, there is an irony in the hardliners' depiction of effeminate and cowardly natives during the Seven Year's War. By the end of that war, some British regular army officers learned to pride themselves on their successes on woodland marches. But they soon forgot their lessons. During the War for Independence, British officers would in vexed frustration accuse the upstart American rebels of using the Native Americans' craven tactics. Schooled in decades of backcountry fighting, Anglo-Americans were better woodland skirmishers than the soldiers of the British regular army. In this respect, the revolutionaries paid their Native American adversaries the highest compliment: adoption of their methods and standards of manly courage in battle.

Similarly, if we return to the seventeenth-century Puritans, their vehemence about "womanish" and "diabolically" inspired Indian dreamwork was meant to underscore the differences between Native American culture and their own. But did they protest too much? As Plane herself points out, Puritan men worried obsessively about their own capacity to master their passions and only partly succeeded in quelling their doubts about divine sanction for their own interpretive practices. Was their vehemence an attempt to externalize their inner doubt? Moreover, not all images of Native Americans were so pejorative. As Anglo-Americans restlessly appropriated more and more territory and displaced real Indians in the late colonial and early national eras, they produced admiring portraits of the noble but vanishing savage. The last of the Mohicans and other cultural icons of his ilk distilled manly virtues that Anglo-Americans associated with an archaic but freer mode of life. Like the pirate, the noble savage was a product of the cultural cross-identifications that emerged from encounters in the borderlands of early America.⁴

The gender frontier also included fraught interactions between European Americans and their slaves. As the essays by Trevor Burnard and Kathleen Brown demonstrate, racialized ideals of manhood were closely intertwined with power differentials between white and black men in early America. In Jamaica, plantation slavery and a racial ideology that barely granted the humanity of blacks produced a rough equality among white men based on their shared patriarchal privileges, especially their nearly unlimited control over the laboring and reproductive bodies of enslaved men and women. A hypermasculine standard of white manhood that openly endorsed "self-aggrandizing," violent conduct, and predatory sexual practices was a central expression of this privilege. By the same token, a sense of common bonds among white men rested on systematically depriving slaves and free blacks of the two resources that Europeans most closely associated with mature manhood: property and the ability to marry. Without access to these resources, what claims to manhood could Africans pursue? Kathleen Brown's answer is that African Americans could use one of the few valued resources still left to them: their laboring bodies. Accordingly, black manhood ideals centered on physical prowess and endurance, on stylizations of body in gesture and movement, and on elaborate sartorial display. This alternative model of masculinity could backfire because it supplied fodder to whites who were all too prone to characterize black men's physicality as a threat and their cultural style as undisciplined, foolish preening. Still, black masculinity was a form of "male self-assertion" and a claim for recognition and dignity. Black men carved out an alternative culture of masculinity and even resistance from the limited social, economic, and cultural resources available to them.⁵

These essays taken together show, then, that early American conditions produced multiple standards of masculinity as men of different classes, "races," and cultures contended with one another. Under such conditions, a single aristocratic ideal of manhood could not dominate or even endure unchanged. But these competing standards of manhood were not born equal. They organized power and access to resources along racialized and class lines: the full privileges associated with preferred manhood were available only to some, not all men.

Several essays in this volume focus on the men who benefited most from the colonial order of things. They suggest that by the middle of the eighteenth century prevailing standards of manhood among Anglo-American elites and middling sorts began to put a new premium on sensibility. Sensibility was the capacity to experience and express feelings, especially the finer feelings associated with good taste and moral conscience. Sensibility had to be cultivated: it involved the formation of the whole man—his character and his comportment. This new emphasis on sensibility or refined feeling transformed the standards by which elites and aspiring elites could claim cultural authority by replacing blood or family lineage with the more flexible criterion of refined character and manners. This new standard blurred distinctions between the titled nobility and men and families whose wealth rested on commerce and the professions. It also suited colonial cultural and political leaders who sought to bolster their cultural authority at home and to enhance their claims to be the social and cultural equals of elites back in England.[6]

The essays in this volume suggest that reformers drawn from a class just below that of provincial and colonial elites were the ones who most actively sought to promote the culture of sensibility and the new model of genteel manhood that went with it. Consider Natalie Zacek's essay on Henry Hulton, the British customs official who described West Indian plantation life in his memoir. Hulton excoriated the planters of the West Indies for their unrestrained display of aristocratic bad habits. He chose an easy target. The West Indies, with its enervating climate and the virtually unlimited power of its slaveholders, was denounced throughout the European world as a sinkhole of temptation and moral danger. Imagined as a modern-day Sodom and Gomorrah, the islands crystallized widespread moral anxieties about the negative effects of commercial wealth and imperial power. Hulton joined a steady stream of critics and condemned his hosts for their excessive expenditures on lavish hospitality, their gaming, their whoring around, and their sheer brutality. He urged on them instead a model of virtuous manhood based on self-restraint and benevolent paternalism. Hulton's new men were to use enlightened agricultural techniques to manage their labor force, and they were also supposed to reform their domestic habits: Hulton touted the merits of sexual fidelity and temperate, affectionate oversight over children and wives, while condemning taciturn, tyrannical, and just plain foolish fathers and husbands. As Zacek points out, this model of reformed manhood was closely linked to the "emerging cultural style of sentiment and sensibility" beginning to take hold among big planters who identified with metropolitan culture.

The men who actively threw themselves into what Jessica Choppin Roney calls "the culture of improvement" in the late colonial era also championed reformed masculinity. These were the middling and elite men who used their all-male clubs and reform societies to strengthen their own business and social connections, but also to build reputations for civic responsibility and stewardship as they created libraries, fire companies, and hospitals to dispense medical care and charity to the poor. In short, Philadelphia's civic improvers, like Hulton and other reformers in England and the colonies, promoted new standards of manhood that they associated with the smooth ordering of domestic and public life in civilized, commercial nations.

Amid the anti-imperial crisis and revolution, the advocacy of reformed manhood had a strong political dimension, as several essays show. When polemicists debated, for example, the wisdom of the economic boycott as a strategy of anti-imperial resistance in 1774, essayists on both sides accused their opponents of failing to embody virtuous manhood. Moderates and loyalists condemned members of the Continental Congress as both weak-minded and too prone to passion. Like the henpecked yet tyrannical southern Congressmen debating his wife in the antiboycott polemic *A Dialogue*, they were unable to perceive clearly the limits of their legitimate public and domestic authority. Patriots in turn said that the opponents of the boycott were fence-sitting sissies: effeminized and morally weakened by their overindulgence in the luxury goods made available by the burgeoning Atlantic trade. These polemical strategies would persist throughout the revolutionary era, and they had strong class dimensions. The inability to master one's passions was in one register associated with lower-class whites and blacks, who were said to be incapable of finer feeling and easily enflamed by demagogues. Like savages, they gave in to their passions and were in that sense less than men.[7] At the other end of the social hierarchy, luxury-loving aristocrats and their emulators were also unmanned by their overstimulated appetites. Their unwillingness to give up their cosmopolitan pleasures feminized them and sapped them of their strength and moral will.

Republican leaders championed a positive model of reformed masculinity that repudiated both kinds of weakness. John Adams used the classical image of Hercules to represent manhood ideals centering on moderation and restraint: a reining in of the passions by reason and moral conscience and a marshaling of inner resources on behalf of civic duty. Like the civic associators of the late colonial era and other patriot leaders, Adams was trying to define standards of manly virtue appropriate to the broad social spectrum of property-owning men entitled to play active political roles in the new republic. At the center of republican civic virtue was the capacity to exercise independent political judgment: a capacity that the ownership of property was said to confer. But virtuous republican citizens were not just landowners: they were, as almost all the essayists point out, married men. Men like Adams welded their model of republican citizenship to the new ideals of companionate marriage advocated by promoters of sensibility on both sides of the Atlantic. Strong civic bonds among the republican "band of brothers" were guaranteed by the orderly expression of the domestic affections at home.

These standards also defined the *limits* of civic inclusion. Unmarried males without property were almost by definition not man enough to rule even in republics—or perhaps especially in republics. Single men were culturally suspect: youths too young to marry were considered restless and morally vulnerable, and older bachelors were sometimes stigmatized as social or sexual outcasts. Poor men, white and black, found it very difficult to marry precisely because they were not property owners. And free blacks suffered under legal liabilities that ensured that most would not get access to the property that would qualify them for civic inclusion or allow them to marry: the republican body politic was both masculine and white.[8] Without property or access to marriageable women, blacks and poor whites were ineligible to share fully in the civic privileges of manhood; they were simply not "visible," "knowable," or "trustworthy" in the eyes of other men.

As this collection amply demonstrates, competing and interconnected standards of manliness structured inequalities among men—disparities in their access to economic, social, and political resources and power. Moreover, emerging new models of manliness, such as those forged in the furnace of evangelical piety and amid war, could herald a realignment in men's relations with one another as new groups gained cultural or political power and others became marginalized.

Still, even this is not the entire story. As any feminist analysis must show, manhood ideals also order relationships among men and women, and these essays provide insight into several dimensions of this process. One is the monotonous frequency with which men used culturally conservative, often pejorative images of women to impugn the manhood of their adversaries. As we have seen, the rhetoric of womanish defeat and cowardice in battle was common coin among Native Americans as well as Europeans. And this was so despite the fact that Native American women were often quite powerful within their own societies, even with respect to the institutions of war. In many, they had, for example, the authority to decide the fates of captives and to validate the ritual transformation of youths into adult warriors. In the face of women's real social power, the charge that one's defeated enemies were feminized reinforced the most culturally conservative assumptions about women on both sides of the gender frontier. So, when the Iroquois called their defeated enemies "old Women," their primary aim was to score points against their adversaries. But they were also casually positing at least for the moment the weakness and vulnerability of (older) women in order to make their point. Similarly, Anglo-American republican discourse held in principle that both women and men could be corrupted by the temptations of the commercial marketplace and the requirements of competitive status display. Nonetheless, republican rhetoric often personified *lux* as a female figure and typically depicted the love of fashion as a female vice to which weak men capitulated. This gambit reinforced the misogynist association of femininity with excessive expenditure, lack of self-control, and foolish fantasy. It also positioned self-disciplined patriots as men capable of exercising tough love—as virtuous men who had enough confidence in their own authority to restrain the sometimes foolish impulses of the women under their benevolent care.

These essays also show that competition and alliances among men were closely linked to disparities in their access to (and power over) women. To take the starkest case, let's return to the shared patriarchal privileges of white men in slaveholding regimes in Jamaica and elsewhere. A central aspect of this privilege is access to the bodies of women, especially slave women. The extreme inequalities that characterized plantation societies in the West Indies led to especially brutal and rapacious behavior on the part of many slaveholders there. Still, chattel slavery almost everywhere gave slave owners almost unfettered access to enslaved women and severely circumscribed their capacity to control the reproductive and sexual use of their own bodies (in stark contrast to the ideological emphasis on mutual consent coming to characterize the institution of marriage among whites in the eighteenth century). At the same time, chattel slavery also made it difficult for enslaved men and women to form stable unions, families, and households: black men took up these privileges of manhood only on the sufferance of their white masters. In short, one of the most fundamental dimensions of inequality between white and black men was their differential access to black women.

The constraints imposed on black women in this extreme case illustrate a more general principle. Masculinity is always implicated in systems of *gendered* power, and dominant standards of masculinity everywhere structured the terms of women's subordination. Among European American settlers, the two main predicates of adult manhood were property *and* marriage, and the civic and political privileges that defined property-owning male householders as a band of brothers also defined the terms of their authority *over* women. Many of the essayists in this volume unhesitatingly say that these propertied white householders wielded "patriarchal" power over their families, servants, and slaves. Certainly, even the most enthusiastic eighteenth-century advocates of reformed manhood expected women to obey their masters, fathers, and husbands, who in any case almost always had superior legal powers to manage their households and dispose of family property. It is true that the late eighteenth-century model of companionate marriage, with its emphasis on consent and mutual affection, did give middling and elite women new languages for asserting their worth as wives and household mistresses.[9] It also required husbands to calibrate carefully how they exercised their authority; they had to steer a careful course between the weakness of the "henpecked" husband and the brutality of the domestic tyrant. But this kinder, gentler model of marriage did little to lessen the legal powers granted to husbands under the common law doctrine of coverture and authorized women's continuing political disenfranchisement, as Abigail Adams vigorously protested. It was also compatible with a new cloistering of domestic women.[10] Women, even the most privileged among them, would need to assert vigorously and against the cultural grain their claim to a place in the civic spaces of the new nation.

These essays on early America, like much of the new scholarship on manhood, emphasize contending masculinities rather than a single dominant standard. Competing definitions of manliness structured the distribution of power and resources among men; they identified men of different classes, races, and ethnicities as more and less deserving of political, economic, and social privileges within the new colonial societies taking shape in mainland North America and the Caribbean. These essays also hit at least two distinctive notes. Strikingly, they update one of the most venerable branches of historical study, military history. They show that war and the military were not simply domains that tested men. Rather, battle and the exigencies of imperial state-building defined and redefined the meaning of honorable and dishonorable manhood. They changed the "test" itself. The essays also single out America's gender frontier: the porous zone of gendered interactions between indigenous and settler societies and between Europeans and Africans. Finally, the collection shows that the history of masculinity is tightly connected to the history of women and gendered power. Contending standards of masculinity differentially defined men's access to women and, as part of a larger complex of related ideas about gender and the family, shaped the allocation of power and resources among women.

NOTES

1. Toby L. Ditz, "The New Men's History and the Peculiar Absence of Gendered Power: Some Remedies from Early American Gender History," *Gender and History* 16, no. 1 (April 2004), 1–35.

2. David Armitage and Michael J. Braddick, eds., *The British Atlantic World, 1500–1800* (New York: Palgrave Macmillan, 2008); "Forum: Entangled Empires in the Atlantic World," *Am. Hist. Rv.*, 112, no. 3 (June 2007), 710–99; and "AHR Exchange," *Am. Hist. Rv.*, 112, no. 5 (December 2007), 1414–31; "Forum: Beyond Atlantic History," *William and Mary Q.*, 3rd Ser., 63 (2006), 675–742.

3. Margaret S. Creighton and Lisa Norling, eds., *Gender and Seafaring in the Atlantic World, 1700–1920* (Baltimore: Johns Hopkins University Press, 1996); Maurice Rediker, *Villains of All Nations: Atlantic Pirates in the Golden Age* (Boston: Beacon, 2004).

4. On gender and warfare between Native Americans and European settlers, see especially Juliana Barr, *Peace Came in the Form of a Woman: Indians and Spaniards in the Texas Borderlands* (Chapel Hill: University of North Carolina Press, 2007); Ann M. Little, *Abraham in Arms: War and Gender in Colonial New England* (Philadelphia: University of Pennsylvania, 2007).

5. Shane White and Graham White, *Stylin': African American Expressive Culture from Its Beginnings to the Zoot Suit* (Ithaca: Cornell University Press, 1998).

6. Richard L. Bushman, *The Refinement of America: Persons, Houses, Cities* (New York: Vintage, 1993); Lawrence E. Klein, "Property and Politeness in the Early Eighteenth-Century Whig Moralists: The Case of the *Spectator*," in *Early Modern Conceptions of Property*, ed. John Brewer and Susan Staves (London: Routledge, 1996), 221–33; Sarah Knott, *Sensibility and the American Revolution* (Chapel Hill: University of North Carolina Press, 2009).

7. Nicole Eustace, *Passion is the Gale: Emotion, Power, and the Coming of the American Revolution* (Chapel Hill: University of North Carolina Press, 2008).

8. Mark E. Kann, *A Republic of Men: The American Founders, Gendered Language, and Patriarchal Politics* (New York: New York University Press, 1998).

9. Susan E. Klepp, *Revolutionary Conceptions: Women, Fertility, and Family Limitation in America, 1760–1820* (Chapel Hill: University of North Carolina Press, 2009).

10. Ruth H. Bloch, *Gender and Morality in Anglo-America* (Berkeley: University of California Press, 2003); Rosemarie Zagarri, *Revolutionary Backlash: Women and Politics in the Early American Republic* (Philadelphia: University of Pennsylvania Press, 2007).

About the Contributors

SUSAN ABRAM is an Independent Scholar and Adjunct Professor of History at Western Carolina University. She is the author of "The Cherokees in the Creek War" in Kathryn H. Braund, ed., *The Creek War and The War of 1812 in Alabama* (forthcoming).

TYLER BOULWARE is Assistant Professor of History at West Virginia University. He is the author of *Deconstructing the Cherokee Nation: Town, Region, and Nation Among Eighteenth-Century Cherokees* (forthcoming).

KATHLEEN BROWN is Professor of American History at the University of Pennsylvania. She is the author of *Foul Bodies: Cleanliness in Early America* and *Good Wives, Nasty Wenches, and Anxious Patriarchs: Gender, Race, and Power in Colonial Virginia*.

TREVOR BURNARD is Professor of the History of the Americas, History, and Comparative American Studies at the University of Warwick. He is the author of *Creole Gentlemen: The Maryland Elite, 1691–1776* and *Mastery, Tyranny, and Desire: Thomas Thistlewood and His Slaves in the Anglo-Jamaican World*.

TOBY L. DITZ is Professor of History at Johns Hopkins University. She is the author of *Property and Kinship: Inheritance in Early Connecticut, 1750–1820*. She is currently at work on a book provisionally titled *Shipwrecked: Manly Identity and the Culture of Risk Among Philadelphia's Eighteenth-Century Merchants*.

CAROLYN EASTMAN is Assistant Professor of History at the University of Texas at Austin. She is the author of *A Nation of Speechifiers: Making an American Public After the Revolution*.

THOMAS A. FOSTER is Associate Professor of History at DePaul University. He is author of *Sex and the Eighteenth-Century Man: Massachusetts and the History of Sexuality in America* and editor of *Long Before Stonewall: Histories of Same-Sex Sexuality in Early America*.

BENJAMIN H. IRVIN is Assistant Professor of History at the University of Arizona. He is now finalizing a social and cultural history of the Continental Congress, to be published by Oxford University Press.

JANET MOORE LINDMAN is Professor of History at Rowan University. She is the coeditor with Michele Lise Tarter of *"A Centre of Wonders": The Body in Early America* and author of *Bodies of Belief: Baptist Community in Early America*.

JOHN GILBERT MCCURDY is Associate Professor of History at Eastern Michigan University. He is the author of *Citizen Bachelors: Manhood and the Creation of the United States*.

MARY BETH NORTON is Mary Donlon Alger Professor of American History at Cornell University. She has coedited three collections of essays on women's history and has written four books about early America, including *Liberty's Daughters: The Revolutionary Experience of American Women, 1750–1800*, *Founding Mothers and Fathers: Gendered Power and the Forming of American Society*, and *In the Devil's Snare: The Salem Witchcraft Crisis of 1692*.

ANN MARIE PLANE is Associate Professor of History at University of California at Santa Barbara. She is the author of *Colonial Intimacies: Indian Marriage in Early New England*.

JESSICA CHOPPIN RONEY is Assistant Professor of History at Ohio University. She is the author of "'Ready to act in defiance of Government': Colonial Philadelphia Voluntary Culture and the Defense Association of 1747–1748," *Early American Studies*.

NATALIE A. ZACEK is Lecturer in History and American Studies at the University of Manchester. She is the author of *Settler Society in the English Leeward Islands, 1660–1776*.

Index

Abolition, 119
Abraham in Arms (Little), 52
"Account of Travels" (Hulton, H.), 116–31. *See also* Hulton, Thomas
Adair, James, 74–75, 77
Adams, Abigail, 215n56, 217; letters to, 229
Adams, John, ix, 4, 202, 217–32, 263; courtship for, 225–27; diaries for, 224–25; early background of, 219; European culture for, 229–30; Hercules story for, 220–24; letters to spouse, 229; as masculine ideal, 218–19; moral uprightness of, 219–20, 223; proper manhood for, 231–32; virtue for, 222–24, 226, 232
Addison, Joseph, 199
African Americans. *See* Black males; Black women
Africanization, of whites: British criticism of, 136; in Jamaica, 148
Algonquian tribe, dreams for, 32, 41
Allen, Thomas, 238, 240, 242, 244
American Revolution, 236–50; Baptist chaplains during, 247–48; boycotts during, 202–4; concept of manhood influenced by, 184; Continental Congress during, 195–98, 202–3; henpecked husbands as symbol for, 197–206; manhood during, 195–211; masculinity during, 237–50; Methodists during, 247, 254n27; military chaplains during, 236–50; Native Americans during, 69n28; patriots during, 211n2; voluntary associations during, 168–69. *See also* Continental Congress
Amherst, Jeffery, 57
"Ancient Planters of Virginia," 24

Anglo-Americans: dream diaries for, 32; ethnocentrism of, 57; masculinity and, 3; Native Americans and, views on, 39, 56; Native American warfare v., 72; "new" masculinity among, 66n4; during Seven Years War, 51–65
Anglo-Cherokee War, 61
Anglo-Indian warfare, 51–65. *See also* Seven Years War, projections of masculinity during
Anglo-Powhatan War, 23
Anglo-Spanish War, 12
Antigua: masculinity in, 116, 119–26; "banes of society" in, 119–26; white hospitality and, 119–20
Appeal (Walker), 187
"Arabella's *Complaint of the* Congress," 198, 200–202, 204–6; consumer boycotts in, 204
Arbuthnot, John, 199, 213n19
Armstrong, James, 240
Articles of Association, 202–3
Asbury, Francis, 247
A ska yv ste qo (Cherokee leader), 75–76
Atkin, Edmond, 51, 60
Attakullakulla, 59, 61, 63
Avery, David, 238
Avery, Henry, 108
Axtell, James, 39

"Banes of society," 119–26
Bangs, Isaac, 240
Baptist chaplains, during American Revolution, 247–48; political maturity of, 255n35
Bartholomeus de Portugees, 100, *101*, 103
Bartram, William, 54

| 271

Battell, Andrew, 176
Battle of Etchoe, 64
Beadle, Gabriel, 19
Bederman, Gail, 6n8
Beggar's Opera (Gay), 115n36
Bialuschewski, Arne, 114n28
Biology. *See* Evolutionary biology
"Blackbeard." *See* Teach, Edward "Blackbeard"
Black males: Christian symbolism of, 146; clothing styles for, 186; desire for white women by, 144; hairstyles of, 186; life at sea for, 185; manhood for, Christian piety and, 183; masculinity among, 4; naming of, symbolism of, 144; patriarchy and, as commonality with white males, 149; in public, response to, 185-86; self-assertion by, under slavery, 180; social views of, 143-44; stereotypes of, 143-46; in white portrait art, 181-82
Black women: Christian piety for, 183; Creole, in West Indies, 118-19; in Jamaica, white male pursuit of, 142-43, 147-48
Blake, William, 145
Bledsoe, Caroline, 148
Bloch, Ruth, 218-19
Blood law, 74
Bolster, Jeffrey, 185
Bonny, Anne, 109-10, *110*
Book of Pirates (Pyle), *111*, 111-12
Bouquet, Henry, 58
Boycotts. *See* Consumer boycotts
Braddock, Edward, 56
Brown, Kathleen M., 4, 10, 33, 259, 261
Brown, Vincent, 150n5
Bucaniers of America (Exquemelin), 96-106; alternative models of masculinity in, 99-100; illustrations in, 97-98, 100-106, *104*; Native Americans in, 106; popularity of, 97-98; printing techniques for, 114n22, 114n24; translations of, 102-3, *105*, 113n5, 114n23
Buccaneers, origins of, 98
Bull, William, 59, 61-62
Butler, Jon, 246

Butler, Judith, 6n8
Butler, Samuel, 195

The Caribbean. *See* West Indies
Carmichael, John, 243
Carter, Landon, 117
Carter, Robert, 97
Chandler, Thomas Bradbury, 195, 198, 206
Chaplains, during American Revolution, 236-50; Baptist, 247-48; British capture of, 254n31; Continental Congress recognition of, 251n5; demographics for, 251n4; as "gender brokers," 236-50, 257; justification of war by, 242-43; literature on, 251n6; Methodist, 247, 254n27; political dissent and, 246-50; primary activities of, 239-40; purpose of, 238-39; religious conversions by, 241; on swearing, 240-41, 252n13; as symbols of manhood, 237-42, 250; war as God's plan for, 244
Chard, Chloe, 220
Charity, 156
Charles I (King), 35
Charles II (King), 35
Cherokee tribe, 54; in Battle of Etchoe, 64; belief systems for, 72; blood law for, 74; civil leaders within, 84; civil life within, 90n58; communication with animals within, 79; community recognition within, for warriors, 83-85; "corn pullers" in, 63; death as spiritual for, 83; eagle dance performances in, war-related, 84-85, 91n74; emasculation of enemies by, 82-83; fire symbolism for, 81; gender roles within, 73-74; geopolitical conflicts within, 74-75; gifting ceremonies for, 85; honoring ceremonies for, 84; hunting for, 74; informants within, 72; manhood within, 63-64, 73; marriage ceremonies within, 87n12; marriage partners within, 73; martial titles within, 75, 85; masculinity within, 71-86; organization within, 73; protection formulas, 77-80, 89n39; recruited by British, 58,

60–61, 68n19; reintegration process into, for warriors, 82; rites of purification for, 81; sanctification rites in, 81; scalping for, 79–80, 85; slavery by, 82–83, 90n64; war as political tool for, 71; war deliberations by, 75; warfare for, 71–86; war fire rituals for, 76–77; war paint for, 79; water symbolism for, 81; women's roles within, 67n7, 80–82. *See also* Protection formulas

Cherokee Women: Gender and Culture Change 1700-1835 (Perdue), 72

"The Choice of Hercules" (Handel), 222–23

Christian piety: black males and, manhood for, 183; for black women, 183; chaplains and, as symbols of manhood, 238–42; manhood and, 237–38; slavery and, 183; of women, men v., 246. *See also* Chaplains, during American Revolution; Evangelical Protestantism

The Clear Sun-Shine of the Gospel Breaking Forth upon the Indians in New England (Shepard), 46n53

Cleaveland, John, 248–49

Cole, B., 107

College of Philadelphia, 164, 167

Colonial America, masculinity in, 2

Connell, Robert, 5n4

Consumer boycotts, 168–69, 202–4; in "Arabella's *Complaint of the* Congress," 204; under Continental Congress, 202–4; women's roles in, during American Revolution, 203–4, 212n11

Continental Congress, 195–98, 202–3; accusations about manhood for, 196–97; Articles of Association under, 202–3; chaplains and, importance of during American Revolution, 251n5; delegitimization of, 196; trade boycotts under, 202

Contributors to the Relief of the Poor, 165–67

Cooper, Anthony Ashley, 177

Cooper, Myles, 206, 215n44

Cooper, Thomas, 44n13

The Coquette, 219

Coverture, 197–98, 210

Creole women, in West Indies, 118–19

Croghan, George, 60

Crooke, William, 103

Cross-dressing, in *A General History of the Pyrates*, 109

"Culture of improvement," 262

Curti, Merle, 38

Custis, Daniel Parke, 133n19

Dale, Thomas, 20–25; "farmers" for, 24; Henrico settlement and, 24

Dane, John, 43n7

David, Ebenezer, 240

Dayan, Joan, 138

Declaration of the Rights of Man and of the Citizen, 184

de Crevecouer, J. Hector St. John, 1

Delaware tribe, 58

De La Warr, Baron, 22

de Montcalm, Louis, 68n15

de Tocqueville, Alexis, 168

D'Ewes, Simonds, 34

A Dialogue Between a Southern Delegate and His Spouse on His Return from the Grand Continental Congress, 198, 200, 206–11; authorship of, 215n43, 216n52; satire of masculinity in, 207; women's roles in, 209

Diaries. *See* Dream diaries

The Diary of Michael Wigglesworth (Morgan), 44n19

Digges, Thomas, 21–22

Donovan, Joan, 170n11

Dorrill, William, 140

Douglass, Frederick, 185–86, 188–89

Drake, Harold, 43n5, 45n30

Drake, Kathy, 43n5

Drayton, William Henry, 248

Dream(s): for Algonquian tribes, 32, 41; analysis of, 42; gender frontier for, 33, 40; heaven in, 36–37; as inconsequential, 32; interpretation of, 259; modern psychoanalytic theories of, 43n10; for Native Americans, 32–33; as natural phenomena, 44n18; religious implications of, 34; about salvation, 36

Dream diaries, 31–43; achievement in, 37; for Anglo-American men, 32; categorization within, 35; hierarchy in, 33; loss of control, 33; power in, 33; purposes of, 32, 45n34; for Sewall, 31–32, 36–38; social status in, 33; by women, 33
Duché, Jacob, 243
Duffield, George, 236–37

Eagle dance performances, 84–85, 91n74
Earl of Leicester, 22
Easton, Peter, 43n7
Edwards, Bryan, 141, 146
"Effective men," 159–66; virtue for, 159–60
Egalitarianism, in Jamaica, 136, 140–41
Elias, Norbert, 139
Eliot, John, 41, 47n59
Elizabeth (Queen), 12
England, Edward, 108
England, manhood in: age of marriage as influence on, 13–14; military rank and, 22–23; during Seven Years War, 51; during sixteenth century, 13–14
English Civil War, 177
Equiano, Olaudah, 182–83
Essay on Plantership (Martin), 127, 130
An Essay on the Treatment and Conversion of African Slaves in the British Sugar Colonies (Ramsay), 125, 130
Ethnocentrism, of Anglo-Americans, 57
Europeans: gender hierarchy among, 55; on Native American warfare, 55–57, 62, 69n27
Evangelical Protestantism, 182, 237
Evolutionary biology, 2
Exquemelin, Alexandre, 96–106

"Farmers," 24
A Father's Instructions (Percival), 51
Fauquier, Francis, 59–60
Female behaviors, research on, 2
Female pirates, 109
Femininity, as weakness, 11
Feminism: masculinity and, x, 1. *See also* Womanhood, masculinity as opposition to
Filmer, Robert, 177

Firefighting: organization of, through voluntary associations, 158, 160, 166–67; Union Fire Company for, 158, 162; as virtue, 160
First Anglo-Powhatan War, 23
Fithian, Philip Vickers, 239, 242
Flynn, Errol, 95
Forbes, John, 58
Foreign service, manhood from enlistment in, 15
Forrest, George, 18
Foucault, Michel, 2
France, Native Americans and, in wars against Great Britain, 68n15
Franklin, Benjamin, 159, 234n46; the Junto and, 161–63
Freeman, Arthur, 128
French and Indian War, 167
French Revolution, manhood influenced by, 184
Friendly Association, 167
Fyffe, William, 71

Gadsden, Christopher, 62
Gano, John, 238, 249–50
Garrard, William, 22
Garraway, Doris, 138
Garrettson, Freeborn, 247
Gaskell, Roger, 98
Gates, Geoffrey, 15
Gates, Thomas, 22
Gay, John, 115n36
Gender: chaplains and, during American Revolution, 236–50, 257; within Cherokee tribe, 73–74; construction of, 6n8; dreams and, 33, 40; in Europe, hierarchy within, 55; historical context for, in Jamestown colony, 10; in Jamaica, relations with white men and, 136–37; among Native Americans, hierarchy for, 55; Native American subjugation and, 10; as performative, 6n8; sex v., 6n8; slavery and, 10; as social construction, 2; studies on, 3; for suppression of other males, 10; in West Indies, academic studies for, 135–36

274 | Index

"Gender frontier," 33, 40, 259–61
A General History of the Pyrates (Johnson), 96, 106–11; cross-dressing in, 109; masculinity as theme in, 106–8; sexuality as theme in, 106–8; translations of, 114n28
Gifting ceremonies, 85
Glover, Lorri, 132n5
Goodwin, Philip, 34; on dream interpretation, 40–41
Gookin, Daniel, 39, 41
Gorges, Fernando, 13
Graeme, Elizabeth, 155–56
Grant, James, 62
Gray's Inn Journal, 199
Great Britain: animal metaphors by, regarding Native Americans, 67n14; Cherokee tribe recruited by, 58, 60–61, 68n19; Jamaican colonials and, as "Africanized," 136; plantation life in West Indies, criticism of, 118; projections of power in, 59–62; during Seven Years War, 51–65; trade between Native Americans, 59; wartime achievements by, 60

Hamilton, Alexander, 158, 220
Handel, George Frideric, 222–23
Harper's Weekly, 111
Hart, Oliver, 242, 248
Hartman, Saidiya, 139
Henpecked husbands, in satirical publications, 197–206, *201*, 212n7; "Arabella's *Complaint of the* Congress," 198, 200–202, 204–6; *A Dialogue Between a Southern Delegate and His Spouse on His Return from the Grand Continental Congress*, 198, 200; literary history of, 199–200; transvestitism and, 212n10
Henrico settlement, 24–25; Dale and, 24
Henry VIII (King), 12
Hercules, story of, 220–24, *229*; in popular culture, 233n16, 233n17; symbolism of, 221, 234n27
The Heroic Slave (Douglass), 188–89
Heywood, Linda, 176

History and Lives of All the Most Notorious Pirates, and Their Crews (Johnson, C.), 107
Hitchcock, Tim, 139
Hoganson, Kristin L., 212n11
Holles, Gervase, 34
Homosexuality, 96, 113n3, 212n7
Homosociality, in Jamaica, 139–43; egalitarianism and, 140–41; violence and freedom and, 140
Honorable Tuesday Club, 158
Hospitality, by whites, in Antigua, 119–21; for Hulton, 119–21; as moral hazard, 120–21
The House Servant's Directory (Roberts, R.), 188
Howard Pyle's Book of Pirates (Pyle), 95
Hull, Hannah, 38
Hull, John, 35, 38, 43n7
Hulton, Elizabeth, 125
Hulton, Henry, 116–31, 262; "banes of society" and, 119–26; in colonial America, 125–26; on defective masculinity, for West Indian white man, 124–26; early background of, 131; fatherhood for, 130; financial security for, as negative focus, 123; hospitality by whites for, 119–21; lust for money and, as negative focus, 123–24; masculine sphere of sociability for, 120; as role model, 130
Hulton, Thomas, 125
Hunt, Lynn, 221
Hunting: for Cherokee tribe, 74; for Native Americans, 66n5
Husbands. *See* Henpecked husbands, in satirical publications
Hutchinson, Lewis, 138–39
Hyde, Edward, 212n10

Inglis, Charles, 215n43
Insurance companies, 162
Interracial sex: in Jamaica, between white men and black women, 142–43, 147–48; patriarchy as foundation for, 142–43; for pirates, 108, 112; in West Indies, 118–19
Irvin, Benjamin H., 4
Isaac, Rhys, 132n5

Jamaica, 134–50; abolitionists in, models of manhood for, 135; Africanization of whites in, 148; black males as rebels in, 145–47; British criticism of, white colonials as "Africanized," 136; early demographics for, 134; egalitarianism in, 136, 140–41; feminine ideals in, 137; gender relations in, with white men, 136–37; homosociality in, 139–43; interracial sex in, between white men and black women in, 142–43, 147–48; libertinism in, 136; mortality rates in, for white males, 141; patriarchal values in, 134, 137–40, 143–44, 147–49; plantation life in, 137–38; slavery in, gender relations influenced by, 138–39; Tacky's Rebellion in, 145–46; treatment of slaves in, 142; white male pursuit of black women in, 142–43; whiteness as factor for mastery, 141–42

The Jamaica Lady (Pittis), 118

James I (King), 24

Jamestown colony, 9–26; Dale in, 20–25; establishment of, 9; gender in, historical context for, 10; historical relevance of, 9–10; manhood in, 9–26; masculine comportment in, 3; as military post, 10; military rank in, social status influenced by, 11–13; political discord within, 19–20; Powhatan tribe and, 19–20; Sandys in, 25; Smith, John, in, 16–20, 25; social status in, military rank as influence on, 11–13; Virginia Company in, 10, 21

Jefferson, Thomas, 89n37, 117, 234n46

Jobson, Richard, 175

Jockey Club, 159

Johnson, Anthony, 178

Johnson, Charles, 96, 106–11. See also *A General History of the Pyrates*

Jones, David, 244–45, 248

Judgment of Hercules (Shaftsbury), 222

The Junto, 161–63

Kann, Mark, 229

Kerber, Linda K., 197, 211

Kimmel, Michael, 2

King George's War, 166

King Philips War, 52

Kohut, Heinz, 43n10

Kongo-Angola region, culture of, 175–77; slave rebellions influenced by, 176–77; warfare as part of, 175–76

Kovitz, Marcia, 11

Lafitau, Joseph-Francois, 53–54

Lahontan, Louis-Armand, 53

Lane, Drury, 199

Lane, Ralph, 13

Laurens, Henry, 117

Lawes Divine, Morall and Martiall (Ruttman), 23

Lee, Jesse, 247

Le Febvre, Jacques, 104

Leonard, Abiel, 244

Leslie, Charles, 140, 142

Lewis, Monk, 144–45

Libertinism: in Jamaica, 136; in Saint-Domingue, 139

Library Company of Philadelphia, 160–61, 166, 170n6

Lindman, Janet, 4, 132n5, 257

Linebaugh, Peter, 106, 221

Little, Ann, 52, 55, 67n12

Littlejohn, John, 249

Loans, through voluntary associations, for women, 164

Locke, John, 177

Lolonois, François, 98

Long, Edward, 139–40, 143

Louverture, Toussaint, 184–85

Lyttelton, William Henry, 62, 69n21, 69n28

Manning, James, 255n34

A Man with a Quilted Sleeve (Titian), 101

Marquis de Sade, 138–39

Marriage: age of, among men in England, 13–14; bachelorhood to, as stage of, 197; within Cherokee tribe, 73, 87n12; coverture and, 197–98, 210; henpecked husbands during, 197–206

Martin, Samuel, 127, 130; as ideal father, 129

Mastery, 11–12; domestic, 11; in Jamaica, whiteness as factor for, 141–42; manhood and, 11–12; masculinity and, 141

Mather, Cotton, 43n7
Mather, Increase, 43n7
Maurice of Nassau (Prince), 21
Mayhew, Thomas, 40
The Mayor of Garratt, 199
McBride, Kari Boyd, 11
McCurdy, John Gilbert, 3, 257
McWhorter, Alexander, 248
Medicine man/woman, 46n45. See also Shamans
Memoirs of Socrates (Xenophon), 222
Methodist chaplains, during American Revolution, 247, 254n27
Military: chaplains, during American Revolution, 236–50; codes, 22; Dale in, 20–25; desertion from, 15; in England, 22; under feudalism, 12; in Jamestown colony, social status influenced by, 11–13; manhood and, 11–16, 22–23; as noble profession in England, 12; as opportunity for lesser-born, 13; order in, 19–20; social rank and, 11–16; swearing within, 240–41, 252n13; Wingfield in, 16–17. See also Chaplains, during American Revolution
Military codes, 22–24; religious edicts under, 23–24
"Military revolution," 28
Mingo tribe, 58
Minor, Thomas, 35, 43n7
Montgomery, Archibald, 61–62
Morgan, Edmund S., 44n19
Morgan, Henry, 99, 258
Morris, Robert, 58
Mullin, Michael, 138
My Bondage and My Freedom (Douglass), 189

Narrative of the Life of Frederick Douglass (Douglass), 189
Native Americans: during American Revolution, 69n28; Anglo-American views on, 39, 56; Anglo-American warfare v., 72; Anglo-Indian warfare v., 51–65; in animal metaphors, by British, 67n14; in *Bucaniers of America*, 106; Christian conversion of, 40; dogs for, 67n12; dream beliefs for, 32–33; European views on warfare by, 55–57, 62, 69n27; feminization of, 40; French and, in wars against Great Britain, 68n15; gender and, as reason for subjugation of, 10; gender hierarchy among, 55; hunting for, 66n5; masculinity for, as concept, ix–x; during Seven Years War, 51–65; shamans among, 39–43; social status among, achievement of fame for, 54; trade with Great Britain, 59; treatment of outsiders by, 54; victory in war as concept for, 64; warfare for, cultural background of, 53–55; warfare retreat by, attitudes toward, 64; warriors among, defamation of, 54; "White people" as label among, 67n8; woodland warfare by, 58. See also Algonquian tribe, dreams for; Cherokee tribe; Delaware tribe; Powhatan tribe; Shawnee tribe
Negro Seaman Acts, 185
Nelson, Francis, 19
Networking, within voluntary associations, 161–63
Newport, Christopher, 17
New York Daily Tribune, 188
Nicken, Edward, 178
Nine Years' War, 12
North America, warfare in, 51–52
Norton, John, 64
Norton, Mary Beth, 10, 203

O'Brien, Karen, 251n5

Paine, Thomas, 200
Parke, Daniel, 133n19
Parke, Lucy Chester, 133n19
Parke, Thomas Dunbar, 133n19
Patriarchy, 147–49; commonality between white and black males and, 149; interracial sex and, between white men and black women, 142–43, 147–48; in Jamaica, 134, 137–40, 143–44, 147–49; within slavery, black men and, 138; social order from, 161

Pawwows, 39–42; Christian conversion and, 41; prohibition of, 47n56; purposes of, 42. *See also* Shamans
Payne, John Howard, 75
Pennsylvania Hospital, 164–65
Pennsylvania Magazine, 200, 204
Pequot War, 52–53
Percival, Thomas, 51
Percy, George, 12, 16–17, 20
Philadelphia, voluntary associations in, 155–69; during American Revolution, 168–69; British models for, 156; capital acquisition by, 163–64, 171n18; charity and, 156; consumer boycotts by, 168–69; dependent protection from, 161; development of, 156, 168–69; economic advancement through, 163–64; economic self-sufficiency as result of, 161; for firefighting, 158, 160, 166–67; governance and, 166–69; insurance companies as, 162; loans through, 164; male monopolization of, 156–57; masculine dominance reinforced by, 157–59; for militias, 167; networking opportunities within, 161–63; political and social purposes of, 161; productivity in, 161; property rights and, 161–65; by Quakers, 167; subscription libraries as, 157; tavern meetings for, 158; variety of, 162; women in, 155–59, 170n6
Philadelphia Contributionship, 162, 164
Philip (King), 36
Pinckney, Eliza, 61, 63, 69n21
Pirates, 95–112, 258; in *Bucaniers of America*, 96–100; buccaneers and, 98; female, 109; in *A General History of the Pyrates*, 96, 106–11; history of, 96–97; in illustrations, 100–106; interracial unions among, 108, 112; in masculinity and sexuality for, 95–112; moral ambiguity in, 112; in popular culture, 95; role in economic development, 97; role in maritime development, 97; Teach, Edward "Blackbeard," 107–8. *See also Bucaniers of America*
The Pirates of Penzance, 95

Pitman, John, 248
Pittis, William, 118
Plane, Anne Marie, 3, 259
Plantation life: British criticism of, in West Indies, 118; female roles in, 150n10; in Jamaica, 137–38; in West Indies, 117–18
Planter (ship), 188
"Pleasures of resistance," 187
Plumstead, Mary McCall, 155–56
Polly: An Opera (Gay), 115n36
Pontiac's War, 67n12
Pope, Alexander, 213n19
Powhatan tribe: Anglo-Powhatan War, 23; in Jamestown colony, 19–20
Presbyterian Ministers Fund, 164
Printing techniques, 114n22, 114n24
Property rights, 161–65; masculinity and, 161; slavery and, as facet of manhood, 178; voluntary associations and, 161–65
Prosser, Gabriel, 185
Protection formulas, 77–80, 89n39; color symbolism in, 78, 90n58
Protestantism, 34; evangelical, 182, 237; radical, 34
Pyle, Howard, 95–96, *111*, 111–12

Quakers, 167; on warfare, 246

Radical Protestantism, 34
The rake, hypermasculinity and, 218
Ramsay, James, 125, 130, 135
Ratcliffe, John, 17–18, 20
Read, Mary, 109
Rediker, Marcus, 106, 221
Reflections on Courtship and Marriage, 226–27
Reformation, 34, 36
Reid, John Phillip, 71, 85
Religion and the Decline of Magic (Thomas, K.), 34
Rembrandt, 101
Reports. *See* Dream diaries
Rivington, James, 198, 200
Robbins, Ammi, 239–40
Roberts, Michael, 28

Roberts, Robert, 187–88
Rogers, William, 248
Rolfe, John, 26
Rotundo, Anthony, 2
"The Runaway" (Lewis), 144
Russell, John, 19
Ruttman, Darrett, 23–24

Saint-Domingue, 138–40; black men in, for white men, 138–39; desire and sexuality in, power relations and, 139; libertinism in, 139; manhood in, revolution in as influence, 184; rebel slaves in, 146
Sandys, Edwin, 9–10; in Jamestown colony, 25
Scalping, 79–80, 85
Scarouady, 56–59
Scrivener, Matthew, 27
Seabury, Samuel, 206
Self Portrait at the Age of 34 (Rembrandt), 101
Self-restraint, manhood and, 33–39
Sensibility, 262
"Separate spheres" ideology, 139
Seven Years War, projections of masculinity during, 51–65, 67n12; distinctions for, 52
Sewall, Samuel, 31–32, 43n7; dream diaries for, 31–32, 36–38; at Harvard College, 45n33
Sexuality: and Adams, John, 217–35; in *A General History of the Pyrates*, 106–8; manhood and, 217–18; among pirates, 95–112; in Saint Domingue, power relations and, 139
Shaftsbury, Anthony Ashley, 222
Shamans, 39–43; Christian conversion and, 41; vilification of, 42, 47n59
Shawnee tribe, 58
Shoemaker, Nancy, 54, 59, 67n14
Shepard, Thomas, 46n53
"Sketches, with a View to Fix Right Principles in the Minds of Children, and Lead Them to Just Sentiments, and a Virtuous Conduct" (Hulton, H.), 130

Slavery: black masculinity and, 172–89; black men as patriarchs within, 138; by Cherokee tribe, 82–83, 90n64; Christian piety and, 183; Evangelical Protestantism and, 182; gender and, as basis of, 10; history of, West African culture and, 174–77; in Jamaica, 138–39, 142; "pleasures of resistance" during, 187; political manhood under, 178; property rights and, as facet of manhood, 178; rebellions against, Kongo-Angola region as influence on, 176–77; self-assertion under, by black males, 180; white male interest in black females under, 180; in white portrait art, 181–82
Smalls, Robert, 185, 188
Smith, Hezekiah, 240–43, 248
Smith, James, 64
Smith, John, ix, 14–20, 25, 257–58; common men v. well-born for, 19; early history of, 16–17; in Jamestown colony, 16–20; order for, 19–20; on personal sacrifice, 18; physical strength for, 18; political betrayal of, 20; style of leadership for, 20
Social order, from patriarchal values, 161
Social rank, military involvement and, 11–16
Social status: in dream diaries, 33; in Jamestown colony, military rank as influence on, 11–13; among Native Americans, achievement of fame for, 54
Sodomy, 96, 113n3, 212n7
Spencer, Elihu, 248
Sproat, James, 239
St. Andrews Society, 155–58; foundation of, 155; tavern meetings for, 158
Stamp Act Crisis, 206
Standish, Myles, 39
Stanhope, Philip Dormer, 133n22
Stedman, John, 145–46
Steele, Richard, 199
Stone, Brown, 79
Struikman, Lorenzo, 102
Stuart, John, 57, 59
Subscription libraries, 157

Sumptuary laws, 38
Sutcliffe, Matthew, 21–22
Swearing, 240–41, 252n13; for Washington, George, 252n12

Tacky's Rebellion, 145–46
Tatler, 222
Taylor, John, 147
Teach, Edward "Blackbeard," 107–8, 115n30
Teedyuscung, 60
ten Hoorn, Jan, 97
Tennent, William McKay, 244–45, 248
Thirty Years War, 21
Thistlewood, Thomas, 140
Thomas, Edward, 172
Thomas, George, 127–29
Thomas, Keith, 34
Thornton, John, 176
Timberlake, Henry, 57
Titian, 101
Toryism, as pacifism, 247
Trabue, Daniel, 241
Trotter, Moore, 155–56
Trout, John, 244

Union Fire Company, 158, 162
Union Library Company, 170n6

Van Horne, William, 240, 247–48
van Rijn, Rembrandt, 101
Vasa, Gustavus, 182
Vecelli, Tiziano. *See* Titian
Vesey, Denmark, 185
Virginia Company, 22–23; in Jamestown colony, 10, 21
Virtue: for Adams, John, 222–24, 226, 232; for "effective men," 159–60; females excluded from acts of, 160, 203; firefighting as, 160; husbands and, 199–200; masculinity and, 217–32; in West Indies, manhood and, 116–33
Volday, William, 20
Voluntary associations, in Philadelphia, 155–69; during American Revolution, 168–69; British models for, 156; capital acquisition by, 163–64, 171n18; charity and, 156; consumer boycotts by, 168–69; dependent protection from, 161; development of, 156, 168–69; economic advancement through, 163–64; economic self-sufficiency as result of, 161; "effective men" in, 159–66; for firefighting, 158, 160, 166–67; governance and, 166–69; insurance companies as, 162; loans through, 164; male monopolization of, 156–57; masculine dominance reinforced by, 157–59; for militias, 167; networking opportunities within, 161–63; political and social purposes of, 161; productivity in, 161; property rights and, 161–65; by Quakers, 167; subscription libraries as, 157; tavern meetings for, 158; variety of, 162; virtue and, 159–60; women in, 155–59, 170n6
von Steuben, Baron, 255n34
V.V., Mary (pseudonym), 210–11, 216n56; gender assumptions by, 210–11, 216n58

Walker, David, 187
Ward, Nancy, 90n61
Warfare: by Cherokee tribe, 71–86; eagle dance performances during, among Cherokee tribe, 84–85, 91n74; as essentially male, among Native Americans, 54; honoring ceremonies during, 84; in Kongo-Angola region, 175–76; manhood and, 14–16; for Native Americans, cultural background of, 53–55; in North America, 51–52; Quakers on, 246; women and, among Native Americans, 54, 67n7
War fire rituals, 76–77
Warner, Thomas, 129
War of 1675, 36
War of Spanish Succession, 97
War paint, 79
Washington, George, 58, 117; swearing for, 252n12
Washington, Martha, 133n19
Watkins, Katherine, 179–80
Wayne, Anthony, 239
Webb, Henry L., 13

Wesley, John, 247
West, Francis, 27
West African culture, 174–77; Kongo-Angola region, 175–77; religion in, 175; slavery and, 174–77
West Indies: abolition movement in, 119; British critique of, of plantation life, 118; Creole women in, 118–19; gender studies of, 135–36; historiography of, 117; interracial sex in, 118–19; masculinity in, 116–31; plantation life in, 117–18; planters in, 117–18
"White people," as label among Native Americans, 67n8
Wibirt, Anthony, 226–27
Wigglesworth, Michael, 35, 43n7
Wilson, Lisa, 33
Wingfield, Edward Maria, 12, 16; military rank of, 16–17; removal from power, 17
Wingfield, Jacques, 12
Winslow, Edward, 42
Winthrop, John, 36, 43n7
Womanhood, masculinity as opposition to, 5n4

Women: during American Revolution, role in consumer boycotts, 203–4, 212n11; black males and, desire for white women by, 144; in Cherokee tribe, 67n7, 80–82; in *A Dialogue Between a Southern Delegate and His Spouse on His Return from the Grand Continental Congress*, 209; dream diaries by, 33; in Jamaica, forced interracial sex with white men, 142–43, 147–48; loans to, through voluntary associations, 164; as pirates, 109; on plantations, 150n10; religious piety of, men v., 246; in subscription libraries, 157; in voluntary associations, 155–59, 170n6; warfare and, among Native Americans, 54, 67n7. *See also* Black women; Creole women, in West Indies
Wood, Gordon, 221
Wood, Marcus, 145
Wood, William, 41–42

Xenophon, 222

Young, William, 124